Understanding Stamp Duty on Property

Related titles available from Law Society Publishing:

Conveyancing Forms and Procedures
Shelley Buckingham and Allyson Colby

Conveyancing Handbook
Frances Silverman

Environmental Law Handbook
Trevor Hellawell

Guide to the National Conveyancing Protocol
The Law Society

Understanding VAT on Property
David Jordan

Titles from Law Society Publishing can be ordered from all good legal bookshops or direct from our distributors, Marston Book Services (tel. 01235 465656 or email law.society@marston.co.uk). For further information or a catalogue call our editorial and marketing office on 020 7320 5878.

Understanding Stamp Duty on Property

7th Edition

REG NOCK

The Law Society

© Reg Nock 2003

ISBN 1 85328 880 2

Sixth edition published in 1995 under the title
Stamp Duties for Conveyancers
by FT Law & Tax (now Sweet & Maxwell).

This seventh edition published in 2003 by the Law Society
113 Chancery Lane, London WC2A 1PL

Typeset by J&L Composition, Filey, North Yorks
Printed by Antony Rowe Ltd, Chippenham, Wilts

Contents

Table of cases

Tables of statutes

Table of statutory instruments

CHAPTER 1

The general principles of stamp duty

1.1 HISTORY OF THE STAMP ACT 1891

Stamp duty is a curious tax, and steeped in the mysterious anomalies of history. First imposed in 1694 (having been copied from the Dutch) it has been at least as unpopular as other taxes, and frequently more capricious in the scope and manner of its operation. Also, somewhat uniquely, three people were executed in 1695 for stamp duty avoidance.

The basic structure of the tax has remained essentially unaltered since 1694. There have been minor modifications from time to time. In 1850 the Stamp Office was given powers to assess the tax and an appeals procedure was introduced. The late Victorian zeal for progressive reform and rationalisation, evident in other areas of the law, resulted in the Stamp Duties Management Act 1891 (SDMA 1891), a short statute dealing with administration and penalties for forgery, and the Stamp Act 1891 (SA 1891).

1.2 STAMP DUTY RESERVE TAX

The Finance Act (FA) 1986 attacked the *loophole* of subsale relief (introduced in the reign of George III) in the case of stock market dealings in shares, by the introduction of a totally new tax of limited range and low quality technical thought known as stamp duty reserve tax. This tax made significant changes in the taxation of share transactions. It is not widely understood because, despite its scope, it is rarely applied in practice to the wide range of off-market share transactions where it is relevant. The current absence of adequate resources to audit the tax means that the many failures to report and pay the tax escape notice.

1.3 DUE DILIGENCE IN CURRENT SUBSALES

The provisions charging contracts for the sale of land in the UK where the land price exceeds £10 million (or £8.5 million plus VAT) have also made substantial changes to the rules relating to subsales of land (FA 2002, s.115 and Sched.36). These new rules and the clawback provisions for certain stamp duty reliefs (FA 2002, s.111 and s.113) have made significant changes in relation to the obligations of solicitors whose errors or omissions in due diligence may affect the stamp duty position of other parties to whom they may now owe a duty of care even though they are not immediate parties to the particular transaction.

Not only are there issues of not proceeding in such a way as to prejudice the recovery rights of previous sellers but also of requiring later parties in the chain to keep them informed so that they are aware of when they can reclaim the stamp duty paid.

Solicitors also have to investigate earlier contracts in order to discover how much of the current consideration is dutiable and how much credit is available to their clients where subsales of part are involved. The new land regime clearly involves a rethinking by solicitors of their role even in relatively small transactions because these may be a small part of a larger deal and, if only as a matter of self protection, they should find out the stamp duty position of earlier transactions.

1.4   THE FINANCE ACT 1999

The heads of charge were *modernised* by the FA 1999, which also tinkered with certain aspects of stamp duty compliance. These alterations have had wide ranging but generally misunderstood implications for solicitors investigating title. However, the SA 1891 (together with numerous subsequent Finance Acts) remains the source of charging provisions and still contains the basic rules for the computation of stamp duty.

Recent years have seen a growth in the utilisation of statutory instruments to supplement the Finance Act, largely but not solely in the context of the administration of the tax. The FA 1999 altered relatively little and has not produced a tax fit for the new millennium.

1.5   STAMP DUTY REFORM IN 2003

An attempt is to be made to modernise stamp duties in relation to land transactions planned to commence in Autumn 2003 (see the consultation document from the Inland Revenue Stamp Taxes Office, *Modernising Stamp Duty on Land and Buildings*, April 2002). This will affect solicitors, who will be primarily accountable for the administration of the tax because of the rules controlling who may prepare land transfers as deeds, and they will have only a very limited time to understand the new provisions (see **Chapter 12** and boxed passages of text throughout this book).

These changes represent essentially another attack on subsale relief modelled upon stamp duty reserve tax, which apart from being defective in its structure, is inappropriate to the more complex regime for conveyancing. The structure is in consequence piecemeal and complex.

1.6   SOURCES OF LAW

The Inland Revenue Stamp Taxes Office has begun to supplement the legislation with details of their interpretations and practices. These appear in a variety of publications:

- *Letters to Customers* which appear from time to time in the *Law Society Gazette*;
- Statements of Practice;
- Contributions to the *Inland Revenue Tax Bulletins*;
- A specialist *Stamp Taxes Bulletin* (published about twice a year); and
- A *Stamp Taxes Manual* (last updated in March 2002).

Certain key issues are addressed in these publications which should be investigated, particularly as they are in many cases available on the Inland Revenue Stamp Taxes website. They will be referred to in the text and certain key statements of practice are contained in Appendix A to this book. However, these can be amended on screen, and this has been done by the Inland Revenue Stamp Taxes Office. So it is necessary both to take a hard copy of the details whenever used, in order to prove what the position was at the time, and to check that nothing has changed since the previous visit to the website.

1.7   STATUTORY INTERPRETATION

It was observed by Vinelott J in *Blendett Ltd* v. *IRC* [1983] STC 17 that:

> in the field of stamp duty ... the presumption that the legislature intended to create a rational and coherent system of taxation is at least weaker than in other fiscal fields.

Furthermore, in *LM Tenancies* v. *IRC* [1996] STC 880 (on appeal [1998] STC 326) Carnwath J commented that in an area as technical as stamp duty the judge should not pay too much attention to the wording of the legislation and he decided the case on the basis that he thought that he had discovered the spirit of SA 1891!

Nevertheless, once the innumerable statutory cross-references have been tagged and traced, a pattern does emerge showing some fundamental principles applicable throughout the operation of the tax, no matter under which separate and distinct head of charge a particular document may fall victim to stamp duty. It is worth noting, however, that stamp duty can be capricious in its operation: either a transaction does or it does not fall within one or more stated head or heads of charge. The structure therefore provides opportunities for stamp duty efficiency, and ample pitfalls so that under-prepared solicitors venture into a transaction at their peril.

This risk is important since the court has, in an unfortunately unreported case, held that solicitors are responsible for the stamp duty efficiency of the implementation of transactions, notwithstanding that accountants and other professionals have been advising on the tax. His duty is, at the least, to alert the client to the likely level of stamp duty costs in relation to the proposed transaction.

As with all Revenue statutes, the SA 1891 and subsequent amendments should be construed according to the plain and ordinary meaning of the words used, and any ambiguity construed in favour of the taxpayer. It must be considered that much of the extant stamp duty legislation is centuries old and that on the whole, the numerous Finance Acts have to be construed *as one* with the Stamp Act 1891, which is itself based upon much older legislation and case law. To further complicate matters for practitioners, some words in the stamp duty legislation have acquired their own special meanings that frequently surprise the unwary.

1.8 STAMP DUTY CONCEPTS

Parties are frequently surprised that their document is stampable because it falls into a special definition, so in this context practitioners are reminded that the terms used in the stamp duty legislation have their own unique meanings which have developed over more than three centuries. Some illustrations are given below.

A company takeover and reconstruction is not in general parlance a *sale* (*Re Westminster Property* [1985] 2 All ER 426) but it is so treated for the purposes of stamp duty (*J&P Coates* v. *IRC* [1897] 2 QB 427; *Great Western Railway* v. *IRC* [1894] 1 QB 507).

Similarly a power of attorney may in certain circumstances be a *conveyance* (*Diplock* v. *Hammond* (1854) 5 De GM & G 320).

In *Eastern National Omnibus Co Ltd* v. *IRC* [1939] 1 KB 161 there was an agreement whereby the vendor, in addition to selling a fleet of buses to the purchaser, also agreed, for a monetary consideration, not to compete with the purchaser in a specified area for a specified time, and to assist the purchaser in obtaining the necessary transport licences. Notwithstanding the way in which the transaction was dressed up, it was held that in substance the agreement included a sale of the vendor's goodwill (now exempt from stamp duty) and as such the consideration attributable thereto was

4

stamp able with *ad valorem* duty under the head of charge *conveyance on sale*.

Consideration of the various heads of charge in subsequent chapters will involve a discussion of the special meaning of the legislation, which should be carefully studied. It will also be observed in later chapters that some heads of charge are specific and others are general sweeping-up charges. Where, however, a specific head of charge is repealed, a later transaction which would otherwise have fallen within the repealed head of charge will be totally exempt and not fall within some residual head of charge (see *Att.-Gen.* v. *Lamplough* (1878) 3 Ex D 214).

1.9   VOLUNTARY TAX

Stamp duty has been described as a *voluntary tax* and this has several aspects which are important when preparing documents.

1.9.1   Oral and written transactions

There is no general stamp duty obligation to carry out a transaction in writing. Subject to the general law, the parties are free to choose whether to carry out their transaction orally or in writing.

1.9.2   Presenting documents

Apart from bearer instrument duty (FA 1999, Sched.15) there is no obligation to present documents to the Inland Revenue Stamp Taxes Office. Although recently the number of situations where, for a variety of reasons, the document may have to be produced to the Inland Revenue Stamp Taxes Office is increasing, with the consequential increased risk of errors being discovered.

For example, where a person in a chain of subsales is seeking a repayment of the stamp duty upon the contract, the special unit in the Manchester Stamp Office (see **Appendix B**) dealing with such claims is likely to require the production of all documentation in order to see whether the conditions for the relief have been strictly satisfied or if there has been some error entitling them to refuse payment (FA 2002, s.115; Sched.36 especially para.9).

There is also increasing evidence that when an assignment of a lease is presented for stamping the Inland Revenue Stamp Taxes Office is calling for the production of the contract, if any, in order to determine whether the contract is dutiable pursuant to FA 1999, Sched.13 para.7 (see **section 5.3**).

1.9.3 Unpaid duty

Apart from bearer instrument duty (FA 1999, Sched.15) the Inland Revenue has no power to sue for unpaid stamp duty (see **Chapter 11**).

1.9.4 Assigning liability

Apart from the special situation of bearer instruments and limited cases of contracts dutiable pursuant to FA 1999, Sched.13 para.7 and FA 2002, s.115 (which imposes liability for duty upon the contractual purchaser, but not for the conveyance) there is no provision setting out who is liable for the stamp duty, late payment interest, or late presentation penalties (see **Chapter 11**).

The other pressures to stamp a document are indirect, and considered in more detail in **Chapter 11**.

1.10 TAX ON DOCUMENTS

The first principle to note is that stamp duty is not a tax on transactions as such, but a tax on documents which record and give effect to certain transactions. The stamp duty legislation itself does not require writing for transactions, but it does identify a wide range of instruments required for other purposes as being subject to stamp duty. This may seem a pointless distinction where the only possible way in which a transaction can be given legal or equitable effect is by some kind or other of written documentation, but stamp duty relies upon other law to require parties to make use of writing.

1.10.1 On sale of land

A sale of land will generally involve a contract that must be:

- in writing (Law of Property (Miscellaneous Provisions) Act 1989 (LP(MP)A 1989), s.2);
- of a formal nature (*First Post Homes* v. *Johnson* [1995] 4 All ER 355);
- inclusive of the need for written exercise of options (*Spiro* v. *Glencrown Properties Ltd* [1991] 2 WLR 931);
- followed by a conveyance, which must normally be by deed (Law of Property Act 1925 (LPA 1925), s.52).

Nevertheless, there may be scope in certain cases to carry out a transaction otherwise than in writing, in which case there will be no piece of paper on which the stamp can be affixed, and no duty payable. Thus, despite the necessity of a deed for a conveyance mentioned above, it may be possible to engineer a situation in which a conveyance, or other transfer of a legal estate or interest, may take effect by operation of law (*Yaxley* v. *Gotts* [1999] 2 WLR

1217). This saving is expressly recognised by LPA 1925, s.52 and s.53(2) and LP(MP)A 1989, s.2(6) (*Neville* v. *Wilson* [1997] Ch 144; *Parway Estates* v. *IRC* (1958) 37 ATC 164; *Walsh* v. *Lonsdale* (1882) 21 Ch D 9). Also, such a contract based constructive trust is not subject to stamp duty (*Angus* v. *IRC* (1889) 23 QBD 579).

Further examples referred to later on in this book include other transactions or courses of conduct into which property rights are implied rather than expressly declared, such as:

- the creation of implied, resulting and constructive trusts;
- the transfer of ownership of chattels by physical delivery;
- certain oral transactions (such as an oral declaration of a trust of personalty).

Although, if voluntary, this last category would in any event be exempt from *ad valorem* duty as there is no longer a charge on voluntary dispositions of property except in relation to transfers of land to a connected company (FA 2000, ss.119–121) or in certain cases, where the property is subject to a mortgage (SA 1891, s.57; Statement of Practice SP6/90 – **Appendix A**).

A notorious example of a resulting trust (of which a legal mortgagee had no actual notice but which took effect as an overriding interest in registered land) arose in the case of *Williams & Glyn's Bank Ltd* v. *Boland* [1981] AC 487 where Mrs Boland, without being in any way a party to the conveyance to Mr Boland of the matrimonial home, was held to have a beneficial interest in the property by virtue of having contributed to the purchase price.

However, it is possible to convert a trust implied by law into a stampable transaction. Turning a constructive trust into an express arrangement for instance, which may mean that the contract has become a conveyance or that it is a contract of the sale of the equitable interest dutiable pursuant to FA 1999, Sched.13 para.7 (*Chesterfield Brewery* v. *IRC* [1899] 2 QB 7; *Peter Bone* v. *IRC* [1995] STC 921).

Other documents required by law which attract stamp duty include:

- returns of allotment pursuant to Companies Act 1985, s.88 (which may be stampable as agreements for sale FA 1999, Sched.13 para.7 or agreements for lease which must be in writing (LP (MP)A, 1989 s.2) (pursuant to FA 1999, Sched.13 para.14);
- notifications to the Land Registry in connection with the surrender of leases (FA 2000, s.128).

The legal adviser should therefore always bear in mind, when there is a choice in the manner of effecting a transaction, that the avoidance of documentation is the avoidance of stamp duty (*Carlill* v. *Carbolic Smokeball Co* [1892] 2 QB 484) and that the drafting and structuring of the documentation can affect the stamp duty costs significantly. It is important to ask whether the document is necessary because it simply states what the law implies or the issue can be dealt with equally effectively by other means. See, for example, *Peter Bone* v. *IRC* [1995] STC 921 where the unnecessary conversion of the constructive trust arising upon sale into an express trust produced a totally unnecessary and avoidable charge to stamp duty. Also see **Chapter 3** on key issues when drafting documentation where stamp duty is involved.

1.10.2   Consequences of documentary nature of tax

Numerous consequences flow from the fact that stamp duty is a tax upon documents and not transactions:

- Whether an instrument is liable to stamp duty depends upon its legal effect at the time when it becomes an instrument (*Carlill* v. *Carbolic Smokeball Co* [1892] 2 QB 484).
- The computation of stamp duty is linked to the effect of the instrument and the surrounding circumstances at the time when it is executed or becomes an effective instrument (see **Chapter 2**).
- The stamp duty charge will depend upon its drafting rather than any incidental consequence arising (see **Chapter 3**).
- The jurisdictional rules which may depend upon the place and time of execution (SA 1891, s.14(4)).
- Late payment interest and late stamping penalties run by reference to the date of execution of the documents (see **Chapter 11**).
- The charge upon contracts for the sale of land in the UK where the consideration exceeds £10 million runs from 90 days after execution (see **section 5.8**).

1.11   EFFECT OF DOCUMENTS

For the conveyancer, the only significant charges to *ad valorem* stamp duty will arise under the heads of charge 'Conveyance or Transfer on sale' and 'Lease' (FA 1999, Sched.13).

Nevertheless, even though no *ad valorem* liability exists, a document might still attract one of the nominal fixed duties. Though nominal, these charges cannot be ignored as, for example, a District Land Registrar will not give effect to an instrument which has not been duly stamped (SA 1891, s.17) and strictly the document is not admissible in evidence (SA 1891, s.14(4)).

Problems frequently arise as to whether a document attracts *ad valorem* duty or a fixed duty only. These difficulties are discussed later on, but the reader should be warned that the apparent classification of a document under a fixed duty head of charge may conceal a much greater liability to *ad valorem* duty (see **Chapter 10**).

The fixed duties in FA 1999, Sched.13 are usually qualified by the condition that they are not dutiable upon sale or that some other instrument has borne *ad valorem* stamp duty. Thus a declaration of trust may, depending upon the facts, be dutiable as a conveyance on sale (*Chesterfield Brewery* v. *IRC* [1899] 2 QB 7; *Peter Bone* v. *IRC* [1995] STC 921).

Some documents merely record the passing of a beneficial interest at an earlier time, and avoid *ad valorem* duty. Others, however, both simultaneously record and effect the change of beneficial ownership which for technical reasons did not pass at an earlier time, thus attracting full *ad valorem* duty (*Oughtred* v *IRC* [1960] AC 206).

This distinction may not be an obvious one. To appreciate the true effect of a document, regard must constantly be had to the substantive rules of property law. Although there are also a number of principles peculiar to the law of stamp duties, to which consideration must be given, this principle does mean that it is also necessary to appreciate the effect of the instrument in general law.

Thus a power of attorney given by the vendor to a purchaser may constitute an equitable assignment and be dutiable as a conveyance on sale (*Diplock* v. *Hammond* (1854) 5 De GM & G 320 – see further **section 4.6**).

1.12   THE *ALL ONE TRANSACTION* PRINCIPLE – THE MEMORANDUM RULE

The documentary nature of the tax gives rise to three basic issues, discussed below, which are not always understood and correctly applied:

1.   *Categorising instruments*: where there is writing it is necessary to categorise the instrument according to stamp duty principles, i.e. whether the document is a *conveyance* within the extended definition of this term in the context of stamp duty. For example, a power of attorney given to a purchaser is an equitable assignment and dutiable as a conveyance on sale (*Diplock* v. *Hammond* (1854) 5 De GM & G 320, but also see **Chapter 4**).

2.   *Requirement for a written document*: in certain circumstances the general law may require writing to pass title. Where the parties have acted orally, the transaction may be uncompleted in law and, in consequence, any written instrument dealing with the property involved in the transaction may operate to complete that transaction (*Oughtred* v. *IRC* [1960] AC 206. However, note the later comments on certain aspects of the case relating to whether writing was necessary in *Neville* v. *Wilson* [1997] Ch 144).

3.   *Documents relating to oral transactions*: where the parties have carried out a transaction orally because writing is not required, any record or memorandum of the transaction may be dutiable (a receipt in *Garnett* v.

9

IRC (1899) 81 LT 633 and a subsequent appointment of a trustee in *Cohen and Moore* v. *IRC* [1933] 2 KB 126).

1.12.1 Meaning of *oral transaction* in stamp duty terms

The first two issues above are concerned with the effect in law of the instrument. In relation to the last of these three areas, a transaction effected orally is not subject to stamp duty, this is a purely stamp duty issue.

For these purposes it is necessary to understand what is an *oral transaction* in stamp duty terms. It is essentially a transaction where the parties have made their contract verbally or by conduct, or have attempted to pass title by delivery. This means that to some extent it is possible to have a certain amount of writing, but this will depend upon the structure of the documentation.

The fact that the contract is based upon a written proposal which later formed the basis of a contract is irrelevant; subsequent events are ignored in relation to stamp duty (*Carlill* v. *Carbolic Smokeball Co* [1892] 2 QB 484), but if there is an oral offer which is accepted in writing there will be a written agreement (see **section 1.13**). This might seem to offer a simple means of avoiding stamp duty where the general law does not require writing. However, the Inland Revenue Stamp Taxes Office is seeking to develop a principle that a document which purports merely to record a prior, non-stampable, transaction may actually carry out the transaction or be read with the earlier transaction so as to be taken to be an integral part thereof, and so dutiable.

In *Cohen and Moore* v. *IRC* [1933] 2 KB 126 a deed of appointment of new trustees, which prima facie then carried only a fixed duty of 50p (now £5 but exempt if certified pursuant to the Stamp Duty (Exempt Instruments) Regulations 1987 SI 1987/516 (see **Chapter 10**), recited an oral settlement of funds which had taken place a few weeks earlier. The deed of appointment was in draft at the time of the settlement, and it was held that:

> ... the transaction was really all one transaction, and ... being one transaction, the whole was recorded in the document – the only document which has been drawn up – which is the settlement.

Each case must turn on its own facts, but it will be appreciated that a later purported written record of an earlier (non-stampable) oral dealing may, if sufficiently proximate and there was the necessary intention of the parties to record their oral transaction in writing, be held to be the true means of effecting the earlier transaction and as such stampable *ad valorem*.

The need for the intention is crucial since the written record and the oral arrangement must form one transaction. In consequence, writing which incidentally records a transaction and is created for unrelated purposes is not dutiable pursuant to this principle.

It should be remembered that a partnership share is either a legal or equitable *chose in action*, and neither interest can be passed by delivery (by virtue

10

of LPA 1925, s.136 or s.53(1)(c)). These dispositions must be in writing, and the necessary documentation immediately attracts duty as a conveyance on sale, or as an agreement treated as a conveyance on sale under FA 1999, Sched.13 para.7.

1.12.2 Memoranda, notes of meeting

Memoranda recording previous oral transactions, which if in writing, would have been treated as conveyances on sale, may be equally so treated either under the *all one transaction* principle or because the oral transaction on its own was ineffective to transfer ownership (*Horsfall* v. *Hey* (1848) 2 Ex 778; *Fleetwood Hesketh* v. *IRC* [1935] 1 All ER 682).

The leading example of the former was *Cohen and Moore* v. *IRC* [1933] 2 KB 126, where there was an oral settlement of funds followed a few weeks later, by a deed of appointment of new trustees reciting the oral settlement. The deed had been in draft when the settlement was made and the court held that there had been just one transaction, all recorded in the deed, which both recited and constituted the settlement, and which was therefore liable to (the now abolished) settlement duty.

On the other hand, if there is a clear gap between an oral transaction and a later written record thereof, the written memorandum should not bear *ad valorem* duty merely because it records an earlier, and non dutiable, transaction (*Eagleton* v. *Gutteridge* (1843) 11 M&W 461).

Property other than goods, bearer instruments and cash is difficult to dispose of orally and there are fairly comprehensive requirements for writing in relation to land transactions. The problems relating to trusts are more fully explored in Chapter 9, but suffice it to say at this stage that a purported oral assignment of an existing beneficial interest under a trust is wholly inoperative, because under the provisions of LPA 1925, s.53(1)(c) such an assignment must be effected in writing although where payment is made the interest may pass without writing by reason of the constructive trust pursuant to LPA 1925, s.53(2) (*Neville* v. *Wilson* [1997] Ch 144).

The memorandum rule may apply even where there has been a written agreement which has not been completed by the transfer of the legal title and the parties are relying upon the constructive trust arising by operation of law following payment of the purchase price in full. Such an arrangement is not subject to stamp duty (*Angus* v. *IRC* (1889) 23 QBD 579; but note the drafting traps as illustrated by *Peter Bone* v. *IRC* [1995] STC 921). However, a subsequent *memorandum* may operate as a conveyance (*Fleetwood Hesketh* v. *IRC* [1935] All ER 682). Great care is therefore required in preparing ancillary documentation.

A rent authority letter by the vendor of a lease directing the tenants to pay future rent for the purchaser is not of itself an assignment of the leasehold interest, but if as frequently happens, the letter contains details of the sale as

11

well as the directions to pay, it may fall into charge as a memorandum operating as a conveyance.

Board minutes do not normally operate as stampable records of the transaction (*Vaughton* v. *Brine* [1840] 1 Man & G 559).

1.12.3   Recitals

Recitals in a deed recording an earlier transaction or a previous step in the same transaction are not stampable as memoranda of that earlier event (*Oughtred* v. *IRC* [1960] AC 206). However, there is a modern drafting technique which could change this position.

Traditionally recitals have appeared at the beginning of the instrument before the operative part of the document, i.e. after the word *Whereas* and before the words such as 'Now this deed witnesseth as follows'. Recently the technique has emerged of setting out the *recitals* in the deed itself, usually after the definitions. This is a high risk approach since by being in the operative part of the instrument they may have a wider effect. It would not require a great deal of ingenuity on the part of the Inland Revenue Stamp Taxes Office to persuade the current judiciary to accept an argument that such a *recital* is really a declaration of trust or other dutiable acknowledgement of title.

1.12.4   Receipts

In *Garnett* v. *IRC* (1899) 81 LT 633 a receipt for payment setting out the details of the transaction was held to be stampable as to the operative conveyance. However, a VAT invoice, which merely sets out the information required by the regulations, is not stampable as it is brought into existence to comply with the legal obligation of the seller and not primarily to record the transaction.

1.12.5   Limits to memorandum principle

At first glance this doctrine appears prospectively to echo the anti-avoidance principles laid down in *W T Ramsay Ltd* v. *IRC* [1982] AC 300, and elaborated in *Furniss* v. *Dawson* [1984] AC 474. The sequentially linked transaction can be regarded as a single composite whole to which the fiscal results of the single composite are to be applied (on the application of this principle to stamp duty see **section 1.17**).

Appearances, however, can be deceptive and the *all one transaction* principle is better regarded as stamp duty's own peculiar creature. It has been applied only where the transaction has been carried out orally but the parties always intended to record the transaction in writing. Since it only applies to post-transaction documents, the principle cannot apply to detailed letters of offer setting out the full terms of the proposed transaction (*Carlill* v. *Carbolic Smokeball Co* [1892] 2 QB 484).

1.13 AN INSTRUMENT IS DUTIABLE UPON ITS STRICT LEGAL EFFECT AT THE TIME OF EXECUTION

An instrument only attracts duty based on the legal effect it produces (*Cory Brothers* v. *IRC* [1965] AC 1082). This means that whether the instrument is liable to stamp duty and the amount of such stamp duty is fixed at the time when it comes into existence; later events are irrelevant on both issues. Hence, in the case of *Carlill* v. *Carbolic Smokeball Co* [1892] 2 QB 484, a written offer accepted by conduct was not stampable because it was not a written contract.

Clearly, this fundamental principle sits uneasily with the *all one transaction* principle. It might seem that with regard to the instruments of the kind in question in *Cohen and Moore* [1933] 2 KB 126 and *Carlill* [1892] 2 QB 484 that neither effects a transaction, both could be produced in court as evidence of the transaction, but only one is stampable.

It is perhaps simplest conceptually to distinguish these principles by viewing the record of the prior transaction as an integral part of the contract or completion process and therefore as having the legal effect it records. Thus, where an oral agreement is later recorded, that instrument may be seen as a part of the contractual process (i.e. the creation of a written contract). It is therefore stampable on this legal effect. This analysis is impossible with regard to the written offer which, at the time of execution, cannot be liable in respect of an agreement that may or may not happen.

1.13.1 No *wait and see*

This up-front, once and for all nature of stamp duty also has the consequence that the amount of the stamp duty is fixed by reference to the circumstance prevailing at the time when the instrument is executed. There is no true *wait and see* in stamp duty. Subsequent events cannot increase or reduce the stamp duty charge. This has given rise to considerable difficulties where the consideration or rent is variable, which is a frequent trap for the unwary because of the arbitrary rules that apply to calculate the tax in such cases (see **Chapter 2**).

1.14 THE *MORE THAN ONE TRANSACTION* PRINCIPLE

On occasion the same document may enshrine and give effect to more than one transaction. Should this happen, care must be taken when looking at the second transaction to distinguish a secondary or accessory purpose from one which in reality is a distinct and separate matter.

The importance lies in the rule that an instrument should be stamped for its leading and principal object, and that the one stamp thereby attracted covers all accessory objectives without the need for further stamping, even though in their own right the ancillary objects, if recorded separately, would attract stamp duty (*Limmer Asphalte Paving Co* v. *IRC* (1872) LR 7 Exch 211).

Before the abolition of the head 'Covenant' by FA 1985, s.85, an example would have been a covenant given by a purchaser to a vendor in the conveyance to the purchaser. A declaration of trust in a conveyance to joint purchasers is another example, and still of relevance. On its own, a declaration of trust bears a fixed duty of £5 (FA 1999, Sched.13 para.17). If it appears in the conveyance it will escape this added impost.

It follows that if the conveyance (or other instrument) is totally exempt from duty, where for example it is certified at £60,000, no duty is payable even on the declaration of trust.

If on the other hand, the objective is clearly capable of standing on its own, divorced from the main transaction, it must be separately stamped. The Stamp Act 1891, s.3(2) states:

> If more than one instrument be written upon the same piece of material, every one of the instruments is to be separately and distinctly stamped with the duty with which it is chargeable.

This is reinforced by s.4(*a*) which stated:

> An instrument containing or relating to several distinct matters is to be separately and distinctly charged, as if it were a separate instrument, with duty in respect of each of the matters.

A situation could arise where a contracting purchaser directs an immediate conveyance from his vendor to a donee. If the purchaser/donor joins in the conveyance, two transactions are enshrined in the one document: the purchase and the subsequent gift. Prima facie (before the abolition of the charge on voluntary dispositions) a case of double duty arose, the first as a conveyance on sale and the second as a voluntary disposition treated as a conveyance on sale (*IRC* v. *Baddeley* [1955] AC 572). In practice the Revenue only sought duty on the consideration paid by the purchaser/donor.

A conveyance incorporating a subsale carries out two separate transactions: the completion of the contract for sale between the vendor and purchaser and completion of the contract for subsale between the purchaser and the subpurchaser. In this case there is express statutory relief from a double charge to duty (SA 1891, s.58(4) and (5) and see **section 6.1**).

However, it appears from the *Inland Revenue Stamp Taxes Office Manual* that if the conditions for the relief in SA 1891, s.58(4) and (5) are not strictly satisfied, the transferee is liable to the aggregate of the stamp duty for all of the transactions completed by the instrument. The professional advisers should therefore insert in any contract a provision that the other party will bear any stamp duty in excess of that which their client would normally expect to pay.

Incorrect implementation of the subsale provisions may also affect the right of earlier parties in the chain to recover all or part of the stamp duty paid upon their land contracts when dutiable pursuant to FA 2002, s.115, so that duties of care may now be owed to prior sellers and subsequent purchasers of the property as well as the immediate client.

1.15 THE *MORE THAN ONE DOCUMENT* PRINCIPLE

1.15.1 Principal instrument only liable to duty

As a direct contrast to one document carrying out two or more transactions, occasionally one transaction may be carried out by more than one document. The usual example arises on the creation of a trust where there is a conveyance of the trust property to the trustees accompanied by a separate deed of trust declaring the beneficial interest such as where a lease is granted to a nominee (*Lady Ingram* v. *IRC* [1999] STC 37; but note the possible *ad valorem* charge pursuant to FA 2000, s.121 where the lease is granted to a connected company – see **section 7.12.4**). In such cases it is usual to have a separate declaration of nomineeship rather than have the untidy conveyancing consequences of such a declaration in the lease itself. It is generally considered to be sound conveyancing practice to keep the equitable interests off the legal title.

By SA 1891, s.58(3), only the principal instrument will bear *ad valorem* stamp duty (and only then if consideration is given) and it is (under SA 1891, s.61(2)) for the parties to determine which is to be the principal instrument.

However, in *Parinv* v. *IRC* [1998] STC 305 the Court of Appeal held that the parties make their selection of what is to be the principal instrument by presenting an instrument for stamping. The first document presented to the Inland Revenue Stamp Taxes Office is in effect the principal instrument. On this view it is not possible for the parties to elect to treat a document as the principal instrument and present some other instrument for stamping as an ancillary instrument. Whichever document reaches the Inland Revenue Stamp Taxes Office first is liable as the principal instrument even though this is not normally the instrument which would bear the *ad valorem* stamp duty and is presented by a person not party to the instrument or transaction.

However, this wide ranging approach is restricted by the principle that an instrument is dutiable only upon its legal effect and the Inland Revenue Stamp Taxes Office cannot charge the stamp duty due upon another instrument even though they are related (*International Power* v. *IRC* (1933) 12 ATC 413). The instruments escaping *ad valorem* stamp duty will almost certainly attract a nominal fixed duty as, for example, a conveyance or transfer not on sale or as a declaration of trust.

Special rules apply to duplicates and counterparts, especially counterpart leases (FA 1999, Sched.13 para.19 and see **section 10.9**).

1.16   MINIMISING LIABILITY – TAX AVOIDANCE

To what extent can potential payers of stamp duty arrange their affairs so as to minimise their liability for the charge? It has already been noted that there is a weaker presumption in the case of stamp duties than in other fields of taxation that there is a rational and coherent system of taxation. Long before the remarks of Vinelott J quoted at the beginning of this chapter, it was observed by Taunton J in *Morley* v. *Hall* (1834) 2 Dowl 494 that stamp duty:

> ... involves nothing of the principle or reason but depends altogether on the language of the legislature.

However, the peculiar nature of stamp duty as a documentary tax gives rise to numerous issues as to how far the Inland Revenue Stamp Taxes Office can go behind the documents and restructure the transaction and/or rewrite the documents where these have been designed to minimise stamp duty.

The principle long held, of general application to all taxing statutes, was that avoidance used to be acceptable in that it was perfectly permissible deliberately to arrange one's affairs with a view to minimising the payment of tax (*IRC* v. *Duke of Westminster* [1936] AC 1).

The resultant mushrooming of tax avoidance in other spheres of taxation by the use of highly complex and artificial schemes resulted in a severe curtailment of the operation of the *Westminster* principle by the House of Lords in the leading cases since *WT Ramsay Ltd* v. *IRC* [1979] 1 WLR 974; *Eilbeck* v. *Rawling* [1981] 2 WLR 449 and *Furniss* v. *Dawson* [1984] STC 153 but this principle has undergone significant revision in later cases. It does, however, permit the courts to take a more robust approach to the legal form of the transaction when analysing matters as regards the tax consequences. To what extent can these principles be held applicable to stamp duty? Historically it has been regarded as a tax of wholly different nature from other taxes.

Previous cases have shown that the courts were only too ready in this field to tax the legal substance of the transaction rather than the form but in this context *legal substance* has a particular meaning, namely the true legal effect of the instrument rather than any *label* which the parties may attach to their document.

Thus a transfer of assets to a company in consideration of an issue of shares may be described as an amalgamation, but in stamp duty terms it is a sale (*Great Western Railways* v. *IRC* [1894] 1 QB 507; *J&P Coats Ltd* v. *IRC* [1897] 1 QB 778, on appeal [1897] 2 QB 423).

In the same way, the grant of some rights over land will be stampable as a lease regardless of the fact that the parties term the instrument a licence, if the legal relationship which the instrument creates is one of lessor and lessee (*Addiscombe Garden Estates Ltd* v. *Crabbe* [1958] 1 QB 513).

However, on occasion the label used by the parties to described their document may tip the balance when interpreting its effect (*British India Steam Navigation* v. *IRC* [1891] 7 QB 165). Yet, in general, the parties' intention is irrelevant in arriving at the legal effect or construction of the document (*Peter Bone* v. *IRC* [1995] STC 921). Thus, the fact that the parties to a contract do not intend to complete by means of a formal transfer does not convert the contract into one for the sale of an equitable interest within FA 1999, Sched.13 para.7 (*Ingram* v. *IRC* [1985] STC 835 and the majority comments in *West London Syndicate Ltd* v. *IRC* [1898] 2 QB 507).

Hence, the substance of an instrument has traditionally meant its strict legal effect looking at all the circumstances; stamping upon a transaction's commercial substance, if this would mean recharacterising legal instruments, has not found favour with the courts as it would run contrary to 300 years of stamp duty principle. In *Littlewoods Mail Order Stores* v. *IRC* [1962] 2 All ER 267; [1961] Ch 597 a series of documents described as *bizarre* and intended to produce a particular tax result were nevertheless held to be stampable solely by reference to their legal effect.

1.17   THE *RAMSAY* APPROACH AND STAMP DUTY

Any initial thought that stamp duty might survive *Ramsay* unaffected as a *sui generis* tax was lost in *Ingram* v. *IRC* [1986] 2 WLR 598 when Vinelott J held that where a taxpayer had entered into a simple composite transaction or a preordained series of transactions with the intention of avoiding stamp duty, the court would disregard the steps which had been inserted for no business purpose. The *Ramsay* principle applies to stamp duty as well as in other fields. The *Ingram* scheme involved the use of an agreement for lease for a term in excess of 35 years at a premium, coupled with a subsale to the ultimate purchaser, both elements of which have in any event been stopped by FA 1984, s.111 and s.112 respectively (with some interesting side effects for purchasers of reversionary interests on unregistered leases – see **section 11.6.1**).

Ingram was decided before the House of Lords clipped the wings of *Ramsay* and *Furniss* in *Craven* v. *White*, and was not applied in practice by the Inland Revenue Stamp Taxes Office after that decision. Moreover the traditional approach to stamp duty as a tax apart was restated recently in the House of Lords in *Westmoreland* v. *McNiven* [2001] STC 237 at p.254. Lord Hoffmann stated:

... stamp duty is payable upon a 'conveyance or transfer on sale' (see FA 1999, Sched.13 para.1(1)). Although slightly expanded by a definition in para.1(2), the statutory language defines the document subject to duty essentially by reference to external legal concepts such as 'conveyance' and 'sale'. If a transaction falls within the legal description, it makes no difference that it has no business purpose. Having a business purpose is not part of the relevant concept. If the 'disregarded' steps in *Furniss (Inspector of Taxes)* v. *Dawson* had involved the use of documents of a legal description which attracted stamp duty, duty would have been payable.

Two concepts are involved here: *sham* and *form and substance*.

1.17.1 Sham

These examples, however, concerned the artificial nature of the end result of the transactions, and provided that they were genuine in themselves it was considered allowable to arrive at their conclusion by a circuitous route provided that the steps taken genuinely had the effect intended. As Lord Wilberforce observed in *Ramsay*, a sham transaction is one which 'while professing to be one thing, is in fact something different'.

There is always the question of whether the documentation represents the true bargain between the parties. As a documentary tax the normal principles of construction involve only the words in the instrument, extrinsic materials such as the parties' intentions are irrelevant (*West London Syndicate Ltd* v. *IRC* [1898] 2 QB 507). This can work both for and against the parties since they are not allowed to contradict their written words (*Peter Bone* v. *IRC* [1995] STC 921). The nature of the transaction and its stamp duty consequences depends upon the drafting. The parties' conduct is not relevant to the analysis unless such conduct shows that the drafting was misleading and intended to produce a stamp duty result different from that which would have applied had the transaction been accurately described (*Lloyds and Scottish* v. *Cyril Lord* [1992] BCLC 609; *Snook* v. *London and West Riding* [1967] 2 QB 783; and *Ingram* v. *IRC* [1985] STC 835).

1.17.2 Form and substance

There is the question of whether the Inland Revenue Stamp Taxes Office can go behind the legal structure and charge stamp duty upon the basis that the same economics and commercial result could have been achieved by means attracting a higher liability to tax. It is clear that in stamp duty no such power exists.

For example, there may be little difference between a sale of rents and a mortgage of land repayable out of the rents in commercial terms, but the former means of fundraising is dutiable whereas the latter is exempt from stamp duty.

A variation of a lease by extending its term differs little from a variation consisting of the introduction of an option to renew. The former attracts a substantial amount of stamp duty as a surrender and regrant, the latter attracts no immediate stamp duty and only a charge in respect of the new lease when exercised (see **section 7.5**).

In all cases the stamp duty has to follow the legal machinery adopted. The Inland Revenue Stamp Taxes Office cannot charge stamp duty upon an alternative economically similar basis.

A taxpayer is entitled to choose between alternative routes to the same commercial end (*Sherdley* v. *Sherdley* [1987] STC 266) and it is permissible for that choice to be made upon the basis of a better post-tax result (*Willoughby* v. *IRC* [1995] STC 143). Tax efficiency in choice of routes is not tax avoidance. This is important in the context of certain reliefs from stamp duty for company reconstructions (FA 1986, s.75 and s.77) where one of the conditions for relief in the absence of a stamp duty avoidance motive. However, it has been accepted by the Special Commissioners that deciding upon a transaction and seeking to implement it with the minimum stamp duty is not a tax avoidance motive for these purposes.

1.18   FORWARD PLANNING

In the light of the above judicial observations there would seem to be no objection, for example, to transferring shares to an offshore company with a view to finding a purchaser at a later date, even though by passing them out in this way a stamp duty liability may be avoided: a series of transactions is not 'preordained' unless it involves a degree of certainty and control over the end result at the time when the intermediate steps are taken *Shepperd* v. *Lyntress* [1989] STC 617.

This remains important in seeking to avoid the application of FA 1965, s.90 on transfers in contemplation of a sale such as where seeking to split the title or to tidy up previous uncompleted sales (see **Appendix A**). Its importance in relation to the anti-avoidance provisions of FA 1930, s.42 and FA 1995, s.151 for intra-group transfers and lease have been substantially diminished by the two year clawback provisions introduced by FA 2002, s.111 and s.113.

Sophisticated schemes were never within the scope of this book, but other straightforward – and hopefully still recognised – side-steps, which can be legitimately and safely employed to avoid major pitfalls or to minimise or avoid duty, are dealt with as and when appropriate in the following chapters.

1.19 JURISDICTIONAL PROVISIONS

It must not be overlooked that stamp duty is a global tax that can apply to foreign property and foreign individuals, so inappropriately drafted or structured documentation can lead to unexpected liabilities to stamp duty.

The jurisdictional provisions of stamp duties are rather obscure and differ fundamentally from all other taxes. They can be found in SA 1891, s.14(4) and s.15(3). Unlike other taxes they are not related to the residence and domicile of the parties nor is there a necessary link between the property involved and the UK property. The former provision provides three tests to determine whether an instrument is prima facie liable to stamp duty.

(a) If an instrument is executed in any part of the UK regardless of the *situs* of the property it concerns, it will potentially be liable to stamp duty. Although there is an exemption for legal (but not equitable interests) in foreign property in the case of written contracts chargeable with stamp duty pursuant to FA 1999, Sched.13 para.7 (see **Chapter 5**) and the charge upon contracts for the sale of land pursuant to FA 2002, s.115 is limited to land in the UK, there is no such exemption for a conveyance of foreign property or leases or agreements for lease of foreign land. In addition, apart from Ireland there are no provisions for relief from multiple stamp duties or double taxation. Hence, bizarre as it might seem, a conveyance on sale of land in Australia executed in the UK will not be duly stamped unless *ad valorem* duty has been paid. Of course, it is hard to imagine that anyone in Australia would refuse to rely on such an instrument for want of a UK stamp, but if the instrument were left unstamped and subsequently required to be presented before an English court or the UK Inland Revenue, stamp duty, interest and penalties would be payable (see **section 11.7**).

(b) An instrument will be liable to duty wherever it is executed if it relates to UK property. This is not limited to the property being sold or leased but extends to the property being provided by way of consideration such as shares being issued by a company incorporated in the UK (*IRC v. Maples (Paris) Ltd* [1908] AC 22) or United Kingdom reference points for valuation (*Faber* v. *IRC* [1936] 1 All ER 617).

(c) A liability will arise on an instrument, wherever executed, if it relates to a matter or thing to be done in the UK. This usually relates to the provision of the consideration in the UK such as the issue of shares (*IRC v. Maples (Paris) Ltd* [1908] AC 22) or payment into the vendor's bank account in the UK. It can usually be side-stepped by arranging for payment into an overseas bank account. The fact that the payment originates in this country is irrelevant – it is the destination that matters. Leaving the consideration unpaid may create a UK *situs* debt and bring the instrument into charge. This principle is, however, wider in scope and may include approval of conditional arrangements by ratification in this country, at least in the view of the Inland Revenue Stamp Taxes Office.

1.19.1 Foreign property

There is no general exemption for foreign property, nor with the exception of Ireland is there any form of double taxation relief for stamp duty. Thus an agreement for lease of foreign land to a UK company for a premium consisting of or including the issue of shares is subject to stamp duty and since Companies Act 1985, s.88 requires production of the written agreement, duly stamped, alongside the return of allotments it is not possible to escape the charge to stamp duty by retention abroad.

In *IRC* v. *Maples (Paris) Ltd* [1908] AC 22, a transfer of French property executed in France in consideration of an issue of shares in a UK company was liable to duty as it both related to UK property (i.e. the consideration) and related to a matter to be done in the UK (i.e. the entry of the consideration shares in the purchaser's register of members). The charge in this type of case could easily be avoided by:

- subscribing cash for the shares;
- acquiring the foreign land for cash;
- executing the documentation offshore; and
- paying money into an overseas bank.

This structure has no connection with the UK and escapes stamp duty.

In *Faber* v. *IRC* [1936] 1 All ER 617 a covenant to pay a sum of money calculated by reference to the profits of a business carried on in the UK was held to be within the scope of s.14(4) and dutiable.

There are a few limited reliefs for foreign property:

- FA 1999, Sched.13 para.7 exempts contracts for the sale of foreign property (other than foreign equitable interests – *Farmer* v. *IRC* [1898] 2 QB 141) but there is no exemption for any subsequent conveyance on sale if the above conditions are satisfied.
- The charge upon contracts for the sale of land for a consideration exceeding £10 million applies only to UK land.
- The late stamping penalties do not begin to run for instruments executed offshore until 30 days after receipt in the UK except where the instrument is part of a transaction which relates to UK land when the 30 days start to run from execution (FA 2002, s.114).

1.20 EXECUTION OFFSHORE

As a result of the recent changes mentioned in this section mitigating stamp duty by execution offshore is becoming less effective, because the arrangement requires retention of the instrument offshore and this is becoming difficult particularly where land requiring registration for the vesting of title is concerned. Indeed where the transaction involves UK land there is, in general, at present no significant benefit in execution offshore because the same rule for interest and penalties as apply for execution onshore now apply to execution offshore. Such a transaction requires careful preparation of the documentation and structuring if problems for other property are to be avoided (FA 2002, s.114).

1.20.1 Foreign property

It will be seen that in appropriate circumstances execution offshore where foreign property is involved may offer a way of escaping from stamp duty altogether provided that care is taken to ensure that nothing is signed or done in the UK and the seller or his solicitors have an overseas bank account into which the consideration is paid. For these purposes the Inland Revenue Stamp Taxes Office take the view that approval in the UK falls within SA 1891, s.14(4). Therefore, where there is a contract which is conditional upon approval by the board of directors and shareholders in the UK the transaction will be dutiable.

1.20.2 United Kingdom property

Execution and payment offshore cannot, however, exclude liability for stamp duty where UK property is involved.

For the sale of land in the UK this technique is unlikely to be particularly helpful, since transfers and leases must be registered at the relevant Land Registry for legal title to pass. Furthermore, for certain transactions if registration is not effected within two months of the transfer, that passing of the legal title may become void (see LPA 1925, s.123 (as amended)). For a variety of other reasons, instruments may be required in the UK; where for example, a company issues shares as consideration for a transfer or property, the contract for sale duly stamped (pursuant to FA 1999, Sched.13 para.7 as an agreement for sale or para.14 as an agreement for lease) is required to be sent to the registrar of companies with the return of allotments (CA 1985, s.88(2)). The document may be required in subsequent litigation in this country and Inspectors of Taxes and other official bodies such as Companies Registry are under pressure from the Inland Revenue Stamp Taxes Office to be more zealous in raising stamp duty issues in relation to documentation produced to them. Where shares are involved, stamp duty reserve tax means that there is no benefit in execution offshore (FA 1986, s.87).

1.20.3 Penalties and interest

The Stamp Act 1891, s.15(3) (as amended) relieves some of the perhaps less equitable aspects of the above by providing that except where the instrument relates to UK land where an instrument potentially liable to stamp duty is executed outside the UK, the liability will only crystallise 30 days after the instrument is brought into the UK, with no penalties payable in respect of the period between execution and entry into UK. This provision allows stamp duty to be mitigated on a daily basis; every day, many agreements liable potentially to duty are executed offshore in jurisdictions which do not raise their own charges.

However, in recent years, this general benefit of execution offshore has been progressively eroded where land is involved, in two ways, in addition to the increasing number of cases where registration in the United Kingdom is involved:

(a) *Penalties*: although the late stamping penalty normally begins to accrue only after 30 days from the document being brought into the UK, the FA 2002, s.114 provides that for instruments executed on or after 24 July 2002 which relate to land in the United Kingdom the late stamping penalty accrues from 30 days after execution notwithstanding that the instrument remains offshore (see **Chapter 11**). The words 'relates to' are words of the widest meaning (*IRC* v. *Maples (Paris) Ltd* [1908] AC 22) and so will apply to options over UK land. It seems that the Inland Revenue Stamp Taxes Office intends to take the point for the early accrual of penalty in relation to any other property involved in the transaction, including foreign property. This is clearly the case where the other property is involved in the same document. It might be thought that the penalty charge might be postponed by arranging for the land and the other property to be dealt with in separate legally independent documents, particularly at the contract stage. In addition to using the wide words 'relates to' the draftsman inserted SA 1891, s.15B(1A) to the effect that an instrument (whether or not it also relates to any other transaction) that relates to a transaction which to any extent involve land in the UK is an instrument within the new penalty regime. It appears from the debates on the provision that the Inland Revenue Stamp Taxes Office intended to apply the charge upon a wide basis and apply it to separate contracts where these are commercially one trans-action, e.g. the parties would not have signed one agreement unless the other document was also signed, but that view has changed and the separate contract is not within the new penalty regime.

(b) *Interest*: for instruments executed offshore on or after 1 October 1999, other than agreements for lease, where the interest charge accrues from 30 days after the execution of the lease (see **section 11.9**) there is an interest charge where the stamp duty is not paid to or deposited with the Inland Revenue Stamp Taxes Office within 30 days after execution (SA 1891, s.15A). This interest charge applies even where the instrument is outside the UK.

CHAPTER 2

Calculating the stamp duty

2.1 COMMON ERRORS

Professional advisers frequently produce larger than necessary stamp duty bills because they forget to apply the correct principles. It is not sufficient to act on the basis that the stamp duty is 4 per cent. The important question is: 4 per cent of what figure?

Since the latter figure is produced by technical stamp duty rules it is not always the same as the basic price or rent. The understanding of these rules is vital to efficient implementation of transactions. Many errors currently escape their consequences of a proper full charge to stamp duty because the correct information is not recorded in the documents themselves or in the various stamp duty forms, which are at present not investigated by the Inland Revenue Stamp Taxes Office. This is changing however and more documents will be finding their way before the Inland Revenue Stamp Taxes Office.

The rules for calculating the stamp duty charge, which involves determining both the appropriate rate of stamp duty and the dutiable amount, are a mixture of both statue and judge made law. These rules are archaic, particularly those relating to the dutiable amount. Also, since stamp duty is a tax upon documents rather than transactions, the rules are linked to the terms of the instrument and the circumstances as they exist at the time when the instrument is *executed* (there being no true *wait and see* principle for stamp duty). The drafting of the documentation is vital on this point, particularly in relation to transactions involving land where there can be some large stamp duty charges and valuation costs unless care is taken in the preparation of the paperwork. In consequence the rules frequently provide a trap for the unwary who have not investigated how the computational principles apply to the transaction and documentation.

2.2 TIMING ISSUE

The time at which an instrument is *executed* can affect not only whether it is liable to stamp duty (*Carlill* v. *Carbolic Smokeball Company* [1892] 2 QB 484) but also the rate of stamp duty and the amount upon which the stamp duty is charged. There is a steady increase in the number of cases where the duty is calculated by reference to market value or market rent at the time when the instrument is executed, therefore delay in completion may increase or reduce the stamp duty costs.

For example, where land is transferred to a connected company, FA 2000, s.119 imposes a charge upon market value. When incorporating a business, the land may increase substantially in value over time and increase the duty. If the transfer of the land to the company is in consideration of the issue of shares in circumstances where s.119 does not apply, SA 1891, s.6 provides that the stamp duty is to be charged upon the value of the shares on the date of the instrument. If the company has prospered between the issue of the shares and the date of the transfer the duty will be correspondingly higher; if the company has been unsuccessful the stamp duty will be lower.

Professional advisers should discuss with their clients when it is appropriate to execute the documents.

2.3 RATES OF STAMP DUTY

The three calculation tables below are correct as of 1 October 2002 (under FA 1999, Sched.13).

The stamp duty is calculated upon the amount including actual and potential VAT (*Glenrothes Corporation* v. *IRC* [1993] STC 74). All sums are rounded up to the next £5.

Table 2.1 Conveyances on sale and lease premiums where the rent does not exceed £600

Rate	Consideration
Nil	Not exceeding £60,000
1%	Not exceeding £250,000
3%	Not exceeding £500,000
4%	Over £500,000

Table 2.2 Special situations

Rate	Situation
0.5%	On the transfer of undertakings in connection with certain corporate reorganisations (FA 1986, s.76).
0.5%	In the cases of transfers of stock and marketable securities (FA 1986, s.79), debts which are not marketable securities in loan capital attract the normal rate of 4% upon sales.
1.5%	Upon the issue or transfer of bearer instruments (FA 1999, Sched.15 para.1).
0.5%	Principal charge to stamp duty reserve tax upon certain dealings in United Kingdom bearer instruments which are exempt from stamp duty upon issue; (FA 1986, s.87).
1.5%	Stamp duty or stamp duty reserve tax in respect of transfers of certain stock and marketable securities into depository and clearance schemes (FA 1986 s.67, s.70, s.93 and s.96).

Table 2.3 The rent (FA 1999, Sched.13)

% of average rent	Term of lease
1%	Up to 7 years
2%	7+ to 35 years
12%	35+ to 100 years
24%	100 years +

2.4 CERTIFICATES OF VALUE

2.4.1 Obtaining the benefit of the lower rates

It is a prerequisite for obtaining the benefit of the nil and lower rates of stamp duty for both conveyance and leases that the instrument contains a certificate. Paragraph 4.9 of *Inland Revenue Stamp Taxes Office Manual* makes the unannounced Inland Revenue Stamp Taxes Office change of long standing practice explicit, that the certificate of value must be included in the instrument and cannot be added later or included in another document unless it was originally omitted by 'mistake'. These rules on the utilisation of certificates of value have acquired a new significance pursuant to FA 2002, s.115 which imposes stamp duty upon a contract for the sale of an interest in land which is part of a larger transaction or series of transactions where the aggregate consideration for the land components in the transaction exceeds £10,000,000 (or £8,500,000 plus VAT).

2.4.2 Transfer of a going concern

Pursuant to the new practice (*Law Society [1999] Gazette* 15 January 1999) stamp duty is claimed upon any VAT paid, if the transaction is not treated as a transfer of a going concern for VAT purposes. In order to avoid delays in stamping land transfers and the consequent delays in registration of title, the Inland Revenue Stamp Taxes Office will stamp the transfer upon the basic price on a provisional basis provided that two letters are produced:

- one from the taxpayer undertaking to represent the transfer for additional stamping if the VAT becomes payable; and
- one from the solicitor indicating that the taxpayer has been advised on the significance of observing undertakings to the Inland Revenue Stamp Taxes Office.

It seems that few solicitors are aware of this practice, but do not encounter difficulties in practice, largely because of the incorrect completion of the PD and TR forms by omitting reference to the undertaking to pay the VAT as part of the consideration (in breach of SA 1891, s.5 (as amended)).

The final stamp duty is calculated at the rate appropriate to the total consideration. Where the relevant basic (net) price is less than £500,000 a certificate of value for the basic price can be inserted even though the addition of the VAT would take the consideration for the purposes of stamp duty over a threshold. In such a case no penalty for the improper use of the certificate of value will be sought pursuant to SA 1891, s.5 (as amended) if the additional VAT is paid and the threshold exceeded. However the additional stamp duty bears the late payment interest charge from the original 30 day period, not from the later date when it becomes settled that there is not a transfer of a going concern and the further consideration becomes payable. (For other issues on stamp duty and VAT see **section 2.16**.)

2.4.3 Safeguards against misuse

The main safeguard against misuse of certificates of value is SA 1891, s.5, but this requires an intent to defraud before the penalties can be imposed so that a bona fide mistake after proper consideration of the issues would not be a breach of s.5.

In *Lloyds & Scottish Finance* v. *Prentice* [1977] 121 SJ 847 the Court of Appeal took a very stringent view of certificates of value. The Court indicated that it was not possible to structure the documentation in such a way that each instrument fell below the threshold, if it was part of a larger arrangement. It went on to say that, in any case where the Court formed the view that the parties had deliberately broken down a transaction into smaller units and improperly used certificates of value for the purpose of saving stamp duty, the whole arrangement might be regarded as a fraud on the

Inland Revenue, with the result that the transaction would be illegal (*Re Wragge Ltd* [1897] 1 Ch 796); and professional misconduct by their professional advisers and persons preparing the documentation (*Saunders* v. *Edwards* [1987] 2 All ER 651).

2.4.4   Testing the propriety

Based on the court's safeguards above, the prudent course for practitioners is therefore to:

- insert a certificate of value, particularly in those cases where the transaction is deemed to be a sale for market value such as transfers or leases to corporate trustees within FA 2000, ss.119 and 121 where the point is frequently overlooked, otherwise the lower rate might be refused when the value is agreed at below £500,000; and
- submit the document to the Inland Revenue Stamp Taxes Office for adjudication.

This has been approved as the correct method for testing the propriety of a certificate of value (*Paul* v. *IRC* [1936] SC 443). Vendors nervous about inserting a certificate of value should be reassured by the undertaking of the purchaser to adjudicate the instrument.

2.4.5   Eligibility

There are two points of principle involved in the utilisation of a certificate of value, namely:

- determining the transaction and its scope (i.e. whether the document is part of a larger transaction or series); and
- determining how much of the total or stampable consideration is to be included when deciding whether a particular threshold has been exceeded or not.

2.4.6   Larger transaction or series

A certificate of value is not permitted for a particular rate of stamp duty where the instrument is part of a larger transaction or series of transactions where the amount or value of the consideration exceeds the relevant threshold.

Before there is such a larger transaction or a series of transactions which precludes the insertion of a certificate of value the various instruments must be contractually linked. If the various documents are in law independent a certificate of value is permissible even though commercially they would not have proceeded unless all were executed. A series or larger transaction does not automatically arise simply because the parties would not sign one contract unless the other contracts were also signed at the same time (*Kimbers* v. *IRC* [1936] 1 KB 132). It will of course, be difficult in some cases to establish that the stages are technically independent as this may be a matter of drafting which could have the consequence of making the contracts interdependent such as by providing that all contacts are to be simultaneously completed and one will not be completed unless all are completed.

2.5 ILLUSTRATIONS OF CERTIFICATES OF VALUE

2.5.1 Same vendor – same purchaser

In general all other property being transferred by the same transferor to the same transferee as part of the larger transaction or series should be taken into account, however improbable it is that all would be conveyed in one instrument, i.e. there is a single contract that is completed by several transfers as in *Saunders* v. *Edwards* [1987] 2 All ER 651. However, that was a case where the parties broke down a single contract into separate transfers.

The position is different where there are separate, independent contracts. For example, the Inland Revenue Stamp Taxes Office has accepted certificates of value for individual contracts pursuant to a *master agreement* which provides a framework upon which the parties may do business but does not commit them to do so. The master agreement is nothing more than a standing invitation to treat, each transaction being based upon separate offers separately accepted would be a separate contract.

However, although the same parties to the transfer are involved, this does not necessarily preclude the utilisation of certificates of value. For example, it has been held that where two properties are purchased from the same vendor by the same purchaser at the same auction in separate lots they do not form part of a series of transactions, and that accordingly a certificate may be given in each transfer without regard for the other (*Att.-Gen.* v. *Cohen* [1937] 1 KB 478).

The ground of the majority decision in this case was that there was no contractual linkage between the two purchases, so that the parties' rights to enforce one contract would not be affected by their conduct under another. This ground could be equally applicable to two sales by private treaty, but the Revenue have intimated that they would require very strong evidence to support treating two simultaneous purchases by private treaty by the same purchaser from the same vendor as being separate transactions, (1954) 18 Conv (NS) 436, but the mere fact that they are commercially linked is not, of itself, sufficient to prevent there being two separate contracts and the right to use certificates of value in both contracts as the decision in *Kimbers* v. *IRC* [1936] 1 KB 132 clearly indicates.

2.5.2 Different parties

Where there are several vendors to different purchasers, or even a single purchaser or a single vendor to several purchasers, in each or all of the relevant
transactions, those in which both vendor and purchaser are not identical or
associated may be disregarded, at any rate if the transactions are not part of
a larger transaction but it is unlikely that there will be a series or larger
transaction in such cases.

For example, if a purchaser subsells part of the property he or she has contracted to purchase, the subpurchaser would feel justifiably aggrieved if a certificate of value was not provided ([1954] 1 LS Digest 62.63). The fact that the
two purchasers are members of the same group of companies does not
preclude the inclusion of certificates of value.

Similarly, it is not a case of a series of transactions for the purpose of
these provisions if one purchaser buys from several different vendors, even
if each contract of sale was conditional on the fulfilment of others. This
view is supported by the observations of Green LJ in *Att.-Gen.* v. *Cohen*
[1937] 1 KB 478, p. 491. Unless the parties are identical, or at least associated in each of the transactions concerned, there can be no suggestion that
the transaction has been artificially split up. Where there are separate contracts with different purchasers a certificate of value is considered proper,
notwithstanding that there is the same vendor and the various purchasers
are associated.

2.5.3 Options

Options raise several stamp duty issues. The Inland Revenue Stamp Taxes
Office has allowed certificates of value to be inserted in options notwithstanding that either the strike or purchase price or the combined option premiums and strike price exceed a relevant threshold. This seems to be correct
since the exercise of the option being uncertain it does not necessarily form
part of a larger, i.e. contractually linked, transaction which is dependent
upon uncertain events under the control of the parties, notwithstanding that
the contract arising from the exercise of the option may be a 'part' of the
larger option contract. The position is, therefore, somewhat unusual since the
option itself is not part of a larger transaction with the contract for sale or
agreement for lease arising upon its exercise whereas the contract for sale or
agreement for lease is part of a larger transaction with the option.

In *Att.-Gen.* v. *Cohen*, [1937] KB 478 Greene LJ instanced a hypothetical
agreement, under which a builder developing land had under one contract an
option to purchase different parts at different times so that each option, when
exercised, would create a separate contract, in which case there would, in his
view, be such an integral relationship between the transactions as to
constitute each indubitably part of a series of transactions.

The *Inland Revenue Stamp Taxes Office Manual* states:

> Several options granted under a single contract exercisable at different times are a series for Certificate of Value purposes. When an option is exercised the transaction concerned may be certified by reference to the total value of the consideration for all the options exercised to date (see *Att-Gen. v. Cohen* [1937] 1 KB 478).

However, this clearly recognises that several options granted under separate independent contracts are not a series or larger transaction.

2.5.4 Ascertaining the threshold

The basic principle is that prima facie, and subject to the special situations considered below, all of the consideration or deemed consideration must be included even where this relates to items of property that are not subject to stamp duty including foreign property where stamp duty is unlikely to be paid.

2.5.5 Variable consideration

There is a potential issue as to whether a certificate of value can be inserted where the consideration is variable or contingent. Provided that it can be shown that the maximum amount potentially payable cannot exceed the relevant threshold because the variable payment has been capped the certificate of value is proper. Where the structure of a variable payment brings the transaction within FA 1994, s.242 (see **section 2.13**) a certificate of value can be included where the market value of the land does not exceed £500,000. Certificates of value can be included where the market value of the consideration is relevant and the parties believe that the relevant value is below that figure and there is no sanction should the final agreed value exceed the relevant threshold. However, if this belief cannot be justified the certificate of value should not be inserted into the instrument.

2.6 EXCLUDED PROPERTY

There are numerous exceptions to the general principle that all of the consideration must be included where part of the consideration can be ignored because it is allocated to relevant assets.

The consideration can be ignored where it is allocated to the areas outlined below.

2.6.1 Goods

The consideration attributable to goods can be deducted in the contract (but not if there is a conveyance of the goods attracting stamp duty) from the purchase price in deciding whether the total consideration exceeds the particular threshold (bearing in mind the potential application of VAT).

This raises important issues as to whether any equipment that is attached to the land is a fixture. This applies to sales of both freehold and leasehold land but there is a particular issue where leasehold interests are involved as to whether it is a *tenant's fixture* or retains its character of a chattel.

In the former case it is stampable and the amount of consideration attributable thereto is included in the consideration when deciding whether the threshold has been exceeded, whereas in the latter case not only is no stamp duty payable under normal circumstances (i.e. the parties avoid American style bills of sales and similar documents) but the amount of consideration attributable thereto can be deducted in considering the level of consideration and the relevant thresholds. The official position has been modified (*Stamp Taxes Bulletin* Issue 1, August 2001, see **Appendix B** – the comments in this *Bulletin* are not necessarily good law and can be challenged by the taxpayer) and the mere fact that an item is attached to the land is no longer regarded as conclusive that it is part of the land. The position is now governed by general land law.

Stamps Form 22 (and presumably Companies Form 88) has been redrafted to remove the words requiring the property to be in an actual state of severance at the time of the execution of the instrument. The correct procedure in relation to these forms is to include the amount of the consideration which the parties regard as applicable in relation to goods and to send a covering letter setting out the reasons why these items although attached to the land are considered to be chattels.

2.6.2 Intellectual property

Intellectual property including goodwill embedded in the intellectual property is no longer subject to stamp duty and the consideration attributable thereto is also deductible from the purchase price when deciding whether the threshold has been exceeded. It should be noted, however, that, whilst knowhow is not subject to stamp duty because it is not *property* (*Handley Page* v. *Butterworth* 19 TC 328), any consideration attributable to the acquisition of knowhow remains within the consideration for the purposes of deciding whether the threshold has been exceeded (FA 2000, s.129; *Stamp Taxes Bulletin* Issue 1, August 2001; see **Appendix B**).

2.6.3 Goodwill

Goodwill itself is exempt from stamp duty as from 23 April 2002 (FA 2002, s.116) and the consideration attributable thereto can be ignored when utilising a certificate of value.

2.6.4 Disadvantaged land

When the disadvantaged land relief is implemented the consideration attributable to such land can be ignored when considering the utilisation of certificate for any other land or assets in the transaction. The relief has not been implemented to date. The *ultra vires* Variation of Stamp Duties Regulations 2001, SI 2001/3746 merely purport to increase the nil rate for such land to £150,000 so that the certificate of value rules are unaffected.

2.7 ALLOCATING THE PRICE

2.7.1 Global consideration

Where there is a global consideration this will require to be allocated between the various assets, but it must not be overlooked that there is an increasing number of cases where the actual consideration is ignored, particularly where land is involved, and the stamp duty is charged upon market value (see **section 2.9**).Where this type of situation occurs not all of the assets will be subject to duty upon their market value so that it will be necessary to allocate the relevant proportion of the actual consideration to those assets dutiable upon the price, and to ignore the actual consideration and substitute market value for the land involved.

However, even where the stamp duty is charged upon the actual consideration there may be problems for the parties in arriving at agreed figures even in an arm's length transaction. All taxes may require a valuation where there is a sale of a bundle of assets for a single consideration and it is necessary to allocate the consideration between the various assets such as on the incorporation of a business or a reconstruction of a company where there is simply an issue of shares as consideration for all of the assets. The vendor may need to allocate the consideration between the assets in order to determine his disposal figures; the purchaser may need to apportion the consideration in order to determine the base costs, opening stock figures, etc.

For stamp duty purposes it is necessary to apportion the consideration between the various assets, i.e. between those assets subject to full stamp duty and those which are exempt or eligible for the lower rate of 0.5 per cent. There is an obligation to apportion the consideration imposed upon the parties by SA 1891, s.58(1). Usually this is done on Stamp Form 22. The Companies Act 1985, s.88 requires a company which has issued shares as consideration for the acquisition of assets to file a return of allotments with the contract or particulars of the contract duly stamped. Form 88(3) requires the consideration to be allocated between various categories of assets; it may, therefore, not be necessary to value every individual asset acquired. However, as the stampable consideration is the market value of the consideration shares issued (SA 1891, s.55(1)), it is necessary to determine market values of relevant assets and to allocate the share value accordingly, even though for other purposes the transaction may be recorded as taking place at the nominal value of the shares issued or the book value of the assets or there may be some form of tax rollover or other relief.

It is obvious that there are likely to be tensions between the vendor and the purchaser as regards the quantification and/or the allocation of the share value and/or price between the assets. The vendor may wish to allocate more to trading stock and less to plant and machinery, but this may affect the purchaser's stamp duty and capital allowances or capital gains tax base value or opening stock figures. There are procedures whereby for certain taxes these disputes can be resolved on a tripartite basis involving the two taxpayers and the Inland Revenue before the Special Commissioners (Capital Gains Tax Regulations 1967, SI 1967/149 Reg. 8) in order to avoid a fiscal impasse. There are, however, no such equivalent provisions for stamp duty.

It should be noted that the basic principle for stamp duty is that the allocation must be made on such basis as the parties think fit (SA 1891, s.58(1) see *Re Brown and Root MacDermott's application* [1996] STC 483). This does not give the parties total freedom to apportion the consideration, which must be on a reasonable basis. Artificial allocation between the assets in order to produce a particular taxation result may be a criminal fraud on the Inland Revenue, (*Re Wragge* [1897] 1 Ch 796) leading to an unenforceable illegal contract, and it is professional misconduct for the parties' advisers to assist in the exercise (*Saunders* v. *Edwards* [1987] 2 All ER 657). Such an exercise may also have unforeseen taxation or contractual consequences (*Re Hollebone* [1959] 2 All ER 152). Where part of the property is eligible intellectual property or goodwill, the Finance Acts 2000 and 2002 require the consideration to be apportioned on a *just and reasonable* basis. These rules will also apply to disadvantaged land if the relief is ever properly implemented.

2.7.2 Land exchanges and certificates of value

The gradual extension of the charge to *ad valorem* stamp duty upon land transactions, both sales and leases (FA 1994, s.241 and FA 2000, s.118) has led to a considerable change in the circumstances where certificates of value may be appropriate. The changes in relation to land *exchanges* have been the most significant.

Prior to FA 1994, s.241 such transactions attracted *ad valorem* stamp duty only upon the equality money, and a certificate of value was permitted where the equality payment did not exceed the relevant threshold. This is no longer possible since the entire value of the consideration and not merely the equality payment is subject to stamp duty. In consequence, certificates of value for the nil or lower rates of stamp duty are permitted only where the total value of the consideration, i.e. the value of the land plus any equality payment, is below the relevant threshold.

This will depend upon the structure of the transaction and depends whether it is an exchange (or double sale) or a single sale. In the former case it will be necessary to consider the certificate value upon both sides of the transaction since, for example, the level of the equality payment may put the transaction into different stamp duty rates. Where both sides of the transaction fall below £60,000 certificates of value for nil stamp duty are permitted. In other cases it depends upon the level of the consideration on each side.

Example

A agrees to transfer property to B worth £70,000 and B agrees to transfer property to A worth £50,000 and pay £20,000 by way of equality. The Inland Revenue Stamp Taxes Office notes on the Finance Bill indicate that *prima facie* and unless there is care in drafting the documents both parties will be paying stamp duty on £70,000. At one time it was contended by certain offices in the Inland Revenue Stamp Taxes Office that a certificate of value was not available even where both properties were below the £60,000 threshold, because the rules required the value of the two properties to be aggregated. This latter point has been abandoned, and both A and B can insert a certificate for the relevant threshold.

In order to obtain the appropriate certificate of value the parties can structure the transaction as being two sales for cash so that A will transfer his property to B for £70,000 and B will transfer his property to A for £50,000. There will be two conveyances and only a cash balance of £20,000 paid over on completion. In this case both properties are clearly entitled to a certificate of value for the relevant threshold.

Where there is an exchange of several properties on each side, the Inland Revenue Stamp Taxes Office may take the point that it is not possible to apportion the consideration in the transfer or subsequently unless this has been done in the contract.

Example

A agrees to transfer Blackacre to B, worth £55,000 plus £45,000 equality money, in return for B agreeing to transfer Whiteacre worth £100,000. It is the basic view of the Inland Revenue Stamp Taxes Office that in this

---

situation, although part of the consideration for the transfer of the value of the larger property is in cash and it is being transferred for the cash, the transfer of the smaller property although representing consideration of only £55,000 is dutiable upon £100,000. In other words, the whole of the value of the property is attributed to the smaller property. It is apparently necessary to draft this transaction as being an agreement to transfer or a transfer of Whiteacre for cash consideration of £100,000 to be satisfied by the transfer of Blackacre and the payment of £45,000 in cash.

It must, it seems, also be made clear in the document that the transfer of Blackacre is in consideration of and related to only part of the value of Whiteacre in order to obtain the certificate of value for Blackacre.

2.8   THE DUTIABLE AMOUNT

2.8.1   Conveyance on sale and lease premium

The amount or value of the consideration (FA 1999, Sched.13 para.1).

For these purposes the rules applicable to the computation of conveyance on sale duty apply to the calculation of lease premium duty (FA 1999, Sched.13 para.12(2); *Quietlece Ltd* v. *IRC* [1984] STC 95).

2.8.2   Lease rent duty

The average rent (FA 1999, Sched.13 para.12(3)).

2.8.3   Special rules

There are many special rules for determining the consideration, premium or the rent for stamp duty purposes, including an increasing number of cases where value is substituted for the actual consideration or rent, which require to be noted since these can increase the duty well beyond the apparent rate.

2.8.4   Basic principles

There are the usual contractual issues of what is the *consideration* or stampable amount. This can give rise to difficulties, such as whether:

- the arrangement is a condition or consideration as in *Eastham* v. *Leigh London and Provincial* [1971] 2 All ER 887;
- a payment to a third party either pursuant to the instrument in question or pursuant to some independent arrangement is part of the consideration such as a lease premium (*Att-Gen* v. *Brown* (1849) 3 Exch.662);

- a payment by a third party to the seller is part of the consideration subject to stamp duty considerations (*Central and District Properties* v. *IRC* [1966] 1 WLR 1015; *Shop and Stores v IRC* [1967] 1 All ER 42);
- VAT is included (*Glenrothes Development Corporation* v. *IRC* [1994] STC 74).

2.9 STAMP DUTY AND VALUE

Situations where there is a stampable consideration other than the cash where a valuation issue arises and situations where market value of some property may be relevant currently include the following.

- *Debts*: the transfer of property in satisfaction and discharge of debts (SA 1891, s.57) when normally the stamp duty is calculated by reference to the face value of the debt. However, where the property is conveyed to the creditor the stamp duty is limited to the market value of the property where this is less than the face value of the debt (FA 1981, s.102).
- *Subject to a mortgage*: the transfer of property subject to a mortgage (SA 1891, s.57) when the amount of the mortgage constitutes and is added to the stampable consideration. However, where the property is transferred to the mortgagee in satisfaction of the debt (FA 1981, s.102), or there is a foreclosure (SA 1898, s.6) the stamp duty charge is limited to the value of the property.
- *Shares and marketable securites*: consideration consisting of shares or marketable securities attracts stamp duty by reference to the market value of the shares and marketable securities (SA 1891, s.55).
- *Right to be issued shares in the future*: for consideration consisting of the right or contingent right to be issued shares in the future the stamp duty is charged upon the value of the shares or marketable securities (SA 1891, s.55(1A); FA 2000, s.126).
- *Transfers and leases*: in relation to transactions involving transfers and leases of land there has been an extension of the chargeable consideration to all other forms of property (FA 1994, s.241) and the stamp duty is calculated by reference to the market value of the property forming the consideration. This normally applies upon exchanges and part exchanges of land, sale and lease back, surrender and regrant of leases and partitions of land and estates.
- *In consideration for other property*: where land is transferred as consideration for the transfer of other property the land transfer is subject to *ad valorem* stamp duty upon the market value of the land subject to reduction where the other property is land (FA 2000, s.118).
- *Securities for qualifying property*: where marketable securities are transferred as consideration for *qualifying property* the *ad valorem* stamp duty

stamp duty is charged upon the market value of the marketable securities (FA 2000, s.122).

- *Subsale relief*: it is necessary, in order to obtain subsale relief pursuant to SA 1891, s.58(4) and (5) (as amended), to establish that the stampable consideration on the final contract for sale is equally the market value of the transferred property.
- *Unascertainable consideration*: in relation to land transactions where the consideration or rent is unascertainable the stamp duty is chargeable upon the market value of the interest in the land conveyed or leased (FA 1994, s.242).
- *In contemplation of a sale*: where there is a transfer in contemplation of a sale the stamp duty is initially calculated by reference to the market value of the property transferred (FA 1965, s.90).
- *Depositary and clearance schemes*: where there is a transfer of shares to a relevant person in connection with the implementation or operation of a depositary scheme or a clearance scheme which is not dutiable as a sale but falls within the head of charge 'Conveyance or Transfer not on sale' the stamp duty is charged upon the value of the securities at the date of execution of the instrument, which is defined as the price which they might reasonably be expected to fetch on a sale at that time in the open market (FA 1986, s.67 and s.70).
- *Transfer or lease to connected company*: where there is a transfer or lease of land to a connected company, whether or not for consideration, the stamp duty is charged upon the market value of the land (FA 2000, s.119 and s121).
- *Transfer or lease to connected company for shares*: where there is a transfer or lease of land to a connected company for a consideration which consists of or includes the issue of shares the stamp duty is charged upon the market value of the land (FA 2000, s.119 and s.121).

It is, therefore, a necessary preliminary to determine whether the stamp duty is chargeable upon the actual consideration or upon the market value.

2.10   UNDERVALUE AND OVERVALUE TRANSACTIONS

Following the abolition of voluntary disposition duty (FA 1985, s.82) stamp duty is now in general chargeable upon the price or the value of the consideration and not the market value of the asset, but there is an increasing number of transactions where the stamp duty is calculated by reference to the value of an asset whether the asset is being sold or leased or acting as the consideration (see **section 2.9**).

It is important to check which asset is to be valued and upon what basis. This can be a problem because:

- there are costs associated with the valuation;
- it may delay registration of title and cause difficulties in making title on later transactions and in giving security or notices;
- there is the important practical issue of whether to make an estimate of the stamp duty and to deposit this with the Inland Revenue Stamp Taxes Office in order to reduce the impact of the late payment interest charge. This runs during negotiations with the Inland Revenue Stamp Taxes Office and can provide an unpleasant surprise when demanded by them when eventually stamping the instrument. However, provided that the document is presented within the prescribed 30 days the late stamping penalty will not run during the negotiations with the Inland Revenue Stamp Taxes Office.

2.10.1   Cash and debt

Where the transaction is a straightforward disposal for a cash sum payable immediately or a cash rent, the calculation of the stamp duty is easy, but where the payment is deferred in whole or in part or is made by instalments particular rules may apply (SA 1891, s.56). Notwithstanding that the charge to stamp duty refers to the amount or value of the consideration, there is no discounting applied to deferred cash payments or instalments for the delay or absence of interest or the risk that some or all of the instalments may not be paid; the conveyance on sale duty is calculated by reference to the full face value of the price (*Hotung* v. *Collector of Stamp Revenue* [1965] AC 766).

The position may be different where the consideration consists of a future payment evidenced by or embodied in a loan note or debenture issued at the time of the transaction so that the consideration consists of a two stage process namely: the issue of a security and the redemption of the loan note when the deferred payment is finally made; in such a case the rules of SA 1891, s.55 apply to determine the amount of stamp duty which depends upon the nature of the loan note (see **section 2.19**).

2.10.2   Foreign currency

With increasing frequency transactions are being undertaken where the price is paid in a non-sterling currency. The Stamp Act 1891, s.6 (amended by FA 1985, s.88) provides that where it is necessary to calculate *ad valorem* stamp duty by reference to foreign currency, the value taken is the value on the day of the date of the instrument according to the current rate of exchange. Section 6 is silent on the question of deferred or contingent consideration payable in a foreign currency. However, the effect of its provisions would seem reasonably clear. Whatever is determined to be the stampable consideration is converted into the sterling equivalent at the relevant rate of exchange.

There will not, it seems, be any argument for converting the deferred and contingent consideration by reference to the forward rate on the date of the instrument for delivery of the relevant date. In addition, there will be no adjustment of the stamp duty if the rate of exchange has moved from that used at the time of stamping when the time for actual payment has arrived. Section 6 (2) provides that where the instrument contains a statement of the current rate of exchange and is stamped in accordance with that statement it is to be deemed to be duly stamped unless and until it is shown that the statement is untrue and that the instrument is in fact insufficiently stamped.

2.10.3 Liabilities

Transactions frequently involve a consideration consisting of or including the assumption of existing liabilities of the vendor such as where property is bought subject to a charge or mortgage or with the assumption of unsecured liabilities of the vendor to creditors on the sale of or incorporation of a business or partnership reorganisation.

SA 1891, s.57 provides that where the consideration (or premium) consists of or includes the assumption of liabilities of the vendor by the purchaser the assumption of the liabilities including contingent liabilities such as guarantees makes the transaction a sale if not otherwise a sale and the consideration for stamp duty comprises or is increased by the full amount of the liabilities.

There are three limbs to this part of SA 1891, s.57 and these are explained below.

TRANSFER SUBJECT TO A CHARGE OR MORTGAGE ON THE PROPERTY TRANSFERRED

Where the transfer relates to property subject to a mortgage, then the face value of the mortgage is added to the consideration paid for the equity of redemption. In cases of sales the amount of mortgage is added automatically to the purchase price whether or not the purchaser agrees to assume or discharge the mortgage (*City of Glasgow Bank* v. *IRC* 1881 8 R (Ct of Sess) 389).

Example

X Ltd is the owner of Blackacre, which is valued at £100,000. It is mortgaged to the bank to secure guarantees given by Y Ltd in respect of the borrowings of its subsidiaries amount to £550,000. On a reorganisation of X Ltd, Blackacre is transferred to Newco Ltd subject to the charge. Stamp duty may be payable on the contingent liability to pay £550,000 under the charge (see *Statement of Practice SP6/90*).

> The charge under SA 1891, s.57 does not extend to liabilities that are inherent in the property transferred (*Swayne* v. *IRC* [1899] 1 QB 335). No liability arises on the assignment of a lease in respect of future rents, nor in the case of partly paid shares in respect of the uncalled liability or the outstanding purchase price upon the assignment of a contract to purchase land.

Slightly different issues arise in relation to gifts of property subject to a mortgage such as where a spouse wishes to put the matrimonial home into joint names (see **section 8.4**).

SATISFACTION OF DEBTS AND FORECLOSURES

A transfer by a debtor to a creditor in satisfaction or discharge of the whole or part of the debt attracts *ad valorem* duty in respect of the face value of the indebtedness discharged. This is without regard to the question of market value or badness of the debt (*IRC* v. *North British Railway* (1901) 4 F (Ct of Sess) 27).

The amount of the charge is limited to the value of the property if less than the amount of the debt:

- where the property is conveyed to a creditor and the value of the property is less than the amount discharged (FA 1980, s.102); and
- in the case of a foreclosure order (FA 1898, s.6).

2.10.4   Assumption of liabilities

The provisions of SA 1891, s.57 also apply where the purchaser (or lessee) agrees to discharge or take over liabilities of the seller (or lessor) to third parties including unsecured and contingent debts such as guarantees, such as frequently occurs on the sale of a business where there is a transfer of debtors and creditors.

There is no netting off of such debtors and creditors. In such cases there is a sale of the debt for the liabilities (in addition to other considerations). Thus where there are £100,000 of debtors and £1,000,000 of liabilities the cash position is nil but the stamp duty is potentially £4,000 – a large sum to pay for nothing.

2.11   PERIODICAL PAYMENTS SUCH AS ANNUITIES (BUT NOT RENT)

The provisions of SA 1891, s.56 deal with transfers of property in consideration of periodical payments, such as transfers of property in consideration of the granting of an annuity or in consideration of royalty or similar payments.

The section provides:

- where the consideration, or any part of the consideration, for a conveyance on sale consists of money payable periodically for a definite period not exceeding twenty years, so that the total amount to be paid can be previously ascertained, the conveyance is to be charged in respect of that consideration with *ad valorem* duty on such total amount;
- where the consideration, or any part of the consideration, for a conveyance on sale consists of money payable periodically for a definite period exceeding twenty years or in perpetuity, or for any indefinite period not terminable with life, the conveyance is to be charged in respect of the consideration with *ad valorem* duty on the total amount which will or may, according to the terms of sale, be payable during the period of twenty years next after the day of the date of the instrument;
- where the consideration, or any part of the consideration, for a conveyance on sale consists of money payable periodically during any life or lives, the conveyance is to be charged in respect of that consideration with *ad valorem* duty on the amount which will or may, according to the terms of sale, be payable during the period of twelve years next after the day of the date of the instrument.

Where the consideration consists of both a lump sum and periodical payments duty is paid in respect of both items (*Martin* v. *IRC* (1904) 91 LT 453). The charge does include sums contingently due (*Underground Electric Railing and Glyn Mills & Co* v. *IRC* [1914] 3 KB 210; [1916] 1 KB 306) but not damages or other sums payable in the event of a default (*Western United Investments Co Ltd* v. *IRC* [1958] Ch 392). Periodical payments require a reasonable degree of recurrence and a few irregularly spread instalments are not within this provision in which case the restriction to the 20 year period does not apply (*Quietlece* v. *IRC* [1984] STC 95).

2.12   SECURITIES AS CONSIDERATION FOR PURCHASE

It should be noted that shares and loan stock of companies are treated as cash, with the result that transfers of property in consideration of the transfer or issue of stock or loan capital ranks as a *sale* for the purposes of stamp duty (*J & P Coats Limited* v. *IRC* [1897] 1 QB 778, on appeal [1897] 2 QB 423). This aspect becomes important when a company is raising funds otherwise than in cash, e.g. an issue of shares for the acquisition of shares or assets linked with a vendor placing or an offer for sale (for the valuation principles for shares and securities see **section 2.19.**)

43

2.13 VARIABLE AND UNCERTAIN CONSIDERATION – EARNOUTS, OVERAGE AND TURNOVER PAYMENTS

It is not unusual for property to be sold or leased for a variable amount. For example, the price for the land may be dependent upon the obtaining of planning permission or the details of the planning permission; the rent for a lease may be linked in whole or in part to the rent received from subletting or the square footage of a building yet to be completed. The documentary nature of stamp duty means that both the liability to stamp duty and the amount thereof has to be determined by the effect of the instrument at the time of its execution; subsequent events are irrelevant upon both issues (*Carlill* v. *Carbolic Smokeball Co* [1892] 2 QB 484). There is no true *wait and see* in stamp duty.

This raises computational problems where the consideration is not fixed but is variable and dependent upon subsequent events. As was stated in *Underground Electric Railway and Glyn Mills* v. *IRC* [1914] 3 KB 210:

> . . . if you cannot ascertain from the instrument a fixed sum which may become payable, though on contingencies, you cannot stamp *ad valorem*.

For these purposes there is a difference between a consideration that is unascertained but is ascertainable (i.e. where all necessary information is available but the necessary calculations or valuations have not been carried out) such as a price equal to the market value on the date of instrument and one that is unascertainable because it depends upon future events such as a price linked to the square footage of a building yet to be constructed.

The former consideration is unascertained but is ascertainable since all necessary information is available so that the Inland Revenue Stamp Taxes Office can *wait and see* whilst the value of the asset is ascertained and agreed but the parties should be advised that they are subject to the late payment interest charge during this process unless the money is deposited on account of the stamp duty. This is, of course, not a true *wait and see* and cannot take into account future developments. The latter consideration is *unascertainable* in the general meaning of this term but special stamp duty principles have been developed to deal with this type of situation.

The computation of the stamp duty upon variable payments where land is involved is a complex process and is frequently dependent upon the drafting of the instrument (FA 1994, s.242).

It is first necessary to determine whether the consideration is wholly *ascertainable* in the special stamp duty meaning of that term pursuant to general stamp duty principles when the land involved is calculated upon that sum; where land involved is wholly or partially unascertainable upon these principles the statutory regime charges stamp duty upon the market value or market rent (FA 1994, s.242(3)(a)). This can give rise to problems, since, depending upon the drafting what appears to be a variable or uncertain sum may, in stamp duty terms, be an *ascertained* consideration or rent. Thus a rent which is reviewable only upwards is *ascertained* and is the basic stampable figure.

It is contended by the Inland Revenue Stamp Taxes Office that where the consideration is related to the future value of an asset, whether or not the asset sold or leased, the present value of the asset concerned is a prima facie sum which can increase or reduce within *ITA* v. *IRC* [1961] AC 427 and is a dutiable ascertained sum. This type of approach has been supported by the Court of Appeal in *L M Tenancies 1 plc* v. *IRC* [1998] STC 326 where it was held that a reference to a future market value was to be construed as a reference to cash sum equal to the market value of the asset at the time when the instrument was executed such sum to be adjusted by reference to the movement in value between the date of the execution of the instrument and the date for the application of the formula as set out in the instrument (see further *Inland Revenue Tax Bulletin* August 1995 and **Chapter 3** on drafting variable consideration).

Again, the instrument may provide for different payments to be made in different circumstances. Provided that there is a formula sufficiently certain as at the date of the document, the higher or highest sum (no matter how remote the possibility that it will actually become payable) is the one to attract the duty. In *Independent Television Authority* v. *IRC* [1961] AC 427 the contingency principle was extended. Fees payable under a bond (a head of charge which no longer exists) and subject to variation downwards as well as upwards were held dutiable on the basic sum payable which was subject to fluctuation.

There was, however, one exception: a provision for financial penalty in a lease. Thus a provision for rent under a lease to be increased to a stated higher rate in the event of late payment will be ignored (SA 1891, s.77(1)).

2.14 THE GENERAL *CONTINGENCY* PRINCIPLE

It is first necessary to determine whether there is an 'ascertained sum' upon general principles. If so, the stamp duty will be calculated upon this figure. These rules apply to all property, not just land. The principle has only been applied however to contingencies in respect of sums payable. It has not, for example, been applied in determining lease terms subject to options to renew (see **section 7.14.4**).

As the above quotation from the *Underground Electric* case indicates if the consideration or rent cannot be determined, there is no liability to *ad valorem* stamp duty. To counteract this, the Inland Revenue has been working to establish a principle that, although the final figures are not known, if they can discover a sum that will or may become payable, albeit contingently, the duty can be charged upon the same. The principle is now established (*LM Tenancies 1 plc* v. *IRC* [1998] STC 326.) and has been applied to variable rents (*Coventry City Council* v. *IRC* [1978] Ch 157).

There is now a general principle that where the consideration or rent is not finally determined at that time, but it is possible to discover a prima facie sum that will or may become payable, even though contingent, *ad valorem* duty is payable upon that sum. Subject to the special rules for land transactions described in the next section, where no figure can be found only a fixed duty of £5 is payable (*Underground Electric Railway* v. *IRC* [1905] 1 KB 174; on appeal [1906] AC 21). The basic position is:

- Where there is a maximum consideration payable the position is quite simple: the stamp duty is calculated upon that sum.
- Where there is a provisional figure which may be increased or reduced, the stamp duty is calculated upon that figure (*Independent Television Authority* v. *IRC* [1961] AC 427).
- Where there is a minimum or basic figure with an unlimited additional payment then stamp duty is charged upon the minimum or basic sum (*Underground Electric Railway* v. *IRC* [1914] 3 KB 210 at p. 220; on appeal [1916] 1 KC 306).

In all cases there is no obligation to pay additional stamp duty if the actual consideration exceeds the amount upon which the stamp duty was paid. Conversely there is no right to a repayment if the final consideration is less than the amount upon which the stamp duty was paid.

Where the prima facie sum is or may be subject to VAT the stamp duty is charged upon the amount of that tax at the current rate applied to the prima facie sum. However, it does not apply to a sum which is payable solely at the option of one of the parties as an alternative method of performance (*Knight's Deep Ltd* v. *IRC* [1900] 1 QB 217) nor a sum payable in the event of default in relation to the main obligation (*Western United Investment Co Ltd* v. *IRC* [1958] 1 All ER 257).

As was stated in *Independent Television Authority* v. *IRC* [1961] AC 427:

> What is necessary is that it should be possible to ascertain from the agreement that there is some specified sum agreed on as the subject of payment which may, perhaps, fairly be called the prima facie or basic payment.

Notwithstanding the reference to the need to find the basic payment in the instrument itself the Inland Revenue Stamp Taxes Office contend that it may be found in the surrounding circumstances but it seems that the commercial predictions of the parties of expected values or rents are not *contingencies*.

Example

In 2003 a property developer, A, agrees to purchase the shares in Whiteacre Ltd from B for an initial consideration of £1,000,000 plus three further instalments of consideration equal to 10 per cent of the profits of Whiteacre Ltd arising on the sale of the houses to be built by Whiteacre in excess of £100,000 for the years ending 31 December 2003, 2004 and 2005.

Subject to the questions of drafting and the effect on construction of the document of *LM Tenancies 1 plc* v. *IRC* [1998] STC 326, the basic stamp duty principles produce the following result.

SHARES TRANSFERRED IN 2003

- stamp duty is assessed on the initial consideration of £1,000,000;
- no further duty is chargeable in respect of the possibility of further payments; and
- the Inland Revenue Stamp Taxes Office cannot recall the stock transfer form for additional duty when the later payments are made.

VARIATIONS

- The shares in Whiteacre are not transferred until 2004 when the initial consideration of £1,000,000 and two instalments totalling £200,000 have been paid. Stamp duty is chargeable on £1,200,000.
- A specifies that the total consideration for the share is not to exceed £1,500,000. On a transfer before the final instalment is ascertained stamp duty will be charged in the view of the Inland Revenue Stamp Taxes Office on £1,500,000. A cannot represent the transfer to reclaim duty if in later years the payments do not reach £1,500,000. On a transfer after the final payment has been ascertained (i.e. 2005) stamp duty will be charged only on the actual amount paid.
- The consideration for the shares in Whiteacre is expressed to be £1,500,000 subject to increase or reduction if the profits are greater or less than £5,000,000. If the transfer is executed before the final figures are known the Inland Revenue Stamp Taxes Office claim duty on £1,500,000. There is no subsequent readjustment of the duty when the final figure is known.

If the transfer of the shares is delayed as in the above illustrations, the charge to stamp duty reserve tax will not be cancelled and interest and penalties will accrue but with a right to repayment as and when the stamp duty is paid (FA 1986, s.87).

2.15   STATUTORY PROVISIONS AFFECTING LAND TRANSACTIONS

Where the transaction is a sale or lease of land, and the above principles produce a sum which is wholly or partially unascertainable, the stamp duty is charged upon the market value or the market rent (FA 1994, s.242).

2.15.1   *Unascertained* in whole or in part

This word bears a special stamp duty meaning, namely, that no prima facie single sum can be found by applying the general contingency principle. In consequence, the position appears to be that the new market value rules do not apply where the general contingency principle produces a prima facie sum (FA 1994, s.242(3)(a)). The basic position is:

- where the consideration is totally unascertainable because no prima facie sum can be found such as a lease of a building yet to be constructed for a rent of '£x per net lettable square foot' with no basic or minimum figure, FA 1994, s.242 will apply;
- where there is a variable figure which has a maximum the consideration is wholly ascertained, FA 1994, s.242 does not apply and the stamp duty is calculated upon the potential maximum, plus any related VAT;
- where there is a basic starting figure which may increase or reduce this is ascertained for the purposes of stamp duty (*Independent Television Authority* v. *IRC* [1961] AC 427) so that FA 1994, s.242 does not apply and the stamp duty is calculated upon the starting figure.

The difficulties arise where there is a minimum or basic figure with an uncertain additional amount. Here the question is whether the uncertain element makes the consideration or rent unascertainable in part. The answer depends upon the drafting. If the consideration or rent formula is for a basic sum plus a variable uncapped amount the latter component in the formula is unascertainable and so FA 1994, s.242 applies. However, if the consideration or rent formula is for the basic sum to be potentially increased in the future it is wholly ascertained (*Independent Television Authority* v. *IRC* [1961] AC 427) and FA 1994, s.242 does not apply; the stamp duty is charged upon the basic price.

For example, where there is a rent with the normal upward reviews, part of the rent is unascertainable. However, it seems that this is an ascertainable sum upon stamp duty principles and the Inland Revenue Stamp Taxes Office will regard this as not falling within the new regime because there is a single prima facie albeit variable sum; it is dutiable under the general contingency rules as a minimum rent. The statutory rules apply where the consideration or rent has two or more separate components, one or more of which is 'unascertainable'. This analysis applies in the special regime so that if a purchaser agrees to pay £x or 5 per cent of the profits on the resale of the property whichever is the greater there is simply a variation on the upwards only rent review and FA 1994, s.242 does not apply; stamp duty is charged upon £x. However, if the formula is for £x plus the overage payment, the latter part of the consideration is unascertainable and FA 1994, s.242 imposes stamp duty upon the market value (see **Chapter 3** for drafting issues.) Obviously, depending upon the time when the instrument is executed the basic price may represent the market value.

Example

A the freeholder agrees to grant a lease to B a developer conditional upon the completion of certain buildings and grants the lease to B at the completion of the building works for a rent equal to one of the following:

- the greater of £5,000 or 25 per cent of the rent received from subletting;
- 25 per cent of the rents received from subletting; or
- £5,000 plus 25 per cent of the rents received from sub letting;
- £5,000 but if the rents received from subletting exceed £50,000 the consideration shall be increased to a rent equal to 25 per cent of the rents; or
- 25 per cent of the rents received from subletting but such rents to be not less than £5,000.

Note that in the illustration the problem arises at two stages; namely, the agreement for lease and the lease (FA 1999, Sched.13 para.14). It seems that:

- the general contingency rules may apply, i.e. there is a single minimum rent of £5,000 upon which the stamp duty is charged;
- the market value rules would apply because no prima facie rent is ascertainable under the general rules;
- the market value would apply because part of the rent (i.e. the excess over the £5,000) cannot be ascertained;
- there is a single increasable rent so that there is no separate unascertainable part and duty is charged upon £5,000;
- there would seem to be a single rent with a minimum and the duty is charged upon £5,000.

If the lease is granted to B before the commencement of the building works and B enters into possession under the lease paying a token rent of £1 per annum during the building with an increase to the greater of £1 or 25 per cent of the rents received on practical completion, it is possible that the District Valuer and the Inland Revenue Stamp Taxes Office will accept that this is a minimum rent for the whole term so that the new rules do not apply

---

and the averaging principle of stamp duty will apply. Considerable practical difficulties may arise because the Inland Revenue Stamp Taxes Office appear to find it difficult to accept that a low initial rent can constitute a market rent as in this case. The position might be helpful for the taxpayer if the minimum rent for practical completion is a reasonable figure rather than a purely token sum. The position will, of course, be potentially different if B merely has a licence during the construction phase (assuming, of course, that this is a licence and does not constitute a periodic tenancy).

2.16 VALUE ADDED TAX

The FA 1989 made a number of changes to value added tax legislation which have had significant effects on stamp duty liabilities. It seems that previously, supplies subject to VAT and stampable transactions had for the most part not coincided, and thus questions of the correct stampable, or for that matter VATable, consideration had rarely arisen. For example, business sale agreements which will usually raise stamp duty liabilities will often fall outside the scope of VAT as transfers of a going concern. It was the application of VAT to transactions involving land which brought matters to a head. Following FA 1989 it was possible to elect to charge VAT on supplies which had until that time been exempt (the relevant legislation is now contained in Value Added Tax Act 1994 (VATA 1994), Sched.10).

Regardless of the apparent unfairness of the payment of tax on tax, it is now firmly established that stamp duty is payable on the VAT-inclusive consideration for a transfer (*Glenrothes Corporation* v. *IRC* [1993] STC 74).

An area of initial concern was that of leases where the lessor could elect to charge VAT at any point during the course of a lease such that rental payments would be liable for VAT. Where the exemption from VAT was waived before the lease grant, stamp duty was clearly to be calculated on the VAT-inclusive rent. However, where the election had not been made, but it was still possible to do so, that situation was less clear. Broadly, it appears to be the view of the Inland Revenue Stamp Taxes Office that VAT which may become payable is a contingent sum and under the contingency principle is liable to stamp duty. The fact that the rate of VAT may change does not mean that the consideration or rent is unascertainable within section FA 1994, s.242. The official views are set out in Statement of Practice SP11/91 (see **Appendix A**) and the broad position is set out under the four headings below.

2.16.1 Basic price and rent

Stamp duty is chargeable upon any VAT which is actually payable upon the ascertained or fixed consideration or rent.

2.16.2 Contingent and deferred sums

It is the contention of the Inland Revenue Stamp Taxes Office that where there is contingent or uncertain future consideration which may attract VAT then if the contingency principle produces a prima facie sum the hypothetical value added tax upon this prima facie sum is also subject to stamp duty.

2.16.3 Option to tax

Where there is an exempt transaction with deferred consideration or an exempt lease with rent and it is possible for the option to tax to be exercised by the landlord then stamp duty will be claimed on the basis that the option to tax has been exercised and the VAT on the relevant amounts or rents is payable at once.

2.16.4 Periodical premium risk

In relation to rent, there is a difficult line between value added tax that is reserved as rent and value added tax that is reserved as an additional sum. Where the rent is contingent within the *Coventry City Council* case [1978] Ch 157 then the VAT is calculated by reference to that contingent sum. The question is, however, whether the value added tax in all cases is stampable as rent or is a periodical payment within SA 1891, s.56. The effect of this can be very important since treatment as a periodical premium will increase the stamp duty. The issue seems to be essentially one of drafting and, it seems, that provided the sum is either included in the rental figures, such as a rent of £117,500 inclusive of VAT or the rent is £100,000 plus VAT, the VAT will be treated as part of the rent and not as a periodical premium where the VAT is a separate sum the total VAT that will or may become payable over the life of the lease or 20 years whichever is the shorter is aggregated and the lump sum so calculated is dutiable as a premium.

Example

A grants a 25 year lease to B for a rent of £100,000 plus VAT (£17,500):

- if the VAT is treated as part of the rent, the stamp duty is £2,350 (i.e. 2% of £117,500); but
- if the VAT is treated not as rent, the stamp duty is £14,000 (i.e. 4 per cent of 20 × £7500) plus £2000 (i.e. 2 per cent of the rent of £100,000) totalling £16,000.

The position is, however, less obvious in relation to exempt rents where, almost by definition, it is difficult to regard that VAT may arise if the option to tax is exercised as being rent. However, it seems that in practice the Inland Revenue Stamp Taxes Office does not often take the point and regard such hypothetical VAT as being contingent rent rather than premium. In general the point rarely arises since it appears to be standard conveyancing practice for any VAT to be reserved as part of the rent so that the landlord has the extra remedies for the recovery of the tax.

2.17 TOGC CHANGE OF PRACTICE

Where the transaction may be a TOGC but the parties provide that should VAT become payable the purchaser will pay it the Inland Revenue Stamp Taxes Office require two letters to be produced with the documents:

- a letter undertaking by the purchaser to re-present the document and pay the additional stamp duty; and
- a letter from the solicitor confirming that purchaser has had the significance of such an undertaking explained.

Subject thereto the Inland Revenue Stamp Taxes Office will provisionally stamp the document upon the basic price (see *Law Society Gazette*, January 1999). Where appropriate a certificate of value for the basic price can be included notwithstanding that if VAT is payable the total price will exceed the threshold. The stamp duty payable upon the VAT will bear late payment interest from 30 days after the execution of the instrument, not 30 days after the VAT is paid or invoiced. Where the VAT takes the instrument into a higher rate of stamp duty the entire consideration is assessed at the higher rate and interest is payable upon the excess payment (on certificates of value in this context see **section 2.4.2**).

2.18 VALUATION ISSUES

2.18.1 The contract price as value

Where the consideration is cash in sterling and no special anti-avoidance provisions substituting market value apply, no valuation is required. However, as the preceding paragraphs indicate there is an increasing number of situations where valuation is important. Unfortunately the stamp duty legislation is seriously deficient in detailed rules for determining market value.

2.18.2 Inland Revenue Stamp Taxes Office practice

Given the economics of the situation the attitude and practices of the Inland Revenue Stamp Taxes Office to matters of valuation is of crucial significance.

The Inland Revenue Stamp Taxes Office itself has no separate valuation department and these matters are passed to the District Valuer and the Shares Valuation Division of the Inland Revenue.

Unfortunately the *Inland Revenue Stamp Taxes Office Manual* does not contain significant guidance on valuation practice so that there are many areas of doubt as to how to deal with these situations. It merely states that where a valuation is required as in the above list, the person submitting the instrument must submit a valuation supported by documentary evidence of how the figure was produced. If the parties are connected an independent professional valuation is required. It seems that if the value is expected to exceed £2.5 million the District Valuer will require a site visit.

In many transactions the parties may, as part of the negotiations leading to the transaction, have agreed a value through valuers. It may be possible to avoid a valuation process by inserting cash figures. The inclusion of a cash sum may avoid the risk of a double charge to *ad valorem* stamp duty upon land exchanges and swaps; it may also be a figure acceptable to the Inland Revenue Stamp Taxes Office as representing the stampable consideration. In other cases the inclusion of a prima facie sum in a variable consideration formula may bring the instrument into charge under the alleged general contingency principle with the consequence that the market value rules will not apply.

Parties wishing to avoid the delay and/or expense of valuations which will preclude registration of title may find it useful to make use of these or other arrangements. In *Stanton* v. *Drayton* 55 TC 286 the parties agreed the consideration as a cash sum to be satisfied by a certain number of shares. The House of Lords held that where parties acting at arm's length agreed a figure that was not a sham or colourable then, at least for capital gains tax, this was the value. However, in *Lap Shun Textiles* v. *Collector* [1976] STC 83 the Privy Council held that arm's length negotiation was evidence of market value but was not conclusive in relation to stamp duties. There is emerging evidence that at least in cases where the amounts involved are not large, the Inland Revenue Stamp Taxes Office is beginning to act upon the basis of the decision in *Stanton* v. *Drayton* 55 TC 286.

This would, of course, apply so that every transfer by way of mutual exchange and as a sale and lease-back at arm's length, is referred to the District Valuer. However, it seems from the Notes on the Budget that the Inland Revenue Stamp Taxes Office will not necessarily refer the transaction to the District Valuer or Shares Valuation Division where the parties are acting at arm's length and the instruments submitted for stamping are accompanied by a professional valuation, at least where the transaction is relatively small.

The Inland Revenue Stamp Taxes Office has indicated that the valuation needs to be reasonably up to date. It is unclear how far this applies where there is a delay between the valuation and preparation of the instrument. This can, in many cases, be quite significant in that there are delays inevitably involved. The parties may have had professional valuations prepared for the purposes of the initial commercial negotiations but these may easily be six months old by the time that the final documentation is executed. It would seem that in such a situation where there are several months between the valuation and the stampable instrument the Inland Revenue Stamp Taxes Office would not be prepared to act on that valuation and the parties would either have to obtain, at their own cost, a new valuation or conduct even more costly negotiations with the District Valuer.

2.18.3   Valuation procedure

Fiscal valuations are a highly artificial process and any negotiations have bizarre structure and it must not be overlooked there are often significant related costs and the late payment interest charge runs throughout such negotiations unless mitigated by the parties making a reasonable estimate of the dutiable amount and depositing an appropriate amount with the Inland Revenue Stamp Taxes Office to prevent or restrict the running of the interest charge.

Normally the vendor or owner of the property will be seeking the highest possible price whereas the taxpayer, although the notional vendor in a sense, will usually be seeking a lower figure and the Inland Revenue will in a sense be occupying the role of an uncommercial seller attempting to achieve the highest possible price. This odd situation frequently exists in the stamp duty valuation of shares.

However, in relation to the new provisions relating to land, as there will frequently have been arm's length negotiations between the parties to the transaction which has generated the documents, there will be a realistic commercial background which may influence the District Valuer, particularly when supported by reports from independent professional advisers.

In the event that it is impossible for the parties to agree a value for land or any other property it would seem that the strict position would be for the Inland Revenue Stamp Taxes Office to issue an assessment based upon the Inland Revenue's valuation and for this to be contested by way of an appeal to the High Court on a case stated pursuant to SA 1891, s.13 where it seems expert evidence can be heard (*Speyer Bros* v. *IRC* [1903] 1 KB 318, reversed on appeal [1908] AC 92). Such a procedure is regarded as unsatisfactory and it is possible to appeal to the Lands Tribunal by consent (Lands Tribunal Act 1949, s.1(5); *Inland Revenue Tax Bulletin* August 1995); such procedures do not appear to be available for other types of property.

2.18.4   Leases and the two valuations

In relation to leases where there is likely to be a delay between the agreement for lease and the lease itself two valuations will almost inevitably be required. As a result of the two stage process for stamping leases this requires:

- a valuation made shortly before the agreement for lease is entered into for the purpose of determining the duty payable upon that instrument; and
- a fresh valuation when the lease is granted for the purpose of determining the stamp duty prima facie payable upon that instrument.

The double valuation would be necessary even where under the new provisions the agreement for lease and the lease are presented together. It must be noted that FA 1994, s.240 merely relates to the date for the running of penalties, it does not affect that date used for the computation of the stamp duty.

2.19 VALUATION OF SHARES AND STOCK

The SA 1891 has the effect that shares and debentures are treated as cash so that both sale and lease premium duty can arise. It is therefore necessary to value shares and loan stock where these form all or part of the consideration:

(a) Where there is a market in the shares or the marketable security the duty is calculated by reference to the average price for such shares on the day of the date of the instrument, of the stock or security. Section 6(2) provides that where an instrument contains a statement of the average price and is stamped in accordance with that price it is, so far as regards the subject matter of the statement, to be deemed duly stamped, unless or until it is shown that the statement is untrue and that the instrument is in fact insufficiently stamped. Two points call for comment:

   – the charge is as at the date of the instrument, not as is normally thought to be the case, the date of the issue of the shares. Thus on a delayed completion of a land transfer the shares may have increased in value because the land has increased in value or been developed, or even, because the company has acquired other assets and prospered generally;
   – it is thought that the references to 'average price' requires some form of market or Stock Exchange listing or alternatives such as the AIM so that section 6 may not apply to companies not quoted on any form of investment exchange (SA 1891, s.6; *Crane Freuhauf* v. *IRC* [1975] STC 51).

(b) Where there is no market and the consideration is or includes shares or marketable securities duty is charged upon the market value of the shares (SA 1891, s.55). This applies even where the consideration is the right to be issued with shares in the future such as on an earnout (FA 2000, s.126).

(c) Where the consideration is non-marketable securities (e.g. private company debentures) the duty is calculated upon the amount that will or may become payable under the security (SA 1891, s.55).

2.19.1 *Marketable security* defined

The question of a *marketable security* is a significant one for a variety of reasons:

- the application of the 0.5 per cent rate;
- availability of certificates of value;
- principles of valuation; and
- the possible availability of exemptions under FA 1971, s.64 (preserved by FA 1999, Sched.13 para.25).

Marketable security is defined in SA 1891 s.122(1) (as amended) as:

> a security of such a description as to be capable of being sold in any stock market in the United Kingdom.

The essence of this is that an actual listing is not necessary, the test is whether the stock is similar to a security that does have a listing or the stock itself could qualify if the parties so wished. The view of the Inland Revenue Stamp Taxes Office is that a provision stating the parties will not seek a listing or the stock is not to be listed will not, of itself, prevent the particular security from being *marketable*. This also means that the mere fact that a stock has a ready market does not make it marketable if it is not suitable for Stock Exchange dealings. The Inland Revenue Stamp Taxes Office accepts in practice that because of the legal restrictions upon public offerings of their shares a *private company* cannot have a marketable security in this sense.

The second aspect of the definition is that of a *security*. This term means nothing more than the recording of an obligation for the payment of money in a written instrument. Security in the sense of a mortgage or charge is not necessary.

There is little guidance in the cases relating to stamp duty as to the application of these and other valuation provisions and principles. The main guidance on the principles to be adapted must, therefore, be derived from case law upon other legislation which uses the similar terminology, such as:

- Inheritance Tax Act 1984, s.160;
- Taxation of Chargeable Gains Act 1992, s.272(1); and
- Finance Act 1894, s.7(5).

There are a few general comments as to valuation where the assets of the company consisted of an annuity in *Faber* v. *IRC* [1936] 1 All ER 617, and in *Crane Freuhauf Ltd* v. *IRC* [1975] 1 All ER 429 at p. 434 Russell LJ indicated that where SA 1891, s.6 does not apply the Inland Revenue Stamp Taxes Office 'must do the best they can'. He also suggested that if the consideration shares are to be issued after the date of the execution of the relevant instrument but are to be issued and listed shortly thereafter the market value at the time of issue would be a good indication of the amount or value of the consideration for the transfers. The effect of these provisions is to draw a distinction in the valuation rules between shares and marketable securities and non-marketable securities and those which are quoted on a stock exchange or similar institution.

2.20 VALUATION OF LAND

No special rules are laid down in the stamp duty legislation for the valuation of the land or other property involved other than that is the open market value of the relevant property at the time when the instrument is executed. Notwithstanding that from 1910 to 1985 the value of land might be relevant in assessing stamp duty under the head 'Voluntary Disposition Duty' and that the value of shares being issued by a company might depend to a considerable extent upon the value of various parcels of land, there is no body of case law to provide guidelines.

There is no equivalent to SA 1891, s.6 or s.55 relating to the valuation of land. The new provisions relating to land exchanges and transfers or leases of land for an unascertainable consideration or rent (FA 1994, s.242) impose stamp duty by reference to the value of land or other property.

The stamp duty valuation provisions merely state that:

- the time for valuation is the time immediately before the execution of the instrument in question;
- the *market value* is to be the price which that property might reasonably be expected to fetch on a sale at that time (i.e. immediately before the instrument is executed) in the open market which would seem to mean the best price possibly obtainable (FA 1994, s.241(2) and s.242(3) and see *Re Hayes* [1971] 1 WLR 758); and
- *the market rent* is the rent which the lease might reasonably be expected to fetch at that time in the open market (FA 1994, s.242(3)(*b*)).

No further guidance is provided as to how one determines the relevant price or the assumptions upon which such hypothetical sale is to be treated as being made. No doubt the District Valuer may be able to make some use of the Particulars Delivered Forms produced to him as comparables but these will frequently offer little direct comparability. Moreover, there are serious difficulties in making use of comparables in valuing shares or seeking to rely upon evidence of actual transactions.

One area that provides a trap is the identification of the property to be valued. When dealing with the exchange regime it is the value of the property forming the consideration for the transfer or lease of the land which is the basis for calculating the stamp duty. In relation to the unascertainable consideration regime it is the value of the land transferred or leased which is used to calculate the stamp duty.

However, the values of these properties may vary between contract and completion. For example, one of the parties may commence and possibly complete extensive building works or where there is an agreement to transfer a freehold the purchaser may, prior to receiving the conveyance of the legal title, direct the vendor to grant a lease to a third party for a premium, or to execute a mortgage in favour of a lender. In the former case the value of the land may have substantially increased in value in the interim period, whereas in the latter two cases the value of the land will have fallen considerably. It is considered that the value of the land is different from the potentially stampable consideration should SA 1891, s.57 apply, i.e. the value is the value of the encumbered equity of redemption. In the latter cases there may, in consequence, be a substantial saving of stamp duty. It will, therefore, be important to consider which property will be potentially vulnerable to change in values and when, subject to commercial considerations, will be the best time to execute the Land Registry transfer or lease.

2.20.1   Other property

The effect of section FA 1994, s.241 in relation to land transactions is that the value of other property such as patents, goodwill, shares and so on may now form the basis of stampable consideration. No express statutory principles are laid down for valuing such property.

2.20.2   Actual transaction

The Inland Revenue Stamp Taxes Office has accepted that what is to be valued in the instrument in the context of the actual transaction, for example, the actual lease with all is covenants, reservations and terms and not a hypothetical lease (*Inland Revenue Tax Bulletin* August 1995).

CHAPTER 3

Drafting

3.1 PRACTICAL APPLICATIONS OF DOCUMENTATION

The documentary nature of the tax has several important practical applications.

3.1.1 No liability to tax

If there is no document there is no liability to tax (*Carlill* v. *Carbolic Smokeball Co* [1892] 2 QB 484. However, the possibility of avoiding writing for land transactions is rare because of numerous provisions in LPA 1925 and 1989 requiring deeds or written contracts. Writing may be required for assignments of equitable interests (LPA 1925, s.53(1)(c)) or to pass legal title to *choses in action* (LPA 1925, s.136). In each case it is necessary to study the provision to see whether it requires writing for the contract or the transfer or both. If the requirement for writing is limited to the formal transfer it may be possible to mitigate the stamp duty or postpone the charge by an oral contract.

3.1.2 Rates and penalties

The structure of the documentation can affect the amount of stamp duty and any penalties and late payment interest. The latter two run from the time of execution where land is concerned but apply only to the amount of stamp duty upon the instrument in question. If the property is conveyed by instalments over time the stamp duty is payable over time and interest and penalties may not accrue or are reduced.

For example, where the transaction affects both United Kingdom and foreign property a single transfer of all property will attract a full charge to stamp duty but it may be possible to mitigate this by arranging for separate transfers of the United Kingdom and foreign property. The latter being executed and retained abroad and hopefully not required in the United Kingdom although it may be necessary to disclose their existence (*Inland Revenue Tax Bulletin 30* (August 1997)).

3.1.3 Stamp duty reliefs

The structure of the documentation may affect the stamp duty reliefs in respect of land contracts, dutiable pursuant to FA 2002, s.115, not only for the immediate parties but also prior and subsequent sellers. As the repayment of the tax requires production of the documentation and full disclosure, errors in sub-sale techniques will now be more likely to be discovered to the cost of the clients.

3.1.4 Unnecessary charges

The drafting of the documentation may attract an unnecessary charge to or help to avoid or reduce the charge to stamp duty as in *Peter Bone Ltd v. IRC* [1995] STC 921. In this case the parties, rather than rely upon the constructive trust which arises automatically and without the need for writing (LPA 1925, s.53(2) and LP(MP)A 1989, s.2(6)) upon payment, chose to include an express declaration of trust. As the document was executed as a deed and the parties went straight from contract to completion this converted the contract into a conveyance; but even if it had retained its character as a contract it would, as drafted, have been dutiable pursuant to FA 1999, Sched.13 para.7. However, there is a problem which could arise in these circumstances, where the vendor retains title and has charges or liens for the unpaid purchase price or balance thereof.

3.2   DRAFTING AT DIFFERENT STAGES OF THE TRANSACTION

The drafting of the documentation at all stages of the transaction including negotiation and post transaction may affect the taxation generally. As solicitors are responsible for the tax efficient implementation of the transaction and have been held to be liable for incurring excessive stamp duty even when not advising upon tax it is vitally important that care is exercised in drafting at all stages of the transaction. The following paragraphs illustrate the tax problems that have arisen because of inappropriate wording.

3.2.1   Pre-contract correspondence

Pre-contract correspondence between solicitors has been used by the Revenue (*Ridgeons Bulk* v. *Customs and Excise* [1994] STC 427).

3.2.2 Clearance letters

Inland Revenue clearance letters may need to be produced to the Inland Revenue Stamp Taxes Office in support of an adjudication particularly in the context of group reconstructions and intra-group transfers (*Swithland* v. *IRC* [1990] STC 448).

3.2.3 Effect upon later transfers

Contracts need to be appropriately drafted as this may affect the stamp duty upon later transfers (*Portman* v. *IRC* (1956) 35 ATC 349, where the parties entered into two contracts for the sale of properties for cash sums. Completion took the form of a single deed of exchange. It was held that the deed was in substance not an exchange but a completion of two sales for cash and attracted two charges to conveyance on sale duty).

3.2.4 Consideration provisions

The amount of stamp duty may be influenced by the drafting of the consideration provisions such as the single sale for land transactions (see **section 4.13.3**) and variable consideration (see **section 2.15.1**).

3.2.5 Classification of documents

Routine documents may, in stamp duty terms, be conveyances and agreements for leases such as notices exercising options to renew a lease and receipts which describe a prior sale have been held to be subject to stamp duty (*Garnett* v. *IRC* (1899) 81 LT 633; *Horsfall* v. *Hey* (1848) 2 Ex 778). Letters of direction may constitute equitable assignments subject to stamp duty (*Re Tyler* [1967] 3 All ER 389).

3.2.6 Post transaction and ancillary documents

Post transaction and ancillary documentation if appropriately prepared may be stampable within the Memorandum Rule. This brings into charge a wide range of documentation (see **section 1.12**). In consequence the preparation of ancillary documentation is an important issue. Solicitors should consider whether their zeal for reducing everything to formal writing and for protecting their client against remote commercial risks is really necessary commercially and does not lead to a stamp duty charge where one would otherwise not arise. Frequently the stamp duty risks involved in such steps are greater than the other risks being covered.

> The consultative documents suggest that drafting will not matter in the revised land stamp duty regime after early 2004, but this may be a naïve view and will depend upon the detailed legislative amendment. The revised stamp duties for land transactions from early 2004 are likely to be linked to 'payment' and there are some important drafting issues as to whether an outstanding consideration has been paid; the difference between an unpaid price and a payment and loan back by way of set-off is likely to have important consequences and turns upon the words used (*Coren* v. *Keighley* 48 TC 370).

3.3 FORM AND SUBSTANCE

A key issue in the preparation of documentation is the question of whether, notwithstanding the legal form of the instrument, the Inland Revenue Stamp Taxes Office can look behind the document and claim the stamp duty upon the basis of the 'economic realities' of the transaction.

> In stamp duty terms, this is a highly limited doctrine and has no real application at present. However, it is a principle that the Inland Revenue Stamp Taxes Office may seek to develop under the revised regime from 2004.

It is clear that the parties cannot dictate the legal nature of the transaction simply by utilising *labels* or particular words. For example, the important issue of lease or licence is not determined by the use of the word 'licence', it is a question of the overall effect of the instrument as to the rights and liabilities created (*Addiscombe Garden Estates Ltd* v. *Crabbe* [1958] 1 QB 513). However, in a borderline case the actual words used may tip the balance (*British India Steam* v. *IRC* (1881) 7 QB 165) so the choice of individual words is important. This is particularly the case in stamp duty, since what matters is the words in the document and what the parties thought or intended is irrelevant and inadmissible in construing the instrument (*West London Syndicate Ltd* v. *IRC* [1898] 2 QB 507; *Peter Bone Ltd* v. *IRC* [1995] STC 921).

Unless what the parties wrote is a 'sham' misdescribing their intended transaction, the legal analysis prevails (*Snook* v. *London and West Riding* [1967] 1 All ER 518). This is important upon issues of form or substance since the fact that there are several methods of implementing a transaction with different legal consequences but which produce the same or very similar commercial or economic consequences does not enable the Inland Revenue Stamp Taxes Office to go behind the documentation. In general the approach of *Ramsay* v. *IRC* [1982] AC 300 and *Furniss* v. *Dawson* [1984] AC 474 does not apply to stamp duty (*MacNiven* v. *Westmoreland Investments* [2001] STC 231).

Taxpayers are free to choose the legal structure they desire (*Sherdley* v. *Sherdley* [1987] STC 217; *Cyril Lord* v. *Lloyd and Scottish* [1992] BCLC 609) and the choice cannot be attacked by the Inland Revenue Stamp Taxes Office simply because the choice was made solely or mainly because it was believed to produce a tax efficient result (*Willoughby* v. *IRC* [1995] STC 143).

For example, a sale of future rents attracts stamp duty but a mortgage of the land is free of duty notwithstanding that it is to be repaid only out of the rents. However, such arrangements may have wider implications for stamp duty and other taxes (see Income and Corporation Taxes Act 1988 (ICTA 1988), Sched.18 para.1(5), which applies to stamp duty groups).

In many respects the financial results over time are similar but the fact that the parties chose the latter route because it was regarded as more stamp duty efficient cannot be used as the basis for the Inland Revenue Stamp Taxes Office to attack the transaction and treat it as a sale of rents. It may, however, be a complex question of construction whether the drafting of the documentation has produced that result (*Lloyds and Scottish* v. *Cyril Lord* [1992] BCLC 609).

The problem of drafting in stamp duty planning is complicated by the fact that over 300 years the tax has developed a terminology of its own and this has been affected by legislative changes. For example, in general terms a transfer of property in consideration of the issue of shares is not a *sale* (*re Westminster Property* [1987] 2 All ER 426) but is so regarded for stamp duty (*J&P Coats Ltd* v *IRC* [1897] 1 QB 778, on appeal [1897] 2 QB 423). An amalgamation may be a sale for stamp duty purposes no matter how the parties describe it (*Great Western Railways* v *IRC* [1894] 1 QB 507). Draftsmen should be aware of the special usages.

3.4   ILLUSTRATIVE DRAFTING PROBLEMS

The following paragraphs are intended to illustrate routine areas where drafting is likely to have a significant impact upon the stamp duty liability.

3.4.1   Certificate of value

It is necessary to include a certificate of value in the instrument itself at execution since according to the *Inland Revenue Stamp Taxes Office Manual* it may not be possible to add it later. When preparing documentation it is necessary to avoid any drafting such as over elaborate cross-referencing to other transactions since this may make the document part of a larger transaction (see **section 2.4.4**).

3.4.2 Powers of attorney

A power of attorney given to a purchaser is a conveyance on sale (*Diplock* v. *Hammond* (1854) 5 De GM & G 320, see **section 4.6**). The risk can be reduced by providing that the vendor will execute transfers when requested by the purchaser but that if the vendor should fail to do so the purchaser is authorised to execute them. Since this power arises only in the event of breach, it is not a conveyance and is ignored when determining stamp duty liability.

3.4.3 Options

It must not be overlooked that options are subject to stamp duty as conveyances on sale where granted for a relevant consideration (SA 1891, s.60; *George Wimpey Ltd* v. *IRC* [1975] 2 All ER 45). Consequently where the premium is below £500,000 a certificate of value is essential if the lower rates are to be obtained (see **section 2.5.3**).

The main trap is the manner in which the purchase price is expressed. As *George Wimpey Ltd* v. *IRC* [1975] 2 All ER 45 clearly indicates, if the option premium is not deducted from the contract price but operates rather like a deposit or a credit against the purchase price the grantee is technically liable to stamp duty twice upon the option premium.

It is the view of the Inland Revenue Stamp Taxes Office that an option can affect the beneficial ownership of an asset, particularly shares with implications for stamp duty group structures and reliefs such as FA 1930, s.42 (as amended). However, much may depend upon the drafting. It seems that beneficial ownership can be lost if the option agreement restricts the taking of dividends pending the exercise of the option; but if there is no such restriction and the agreement provides that the price will be reduced to take account of dividends paid during the period this does not affect beneficial ownership (*J Sainsbury* v. *O'Connor* [1991] STC 516). The economic result is the same, but the legal consequences may differ.

3.4.4 Land exchanges

The FA 1994, s.241 enlarged the definition of 'sale' and 'premium' for land transactions. It was clearly the intention of the Inland Revenue Stamp Taxes Office that upon a land exchange there should be two charges to *ad valorem* duty upon the market value of the land plus equality money and both payments of VAT (see **section 4.13.3**). However, they were forced to accept that with appropriate drafting it was possible to create a 'single sale' (*Connell* v. *Begej* [1993] 39 EG 123) with only one charge to *ad valorem* stamp duty and a fixed duty charge of £5 upon the other property. The position has been somewhat modified by FA 2000, s.118 (see **section 4.13.3**) which has the incidental effect of cancelling the £5 charge. The position does depend upon the drafting and inappropriate wording can easily cause the client to incur an unnecessary charge to stamp duty or to lose the credit conferred by s.118.

> It is clear that the Inland Revenue Stamp Taxes Office intends to bring back the double charge in the revised stamp duty regime for land in early 2004.

It is important that drafting begins at the contract stage since those terms dictate the nature of the transaction, and even before FA 1994, s.241 it was possible to convert an exchange which was the subject of a very limited charge to stamp duty into a double sale simply by drafting (*Portman* v. *IRC* 35 ATC 349).

To obtain the single sale treatment it would seem that it may be necessary to express the transaction as an agreement to transfer or the actual transfer of Blackacre in consideration of '£X (a cash sum) to be satisfied by the transfer of Whiteacre and the payment of £Y' (*Inland Revenue Tax Bulletin* August 1995) The Tax Bulletin indicates that the single sale treatment is available only where there is the payment of cash balance. A simple exchange of two or more properties of equal value will not be regarded as a single sale notwithstanding that the agreement is drafted in the terms discussed above; double stamp duty will be payable. Fortunately in exchanges it is rare for the properties on each side to be of precisely the same value and some cash adjustment will almost always be required in practice. The present position must depend entirely upon the drafting and merely to refer to cash sums may not be sufficient such as where the parties merely refer to agreed values rather than a price.

It is, presumably, necessary to carry this drafting fiction through from the contract to the conveyances at completion including the Land Registry TR1. The final transfer may need to work around the wording which has been accepted by the Inland Revenue Stamp Taxes Office and the Land Registry:

> In consideration of the satisfaction of the obligations in the agreement dated . . . by the transfer of Whiteacre and the payment of £Y by B, the transfer and receipt whereof A hereby acknowledges . . .

This should not, however, be expressed as being in satisfaction of the obligation to pay the cash sum since this may operate to bring the Stamp Act 1891 s.57 into operation (see *Inland Revenue Tax Bulletin* August 1995; but note *Re Bradford Investments (No. 2)* [1991] BCLC 688 that this is not a cash and debt transaction). It will be appreciated that where there are multiple properties involved in the exchange the contract drafting, which is pedantically required to reflect the allocation of the consideration property and cash to each individual parcel of land, will be of considerable complexity; block transfers are not, it seems, acceptable to the Inland Revenue Stamp Taxes Office.

It must also be noted that since the credit relief from the double charge to *ad valorem* stamp duty is dependent upon the documentation qualifying for the single sale treatment it is necessary to adopt this type of drafting. The credit pursuant to FA 2000, s.118 applies only where the land is transferred otherwise than on sale, i.e. as consideration for the other land. A straight exchange even with an equality payment is a double sale and so not being within s.118 does not attract the credit (see **section 4.13.3**).

Where the transaction involves charges to VAT there is the risk that the Inland Revenue Stamp Taxes Office will seek to subject both cash sums to *ad valorem* stamp duty and to utilise them as a basis for refusing to accept the single sale treatment. It is, therefore, essential to comply with the statements made to the Institute of Chartered Accountants in England and Wales Tax Faculty in 1995 so that the two VAT payments are netted off and only one single cash payment is made, modifying, if necessary, the amount of the cash equality payment. However, treating the two sums as being due but dealt with by way of set-off has been treated by the Inland Revenue Stamp Taxes Office as two cash payments (see *Coren v. Keighley* 48 TC 370).

It will be appreciated that the property exchange provisions apply to a wider range of transactions that simple exchanges such as transfers and lease back. It is thought that the drafting techniques suggested above might also be effective to reduce the double charge upon such transactions, but these prima facie do not qualify for the credit relief pursuant to FA 2000, s.118 which does not apply to leases.

3.4.5 Unpaid consideration

In certain contexts there may be important stamp duty consequences turning upon whether or not the consideration has been paid or consists of cash. For example, it is not possible to extend the 90 day period for contracts for the sale of land where the consideration exceeds £10 million where substantially all (i.e. 90 per cent or more) of the consideration has been paid. This raises issues where the vendor is prepared to leave the consideration outstanding possibly secured by a charge over the land or where the vendor makes a loan to the purchaser. Similarly the 0.5 per cent relief for reorganisations pursuant to FA 1986, s.76, is dependent upon any consideration consisting only of cash not exceeding a limited amount. Where the transaction does not qualify as a transfer of a going concern, the payment of the VAT will cause a loss of the relief. The drafting may affect whether there has been a payment of cash by way off set-off or merely an unpaid consideration (*Coren v. Keighley* 48 TC 370).

Dividends *in specie* may also require special drafting (Table A (1985) art.105); dividends usually need to expressed in cash terms. It will remain exempt from stamp duty and outside the *connected company* charge of the FA 2000, s.119 if the resolution is for a cash sum to be satisfied by the transfer of the property but not if the resolution creates a debt which is separately discharged by the transfer (SA 1891, s.57).

3.4.6 Contingencies and variable consideration

Drafting may be important when dealing with the interaction of the general contingency principle and the new statutory regime of FA 1994, s.242. As described elsewhere (see **section 2.13**) variable payments can produce a substantial charge to stamp duty in excess of 4 per cent of the commercial value of the transaction and where FA 1994, s.242 applies parties are likely to incur substantial costs of valuation as well as the late payment interest charge which continue to run during the negotiations on value except to the extent that a sum on account of stamp duty has been deposited with the Inland Revenue Stamp Taxes Office. However, it is possible by suitable drafting to avoid the valuation costs and limit the amount of stamp duty payable (*Inland Revenue Stamp Taxes Bulletin,* August 1995). The drafting turns upon the meaning of *unascertainable* and *in part* and the effect of FA 1994, s.242(3)(a).

3.4.7 Unascertainable

The main difficulty is deciding when the consideration, or part thereof, cannot be ascertained. Subsection 242(3)(a) provides that the provision does not apply:

> . . . where the consideration or rent could be ascertained on the assumption that any future event mentioned in the instrument in question were or were not to occur.

In consequence the new provisions do not apply where there is a single prima facie sum determined in accordance with the general contingency principle which may become payable upon the happening of the future event (see **section 2.13**). It is clear that where the general contingency principle produces a maximum possible consideration or rent because, for example, it is capped the stamp duty will be claimed by reference to that maximum.

The difficulties arise where the general contingency principle produces no sum at all or a minimum or other sum capable of increase. This depends upon drafting. For example, in relation to rent reviews with the normal upward reviews, part of the rent is in a sense unascertainable. However, this represents a single prima facie minimum figure and seems that the Inland Revenue Stamp Taxes Office will regard this as not falling within the new regime but dutiable under the general principle rule upon the minimum rent. This means that there is a fundamental difference between a single sum with a minimum amount capable of increase and a composite sum with at least one component that does not produce a single ascertainable sum. The difference is between broadly a variable sum which is to be not less than a specified sum

UNDERSTANDING STAMP DUTY ON PROPERTY

or a consideration premium or rent which is to be the variable sum or a fixed amount 'whichever is the greater' and a consideration or rent which is a basic sum plus a variable amount.

There is, therefore, a vital difference between a consideration or rent which is expressed as '£X or Y per cent of the value whichever is the greater' and '£X plus W per cent of the value'. The latter case provides a sum which is unascertainable as to part, the former produces a single minimum sum which is wholly 'ascertainable'. Stamp duty is charged upon that minimum sum and the valuation and interest costs are avoided in the former case; in the latter case the FA 1994, s.242 charge upon market value or rent rules apply with the related costs and inconveniences.

Another problem arises in relation to the possible application of the new rules where there are alternative considerations where only one of the alternative consideration is unascertainable, such as where under a lease the rent is either a fixed rent or a share of the rent received from subtenants whichever is the greater. It is difficult to see how this can be regarded as a case where *part* of the consideration is unascertainable – alternative sums are not necessarily *part* of a larger whole. This differs from the situation where the rent is a basic sum plus a share of the rents received since the latter is a separate component which is unascertainable.

3.4.8 Intra-group reliefs

Lending documents may affect stamp duty. For example, there have been difficulties from time to time in obtaining relief for transfers and leases within a corporate group pursuant to FA 1930, s.42 and FA 1995, s.151 respectively where the consideration or premium is diSchedarged out of borrowed money. Although Statement of Practice SP3/98 (see **Appendix A**) indicates a relaxation of the former practice in this area difficulties can still arise. It is, however, a precondition to the application of the anti-avoidance provisions that there is an *arrangement* and on this point there is a long standing practice that the exemption will not be prejudiced provided that the loan is obtained from outside the group without strings attached. This usually means that the loan agreement should not contain a purposes clause which specifically states that the loan is to be used to pay for the land transferred or leased. Ideally there should be no purposes clause, but should one prove necessary it is best left as a loan *for general corporate purposes*. Similarly an undertaking to charge the land has given rise to occasional difficulties which can be avoided by stating that the ability to draw down the loan is conditional upon the borrower tendering suitable but unspecified property as security. In ways such as these the risks of tying the loan into the internal arrangements within the anti-avoidance provisions is reduced.

3.4.9 Execution offshore and drafting: 'long division'

Careful planning of the documentation may achieve some degree of stamp duty planning when executing offshore. Moreover, where United Kingdom land is involved the penalty regime introduced by FA 2002, s.114 means that it will rarely be beneficial to execute offshore unless substantial foreign assets are also involved and the documentation is carefully prepared. A document can only be stamped by reference to what it achieves; the Inland Revenue Stamp Taxes Office cannot impress the stamp duty chargeable upon one document which is properly chargeable upon another document even where the documents are related and form part of the same transaction (see *International Power* v. *IRC* (1933) 12 ATC 413).

Where there is a single conveyance of the entire property by one instrument the entire transaction will be dutiable even in respect of the foreign property but by structuring the document in an appropriate way it may be possible to reduce the amount of stamp duty payable. For example by assigning the United Kingdom property in a separate instrument from the foreign property transfer it is usually possible to obtain registration of title in the United Kingdom paying duty only upon those assets and, in practice, avoiding the charge on the foreign assets provided that these can be retained offshore which is becoming increasingly difficult and is likely to prove impossible where the document relates to both United Kingdom and foreign property.

This ability to retain documents outside the United Kingdom because they relate to foreign property has become important because of the imposition of the late payment interest charge where the document is held offshore (SA 1891, s.15A) and of the late stamping penalty upon all documentation where the transaction relates to United Kingdom land (FA 2002, s.114). Solicitors should, however, remember that the Inland Revenue Stamp Taxes Office takes the view that failure to disclose the existence of documents offshore which may have relevance to the stamping of documents produced to them may amount to fraud within SA 1891, s.5 (*Inland Revenue Tax Bulletin 30* (August 1997)).

CHAPTER 4

The conveyance on sale

4.1 CONTRACT AND CONVEYANCE

Throughout the next two chapters, the fact that a transfer of any form of property under English law may involve two stages, contract and completion, should be borne in mind. (Scottish law and other legal systems do not always have such a clear distinction between the two stages). In consequence, since transactions with a foreign element may be subject to stamp duty (SA 1891, s.14(4) see **section 1.19**) the effect of any foreign law governing the transaction will require investigation of this issue of whether the instrument is a contract or conveyance, i.e. broadly whether anything remains to be done to vest the title in the purchaser since, in general, contracts are not always subject to stamp duty, whereas conveyances are dutiable (see **Chapter 5**).

Although conveyancers usually consider the stamp duty liability to arise only on the instrument of completion, this is by no means always the case. The question of contract or conveyance is important in this area of stamp duty and the answer frequently depends upon the drafting of the documentation (*Peter Bone Ltd* v. *IRC* [1995] STC 921).

In addition certain contracts are stampable as if they were conveyances; for example:

* FA 1999, Sched.13 para.7 charges many contracts to *ad valorem* duty as if they were conveyances.
* SA 1891, s.60 treats the creation by contract of certain rights (e.g. options and annuities) as conveyances.
* FA 2002, s.115 applies a charge to contracts for the sale of land for a consideration exceeding £10 million where a duly stamped transfer is not produced within 90 days or such longer period as the Inland Revenue Stamp Taxes Office may permit upon application.

Moreover, it must not be overlooked that *written contract* for the purposes of stamp duty is not limited to a single written agreement signed and exchanged by the parties. Stampable documents can include written acceptance of offers (*Hegarty* v. *Milne* (1854) 14 CB 627; but note *First Post Homes* v.

Johnson [1995] 4 All ER 355 on what is required to constitute a valid contract pursuant to LP(MP)A 1989, s.2) or notices exercising options to purchase or to grant leases (on the need for writing see *Spiro* v. *Glencrown* [1991] 2 WLR 931). In addition, the impact of Companies Act 1985, s.88 requiring the filing of stamped documentation must be noted in this context.

4.2 THE CHARGE ON CONVEYANCES ON SALE

FA 1999, Sched.13 para.1 imposes *ad valorem* duty on a 'Conveyance or Transfer on sale of any property'. This involves three main elements; namely:

- a *conveyance* or deemed conveyance;
- property; and
- a *sale* or deemed sale.

4.3 *CONVEYANCE*

To the conveyancing practitioner the words *conveyance* and *transfer* tend to attract limited meanings, almost as terms of art, the former being reserved for the sale of a legal unregistered freehold and the latter for the sale of a legal estate, leasehold or freehold, registered at HM Land Registry. Nothing could be more misleading in the context of dutiable transactions.

FA 1999, Sched.13 para.1(2) reads:

> For the purposes of this Act the expression 'conveyance on sale' includes every instrument, and every decree or order of any court or of any commissioners, whereby any property, or any estate or interest in any property, upon the sale thereof is transferred to or vested in a purchaser, or any other person on his behalf or by his direction.

It was suggested, though not decided, in *Oughtred* v. *IRC* [1960] AC 206 that paragraph 1(2) by using the word *includes* may not contain an exhaustive definition, and that the head of charge in the Schedule may cover instruments not within the paragraph. Be that as it may, the definition is certainly wide enough to encompass much more than the conveyancing practitioner ordinarily understands by the word *conveyance* which over the centuries has acquired a special and extended meaning for the purpose of the charge to stamp duty.

The term *instrument* covers every document whereby a *conveyance on sale* is effected. A conveyance of a legal estate in land must generally be by deed (LPA 1925, s.52), whereas other property may equally be transferred simply by writing, without complying with such formalities. Some property however, does not require any form of writing (e.g. goods where title passes by delivery).

However, if the parties produce a unnecessary *conveyance* of goods, this is subject to stamp duty (*Att.-Gen.* v. *Eastbourne Corporation* [1902] 1 KB 403) and will incidentally destroy the benefit of the exclusion of goods from the charge to stamp duty and of the exclusion of the consideration attributable to them for the purposes of certificates of value for the lower rates of stamp duty, see **section 2.6.1**).

An example of a court order which must be stamped once it has been drawn up in writing is a decree of foreclosure, vesting the mortgagor's property in the mortgagee freed from all rights of redemption. FA 1898, s.6 (not amended by FA 1999) for the removal of doubt, declares unambiguously that 'the definition of 'conveyance on sale' includes a decree or order for . . . foreclosure'. The order is executed when it is drawn up, passed and entered, and until stamped cannot be looked at (*Sun Alliance Insurance Ltd* v. *IRC* [1972] 1 Ch 133).

4.3.1 Drafting

The first and fundamental point to note is that the question of whether a document is a *conveyance* is a matter of drafting in many cases. There is a vital and potentially expensive difference between an instrument whereby someone *agrees to transfer* in the future (contract possibly not stampable) and an instrument whereby he *hereby transfers* (potentially dutiable conveyance).

The practice of proceeding immediately from contract to completion puts great pressure upon the drafting of the instrument and any related documentation since if there is effectively nothing left to be done to pass title the instrument is likely to be a *conveyance* (*Peter Bone Ltd* v. *IRC* [1995] STC 921).

4.3.2 Transferring or vesting

It is an essential ingredient in the definition of a *conveyance* that it transfers or vests property. The word *transfer* requires a movement of property from one person to another. This does not occur upon the initial creation of property where property does not leave the grantor – this situation is covered by the word *vest*, which applies to the creation of property *de novo* such as the grant of an option (*George Wimpey Ltd* v. *IRC* [1975] 2 All ER 45).

The *disappearance* of property does not necessarily vest property, for example the redemption of preference shares or the release of options and restrictive covenants. A release of a debt or contract does not convey property back to the debtor (*Cormack's Trustees* v. *IRC* [1924] SC 819). However, in some cases releases or surrenders may transfer or vest property such as surrenders of leases or release of life interests in settlements which may operate to vest property in the next beneficiary. In certain cases statute may deal with the disappearance of property such as FA 1986, s.66 (purchase of own shares by a company) (on *releases* see **section 10.13**).

It is impossible to convey to oneself (*Rye* v. *Rye* [1962] 1 All ER 146) and it is not possible to sell to oneself. These principles may be important where one of the parties is on both sides of the transaction, such as where one partner sells to himself and his co-partners. In such a case the sale is limited to that proportion of the beneficial interest passing, i.e. to the co-partners only.

Provided that beneficial interest passes it is not necessary that it passes to the person providing the consideration. Thus a transfer from A to C at the direction of B who is paying cash to A is a conveyance on sale. Whether any other duties arise will depend upon the nature of the relationship between A, B and C (see for example subsales in **Chapter 6**).

The straightforward conveyance of a freehold estate in land calls for no comment. It is interesting, however, to note that it has been suggested, in *Littlewoods Mail Order Stores Ltd* v. *IRC* [1961] Ch 597, at p. 622, that, notwithstanding the separate head of charge in FA 1999, Sched.13 under 'Lease or Tack' imposing *ad valorem* duty on both premium and rent, a lease can also fall within the definition of a conveyance for certain limited purposes (*Escoigne Properties Ltd* v. *IRC* [1958] 1 All ER 406).

4.4   DUTIABLE INSTRUMENTS ILLUSTRATED

Other instruments held to be conveyances on sale include the following (see also **Chapter 10** on the borderline between fixed duties and sales).

4.4.1   Declarations of trust

A fixed duty of £5 is levied by Sched.13 para.17 on a declaration of trust (see **Chapter 10**). However, this is misleading and only applies when the declaration does not involve the transfer of beneficial ownership of the trust property upon sale.

In *Chesterfield Brewery Co* v. *IRC* [1899] 2 QB 7 it was held that an express declaration of trust in a contract in favour of the purchaser is a conveyance, though the implied trust that arises on the creation of a specifically enforceable contract for sale is not (*IRC* v. *G Angus & Co* (1889) 23 QBD 579).

The fact that the equitable interest passes, at least upon payment (see *Michaels* v. *Harley House (Marylebone)* [1999] 3 WLR 244 for the interests of a vendor or purchaser when the whole of the price has not been paid) does not make the contract a conveyance.

Where a contract ostensibly for the sale of legal and beneficial ownership of property contains a statement that it also represents the instrument of completion of the sale (e.g. in circumstances where subsale relief is anticipated), it may be liable as a conveyance of an equitable interest in the property; converting the constructive trust arising by operation of law into an express trust by writing in an instrument can lead to a stamp duty charge (see *Peter Bone Ltd* v. *IRC* [1995] STC 921).

However, a declaration in a contract that pending completion the vendor will hold upon trust for the purchaser, such as where the vendor anticipates delay in obtaining the consent of some party to the transaction does not give rise to stamp duty since it contemplates only a temporary arrangement pending the final delivery of the legal title (*West London Syndicate Ltd* v. *IRC* [1898] 2 QB 507; but note *Warmington* v. *Miller* [1973] 2 All ER 372 on the effect of dealing in such situations without the appropriate consent). The formalities for declaring a trust are explored in greater detail in **Chapter 10**.

4.4.2 Options

An option is an offer to sell which remains irrevocable except in accordance with its terms. As a matter of prudence there is often a time limit annexed for its exercise but if not, care must be taken not to offend the rule against perpetuities which, with certain exceptions relating to the tenant's right to a new lease or to acquire his landlord's reversion, provides that an option to acquire for valuable consideration any interest in land must be exercised within 21 years from the date of its grant (Perpetuities and Accumulations Act 1964, s.9(2)).

For an option to be binding it will have to be granted for consideration (i.e. a contract), or executed as a deed. The cases upon the legal nature of options vary in their views as to whether an option is simply an irrevocable offer or is some form of conditional contract sufficient to pass an equitable interest in the subject matter. However, it is clear that the cases all depend upon the particular legislation and the context, and are not to be regarded as laying down a general principle. An option would seem to constitute a form of property, but it is not an equitable interest in the subject matter (*Spiro* v. *Glencrown Properties Ltd* [1991] 2 WLR 931). In the context of sales it seems that, as a matter of general principle, an option is not an agreement to sell or buy (*Helby* v. *Matthews* [1895] AC 471).

In consequence, although options are stampable pursuant to SA 1891, s.60, they are not dutiable as agreements to sell within FA 2002, s.115 or FA 1999, Sched.13 para.7. They offer an opportunity of deferring the payment of the main stamp duty without late stamping penalty or late payment interest for that payment although these apply to the stamp duty upon the premium for the option. The notice exercising the option will, of course, be dutiable as a contract for sale or an agreement for lease. It will also relate to the UK for the purposes of the new provisions for penalties for offshore execution in FA 2002, s.114.

Where the option is exercisable over a period of time it is not unusual to include certain provisions intended to restrict the powers of the grantor from dealing with the subject matter of the option during that period. Failure to include such restrictions or provisions dealing with possible events can produce bizarre consequences (*Thompson* v. *ASDA-MFI* [1988] 2 All ER 722; *Forsayth* v. *Livia* [1985] BCLC 378).

However, care is needed in the structuring and drafting of these restrictions since they may affect the grantor's beneficial ownership of the asset, which can be a vitally important issue in relation to the existence or otherwise of stamp duty groups within FA 1930, s.42 and FA 1995, s.151 when reorganising assets prior to the sale of a company out of the group.

The Inland Revenue Stamp Taxes Office contends that a restriction upon the right to enjoy the income arising from the subject matter deprives the grantor of the beneficial ownership (relying upon *Wood Preservation* v. *Prior* [1969] 1 All ER 364) which may affect group structures; but where the grantor has the right to the income arising this does not appear to affect beneficial ownership, notwithstanding that the price may be adjusted to take account of any income received (*J Sainsbury plc* v. *O'Connor* [1991] STC 516).

Options raise stamp duty issues at three stages; namely:

- whether there is stamp duty upon the grant of the option;
- whether there is stamp duty upon the written exercise of the option; and
- whether there is stamp duty upon the ultimate transfer or lease of the property which was the subject matter of the option.

GRANT OF THE OPTION

From the point of view of stamp duty, options are a complex area. An agreement to grant an option at a future time, entered into for consideration, was suggested, in *George Wimpey Ltd* v. *IRC* [1975] 2 All ER 45, to be liable as a conveyance on sale under SA 1981, s.60. However, an actual grant has been held by the same case to be a conveyance of property within FA 1999, Sched.13 para.1 even though property (i.e. the option) is created rather than transferred and a contract has been held not to be a conveyance (*IRC* v. *G Angus & Co* (1889) 23 QBD 579).

As described at **section 2.5.3**, it is possible to include a certificate of value in the grant of an option provided that the consideration for the grant of the option is below the relevant threshold. The fact that the premium for the option plus the consideration payable for the asset, if the option should be exercised, exceeds the threshold is irrelevant at the option stage because there is at that time no larger transaction or series of which it is part.

It is necessary to draw the attention of the Inland Revenue Stamp Taxes Office to the existence of the option when presenting any subsequent agreement or transfer for stamping since it may have a bearing on the rate of stamp duty upon such instrument (SA 1891, s.5 (as amended)). This is particularly so where the option is held offshore (Inland Revenue Ruling 171).

EXERCISE OF THE OPTION

When exercised, the option becomes a fully fledged contract in respect of which, with the benefit of hindsight, equity has from the outset been pre-pared in suitable cases, if asked, to order specific performance. As with a sale, it thus creates an equitable interest in the property, the subject of the option.

In the case of land it must, therefore, also satisfy LP(MP)A 1989, s.2 and be in writing duly signed by both parties; accordingly, it would seem that an option in respect of land cannot be exercised orally (*Spiro* v. *Glencrown Properties Ltd* [1991] 2 WLR 931). Moreover, like any other contract for the sale of land, the equitable interest created thereby should be protected by registration as an estate contract or by noting on the Land Register, as the case may be.

The option notice will require to be stamped if it gives rise to a contract dutiable pursuant to FA 1999, Sched.13 para.7 or a contract for the sale of land for a consideration exceeding £10 million where there is no stamped transfer within 90 days or any extended period. As between landlord and tenant the option notice may give rise to a dutiable agreement for lease.

Completion of a sale agreement arising on the exercise of an option is, as would ordinarily be the case, a conveyance on sale.

RELEASE OF OPTIONS

The release of an option being the cancellation of a purely contractual right is not a conveyance since it does not transfer property back to or vest property in the grantor and is not dutiable even where the grantee receives consideration for the release (*Cormack's Trustees* v. *IRC* [1924] SC 819).

4.4.3 Pre-emptive rights

The Land Charges Act 1972, s.2(4)(iv) includes with options 'a right of pre-emption or any other like right' within the definition of an estate contract. It would be forgivable in the circumstances to imagine that a right of pre-emption would be similarly dealt with for stamp duty purposes.

However, the Court of Appeal held in *Pritchard* v. *Briggs* [1980] Ch 338, following the earlier decision in *Murray* v. *Two Strokes Ltd* [1973] 1 WLR 823, that a right of pre-emption confers a personal contractual right, not an interest in land. This is notwithstanding the provisions of the Land Charges Act 1925, which creates no more than a right of first refusal, without any certain obligation to sell. As such no property passes and no duty can be payable for whatever consideration is paid by the donee for the right.

4.5   GENERAL AND LIMITED PARTNERSHIPS

Partnerships present particular problems for stamp duty since notwithstanding that the partners, in a broad sense, own the assets of the firm, their share or membership in the firm is a separate asset from their interests in the assets. Thus a partnership share is not an interest in land for the purposes of FA 2002, s.115. Similarly where the partnership is established under a foreign legal system the partnership share will be foreign property. It is, therefore, always necessary to be clear whether the transaction relates to partnership assets or partnership shares.

Although, apart from limited liability partnerships, ordinary partnerships are not bodies corporate, the views of the Inland Revenue Stamp Taxes Office on the connected company issues of FA 2000, s.119 and s.121 where there are corporate partners is unclear. It is considered that when dealing with partnership assets, the partners are not connected companies but care is needed when dealing with nominee companies owned by a partnership for these purposes. Limited liability partnerships are bodies corporate for these purposes.

Partnership property is always held by whichever partner, or partners, have the legal estate or interest vested in them on trust for the partnership. Equity dislikes the right of survivorship operating on the death of a business partner, so it is presumed that the individual partners (who may or may not also hold the legal estate) hold beneficially between themselves as tenants in common in proportion to their partnership shares.

When a new partner is introduced and he gives the existing partner or partners monetary consideration, or other consideration deemed as such for the SA 1891 (for which see below) for a share of the business, and this is recorded in the partnership deed or agreement, the document is, generally, stampable as a conveyance on sale to the new partner of his share. As the share is intangible (whether legal or equitable), an executory contract for its sale will also be stampable under FA 1999, Sched.13 para.7 as an agreement for the sale of an intangible interest in any property.

It may be possible to draft round these charges on acquisitions of partnership shares. For instance, if the incoming partner, instead of paying the existing partner or partners personally, pays a capital sum into the partnership, thereby augmenting the partnership assets there is no sale.

If, however, at the same time another partner leaves the partnership taking out cash, the Inland Revenue Stamp Taxes Office regard this as evidence of a sale, and *ad valorem* duty may be payable. They apply special concessionary rules for computing the stamp duty. The *Manual* states:

4.448. Evaluating a Document Effecting the Introduction of a New Partner
When a document is submitted for stamping which effects the introduction of a new partner we need the following information:

- the amount paid or payable by the incoming partner for his share of the partnership
- whether this sum was paid direct to the existing partner or to the capital of the partnership
- the amount of any simultaneous withdrawal of money by the existing partner
- the shares in which the partners are entitled to the assets and liable to the debts of the partnership
- the total amount of the liabilities secured by mortgage or charge
- the total amount of the trade liabilities
- the total amount of the liquid assets, i.e. stock in trade, cash and book debts.

4.449. In all Offices, except Edinburgh, a standard letter is provided which sets out these questions and provides space for the customer to enter the appropriate answers and return it to Stamp Taxes.

4.450. Duty is due on the amount or value of the consideration but to arrive at that consideration we need to know the share of the liabilities of the business, if any, assumed by the new partner. That share is also liable to ad valorem Conveyance or Transfer on Sale duty but after having allowed a set-off of any liquid assets of the firm such as stock in trade, cash and book debts against trade liabilities. Work in progress is not to be deducted.

4.451. Examples
The two examples which follow illustrate the calculation of stamp duty in the case of an incoming partner. You will also need to consider the interest and penalty position . . .

Example 1
The following information is provided in answer to the questions raised in our standard letter:

1. £48,000 paid by the incoming partner.
2. Paid direct to two existing partners.
3. No withdrawal of any other money by existing partners.
4. Partners, including new partner, entitled and liable to ⅓rd of assets and debts each.
5. £18,000 liabilities secured by mortgage.
6. £30,000 trade liabilities.
7. £6,000 liquid assets.

The chargeable consideration therefore amounts to the sum paid by the incoming partner plus his share ($\frac{1}{3}$ of the secured liabilities and net trade liabilities). In other words £48,000 + ($\frac{1}{3}$ of £18,000)+ $\frac{1}{3}$ (£30,000–£6,000) = £48,000 + £6,000 + £8,000 = £62,000. Duty of £620 is therefore payable with a £250,000 Certificate of Value.

Example 2
The following information is provided in answer to the questions raised in our standard letter:

1. £48,000 paid by the incoming partner.
2. Paid direct to two existing partners.
3. No withdrawal of any other money by existing partners.
4. Partners, including the new partner, entitled and liable to $\frac{1}{3}$ of assets and debts each.
5. £39,000 liabilities secured by mortgage.
6. £5,000 trade liabilities.
7. £10,000 liquid assets.

The chargeable consideration therefore amounts to the sum paid by the incoming partner plus his share ($\frac{1}{3}$) of the secured liabilities. There are no net trade liabilities to take into account because the liquid assets value exceeds the amount of trade liabilities. You should not off-set that excess against any other chargeable figure. In other words, duty is due on £48,000 + ($\frac{1}{3}$ of £39,000) = £61,000. Duty of £610 is therefore payable with a £250,000 Certificate of Value.

In general the contribution of capital to a partnership is not a *sale* and is normally dutiable with the fixed stamp duty of £5 where the capital is contributed in kind rather than in cash. It may be that the assets contributed have a value exceeding the amount of capital to be contributed and a loan account may be created. The Inland Revenue Stamp Taxes Office may take the view that this involves a sale at least to the extent of the loan account, or to the extent that any liabilities are also assumed such as where on a partnership merger the merging firm contributes its business as a going concern and SA 1891, s.57 is likely to apply to create a liability to *ad valorem* stamp duty.

Particular problems arise in relation to land. In addition to the problems of holding land for partnerships and joint ventures though nominees companies which may fall into the connected company charges (see **section 4.14**) there are issues in relation to the contribution of land into a partnership by way of capital. Where land is contributed in return for a share in the partnership it is arguable that the partnership share is other property for the purposes of the charge to stamp duty pursuant to FA 1994, s.241 and FA 2000, s.118. The Inland Revenue Stamp Taxes Office has indicated that it does not intend to take this point in practice.

However, to guard against the risk of the Inland Revenue Stamp Taxes Office changing its practice without warning, it is considered prudent for the incoming partner to contribute £100 to the capital of the firm for the partnership share and then increasing his share by contributing the land. Such increase in value of the partnership share is not *other property* for the purposes of FA 1994, s.241 and FA 2000, s.118 and, subject to the question of nominee companies charges where the land is transferred directly to a nominee company which holds for all of the partners and not just the transferor as permitted by FA 2000, s.120 the stamp duty is £5 as a conveyance or transfer not on sale.

The connected company rules of FA 2000, s.119 and s.121 are particularly obscure in their potential application to partnerships where some or all of the members are bodies corporate and whether it matters that they may be in the same stamp duty group, so that FA 1930, s.42 (as amended) may apply, which is itself a topic upon which the Inland Revenue Stamp Taxes Office views are confused.

Partners are connected persons for certain purposes but not for the bona fide acquisition of assets of the firm. It is, therefore, thought that the connected company charges should not apply to contributions of land to capital; but there is a risk that where the above route to escape the land exchange rules has been adopted because the parties are partners before the land contribution. If this route has not been adopted the parties will not be connected before the transaction and so outside the charge but it raises the risk of the land exchange rules applying if the Inland Revenue Stamp Taxes Office change their practice as frequently happens without warning. However, it appears possible to adopt this alternative route without the prior contribution and escape from FA 1994, s.241 at present.

4.5.1 Dissolution and retirement

On dissolution of a partnership, the agreement may also operate as a conveyance on sale by an outgoing partner to a continuing partner in respect of whatever is paid by a continuing partner for the outgoing partner's share (*Christie* v. *IRC* (1866) LR 2 Ex 46). The agreement in effect is no more than the sale of one partner's share to another partner, paid for by the continuing partner out of his or her own pocket. If, however, the outgoing partner takes his share out of the firm's capital assets, leaving a reduced capital for the remaining partner or partners, the dissolution ranks as a division or partition of the firm's assets, and a partition is not stamp able *ad valorem* unless on sale. Nevertheless, under FA 1999, Sched.13 it does bear a fixed duty stamp of £5 (see *MacLeod* v. *IRC* (1885) 12 R (Ct of Session) 1045). The *Manual* states:

> **4.452. Evaluating a Document Effecting a Dissolution of Partnership or Retirement of a Partner**
>
> When a document is submitted for stamping which effects the dissolution of a partnership we need the following information. You should call for a

copy of the original partnership agreement and of the balance sheet or statement of account between the partners as at the date of dissolution. The original partnership agreement may have been amended over the years if the partnership has been in existence for some time and of course any amending documents should also be submitted and taken into account. If the balance sheet as at the date of dissolution has not been prepared when the dissolution document is sent for stamping the previous years balance sheet should be requested. Although not always essential in straightforward cases the above documents should always be called for, especially when a document effecting a dissolution of a partnership is lodged for adjudication.

4.453. You should also ask for the following information:

- the amount paid or payable to the outgoing partner (if not already stated in the instrument);
- the shares in which the partners were entitled to the assets and liable for the debt of the partnership;
- the total amount of the liabilities secured by the mortgage or charge;
- the total amount of the trade liabilities;
- the total amount or value of the liquid assets, i.e. stock in trade, cash and book debts.

4.454. In all Offices, except Edinburgh, a stock draft letter is provided for this which sets out these questions and provides space for the customer to enter the appropriate answers and return it to Stamp Taxes.

4.455. The procedure of setting off liquid assets against trade liabilities for the purpose of arriving at the dutiable consideration applies equally to a dissolution of partnership. This procedure is not however applied where, for example, it is narrated that the retiring partner has already passed his share of goods, chattels, etc capable of manual delivery, and the document only concerns assets of the partnership other than these. In other words there is no set-off in such cases.

4.456. Examples

The two examples which follow illustrate the calculation of stamp duty in the case of a dissolution or the retirement of a partner. You will also need to consider the interest and penalty position.

Example 1

The following information is provided in answer to the questions raised in our standard letter:

1. £50,000 paid to the outgoing partner.
2. Partners entitled and liable to half of the assets and debts each.
3. £24,000 liabilities secured by charge.
4. £42,000 trade liabilities.

5. £22,000 liquid assets.

The chargeable consideration therefore amounts to the sum paid to the outgoing partner plus his share (half) of the secured liabilities and net trade liabilities. In other words £50,000 + (½ × £24,000) + ½ of (£42,000 – £22,000) = £50,000 + £12,000 + £10,000 = £72,000. Duty of £720 is therefore payable with a £250,000 Certificate of Value.

Example 2
The following information is provided in answer to the questions raised in our standard letter:

1. £50,000 paid to the outgoing partner.
2. Partners entitled and liable to half of the assets and debts each.
3. £24,000 liabilities secured by mortgage.
4. £12,000 trade liabilities.
5. £22,000 liquid assets.

The chargeable consideration therefore amounts to the sum paid to the outgoing partner plus his share (half) of the secured liabilities. There are no net trade liabilities to take into account because the liquid assets value exceeds the amount of trade liabilities. You should **not** off-set that excess against any other chargeable figure. In other words, duty is due on £50,000 + (½ × £24,000 = £62,000. Duty of £620 is therefore payable with a £250,000 Certificate of Value.

4.5.2 Limited liability partnerships

The new limited liability partnerships permitted by the Limited Liability Partnerships Act 2000 (LLPA 2000) raise separate issues for stamp duty because they are in general law bodies corporate. The normal rules for partnerships are therefore not applicable. The transfer of assets to such a partnership involves a total change of ownership and it seems that the interests of partners will be *other property* within FA 1994, s.241, and possibly *shares*, and so cash for stamp duty purposes (*J&P Coats Ltd* v. *IRC* [1897] 1 QB 778, on appeal [1897] 2 QB 423), *ad valorem* stamp duty will, prima facie, arise.

An exemption from stamp duty is provided under LLPA 2000, s.12 upon the initial incorporation of an existing partnership, provided that the assets are transferred within 12 months of the incorporation and there is no change in the partners involved in the existing and the new firms. The Inland Revenue Stamp Taxes Office accepts that the incorporation may frequently coincide with changes of partners. It has indicated that such related changes will not necessarily preclude the relief being obtained, but that it will investigate any changes carefully in order to ensure that any stamp duty arising has been paid (*Inland Revenue Tax Bulletin 50*, December 2000).

There are great areas of uncertainty concerning the ongoing position of limited liability partnerships. In the *Inland Revenue Tax Bulletin 50*, December 2000, the Inland Revenue Stamp Taxes Office appears to be putting forward the view that the limited liability partnership is not a legal entity but is to be treated upon the same basis as other partnerships as set out above. This view is clearly incorrect in law so there may be benefits in challenging these views when there is an attempt to charge 4 per cent stamp duty upon partnership changes, which may not be dutiable since there are cancellations of partnership rights in the company that are not purchases of own shares within FA 1986, s.66. It will clearly take time before the detailed views of the Inland Revenue Stamp Taxes Office are discovered and tested. In consequence dealings involving such entities will need to be approached with great caution in the intervening period.

4.6 POWERS OF ATTORNEY

The specific head of charge upon letters or powers of attorney has been repealed (FA 1985) but this does not mean that powers of attorney escape stamp duty altogether.

In the aftermath of the changes introduced by the Powers of Attorney Act 1971, a practice developed of delaying the execution of transfers of land thereby delaying the payment of stamp duty without penalty. However, in order to be legally irrevocable and protected from the death or incapacity of the vendor/grantor of the power, this Act requires the power of attorney to be given to the purchaser to secure his or her interest (or to a mortgagee) (Powers of Attorney Act 1971, s.4).

This essentially reflects the position at common law that an authority coupled with an appropriate interest in the transaction cannot be withdrawn (*Smart* v. *Sanders* (1848) 5 CB 895). A mere contractual provision against revocation is not sufficient. Such a provision may make the revocation a breach of contract but it does not prevent the ability to act upon the power of attorney from being cancelled.

As a result of the irrevocable nature of the power of attorney the Inland Revenue Stamp Taxes Office has from time to time sought stamp duty upon powers of attorney given to the purchaser as a conveyance on sale (*Diplock* v. *Hammond* (1854) 5 DeGM&G 320). Powers of attorney to third parties are not *irrevocable* in this sense and so are not equitable assignments or conveyances (*Roddick* v. *Gandell* (1852) 1 DeGM&G 763).

Contracts for sale, particularly of land, frequently contain a provision to the effect that if the vendor fails to deliver a duly executed conveyance in favour of the purchaser or as it may direct, the purchaser is appointed the agent of the vendor to execute the transfer. Such an authority may be irrevocable but it is not dutiable as an assignment. Stamp duty is not chargeable in respect of documents dealing with what is to happen in the event of a breach of contract (*Western United Investments Ltd* v. *IRC* [1951] Ch 392) and as the power to execute in the vendor's name is dependent upon breach and is not intended to be the completion arrangement it does not make the contract containing the power dutiable as a conveyance.

In addition, the use of powers of attorney can give rise to a loss of subsale reliefs whether pursuant to SA 1891, s.58(4) and (5) or the provisions in relation to contracts for the sale of land in the UK for a consideration exceeding £10 million pursuant to FA 2002, s.115 Sched.36. It is one of the conditions for that relief to apply that the first purchaser has not received a *conveyance*, which will include a power of attorney. The existence of such a power of attorney, even though not relied upon by the first purchaser, nevertheless affects the subsale treatment adversely and solicitors acting for subpurchasers have considerable due diligence obligations in the new compliance regime in order to protect their client who may be exposed to multiple charges to stamp duty or unable to recover the subsale credit in relation to the charges upon contracts for the sale of land for a consideration exceeding £10 million (see **section 5.8**). In addition failure to bring the existence of the power of attorney to the attention of the Inland Revenue Stamp Taxes Office or not referring to it in the Land Registry Transfer would appear to be a potential breach of the disclosure obligations imposed upon parties and professional advisers preparing documents by SA 1891, s.5.

4.7   LETTERS OF DIRECTION

Letters of direction are, for the purposes of stamp duty potentially subject to *ad valorem* stamp duty. They are closely related to powers of attorney and frequently are simply the other side of the same coin. For example, a power of attorney to a creditor to collect money arising to the donor of the power from a third party in full or partial discharge of the donor's indebtedness to the creditor is dutiable as a conveyance of the debt upon sale (SA 1891, s.57; *Diplock* v. *Hammond* (1854) 5 De GM&G 320).

Similarly a letter of direction by the person directing his or her debtor to pay a third party to whom money is owed is an assignment of that debt (*Re Tyler* [1967] 3 All ER 389) and dutiable accordingly. The liability to stamp duty may turn upon the drafting of the letter. For example, a letter directing a nominee for the vendor to hold the property to the order of the purchaser is an assignment dutiable *ad valorem*. However, a letter directing the nominee to transfer the legal title to the property to the purchaser is not an assignment since the direction contemplates the performance of a further act, i.e. the execution of the transfer, and so is not considered to be a dutiable assignment. It is for this latter reason that in a subsale situation a written direction from the first purchaser or his or her advisers to the original vendor to transfer the property to the subpurchaser is not a conveyance for the purposes of stamp duty.

It should not be overlooked that a declaration of trust or similar acknowledgement of title by the vendor or the nominee in favour of the purchaser or subpurchaser would be a conveyance on sale (*Chesterfield Brewery Ltd* v. *IRC* [1899] 2 QB 7).

Letters of direction may take many forms and the drafting of them requires consideration of the potential stamp duty implications since although they may not be equitable assignments they may operate as a *memorandum* of the transaction and be dutiable accordingly (see **section 1.12**).

4.8   RECEIPTS AND MEMORANDA

As described above (see **section 1.12**) the Memorandum Rule can apply to charge records of oral transactions with stamp duty as if they were an actual conveyance. For example, attempts have been made to avoid the consequences of a formal deed of dissolution, whereby one partner buys out another, by recording the terms in the form of a receipt given by the outgoing partner for the payment of his share.

In *Garnett* v. *IRC* (1899) 81 LT 633, a deed containing, among other things, a declaration by the outgoing partner that a promissory note given by the continuing partner was accepted in full discharge of the outgoing partner's claim against the partnership property was held to be a conveyance on sale, as was a receipt for purchase money in *Fleetwood Hesketh* v. *IRC* [1936] 1 KB 351.

4.9   WHAT IS PROPERTY OR *ANY ESTATE OR INTEREST IN* IT?

It will be appreciated by now that the term *property* has wide application. Property has been described as 'that which belonged to a person exclusive of others, and which could be the subject of bargain and sale to another' (*Potter* v. *IRC* (1854) 10 Exch 147). The following rights have been held to be property for the purposes of assessing *ad valorem* duty on a conveyance on sale thereof.

4.9.1   Land

Land can only be transferred at law by deed (LPA 1925, s.52(1)) subject to a few exceptions where a legal interest or estate can pass under hand (assents by personal representatives, mortgage receipts LPA 1925, s.52(2)) or even orally (leases for three years or less taking effect in possession at the best rent without a fine: LPA 1925, s.54(2)). It is thus virtually impossible to avoid *ad valorem* duty (subject to the nil rate allowable on a certificate of value at £60,000) on a conveyance on sale of land.

A contract for sale of a legal estate in land is not a conveyance on sale, nor is it a contract chargeable as a conveyance on sale under FA 1999, Sched.13 para.7 (see **Chapter 5**); but may be dutiable pursuant to FA 2002, s.115 where the relevant consideration exceeds £10 million (see **section 5.8**). The contract does, however, pass a beneficial interest capable of protection by registration of a land charge as an estate contract, class C(iv), if title is unregistered; otherwise by notice or caution on the register of the title affected.

Passing of the equitable or beneficial title pursuant to the contract does not of itself make the contract a conveyance, nor does it make the contract one *for* the sale of the equitable interest within FA 1999, Sched.13 para.7 (*Angus* v. *IRC* [1935] All ER 682), but the drafting of the instrument may affect the analysis (*Peter Bone* v. *IRC* [1995] STC 921).

Where the parties are closely associated it may be possible to defer payment of stamp duty by the purchaser choosing to rely upon equitable rights instead of calling for a (dutiable) conveyance of the legal estate. Payment of the full purchase price before completion makes the vendor a bare trustee for the purchaser. If necessary, a conveyance can be taken at a later stage, and duty then paid, though if the only reason for a conveyance is to allow the purchaser to sell, a subsale should be contracted for instead. In this case, only one conveyance will be needed: from the vendor to the sub-purchaser. Provided the property is the same (*Fitch Lovell Ltd* v. *IRC* [1962] 1 WLR 1325) only one payment of duty will be exacted, and that will be from the subpurchaser on transfer of the consideration (SA 1891, s.58(4) discussed at **section 6.1**).

4.9.2 Goods and merchandise

It is trite to say that these are property and that a conveyance on sale thereof will be dutiable. Title to property of this nature is equally transferable by delivery as by document, and such property should not, therefore, be included in a written conveyance or transfer. Of course, if chattels are annexed to the land so that they become fixtures, they will pass with the land.

There is no danger of a liability arising where the parties enter into a written agreement for sale, so long as title does not immediately pass there-under, as such an agreement is expressly excluded from the provisions of FA 1999 Sched.13 para.7 charging certain contracts for sale as conveyances (see **section 5.3**).

A receipt for goods will not result in a chargeable memorandum for it is not necessary to perfect the purchaser's title. Moreover, if not included in the conveyance the consideration attributable to the goods can be ignored when arriving at the threshold for the obtaining of the lower rates of stamp duty (see **section 2.4** on certificates of value). Nevertheless, the general principle remains that an instrument is stamped on its effect, and if goods are conveyed by an instrument, because, for example, they are included in a conveyance of property requiring an instrument of completion, a charge may arise if title has not already been passed by delivery (*Eastbourne Corp* v. *Att.-Gen.* [1904] AC 155).

4.9.3 Cash

Cash in hand can be transferred by delivery, whereas cash in the bank represents a debt due from the bank to its customers. As such it is a *chose in action* and should be transferred by writing (LPA 1925, s.136). Such a written transfer is a conveyance on sale and a contract for its sale at a future date will fall within FA 1999, Sched.13 para.7. In practice the Revenue does not seek to charge duty on a transfer of cash held on current account, as opposed to cash held on deposit account. If there is any doubt, the moral is to withdraw the cash from the bank and hand it over.

4.9.4 Stock and marketable securities

Except for bearer securities, legal ownership on sale can only be transferred by registration of a properly stamped stock transfer form (Stock Transfer Act 1963). Unusually, certificates of value are not available where the consideration is £60,000 or less (FA 1963, s.55(1A)).

As with other property the beneficial interest can be severed and dealt with separately by way of a declaration of trust, which will also rank as a conveyance on sale if in writing and for consideration. Since, however, the nature of this property is pure personalty, an oral declaration can be made, thus avoiding duty (*Paul* v. *Constance* [1977] 1 WLR 527).

Since 18 March 1986 the *ad valorem* rate on stock and share transfers has been reduced to 0.5 per cent, but there is now a separate tax that applies to contracts for the sale of shares (FA 1986, s.87). It is important to note that the principal charge to stamp duty reserve tax applies to the contract stage, whereas stamp duty applies at the transfer stage.

The detailed consideration of the complex provisions and payment regimes required to deal with the duplication of taxes is outside the scope of this book but any stamp duty reserve tax paid in advance of stamping the transfer (e.g. on a prior agreement, oral or written, to sell securities) will be repaid, FA 1986, s.92(2). However, solicitors dealing with share transactions should be aware of the tax because it is directly enforceable and penalties are imposed for failing to report and pay the tax within a very short time after the contract.

4.9.5 Mortgages

A mortgage is property and at one time was subject to a separate head of charge. Since the introduction of FA 1971, s.64 (preserved by FA 1999, Sched.13 para.25) duty is no longer payable on the creation, sale or redemption of a mortgage, be it legal or equitable. Transfer of property subject to the mortgage will prima facie be within SA 1891, s.57 and the amount of stamp duty upon the sale of the property will be calculated including the amount of the mortgage (SA 1891, s.57 but note the exclusions in Statement of Practice SP6/90, see **Appendix A**).

4.10 SALE

4.10.1 Compulsory purchase

It is noteworthy that the element of consent in the context of a compulsory purchase order is somewhat fictitious, particularly where the Lands Tribunal determines the compensation. A compulsory purchase is nevertheless a sale for stamp duty purposes at such consideration as may have been agreed or ascertained at the date of the sale where there is a general vesting declaration before the compensation has been agreed it would appear that the stamp duty is chargeable upon the market value. This is either because the consideration, i.e. compensation, is *unascertainable* until fixed by the Lands Tribunal, so that FA 1994, s.242 applies, or because the consideration is *ascertainable but unascertained* if all of the information is available but has not yet been processed.

The Inland Revenue Stamp Taxes Office appears to incline to the former view, since prior to the 1994 changes such a declaration was charged with only the fixed duty, i.e. as a conveyance for a consideration which could not be ascertained; but whichever view is adopted there is likely to be considerable delay, costs and related late payment interest issues pending the outcome of the negotiations.

In some situations other than land there may be an element of compulsion, but this is not inconsistent with the transaction being sufficiently consensual to be a sale such as on a company takeover where the minority shares are acquired pursuant to statute (*Ridge Nominees* v. *IRC* [1961] 3 All ER 1108).

4.11 *SALE* – THE CONSIDERATION

The consideration for the transaction is important for stamp duty for two reasons, namely:

- it is, usually, the basis for calculating the stamp duty; and

- it determines whether the instrument is dutiable as a *sale* or is subject to the fixed duty of £5 or exempt as a 'conveyance or transfer not on sale' or otherwise within the list of instruments in FA 1999, Sched.13 Part III.

The former issue of computing the stamp duty is dealt with in Chapter 2. This section is concerned with the latter issue of what is a *sale* which in turn, depends upon the nature of the consideration. In practice, there are two special definitions of *sale* for the purposes of stamp duty, namely:

- the general definition of *sale* for all property including land; and
- the special definition of *sale* extending the charge in relation to land transactions.

Each of these requires separate consideration.

4.12 THE GENERAL DEFINITION OF *SALE* FOR ALL PROPERTY INCLUDING LAND

The question of whether an instrument transferring property is dutiable as a *sale* depends upon the nature of the consideration. Those items which make a transaction a stamp duty sale include:

- money;
- stocks and shares;
- debts and liabilities;
- satisfaction of debt;
- assuming liabilities and equities of redemption; and
- periodic payments (other than rent).

4.12.1 Money

Duty is attracted by a conveyance on sale on the 'amount or value of the consideration for the sale'. A necessary ingredient of any sale is a price. In ordinary language this means money (including any element of VAT, see **Chapter 2**). In *IRC* v. *Littlewoods Mail Order Stores Ltd* [1963] AC 135 it was held that the exchange of a lease in the same property for the freehold reversion was not a sale of the freehold for a consideration recognised as such for the purposes of the SA 1891, and was not therefore a conveyance on sale (this would no longer be the case following FA 1994, s.241).

Money includes 'any money in any foreign or colonial currency' (SA 1891, s.6) and duty is calculated on the value on the day of the date of the instrument according to the then current exchange rates (see **section 2.10.2**).

4.12.2 Stocks and shares

In addition to money, stampable consideration for stamp duty purposes has included stocks and securities (SA 1891, s.55). Section 55(1) states that where the consideration or any part thereof consists of any stock or marketable security, the conveyance is to be charged with *ad valorem* duty in respect of the value of the stock. *Stock* includes units under unit trust schemes. This computational provision has been held to mean that a transfer of property in consideration of the issue or transfer of shares, stock, debenture or loan stock must be treated as a *sale* (*J&P Coates* v. *IRC* [1897] 2 QB 427). The effect of this is that many transactions that would in ordinary parlance be regarded as incorporations, takeovers and reconstructions of companies are sales for the purposes of stamp duty.

The collection of stamp duty is this area is assisted by Companies Act 1985, s.88, which requires a limited company to file the duly stamped written contract and duly stamped particulars in the prescribed form where there is no written contract where assets other than cash are acquired in consideration of the issue of shares.

A certain amount of stamp duty upon certain business assets such as book debts and work in progress can be mitigated in the context where the acquiring company is unlimited and relying upon the principles of *Carlill* v. *Carbolic Smokeball Company* [1892] 2 QB 484. There is a letter offering to sell the business which is accepted by conduct such as the issue of shares thereby avoiding a stampable contract and is not required to file a return of allotments pursuant to Companies Act 1985, s.88 notwithstanding that it is intended to apply to reregister the company as limited shortly after the consideration shares are issued. This route is of no benefit where writing is required such as in relation to land, nor for shares where the principal charge to stamp duty reserve tax applies (FA 1986, s.87).

Valuation is by reference to the average price of the security on the day of the date of the instrument (SA 1891, s.6). In practice the Board of Inland Revenue adopts the basis of valuation for assessing capital gains tax: one-quarter up on the difference between the day's quotations, or halfway between the highest and lowest prices at which bargains were actually done (whichever is the lower).

Section 55(2) states that where the consideration consists of any security, which is not a marketable security, duty is payable on the amount due on the day of the date of sale for the principal and interest upon the security.

Where one stock or security is transferred or exchanged for another, there is a sale each way, and both attract duty, i.e. there is a double charge (on the value of the respective securities involved) at the rate of 0.5 per cent. It may, however, be possible to avoid this double charge where one party is required to pay some equality money and the transaction is drafted as a sale of the more valuable shares to be satisfied partly in cash and partly in kind (see **section 10.10**).

4.12.3   Debts and liabilities

A transfer for a consideration left outstanding as a debt, whether or not secured by a charge on the property, is a sale and is dutiable upon the amount of the face value of the debt without any discount for the delayed payment, absence of interest or risks of non-payment in due course. However, if the unpaid consideration is represented by a loan note or debenture the stamp duty is charged upon the market value of the loan note if it is a marketable security but upon its face value if it is a non-marketable security (SA 1891, s.55 and s.122).

4.12.4   Satisfaction of debt

A completely different kind of consideration attracting duty is a conveyance in consideration, i.e. in satisfaction or discharge of a debt. SA 1891, s.57 reads:

> Where any property is conveyed to any person in consideration, wholly or in part, of any debt due to him, or subject either certainly or contingently to the payment or transfer of any money or stock, whether being or constituting a charge on encumbrance upon the property or not, the debt, money, or stock is to be deemed the whole or part, as the case may be, of the consideration in respect whereof the conveyance is chargeable with *ad valorem* duty.

The acceptance, therefore, by creditors of property belonging to their debtor in release and satisfaction of the debt is a conveyance on sale of the property. A conveyance to a mortgagee of mortgaged property consequent upon fore-closure falls within this principle (*Huntington* v. *IRC* [1896] 1 QB 422). The section says that the debt is to be the consideration, and in certain circum-stances, where for example the creditor has decided to cut his or her losses, this may exceed the value of the property received in satisfaction. Any argu-ment as to whether liability should be limited to the value of the property (as suggested in *Huntington* v. *IRC)* has been settled in the taxpayer's favour, in the case of foreclosure, by FA 1898, s.6 and in other cases by FA 1980, s.102; such conveyances must be submitted for adjudication. It will be remembered (**section 9.2.2**) that the satisfaction of a pecuniary legacy by appropriation of property with consent used to be treated as a conveyance on sale in satisfaction of a debt (but see now FA 1985, s.84).

4.12.5   Assuming liabilities and equities of redemption.

A purchaser of a business who undertakes to discharge the vendor's trade debts is taking property '. . . subject either certainly or contingently to the payment or transfer of any money' and the quantum of these debts will therefore form part of the consideration, and thus increase the duty payable.

As mentioned elsewhere in this book, the problem can be avoided by requiring the purchaser to pay off the vendor's debts out of the debts due to the vendor and collected by the purchaser as agent.

Section 57 also applies to a charge or encumbrance upon the property conveyed. Its amount or value will form the whole or part of the consideration. It follows that a purchaser of property subject to an existing mortgage will pay duty, not merely on the amount he pays the vendor for the value of the equity of redemption, but also on the amount outstanding on the mortgage. Where there is a mortgage debt which represents virtually the whole of the value of the property, the conveyance will, on the face of it be at a low or nominal consideration, but duty will be extracted on the combined values of the equity of redemption and the mortgage debt.

Unless the implications of this are fully appreciated an otherwise unanticipated stamp duty demand may arise on the transfer by one co-owner of their interest to a fellow co-owner, particularly where there is a gift, as for example from one spouse to another. The abolition of duty on voluntary dispositions only applies to the gift element in the transferor's interest in the equity of redemption, and the size of the transferor's erstwhile share of the mortgage debt will attract duty if, as is commonly the case, the transferee indemnifies the transferor against liability thereon. Transfers on matrimonial breakdown, however, are totally exempted by FA 1985, s.83.

Another unpleasant surprise can arise where land is held by a member of a group of companies where there are numerous cross charges to secure group borrowings or the property of the shareholders has been charged by way of guarantee of the company's borrowings. Unfortunately SA 1891, s.57 requires the stamp duty to be charged upon the amount of indebtedness being guaranteed at the time of the instrument notwithstanding that the liability is contingent and the risk of payment is commercially remote. Failure to mention the guarantee charge upon the family home may involve a breach SA 1891, s.5 (as amended).

A conveyance in consideration of the assumption of a liability wholly unrelated to the property transferred will also be liable under s.57, which does not require the liability assumed to be an encumbrance on the property transferred.

Where the property is sold subject to financial obligations which are inherent in the property, such as land subject to a rent charge or rent due under a lease or there is an assignment of the benefit of a contract to purchase land where the consideration is wholly or partially outstanding and the assignee becomes liable to pay, s.57 does not apply (*Swayne* v. *IRC* [1899] 1 QB 335). Rent reserved on the grant of a lease is of course dutiable once only (under the head of charge 'Lease or Tack').

Where there is a sale of a local authority or other public sector dwelling house to a sitting tenant, (including a sale by a housing association or by a housing action trust set up under the Housing Act 1988, Part III), discount is invariably allowable, the size of which depends upon the length of the tenant's previous occupation of that or another local authority public sector dwelling house. In the event of a sale within three years from the date of the tenant's purchase, the whole or part of the discount must be repaid (Housing and Planning Act 1986, s.155). Prima facie this potential liability would rank as a contingent debt under s.57 to be aggregated for stamp duty purposes with the discounted price. To cover the position FA 1981, s.107(1) states that, notwithstanding SA 1891, s.57 any money contingently repayable (i.e. the discount) shall not be deemed to be part of the consideration in respect of which the conveyance or transfer is chargeable with *ad valorem* duty.

Following the Housing and Building Control Act 1984 (the relevant provisions of which were consolidated in the Housing Associations Act 1985, s.45(3)) and regulations made thereunder, a tenant of a housing association may enjoy a similar discount on the purchase, with the approval and assistance of the housing corporation, of a property other than the one subject to the tenancy. The tenant chooses a property on the open market, subject to overall financial limits, the property is then acquired by his housing association at the agreed price, and then subsold to the tenant at the discounted price. The discount is ignored in accordance with FA 1981, s.107 above, and provided that the discounted price does not exceed £60,000, no stamp duty will be payable. The anti-avoidance provisions on subsale requiring duty to be charged on no less than the value of the property immediately before the subsale does not apply to a sale by a local authority or other public body at a discount (FA 1984, s.112(1)(*b*)).

The discount is also ignored on the grant of an equity sharing lease on a shared ownership transaction in the case of leases (FA 1980, s.87 (as amended)).

4.12.6   Periodic payments (other than rent)

Occasionally the consideration may take the form of payments spread over a number of years, either fixed or uncertain such as annuities or royalties. In these circumstances, SA 1891 s.56 lays down various formulae for calculating the dutiable consideration which, of course, indicates that it is stampable as a *sale* (see **section 1.12**).

4.13   THE EXTENDED DEFINITION OF *SALE* FOR LAND TRANSACTIONS

Conveyances and contracts in consideration of the transfer of other forms of property were, generally, liable to fixed duty of £5 under the head 'Conveyance or Transfer not on sale'. However, this all changed with the FA 1994, s.241which provides that with regard to transfers of estates or interests in land or grants of leases, any property will be stampable consideration. This potentially has far-reaching effects and many transactions previously liable to a £5 stamp will now suffer *ad valorem* duty. Worse still, exchange of interests in land may now be liable to 4 per cent *ad valorem* duty on each side of the transaction.

4.13.1 Exchanges involving land

As a reaction to some fairly aggressive tax planning involving exchanges of interests in land FA 1994, s.241 provides that where the consideration for a transfer of any estate or interest in land or the grant of a lease includes any property, the transfer or grant will be liable to *ad valorem* duty based on the market value of property given as consideration immediately before the instrument is executed.

It is unclear how wide a provision was intended by the drafting of this section, but based on the fact that the potential difficulties were highlighted during the committee stage of the Finance Bill 1994 and no substantive changes were made, it should perhaps be assumed that all the effects were intended. Accordingly, not only are exchanges of interest in land now potentially liable to double *ad valorem* duty (each interest being chargeable consideration for the transfer of the other), but all forms of property given in consideration for transfers of land are stampable consideration. Thus the transfer of a house by a husband to a wife in exchange for the assignment of an insurance policy is a sale of the house, but not of the policy, and *ad valorem* duty is payable subject to possible relief for matrimonial breakdown pursuant to FA 1985 s.85.

4.13.2 Problems

These provisions are extremely wide ranging and are not limited to simple exchanges of freehold land. The charge extends to sale and lease back and the variation of leases such as where the term of the lease of a flat is extended beyond 60 years and involves a surrender and regrant (see **section 7.15**).

4.13.3 Drafting issues – double sales and premiums

Prima facie, the effect of the provision in relation to mutual transfers of land, is to treat the transfer of each parcel of land as being made for a notional cash sum equal to the market value of the property received plus any cash equality payment. The same issue arises when land is transferred in return for the grant of a lease whether of the same land or other land where the relative property is treated as *cash* consideration for the transfer and the lease premium, prima facie there is an *ad valorem* charge upon both the transfer and the lease.

94

This is clearly the initial thinking of the Inland Revenue Stamp Taxes Office as is evidenced by its *Notes on the Finance Bill 1994* and *The Stamp Taxes Manual*. This approach does seem to be a little harsh; but there does seem to be a suggestion that if the instruments are properly drafted there may be only one *ad valorem* charge and a £5 duty upon the other instruments or nil where FA 2000, s.118 applies.

Example

It would seem that it may be necessary to express the transaction as an agreement to transfer or the actual transfer of Blackacre in consideration of the sum of £x to be satisfied by the transfer of Whiteacre and the payment of a cash sum by way of equality. The wording of the provisions relating to the disposal of Whiteacre will in consequence need to be carefully drafted. It seems that such wording will be regarded as producing ad valorem stamp duty at the appropriate rate by reference upon the transfer of Blackacre and £5 fixed duty upon the transfer of Whiteacre (See *Connell* v. *Begej* [1993] 39 EG 123).

1. A enters into a contract to transfer Blackacre to B 'in consideration of the transfer by B of Whiteacre'. B in the same contract agrees to transfer Whiteacre to A 'in consideration of the transfer by A of Blackacre'. When the formal deeds of transfer are prepared for the purposes of the Land Registry those words are repeated. The Inland Revenue Stamp Taxes Office has indicated that in this situation it will be seeking to charge two amounts of *ad valorem* stamp duty.

2. A agrees to transfer Blackacre to B 'in consideration for the transfer of Whiteacre', nothing further being said in the contract. When the formal deeds of transfer are prepared, A transfers Blackacre 'in consideration of the transfer of Whiteacre' but B transfers Whiteacre 'as consideration for' the transfer by A of Blackacre. The Inland Revenue Stamp Taxes Office has indicated that in this situation it will be seeking to change two amounts *of ad valorem* stamp duty.

3. A agrees to transfer Blackacre 'in consideration of the sum of £x be satisfied by the transfer of Whiteacre' plus the payment of a sum of money, if any. The Inland Revenue Stamp Taxes Office has indicated in the *Inland Revenue Tax Bulletin* for August 1995 that where this wording appears the transaction can be regarded as a single sale rather than a double exchange. There is a further consequence and drafting issue of how to deal with the conveyance of Whiteacre. Presumably this will need to take the form of a transfer 'in satisfaction of' B's obligation. To refer to the transfer as being in consideration of the transfer of Blackacre would presumably immediately raise the risk of the double charge to *ad valorem* stamp duty.

The effect of successful drafting is that one parcel of land is being *sold* and the other property is not being sold but transferred as consideration otherwise than on sale and prior to FA 2000 was dutiable £5. However, changes have been made in relation to land transferred as consideration in this type of situation.

The changes in FA 2000, s.118 are concerned with situations where land is transferred as consideration for the acquisition of other property. It applies where:

- an instrument transferring or vesting an estate or interest in land ('the purchased land') would not otherwise be or fall to be treated as a 'conveyance or transfer on sale' for the purposes of stamp duty; but
- the transfer or vesting of the estate or interest is for consideration; and
- the consideration is or includes any property ('the other property' which will usually be 'the purchased land').

Then the instrument transferring or vesting the consideration land is deemed to be a transfer on sale of the estate or interest for the purposes of FA 1999, Sched.13 Part I. The stamp duty is, subject to s.119(5), charged upon market value of the land and not the consideration if this is greater than the market value. The market value of property at any time is the price which that property might reasonably be expected to fetch on a sale at that time in the open market.

It appears to provide that where land is transferred not on sale but as consideration for the transfer of other property the land transfer is to be treated as a conveyance or transfer on sale and stamped accordingly. Thus where A agrees to sell £1 million of gilts (exempt from stamp duty) to B for £1 million to be satisfied by the transfer of B's land plus a cash balance, the transfer of the land is treated as a conveyance on sale dutiable *ad valorem*.

However, where the other property is itself *land* the amount of *ad valorem* stamp duty on the land transferred by way of consideration is to be reduced by the amount of stamp duty paid upon the purchased land transfer but it is not to be reduced below nil. Thus where A agrees to transfer to B for a consideration of £1 million to be satisfied by the transfer of B's land plus a cash balance, the transfer of A's land will be dutiable as a sale, as will the transfer of B's land but the duty upon the latter will be reduced by the duty chargeable upon the transfer of A's land. In most cases there will, therefore, be one charge to *ad valorem* stamp duty imposed upon the transfer of the more valuable property; the duty on the less valuable property will usually be reduced to nil.

It must be noted that the charge pursuant to FA 2000, s.118 does not apply where the transfer of the consideration land is already a *sale* for the purposes of stamp duty such as on a straightforward exchange so that the reduction relief will not be available and a double charge arises. It would therefore appear to remain necessary to draft land swaps as *single sales* so as to fall into charge pursuant to FA 2000, s.118 in order to fall out again by obtaining the reduction relief.

4.14   TRANSFERS OF LAND TO CONNECTED COMPANIES

FA 2000, s.119 applies to instruments executed on or after 28 March 2000 where either:

(a)   an estate or interest in land is transferred to or vested in a company connected with the transferor pursuant to ICTA 1988, s.839; or

(b)   an estate or interest in land is transferred to or vested in a company (A) and some or all of the consideration for the transfer or vesting consists of the issue or transfer of shares or securities in a company with which B is connected.

In such cases for the purposes of the charge to conveyance upon sale duty, an instrument transferring or vesting the estate or interest is deemed to be a transfer on sale of the estate or interest for a consideration equal to the market value of the estate or interest immediately before the execution of the instrument transferring or vesting it; but reduced by the value of so much of any actual consideration as does not consist of *property* where this is greater than the actual consideration.

The charge applies where land is conveyed; leases are dealt with separately in FA 2000, s.121. It will also apply to land contracts dutiable as conveyances i.e. those within FA 1999, Sched.13 para.7 and FA 2002, s.115. It applies whether or not the transfer is for a consideration, i.e. this limb applies to gifts and to transfers under which no beneficial ownership passes subject to a limited range of exemptions for trustees and nominees.

This is an extremely wide charge because of the definition of connected company which includes companies under common control, certain corporate trustees, nominee companies holding for partnerships and joint ventures. It represents a trap for the unwary because it applies to gifts to corporate trustees unless within the below exclusions and to gifts to companies such as where upon an incorporation the parties are relying upon Taxation of Chargeable Gains Act 1992, s.165 rather than the extremely stamp duty expensive s.162 thereof.

It also applies to intra-group transfers and reconstructions but in such cases there are limited exclusions and the charge is subject to the normal reliefs for corporate reorganisations (see **Chaper 6**). *Company* includes a *body corporate* and so applies to foreign incorporations. This section prevails over FA 2000, s.118 to produce a higher charge than would otherwise be the case and to cancel the credit upon land exchanges.

4.15 EXEMPTIONS

FA 2000, s.120 provides that s.119 does not apply to transfers to connected companies where the consideration, if any, does not consist of or include shares or securities in the following seven cases.

4.15.1 Nominees and bare trustees

- Case 1 is where B holds the estate or interest as nominee or bare trustee for A;
- Case 2 is where A is to hold the estate or interest as nominee or bare trustee for B;
- Case 3 is where B holds the estate or interest as nominee or bare trustee for some other person and A is to hold it as nominee or bare trustee for that other person.

4.15.2 Trusts and settlements

- Case 4 is where:

  (a) the transfer or vesting is a conveyance or transfer out of a settlement in or towards satisfaction of a beneficiary's interest;
  (b) the beneficiary's interest is not an interest acquired for money or money's worth; and
  (c) the conveyance or transfer is a distribution of property in accordance with the provisions of the settlement.

- Case 5 is where A:

  (a) is a person carrying on a business which consists of or includes the management of trusts; and
  (b) is to hold the estate or interest as trustee acting in the course of that business.

- Case 6 is where A is to hold the estate or interest as trustee and, apart from Taxes Act 1988, s.839(3) (trustees as connected persons), would not be connected with B.

4.15.3 Distributions by companies

- Case 7 is where:

  (a) B is a company;
  (b) the transfer or vesting is, or is part of, a distribution of assets. This applies whether or not in connection with the winding up of the company and so will apply to a dividend *in specie*; and

(c) the estate or interest was acquired by B by virtue of an instrument which is duly stamped. This would appear to require a transfer of the legal or other title so that the relief may not apply where B is holding the interest under a constructive trust pursuant to an uncompleted contract.

4.16 PARTITIONS

The partition provisions in FA 1999, Sched.13 para.21 now apply to all partitions of land whether freehold or leasehold where there is a cash equality payment of more than £60,000. Therefore, partition of leasehold premises now attracts stamp duty in the same way as a partition of freehold land used to and still does. The problems are:

- identifying a partition: and
- drafting since it would be very easy to fall into the trap of creating a charged double duty on the whole value.

Example

A and B are tenants in common of Blackacre which consists of 10 acres. It is decided that A will have 5 acres and B will have 5 acres in their own individual ownership. Stamp duty consequences could be quite different depending on how the document is drafted:

1. A and B agree to partition the land and allocate it between themselves. In the situation of the partition treatment the duty only upon the cash equality, if any, would arise. Prima facie the stamp duty is the fixed conveyance duty of £5; or

2. As part of the arrangements A could agree to transfer his or her equitable interest in B's 5 acres in consideration of B transferring to A his or her half interest in A's property. In this situation there is a danger that the Inland Revenue Stamp Taxes Office will take the view that there are mutual transfers of interests in land falling under s.241 both subject to *ad valorem* tax since each is in consideration of transfer of the other. In consequence it falls to be treated as an exchange under s.241 rather than as a partition under para.21.

4.16.1 Part exchange scheme

The potential double hit on exchanges of interest in land caused immediate concern to conveyancers; house builders who had been struggling to keep the market moving through the recession by accepting part exchanges from purchasers, were suddenly confronted by a charge of 2 per cent on the more valuable property as opposed to 50p on the whole transaction. Because s.241 states that where the consideration consists of *or includes* any property, stamp duty shall be charged on the open market value of that property, where a property worth £50,000 plus £50,000 cash is exchanged for a property worth £100,000, the transfer of the cheaper property will be stampable based on the *whole* value of the dearer property. Section 241 does not provide for any form of apportionment, but does make subsale relief available with careful planning (see **section 6.1**).

It is understood that the Inland Revenue Stamp Taxes Office has since retreated from this position where the parties make it clear in the documentation effecting the transfer that the consideration should be apportioned between the cheaper property and the cash. Where, however, they do not make this clear, the possibility of this charge remains. Nevertheless, it would seem that with careful drafting, the liability can be further reduced: if instead of an exchange, the transaction is drafted as a sale of the more expensive property in consideration of a cash sum to be satisfied partly in cash and partly in kind, the transfer of the cheaper property will not be *on sale* and liable to *ad valorem* duty, but will be chargeable under the head 'Conveyance or Transfer not on sale' with £5. Where the transaction to be effected involves an exchange without either party providing equality money, the above drafting may not be possible. In this regard, the parties would do well to find a difference in values of their properties, otherwise, double *ad valorem* duty may be payable.

Accordingly FA 1994, s.241 may prove costly to the taxpayer. It should also be noted that other transactions are at risk: for example, variations of leases taking effect in law as surrenders and regrants, as well as lease enfranchisement schemes will require careful consideration of drafting as they involve exchanges of interests in land. As a cautionary note, it will be crucial to draft the transaction in the most efficient way at both contract and completion (see *Portman* v. *IRC* [1956] TR 353).

CHAPTER 5

Contracts for sale

This chapter deals with contracts for the sale of existing leases; contracts to grant new or to renew leases are covered by a separate regime dealt with in Chapter 7.

5.1 CONTRACT OR CONVEYANCE

The charge to stamp duty upon sales is prima facie limited to *conveyances*. Although this term is widely defined in stamp duty (see **section 4.3**) it was clearly established in *IRC* v. *G Angus & Co* (1889) 23 QBD 579 that a contract for the sale of property is not a conveyance on sale, at least if it is executory and ownership in the subject matter of the sale does not pass immediately (*Peter Bone* v. *IRC* [1995] STC 921).

It should be remembered that equity (subject to the proper exercise of its discretion) will order specific performance of a contract for a sale of land as a matter of course, and for the sale of property other than land where the common law remedy of damages does not afford an adequate remedy to the aggrieved party.

There does therefore pass, by implication, a beneficial interest in most property, particularly land, on the creation of a contract for its sale (*Parway Estates Ltd* v. *IRC* (1958) 45 TC 135 and *Sainsbury plc* v. *O'Connor* [1991] STC 516; *Neville* v. *Wilson* [1997] Ch 144). The interest recognised by equity is qualified until the full purchase price is paid, (*Michaels* v. *Harley House* [1999] 3 WLR 244) which can be done at any time prior to completion if the parties so choose, whereupon the beneficial interest becomes absolute. However, the passing of the equitable interest pursuant to the constructive trust (which does not require separate writing LPA 1925, s.53(2); LP(MP)A 1989, s.2(6)) does not make the contract into a conveyance (*IRC* v. *G. Angus & Co* (1889) 23 QBD 579).

Care must be taken to distinguish between the beneficial interest passing by automatic operation of the rules of equity, and an express declaration of trust in the contract. It has already been noted that the latter has been held to be a conveyance on sale of a beneficial interest and dutiable accordingly (*Chesterfield Brewery Co* v. *IRC* [1899] 2 QB 7).

Moreover, although relying upon the constructive trust arising pursuant to the contract does not attract stamp duty, converting the constructive trust into an express trust by the terms of the contract may create a stampable document (*Peter Bone* v. *IRC* [1995] STC 921). It is, therefore, a question of the construction of the drafting whether there is a contract or conveyance (*Peter Bone* v. *IRC* [1995] STC 921). Where the contract is governed by foreign law, including Scots law, the question of contract or conveyance will be governed by that law.

5.2   CONTRACTS TREATED AS CONVEYANCES

When linked with subsale relief (SA 1891, s.58(4) and (5) – see **section 6.1**) the absence of stamp duty upon most contracts for the sale of land and other property meant that it was relatively easy to avoid stamp duty by resting upon contract and directing a transfer to the subpurchaser in due course, provided that the terms of the contract, including any relevant standard conditions, do not prohibit subsales.

This has been attacked in several ways:

- Stamp duty reserve tax applies to all contracts for the sale of shares where there is not a duly stamped transfer to the purchaser (FA 1986, s.87).
- FA 1999, Sched.13 para.7 charges stamp duty upon a wide range of property other than legal interests in land.
- FA 2002, s.115 charges stamp duty upon contracts for the sale of land where the amount or value of the consideration for the land exceeds £10 million (or £8.5 million plus VAT).

5.3   CONTRACTS DUTIABLE PURSUANT TO PARA.7

Because an unconditional contract for sale passed almost all the benefits of ownership to the purchaser without raising a liability to *ad valorem* duty as being a conveyance on sale (*IRC* v. *G Angus & Co* (1889) 23 QB 579), what is now FA 1999, Sched.13 para.7 was introduced. It provides that certain contracts or agreements shall be treated as full transfers or conveyances prior to actual completion. It was particularly aimed at forms of property that do not necessarily require formal assignment. Paragraph 7 states:

7.   (1)   A contract or agreement for the sale of –

      (a)   any equitable estate or interest in property, or

      (b)   any estate or interest in any property except –

            (i)   land

            (ii)   goods, wares or merchandise

      (iii)   stock or marketable securities

      (iv)   any ship or vessel, or a part interest, share or property of or in any ship or vessel, or

      (v)   property of any description situated outside the United Kingdom.

is chargeable with the same *ad valorem* duty, to be paid by the purchaser, as if it were an actual conveyance on sale of the estate, interest or property contracted or agreed to be sold.

This list of exclusions from the charge has been enlarged to include relevant intellectual property (FA 2000, s.129) and goodwill (FA 2002, s.116).

> It is expected that other assets will be excluded in Autumn 2003 when stamp duty will be restricted to shares and land.

The first thing for the conveyancer to note is that FA 1999, Sched.13 para.7 should not pose too many hazards for him or her in the course of ordinary transactions. Land is expressly excepted, as are, for example, goods.

However, pitfalls do exist for the uninitiated. The words of exception in para. (b) do not apply to a contract for the sale of 'any equitable estate or interest' within para. (a) (*Farmer & Co Ltd* v. *IRC* [1898] 2 QB 141), and are thus restricted to a contract for the sale of the legal estate or interest, but that is the commonest of all contracts for the conveyancer. No duty is, therefore, payable on a contract to buy or sell a legal freehold or leasehold, subject to the issue of 'tenant's fixtures' (below) (other than a contract for the grant of a new lease, which is stampable as a legal lease, regardless of the length of the agreed term (FA 1999, Sched.13 para.14) or any other hereditament such as a legal easement. The same applies to any apportionment in the contract for the sale of carpets, curtains and other fittings, as *goods* are also exempted from the effect of FA 1999, Sched.13 para.7.

However, a contract for the sale of an equitable interest in land is dutiable pursuant to para.7 (*Peter Bone* v. *IRC* [1995] STC 921). Similarly the exclusion for foreign property does not apply to foreign equitable interests (*Farmer* v. *IRC* [1898] 2 QB 141).

5.3.1   Chattels and fixtures

The question of fixtures has undergone a fundamental change in general law (*TSB* v. *Botham* [1996] EGCS 149) and this has led to a change of practice in stamp duty (*Stamp Taxes Bulletin Issue* 1 August 2001) and Stamps Form 22 has been amended to remove the reference to an actual state of severance. It is now accepted that simply because a piece of equipment is attached to the land it is not automatically a fixture and, therefore, part of the land.

The question whether it has retained its character as a chattel or become a true fixture and part of the land depends upon the purpose of the annexation and the degree of annexation. If it can be detached and removed without significant damage to the land and buildings this is a good indication that it is a chattel. Similarly if it is attached to the land for reasons of industrial safety it remains a chattel.

This is important not only for the exemption from charge upon the contract, it affects the duty upon the conveyance. If chattels are included in the conveyance they are dutiable even though title may pass by delivery. However, if they are not included in the conveyance the consideration attributable to them can be ignored when utilising certificates of value (see **section 2.6.1**), and in determining whether the contract falls into charge where the consideration exceeds £10 million pursuant to FA 2002, s.115 (see **section 5.8**). Special rules apply to *tenant's fixtures* on the sale of leases (see **section 7.20**). Where parties are uncertain whether assets are chattels or fixtures they can submit the document (including any certificate of value that may depend upon the outcome of the analysis) for adjudication on this point.

5.3.2 Sale of shares and securities

Contracts for the sale of shares and marketable securities are also exempted, but since 27 October 1986 are subject to the separate impost of a stamp duty reserve tax, unless within the prescribed time limits and the 60 day concession operating in practice (*Stamp Taxes Manual 2002,* para.11.24) from the date of the agreement an instrument of transfer is executed pursuant to the agreement and stamped in accordance with the SA 1891, unless otherwise exempt from duty. Notwithstanding its name, stamp duty reserve tax is a separate tax from stamp duty; it is not governed or construed by reference to the SA 1891; and administration of it is governed by the provisions of the Taxes Management Act 1970 and the Stamp Duty Reserve Tax Regulations 1986 (SI 1986/1711).

5.4 IMPORTANCE OF APPORTIONMENT OF THE CONSIDERATION

Since only certain assets are subject to stamp duty at the written contract stage it is necessary to apportion the consideration between the various categories of assets. This is usually done utilising Stamps Form 22 or Companies Form 88.

The consideration is to be apportioned upon such basis as the parties think fit (SA 1891, s.58(1)) except where the assets include intellectual property, disadvantaged land or goodwill (FA 2000, Sched.34; FA 2001, Sched.30 and FA 2002, Sched.37) when it must be allocated to such assets on a *just and reasonable basis* and the Inland Revenue Stamp Taxes Office is empowered to adjust the consideration.

However, if the consideration is allocated on an unjustifiable or totally artificial basis intended solely to influence the stamp duty this may be fraud by the parties and the persons preparing the instrument (SA 1891, s.5; *Re Wragge* [1897] 1 Ch 796; *Saunders* v. *Edwards* [1987] 2 All ER 651).

The significance of making an apportionment is that stamp duty, being a tax on documents, is not attracted to a transfer of ownership which can be effected without documentation, and an apportionment of the purchase price is commonly made where the sale includes contents which have not become fixtures. Care must, however, be taken to ensure that the ultimate transfer of ownership is not effected by a document, e.g. by including the chattels in the conveyance, as if so, there will be a full charge to duty. (*Eastbourne Corp* v. *Att.-Gen.* [1904] AC 155). For the same reason, the contract for sale should be executory and not actually transfer the ownership, otherwise it ceases to be an exempt contract under FA 1999, Sched.13 para.7 and instead becomes a full-blooded conveyance on sale under FA 1999, Sched.13 para.1.

Sometimes an apportionment of the purchase price will reduce the price paid on completion for the land sufficiently to allow the purchaser to take advantage of the nil rate of duty. Prima facie the concurrent sale of the chattels is an associated transaction thus preventing the giving of the appropriate certificate of value, but FA 1999, Sched.13 para.6 specifically states that in giving a certificate of value, any sale or contract for the sale of goods shall be disregarded, unless the goods are sold by an actual conveyance or transfer.

Fixtures cannot be the subject of apportionment, as by their nature they form part of the land and pass automatically with it on transfer. If, on the other hand, they are severed and regain their former status as chattels, they once again are exempt as goods. To this there is one unpleasant exception. As long ago as 1834 (*Hallen* v. *Runder* (1834) 1 CrM&R 266) it was held that tenants' fixtures (which, if trade, domestic or ornamental they have a right at common law to remove at the end of the lease) are neither goods nor land, severed or unsevered; accordingly, they are not specifically exempted from charge under para.7. A contract for the sale of a lease which includes such fixtures must, it follows, be stamped on the extent that the consideration is apportioned in respect of them.

5.5   APPLICATION OF PARA.7

Occasionally a conveyancer will be faced with a contract which either exclusively or in part deals with the proposed sale of property which falls within para.7. The subject matter of the sale may be an equitable estate or interest, or a legal interest (carrying with it the beneficial interest) in property other than land, goods, marketable securities or property situate out of the UK.

The question of equitable interests is of considerable importance given the linkage of para.7 to subsale relief and to the new land sales provisions in FA 2002, s.115. In some cases the position will be obvious, such as where the seller is a life tenant of a settlement who has only an equitable interest to sell. (The position may be different where the trust is governed by foreign law and is an interest in an unadministered residuary estate where there may be rights against the trustees or executors of a personal nature but there is no interest in the underlying assets (*Baker* v. *Archer Shee* [1927] AC 844; *Archer Shee* v. *Garland* [1931] AC 312; *Commissioner of Stamps* v. *Livingstone* [1964] 3 All ER 692; see also *MEMEC* v. *IRC* 71 TC 77 on the possible nature of the interest of a silent partner under German law).

The contract must be one *for* the sale of the equitable interest. This requires that all that the purchaser is entitled to is the equitable interest; if the purchaser is entitled to call for the legal title the contract is outside the charge of para.7 (*Peter Bone* v. *IRC* [1995] STC 921; *Ingram* v. *IRC* [1985] STC 835). This is important since the intention not to complete by taking a transfer directly and to deal with the matter by way of subsale does not make the contract one *for* the sale of the equitable interest. It remains a contract for the sale of the legal title as and when called for (*Ingram* v. *IRC* [1985] STC 835). The surrounding circumstances are not relevant in construing the instrument. Certain remarks of Rigby LJ in *West London Syndicate* v. *IRC* [1898] 1 QB 507 at p. 520 are sometimes referred to as authority for the proposition that extrinsic evidence of the subsequent conduct of the parties can be admitted to make the contract stampable. This view was not only rejected by the other judges (pp. 512 and 527) it has been subsequently effectively repudiated in cases such as *Ingram* v. *IRC* [1985] STC 835 and *Peter Bone* v. *IRC* [1995] STC 921. In consequence an intention not to complete does not of itself bring para.7 into operation. The contract must provide for something like a declaration of trust for completion before the charge applies.

In some cases the issue of whether there is to be the sale of an equitable interest is not clear, such as where the sole owner is proposing to sell a part interest in the property or one of the co-owners is proposing to sell his or her interest. Here the stamp duty may depend upon the drafting. If the contract provides solely for the sale of the equitable interest para.7 will apply, but if the contract provides that the legal title is to be transferred into joint names or the purchaser is to be added to the legal title (subject to the limit of four holders of the legal title) para.7 would not appear to be applicable and the contract is not stampable provided that the consideration does not exceed the £10 million threshold.

5.6   OTHER PROPERTY WITHIN PARA.7

Other examples may arise on the sale of a business where the purchaser, in addition to acquiring the vendor's premises, may also wish to take over stock in trade, goodwill, existing book debts, cash at the bank, any trademarks, patents, licences, copyrights or similar stock. Apportionment on Form 22 with regard to the business sale agreement will be necessary to determine the instrument's liability under para.7. A written agreement for the sale of the land and stock in trade will escape the operation of para.7, but not to the extent that it also provides for the sale of any one or more of the other assets mentioned below if they are situated in the UK.

5.6.1   Trading debts

With trading debts there are two aspects to consider:

- debts which are owed to the vendor (thus constituting assets); and
- debts owed by him or her constituting liabilities.

If the sale agreement provides for the purchaser to take over the book debts owing to the business, their value will be dutiable. Similarly, if the purchaser agrees to discharge the vendor's business debts, the costs of so doing will be added to the stated consideration by SA 1891 s.57 (conveyance subject to the payment of money, etc). In this case, the agreed consideration will presumably be reduced to reflect the purchaser's obligations.

Thus if premises and other assets apart from debts are valued at, say, £100,000, liabilities at £20,000, and debts owed to the vendor at £20,000, a purchaser will, if taking over both benefit and burden respectively of both sets of debts, pay a net price of £100,000. The purchaser will, however, be charged duty on a consideration of £120,000.

The problem can be avoided by a stipulation that the purchaser will not buy the book debts, but will collect the debts due to the vendor on behalf of the vendor as an agent, and apply them in paying off the vendor's own trade debts. The purchaser should be careful not to enter into an agreement to make up any deficit should the debts paid off exceed those due, as this will amount to a contingent liability, albeit remote, to pay off the whole of the vendor's debts, and it has already been noted in **Chapter 2** that the contingency principle makes dutiable the maximum ascertainable sum payable, even though less may in fact be paid (see **section 2.14**).

Foreign debts, i.e. those where the debtor is resident outside the UK, are within the exemption for foreign property. It must not be overlooked that specialty debts are located where the deed is to be found and from time to time and this may affect the duty upon any sale contract.

5.6.2 Cash in the bank

Cash in the form of notes and coin is *goods* within the exemption even where it is foreign currency.

Cash in the bank is technically a debt due from the bank to its customer and a transfer is dutiable on the consideration apportioned thereto. In practice, the Revenue does not attempt to claim duty on cash on current accounts, but duty is claimed upon deposit and other accounts. The problem can be simply resolved by withdrawing the cash and passing it over by delivery, or alternatively by the vendor retaining the cash and making an appropriate allowance against the consideration.

5.6.3 Sale of mortgage debts

It is also Revenue practice not to claim duty on an agreement to sell a mortgage debt, the implication being that in theory such an agreement is dutiable notwithstanding that an outright sale of a mortgage, not preceded by a contract, is no longer subject to stamp duty (FA 1971, s.64 preserved by FA 1999, Sched.13 para.25). So long as the Revenue make no claim for duty the point is academic, but in principle it would appear that there is no justification in any event for even suggesting that an agreement to sell a mortgage debt is dutiable, at least if the transaction is to take the form of a transfer of mortgage; a mortgage is an interest in land conferring upon the mortgagee the rights of the owner of a long term of years, and land is exempt from the effect of para.7.

No charge arises upon the sale of a debt which is loan capital within the exemption in FA 1986, s.79.

5.6.4 Options and trust interests

Apart from the benefit of existing contracts to acquire a legal estate in land, goods and stock, other examples of a stampable interest within para.7 can be found in options and interests under a trust. Most option agreements in practice do not fall within the section as they are not executory agreements at all. The agreement results in the immediate creation of the option conferring upon the donee a complete title thereto, and is instead dutiable as an immediate conveyance on sale (*George Wimpey & Co Ltd* v. *IRC* [1974] 1 WLR 975). A contract for the sale of an existing option is, however, clearly a contract for the sale of an intangible *chose in action,* being the sale of a benefit of a contract. Agreements to sell a subsisting interest under a trust are equally within para.7, and it seems that an agreement whereby the owner of a legal interest free from prior trusts (i.e. the legal ownership carries with it the beneficial ownership) will execute in the future a declaration of trust in favour of a purchaser, is a contract 'chargeable as a conveyance on sale', at least if the trust will upon the execution of the promised declaration become completely constituted (see *Chesterfield Brewery Co* v. *IRC* [1899] 2 QB 7). The various ways in which an interest under a trust can be created and assigned have been dealt with in greater detail in **Chapter 9**.

5.6.5 Insurance policies and the benefit of contracts

The essence of the charge pursuant to para.7 is upon intangible property and *choses in action* locally situate in the UK. In consequence it will apply to contracts for the sale of the benefit of contracts such as insurance policies, equipment leases and hire purchase agreements and long-term contracts and supply agreements. Work in progress or professional firms will represent the benefit of contracts such as debt owing and accruing, and this falls within para.7. The sale of a contract to acquire land or an interest in land is within para.7 (*Western Abyssinian Mining Syndicate* v. *IRC* (1935) 46 TC 407).

5.6.6 Subsequent conveyance

Where, however, a contract on which *ad valorem* duty has been paid is in fact followed by a conveyance, para.7(3) provides that the final conveyance is not to be chargeable with any duty, but shall be denoted, or else the duty paid on the contract shall be transferred to the conveyance or transfer.

An important concession where it is likely that the contract will be completed within a reasonable time is to be found in FA 1999, Sched.13 para.8, which states that the contract does not have to be stamped, provided:

> . . . a conveyance or transfer made in conformity with the contract or agreement is presented to the Commissioners for stamping with the *ad valorem* duty chargeable thereon within the period of six months after the first execution of the contract or agreement, or within such longer period as the Commissioners may think reasonable in the circumstances of the case . . .

Moreover, if the agreement is subsequently rescinded or annulled, or for any other reason is not carried substantially into effect, any *ad valorem* duty paid on the agreement shall be returned by the Commissioners (FA 1999, Sched.13 para.9).

There is no time limit imposed, unlike the two-year time limit for claiming reimbursement of wasted stamps under Stamp Duties Management Act 1891, s.9.

5.7 SUBSALES AND PARA.7

5.7.1 Assignments and subsales

Contracts of the kind discussed above invariably deal with the sale of the legal estate or interest in the assets to be transferred and, as has been already seen, equity's willingness to give specific performance confers a beneficial interest upon the purchaser prior to completion of the legal transfer.

If a purchaser wishes in turn to realise this interest before completion, this can be done either by an outright assignment of the benefit of the contract, or by a subsale where the purchaser enters into a fresh executory contract to convey to the subpurchaser the legal interest to which he or she is entitled, but has not yet received. In either case the original contract must not contain an express prohibition against assignment or subsale. If the second or sub-purchaser proceeds by way of an agreement to take an assignment of the benefit of the first purchaser's contract, the contract will be dutiable under FA 1999, Sched.13 para.7 (*Western Abyssinian Mining Syndicate* v. *IRC* (1935) 14 ATC 286) as being an agreement to sell intangible property.

A subsale, in so far as it deals with property exempt from para.7 (land, goods, goodwill, intellectual property, stock, etc.) will carry no such burden, as it will take the form of an ordinary contract to convey to the subpurchaser the legal estate in the property concerned. That the first purchaser does not yet have the legal title is immaterial, as they can compel the concurrence of the vendor by requiring them to convey directly to the subpurchaser.

Where there is a contract, which has been properly stamped, for the purchase of property within the scope of the section and the original purchaser enters into an agreement for a subsale before they take a conveyance or transfer, the subsale agreement is only chargeable to duty on any consideration in excess of that stated in the original contract (para.7(3)). Again, the final conveyance to the subpurchaser will not be dutiable, the previous payment(s) being denoted or transferred.

The above will apply where, for example, the subject matter of the sale is a debt, goodwill or an equitable interest. It will be remembered that an executory contract to sell land, stock or goods is not itself dutiable, but that an assignment of the benefit (as opposed to a subsale) is dutiable. In these circumstances, although duty has been paid on the assignment of the benefit of the contract, no further duty is payable on any conveyance to the *subpurchaser* from the original seller not only a fixed duty of £5 chargeable on a conveyance of any other kind.

In other words, the advantage of proceeding by way of genuine subsale (i.e. a further contract to convey the legal estate) instead of by way of assignment of the benefit of the existing contract, is that, in the former case, duty can be postponed indefinitely, whereas, in the latter case it must be paid on time, with the maximum deferral of six months if the conveyance is taken within that time. In either case only one full *ad valorem* charge is made.

5.8 CONTRACTS EXCEEDING £10 MILLION

FA 2002, s.115 provides that where there is a contract for the sale of an estate or interest in United Kingdom land where the consideration for the land exceeds £10 million and such contract is not otherwise subject to stamp duty the contract is stampable in respect of the consideration allocated to the land unless a conveyance or transfer in conformity with the contract is presented for stamping within 90 days after execution of the contract or such longer period as the Inland Revenue Stamp Taxes Office.

This applies to contracts for the sale of legal interests in land not dutiable pursuant to FA 1999, Sched.13 para.7.The interest and penalties upon the contract accrue from 30 days after the expiration of the 90 day or longer period. The contract ceases to be admissable in evidence after the 90 days unless and until stamped. If the contract is adjudicated within the 90 days the adjudication ceases to be valid on that date.

The first question is to determine whether the contract falls into the £10 million threshold. Where the contract is for a fixed price the position is usually clear but it must not be overlooked that consideration for stamp duty includes VAT (*Glenrothes Corporation* v. *IRC* [1993] STC 74) so that the threshold drops to £8.5 million where VAT is involved.

Consequently where the basic consideration exceeds £8.5 million but might exceed the £10 million threshold if it is not a transfer of a going concern, solicitors should apply for an extension of the 90 day period pending the decision of Customs and Excise if the parties are not proceeding to a conveyance within the 90 days.

In certain cases the actual consideration is replaced by market value such as where the transfer is to a connected company (see for the list of such situations at **section 2.9**). In such cases the new charge will apply to the contract if the market value at the time of the contract exceeds the £10 million figure, regardless of the price.

Variable payments such as overage or earnout arrangements are involved. If the consideration is variable but there is a cap or maximum consideration which is greater than £10 million, s.115 applies. The charge does not arise if the maximum consideration is below £10 million. The difficulties will arise mainly where there is a minimum figure below £10 million but it can increase without limit.

If the consideration formula is such that part of the price is unascertainable and the transaction falls within FA 1994, s.242 (see **section 2.15**) the charge will apply to the contract if the market value of the property exceeds £10 million. However, if the formula produces a single prima facie minimum sum which is capable of increase and the minimum sum is below the £10 million threshold the charge will not apply (see **section 3.4.6** on the drafting).

The £10 million threshold is limited to the consideration attributable to land in the UK. The consideration for all other property is ignored. However, where the contract forms part of a larger transaction or series of transactions the consideration attributable to all of the UK land in the related contracts is aggregated for the purpose of determining whether this charge applies.

The 90 day period is capable of extension at the discretion of the Inland Revenue Stamp Taxes Office unless substantially the whole of the consideration (i.e. more than 90 per cent) has been paid or transferred. The time runs where the contract is conditional. The charge does not apply to options but time will begin to run when the option is exercised. Application for extension should be made within 60 days after the execution of the contract to the special unit in Manchester Stamp Office.

If the duty has been paid and the contract is subsequently rescinded annulled or not substantially performed or carried into effect the duty is repayable presumably with interest pursuant to FA 1999, s.110. If a transfer is executed to the purchaser in conformity with the contract it is chargeable with stamp duty only if, and to the extent that, the duty chargeable upon it exceeds the stamp duty paid upon the contract (FA 2002, Sched.36 paras. 5 and 6) such as where the overage payment has been determined below the maximum figure or the market value has fallen for some reason.

The basic structure of the charge pursuant to FA 2002, s.115 would give rise to difficulties in relation to subsales. These difficulties are dealt with in FA 2002, Sched.36. This defines a *subsale* as a situation where B has contracted to purchase land from A and, without having obtained a conveyance contracts to sell all or part or parts of the property to one or more third parties so as to entitle the third party to call for a transfer from A, the original seller.

The definition extends to a chain of subsales and includes situations such as: A contracts with B who contracts to sell to C who in turn sells on to D and so on. It includes subsale of part such as where, as in the above chain, D sells part to E and F and F on-sells his part to G and H, and so on.

Whilst many of these terms appear in SA 1891, s.58(4) and (5) it will be observed that the wording of the provision differs from these subsections. These differences need to be carefully noted and taken into account because the credit and repayment mechanism are dependent upon both sets of provisions being strictly complied with. The meaning of the basic terms and the traps and pitfalls related thereto are considered at **section 6.1** where the subsale provisions for the transfer of the legal title are described.

One particular condition does, however, call for specific comment since it is unique to the subsale relief for the contract. This is the requirement that the subsale contracts must entitle the subpurchaser to call for a conveyance from the original seller. This seems an odd requirement since the subsale contract will not usually give a direct contractual right to call for completion as between subpurchaser and the original seller. It remains to be seen how the Inland Revenue Stamp Taxes Office intends to operate this condition in practice and whether the normal machinery of the first purchaser directing a subsale at the request or pursuant to the contract with the subpurchaser.

5.9 SUBSALE AND THE CONTRACT

Schedule 36 deals with two situations, namely subsale of the whole of the land and subsales of the land in to several parts. It is, however, fundamental to the understanding of these provisions to remember that there are two separate regimes: the subsale rules relating to the contract and the subsale rules relating to the transfer of the legal title before investigating how they interlock.

Looking first at subsales of the whole of the land, in relation to the contract the stamp duty payable by the subpurchaser is limited to the amount by which the consideration exceeds that payable by the original purchaser. For example where A contracts to sell to B for £12 million (duty £480,000) and B sells to C for £15 million and C sells to D for £20 million, C pays stamp duty upon £3 million (i.e. £15−12 million) and D pays duty upon £5 million (i.e. £20−15 million).

If A transfers the legal title to D and the condition for subsale relief in SA 1891, s.58(4) are satisfied (see **section 6.12**) D is liable to stamp duty upon only his consideration, i.e. £20 million. However Sched.36 para.5 provides that the stamp duty upon the transfer is limited to the amount by which that duty exceeds the aggregate stamp duty upon the contracts. In these circumstances D will not pay duty upon the transfer. If, for example, D has not paid duty upon the contract with C because he has received a transfer within the prescribed 90 days, his duty will be limited to £5 million. D's stampable consideration upon the transfer may exceed £20 million because of earnout or market value increases. In such a situation duty will be payable, but limited to the excess over £20 million (or £15 million if D's contract is not stampable).

Schedule 36 para.6 deals with the situation where the consideration for the transfer of the legal title produces a lower charge to stamp duty, such as where the final subsale is pursuant to an overage consideration where the consideration is less than the maximum amount or *cap*. If the stamp duty upon the transfer would be less than the aggregate stamp duty upon the contracts the excess is repayable to the person who paid the stamp duty upon the original sale. If there are several intervening sales the excess duty is returned to the various purchasers on a just and reasonable basis. It would seem that this repayment arises notwithstanding that the amount of stamp duty upon the transfer is nil or low because of some exemptions or relief available to the ultimate transferee such as a charity or registered social landlord or a company reconstruction qualifying for relief.

5.9.1 Subsale of part

The position becomes more complicated where the purchaser, having contracted to acquire land for a consideration above the threshold, contracts to sell the land in parcels which may or may not exceed the threshold. An obvious illustration is a developer who has contracted to purchase land constructs houses which he subsells. Failure by any solicitor in the chain, even one acting for the ultimate house purchaser or lessee, to observe the requirements of both Sched.36 and SA 1891, s.58(5) can prejudice the stamp duty position of many parties and may involve failure to notify fully the Inland Revenue Stamp Taxes Office as required of parties preparing as well as executing documents by SA 1891, s.5. As the new relief requires production of documentation, the risks of the many common errors in this area being discovered to the cost of clients in terms of stamp duty, penalties and interest, is, in consequence, greatly increased.

In relation to contracts to subsell part of the property agreed to be purchased pursuant to a contract dutiable within s.115, each of the individual subpurchasers is liable to stamp duty if the consideration exceeds the relevant £10 million threshold, but their duty is limited to the duty upon the amount by which consideration upon the contract exceeds the appropriate proportion of the consideration paid under the original or any subsequent purchases earlier in the chain.

For example if A contracts to sell to B for £18 million and B contracts to sell one half of the property to C for £12 million, C's stamp duty is charged upon the excess of £12 million over £9 million (i.e. one-half of B's consideration of £18 million). Obviously, the apportionment of the consideration will not necessarily be a simple division of the original price by reference to area since the various parcels of the land are not all of equal value. Parts of the land may have different planning permissions and conditions.

There are, therefore, likely to be significant disputes with the new unit in Manchester Stamp Office as to the level of credit for the earlier considerations to be allocated to subpurchasers of part. Moreover, such subpurchasers will have their own views as to how much credit he should be allowed, which will not necessarily be consistent among all subpurchasers.

No procedure is provided for reconciling such conflicts, and, in consequence, solicitors will need to investigate not merely the consideration paid to the previous vendor by the immediate seller to their client and any prior transactions, but also whether there have been any earlier subsales of part by their seller and whether and, if so, how the earlier consideration has been allocated. They will face enquiries from later subpurchasers seeking information as to their credit level. The opportunities for problems in the absence of proper investigation are obvious. Clearly undertakings from subpurchasers to keep the relevant seller informed of all subsequent dealings in the land will be required as routine because these dealings will affect whether the relief is available and, if so, when the claim for repayment can be made.

A similar allocation is required where a subpurchaser of part subsells that part in several distinct parcels. The credit for the earlier consideration as allocated to the subseller of part has to be apportioned on an appropriate basis to the subpurchasers of parts of the part. This will again require detailed investigation by solicitors for the sub-subpurchaser of part and debates with others in the same position who may have conflicting views upon how the credit should be allocated.

Obviously by the time that the property has been subdivided in this fashion the contracts may well be below the £10 million threshold, but this is not necessarily the case where, for example, the sale is linked to a building contract which forms part of the stampable consideration.

5.9.2 The transfer of legal title

The actual transfer of the legal title to the part subpurchased is subject to stamp duty but if the conditions of SA 1891, s.58(5) are satisfied the duty is limited to the consideration provided by the subpurchaser, with the benefit of the lower rates if a certificate of value for the relevant threshold can be and is inserted (see **section 2.5.2**). However, where stamp duty has been paid upon all or any of the intermediate contracts for sale of the part of the land (or the appropriate proportion of the duty) the transfer duty pursuant to SA 1891, s.58(5) is limited to the amount by which the duty that would otherwise be payable exceeds the aggregate stamp duty paid related to that parcel of the land.

In many situations, such as in retail or social housing, the ultimate transfer of the various parts will be free of stamp duty or subject to the lower rates of stamp because certificates of value are appropriate.

In such a situation, it is provided by Sched.36 para.6 that if, when all of the land has been transferred pursuant to the various sales and subsales and the transfers have all been stamped and the aggregate amount of stamp duty on the various transfers would, apart from the credit, have been less than the aggregate stamp duty upon the intermediate contracts, the difference is repayable to the person who paid the stamp duty upon the contracts and is to be apportioned to them on an appropriate basis.

In a simple case where A contracts to sell to B for £12 million and B constructs numerous houses which he subsells for less than £60,000 each so that the transfer of each house attracts nil stamp duty, upon the *stamping* of all of the transfer, B will be entitled to a full repayment of the stamp duty upon his contract together with interest at 2.5 per cent (tax free) pursuant to FA 1999, s.110.

It is, however, fundamental to the relief that the conditions set out in both Sched.36 and s.58(5) are strictly satisfied. Solicitors will be easily able to identify the areas of risk not only to their own clients but also prior and subsequent purchasers of the property in terms of questions to ask relating to the credit and contractual arrangements. It may be necessary to include restrictions upon subsequent dealings in the property or the relevant part thereof so that the client's credit or that of any predecessor is not prejudiced. This will apply even to those solicitors whose clients are not within the £10 million charge. Residential conveyancers will need to be alert to the possibilities that other parties may have a stamp duty interest in their transactions and act accordingly. It is clearly imprudent to continue to operate such conveyance for new properties without a review of procedures and asking the right questions and taking the right steps.

CHAPTER 6

Exemptions or reliefs from conveyance upon sale duty

6.1 SUBSALE ARRANGEMENTS

The increasing complexity of modern stamp duties has produced a multiplicity of subsale transactions, i.e. situations where there is a chain of transactions which are stamped not cumulatively but upon a basis allocating the stamp duty to particular parties in the chain. This complexity and the provisions requiring the stamping of contracts rather than conveyances means that there are the following separate regimes:

- sales of chargeable securities where there is a subsale relief for stamp duty upon the transfer of legal title but the benefits of the relief are cancelled by the principal charge to stamp duty reserve tax (FA 1986, s.87);
- contracts for the sale of equitable interests and certain other property dutiable pursuant to FA 1999, Sched.13 para.7 (see **section 5.3**);
- contracts for the sale of land for consideration in excess of £10 million pursuant to FA 2002, s.115 (see **section 5.8**);
- transfer of the legal title on the sale of land with its special rules for interaction with the charge upon land contracts (SA 1891, s.58(4) and (5) and FA 2002, Sched.36).

6.1.1 Changes of practice and role of solicitors

The Inland Revenue Stamp Taxes *Office Manual* makes a fundamental change to very long standing practice. Henceforth if a transfer is pursuant to arrangements which do not satisfy the Inland Revenue Stamp Taxes Office view of the conditions imposed by SA 1891, s.58(4) and (5) then the transferee may be liable for the stamp duty in respect of all transactions in the chain, relying upon *Fitch Lovell* v. *IRC* [1962] 3 All ER 685 and *Escoigne Properties Ltd* v. *IRC* [1958] 1 All ER 406 .

It would seem appropriate in such situations for a purchaser to refuse to accept a subsale or to require an undertaking from the immediate seller to bear any additional stamp duty. The SA 1891, s.117 may make an indemnity inappropriate but an agreement to bear part of the stamp duty does not fall within the restrictions of this provision. Moreover, there are many possibilities of failing to qualify for the relief, and solicitors should be carrying out appropriate enquiries to protect their client and themselves, since where there are technical defects on the structuring of the subsale arrangements, failure to draw them to the attention of the Inland Revenue Stamp Taxes Office may involve a breach of SA 1891, s.5 (see **section 11.3.1**).

6.1.2 Sales of legal titles

For subsales of legal interests in land there are two interlocking regimes; namely:

- for all transfers of legal title; and
- for transactions where the consideration exceeds £10 million or where the particular transaction is part of a chain of contracts where the initial contract falls within the charge pursuant to FA 2002, s.115.

These rules permeate the whole chain including later transactions below the threshold which impact upon earlier sales retrospectively and which have to comply with the special rules for contracts and transfers of legal title within the general regime.

It is important that both sets of conditions are properly understood and for each of the parties to appreciate precisely where they fit into the overall transaction, since failure to do so can result in other parties unnecessarily incurring stamp duty.

The various reliefs for the sale of legal title to land depend upon whether there is an onward sale of the whole of the property or several separate parcels. The rules differ significantly with consequent differences in the role of the solicitor.

6.1.3 Subsale of whole property

Subsale relief is available for transfers of legal title in land transactions pursuant to SA 1891, s.58(4) where:

- A contracts to sell property to B;
- B subsequently contracts to sell the same property to C;
- before B obtains a conveyance the same property is transferred to C;
- C pays a fully stampable consideration equal to the value of the property.

Provided that these conditions are satisfied the transfer of the legal title to C will be stampable only in respect of the consideration paid by C (subject to any adjustment that may be required where any of the prior agreements is stampable pursuant to FA 2002, s.115, see **section 5.8**).

Each of these points is important and failure upon any one causes the relief to be forfeited and a potential liability to the aggregate stamp duty created (*Fitch Lovell* v. *IRC* [1962] 3 All ER 685). It should, however, be noted that the relief is not limited to the three-party situation above. The relief applies where C contracts with D who contracts with E and so on. There is no limit to the number of parties in the chain of title, nor is there any time limit upon the relief.

For land transactions this is a useful relief, provided that each of the conditions is carefully observed. Some of the conditions are explored in the following paragraphs. Every transaction must be a sale for stamp duty purposes. This includes land exchanges which are usually dutiable as *sales* pursuant to FA 1994, s.241 and FA 2000, s.118 and transfers to connected companies within FA 2000, s.119.

The order in which the sale/exchange takes place can be vital. The contracts for sale must be entered into in the proper sequence, which can provide a trap where the earlier agreements involve options which have not been exercised at the time of the later contracts.

Each of the contracts must be for the sale of the legal estate and fall outside FA 1999, Sched.13 para.7. The *Peter Bone* [1995] STC 921 drafting trap must be avoided.

There must be no *conveyance* such as a declaration of trust. This is probably the most frequent area of technical failure to implement the relief correctly. This arises because solicitors fail to appreciate the wide meaning of *conveyance* for the purposes of stamp duty (FA 1999, Sched.13 para.1; see **section 4.3.2**). Thus a desire to protect a client by means of an irrevocable power of attorney or taking delivery of an undated or otherwise incomplete Land Registry Transfer can destroy the reliefs. The point usually escapes official scrutiny because of the failure to report the existence of the power of attorney to the Inland Revenue Stamp Taxes Office as required by SA 1891, s.5. However, the provisions linking the relief to the subsale provisions for sales of land for a consideration in excess of £10 million means that more documentation will be before the Inland Revenue Stamp Taxes Office enabling them to raise points in order to refuse relief or credit. Failure to set up the transaction properly could affect the stamp duty position of several parties, even where the particular transaction itself falls below the £10 million threshold.

The final consideration must be equal to market value. The Inland Revenue Stamp Taxes Office has great difficulty in giving the relief where the price on the last contract is lower than the price in any earlier agreement. This appears to be a failure to understand market forces and how certain transactions such as part exchanges or relocation arrangements work. Usually its position will be wrong and the fact that the second or final price is lower than the original price does not preclude the relief provided that it is the proper value. This condition may also be satisfied where the actual consideration is low but the consideration for the purposes of stamp duty is deemed to be market value, such as land exchanges or transfers to connected companies.

Solicitors acting for subpurchasers should investigate all prior transactions in order to ensure that these conditions have been satisfied, and in particular whether there have been any documents that are *conveyances* for the purposes of stamp duty, since this could affect their client's liability to stamp duty and penalty pursuant to SA 1891, s.5 (as amended). It may affect their ability to obtain registration of the title since the Land Registry may query their documentation and/or his mortgagee may be reluctant to advance funds where there are unstamped instruments in the title (see **Chapter 11**).

6.1.4 Subsales of part

The relief is available where A contracts to sell the land to B and who contracts to sell part to C and part to D. In this situation the transfers to C and D attract stamp duty only upon their respective consideration provided that the conditions of SA 1891, s.58 are satisfied.

Example

The conditions are the essentially same as the basic relief set out in subsection (4) above, namely:

A person has contracted to purchase the property, but before obtaining a conveyance, contracts to sell part or parts to other persons. The property is conveyed directly to the subpurchasers, and the aggregate consideration for the subsales is not less than the value of the whole property immediately before the first subsale.

This last condition raises theoretical problems since it implies that the relief is not available and the transfers of part cannot be stamped until all plots have been sold. However, the Inland Revenue Stamp Taxes Office does not take this point in practice and stamp each individual transfer upon its consideration as and when presented.

Where A retains part of the land for his or her own purposes the conveyance to him or her bears *ad valorem* stamp duty upon the proportion of his or her purchase price that the retained land bears to the entire land not just the balance of the original purchase price (*Maples* v. *IRC* [1914] 3 KB 303).

6.1.5 A possible trap

Subsales differ in many ways from assignments of contracts and this has trapped the unwary on many occasions. Whilst subsale arrangements escape the charge because they relate to the legal title to land, the charge under FA 1999, Sched.13 para.7 applies to contracts for the sale of the benefit of agreements relating to land such as agreements to assign contracts to purchase land agreements to assign licences or similar interests in land (*Western Abyssinian Mining Syndicate* v. *IRC* (1935) 14 ATC 286; see **section 5.3**). This can lead to substantially increased stamp duty.

6.2   SUBSALES AND CONTRACTS FOR THE SALE OF LAND FOR £10 MILLION

A subsale for the purposes of FA 2002, s.115 is specially defined and contains conditions restricting the relief somewhat similar to those for SA 1891, s.58(4) (see **section 6.1.2**). The relief requires a situation where a purchaser of United Kingdom land has, before obtaining a conveyance, contracted to sell the land or part thereof to another person so as to entitle that person to call for a transfer directly from the original seller. This final condition relating to the right to call for a transfer directly is somewhat obscure in subsale terms and it remains to be seen in practice what, if any, significance the Inland Revenue Stamp Taxes Office intends to apply to it. Subsales extend to sub-subsales and beyond.

6.3   SUBSALES OF WHOLE INTEREST

The FA 2002, Sched.36 introduces a variation of subsale relief rather like that for contracts that are stampable pursuant to FA 1999, Sched.13 para.7 (see **section 5.3**). That is to say the first contract attracts the full amount of stamp duty and subsequent contracts that fall into charge are stampable only by reference to the amount by which the consideration on the later contract exceeds the consideration upon the first contract; but this structure is more complicated since the stamp duty upon the contract may be subsequently adjusted by reference to the stamp duty paid upon the ultimate transfer of the legal title, which may itself be influenced by stamp duty paid upon the contracts.

> **Example**
>
> A contracts to sell land to B for £12,000,000. There will be a charge to stamp duty of £480,000 upon the contract. If, before obtaining a conveyance, B contracts to sell the land to C for £15,000,000 C's contract will be stampable upon £15,000,000 but with a credit for the stamp duty paid upon the initial £12,000,000. In other words, C will pay stamp duty only upon £3,000,000.

This means, of course, that any solicitor acting for a subpurchaser must now enquire as to the level of consideration paid on the immediate seller's contract and the amount of stamp duty paid in respect thereof. Where there is a chain of contracts, then the enquiry as to stamp duty must relate to all of the contracts in the chain executed on or after 24 July 2002. This will no doubt be an embarrassment for many sellers who, not unreasonably, would like to keep their acquisition cost a secret.

It is also important to ensure that the earlier stamp duty has been paid, otherwise subpurchasers or their mortgagees may find that the 90 days or extended period has expired without the duty having been paid and the contract becoming *retrospectively* unstamped document in the chain of title. This being inadmissible in evidence may affect their ability to obtain specific performance or damages and will make their mortgagees and subsequent purchasers justifiably nervous about their position. Where the 90 day period has not expired at the time when the subsale contract is executed, the solicitor must seek some form of protection or undertaking to stamp for the comfort of his client, bearing in mind that certain arrangements by way of indemnity will be rendered void by SA 1891, s.117.

6.3.1 The subsale transfer of whole legal title

Where there is a conveyance of the legal title from A to C, if the conveyance satisfies the conditions of SA 1891, s.58(4) above, it bears stamp duty only if and to the extent that the stamp duty upon the conveyance exceeds the aggregate stamp duty paid upon the contracts.

Example

A contracts to sell to B who pays the duty and then contracts to sell to C who takes a conveyance from A within the 90 day period after his/her contract with B.

In this situation C's transfer will pay stamp duty upon £15,000,000 but reduced by the stamp duty upon the £12,000,000 paid by B. If C delays taking a transfer and cannot obtain an extension of the 90 day period, then the contract is stampable upon £3,000,000 and it would seem that the conveyance from A to C will not be subject to stamp duty since the stampable consideration will have already borne stamp duty upon the contract.

6.3.2 Refunds

In an extremely odd provision in FA 2002, Sched.36 para.6 where C takes a transfer which falls within SA 1891, s.58(4) the stamp duty upon the consideration provided by C is less than the amount of stamp duty paid or the aggregate amount of stamp duty paid, upon any preceding contract or contracts there will be an entitlement to a refund of the additional excess stamp duty.

Example

If C should be a charity or registered social landlord eligible for relief, not only will the contract be free of stamp duty but upon any conveyance of the land B will be entitled to recover the stamp duty paid by him together with interest (FA 1999, s.110).

Similarly, if the final transfer is eligible for exemption upon other grounds, such as a transfer in connection with a company reconstruction, so that the rate of stamp duty upon the transfer is nil or 0.5 per cent, the execution of the conveyance will entitle B to an appropriate refund together, it would seem, with interest from the date when paid by B.

6.3.3   The role of the solicitor

This refund mechanism represents an important problem for solicitors. Just as outlined above, it is essential for solicitors to ensure that all prior transactions have been carried out properly so that their clients are not exposed to multiple stamp duty which cannot easily be covered by indemnities because of SA 1891, s.117. It is crucial that the solicitor obtains for the client appropriate comfort that all subsequent transactions will be properly carried out so that the client's refund position will not be prejudiced. It is also essential to ensure a proper flow of information so that the client knows when the final transfer of the legal title has been made in order to claim the refund. Details of duty paid and of negotiations relating to value must also be requested.

6.4   SUBSALES OF PART

6.4.1   The sub-sale contract

The new regime obviously raised problems in its original form for subsales of part. A not infrequent situation is for a developer to agree to acquire land, rest on contract, and subsell the various houses with transfers directly from the original seller to the ultimate purchaser of the individual house. Numerous sets of problems arise with significant practical problems for the solicitor including those set out immediately above.

6.4.2 The second contract threshold

Where the second contract, i.e. the one between B and C exceeds the threshold which relates to only part of the land originally agreed to be acquired, there is the question as to how the subsale relief is to apply. In these cases the stamp duty liability of the subpurchaser is reduced by the appropriate proportion of the stamp duty paid by the initial or prior purchasers.

Example

If A agrees to acquire land for £45,000,000 and agrees to sell one-third of that land to C for £18,000,000 then, assuming that C's contract becomes stampable, there is the question of how much *credit* C is entitled to in respect of the stamp duty paid by B. C's credit is linked to an appropriate proportion of the initial purchase price. In this situation C, agreeing to purchase one-third, would *prima facie* be entitled to credit in respect of one-third of the stamp duty paid by B, namely £15,000,000. C's contract would be dutiable in respect of £3 million.

This is, however, a basic illustration and a simple arithmetic apportionment of the initial purchase price by area may not be appropriate since not all part of the land will be equally valuable. The physical conditions and the terms of the planning permission may affect the situation. This is a matter of interest to all potential purchasers of part.

6.4.3 Solicitor's role

The solicitor will face additional problems to those set out above. These include:

- determining how much credit is available upon the contract or transfer in respect of the particular parcel whether at the contract or the transfer stage;
- obtaining regular information where the immediate seller is negotiating with the Inland Revenue Stamp Taxes Office about his or her stamp duty because of earnout or overage arrangements or level of credit;
- estimating the stamp duty payable for deposit with the Inland Revenue Stamp Taxes Office to reduce the late payment interest charge;
- monitoring the progress of subsequent subsales to protect the repayment claim and the time when it can be made;
- supplying appropriate information requested by subpurchasers;
- identifying subpurchasers of other parts of the land who will be interested in the discussions concerning credit and the timing of whose transfers are relevant to repayment claims.

6.1.4 Subsale contracts for part below the threshold

In many situations of part subsales the second or subsequent limbs and the contract will be below the threshold and will not be subject to this stamp duty. However, the progress and proper implementation of these will be crucial for the possible repayment of stamp duty upon earlier contracts

6.4.5 Subsale transfer of part

Where there is a transfer of the legal title to a subpurchaser of part then if the conditions of SA 1891, s.58(5) are satisfied the transferee pays stamp duty only upon his or her consideration. However, where some of the contracts prior to the transfer have borne stamp duty pursuant to FA 2002, s.115 the stamp duty upon the transfer is restricted to the excess, if any, of the stamp duty which would ordinarily have been payable over the aggregate stamp duties upon the contracts.

6.4.6 Refunds

Frequently the transfer of the legal title on subsale of part will qualify for the nil or lower rates of stamp duty. In such a case once all of the parts have been transferred and the aggregate stamp duty upon them is less than the stamp duty upon the contracts the parties to the original and intermediate contracts will be entitled to a refund. In relation to transactions such as housing where the houses fall below £60,000 or £250,000 there is considerable pressure upon solicitors to ensure that their leg of the transaction is properly implemented otherwise prior parties may be disappointed in their expectations and there may be claims for breach of contract if earlier parties have prudently sought undertakings as mentioned above concerning not prejudicing their stamp duty position.

The subsale provisions for stampable agreements are subject to various restrictions which track SA 1891, s.58(4) and (5) as well as having certain overtones of FA 1999, Sched.13 para.7 the parties should, therefore, note this timing and compliance trap as well as the potential risk of extra duty. Where a credit for earlier contracts is claimed and the parties are seeking a refund, the Inland Revenue Stamp Taxes Office special unit in Manchester may ask to see all of the documentation. In consequence errors in setting up the subsale structures which currently are not reported and escape unnoticed may be discovered to the cost of the client and to the possible cost of other parties in the chain who are expecting to receive a repayment (see also *Customer Newsletter,* July 2002).

6.4.7 Other routes

> **Example**
>
> Although C as subpurchaser pays stamp duty only upon the amount of the increase in the consideration the rate of stamp duty is calculated by reference to the total consideration price. Therefore, if A contracts to sell to B for £12,000,000 and B agrees to sell to C for £12,400,000 although C's stamp duty is upon £400,000 it will be charged at the rate of 4 per cent and a certificate of value for £500,000 threshold is not appropriate. However, in this situation the stamp duty upon an assignment of B's contract with A for £400,000 would be dutiable but a certificate of value for the 3 per cent rate would be permissible. In such a situation since C takes an assignment of B's contract any assignment from A directly to C would be pursuant to the contract with B and having borne stamp duty at the contract stage would bear no further stamp duty. Assignment of land contracts may, therefore, have certain advantages provided that they are approached with caution (see **section 6.1.4**).

A novation involves the release of the existing contract and the creation of a new contract with a third party. It would seem that upon the release the original stamp duty paid would become repayable but the new contract with the third party would be dutiable in full and not merely upon the increased amount.

However, the question is whether the release of the original contract is eligible for the refund since this requires that the contract should not have been substantially performed. Where the consideration has been paid in full so that the equitable interest will have passed by reason of constructive trust the Inland Revenue Stamp Taxes Office may seek to resist the repayment of the stamp duty upon that contract and it is not unknown for them to contend that this is not a release but a contract to *re-sell* the equitable interest to the original vendor. The contract would be dutiable pursuant to FA 1999, Sched.13 para.7. Since it would be the contract to sell the property back to the person who had already has the legal title it would seem that it must be a contract for the sale of the equitable interest and dutiable under the old provisions with the stamp duty interest and penalty accruing from 30 days after the contract not at the expiration of the 90 day period.

6.5 SUBSALES AND FA 1999

This provides yet another subsale regime which needs to be investigated where the contract is stampable pursuant to FA 1999, Sched.13 para.7 because for example it relates to an equitable interest or a contract to assign an option over land or the benefit of a contract to purchase land. It is provided by para.7 (2) that where stamp duty has been paid upon the prior agreement the subsequent contract is dutiable only to extent the consideration exceeds that previously stamped provided that the second contract is for sale of the same property and is entered into prior to any conveyance being received by the subseller.

These conditions are similar to but not as stringent as the basic subsale rules (see **section 6.1**). As para.8 provides that where the agreement had been stamped the formal conveyance is not dutiable there are no complex provisions for credit and repayment needed.

6.6   OTHER EXEMPTIONS

Other exemptions are:

- transfers to charities and certain similar bodies are exempt from all stamp duty but adjudication is required (FA 1982, s.129);
- transfers and leases to registered social landlords (FA2000 s.130);
- transfers on divorce (FA 1985, s.83) (see **section 10.5**);
- transfers in connection with the varying of an estate of a deceased person (FA 1985, s.84) (see **section 9.2.1**);
- certain transfers in the course of administering an estate (FA 1985, s.84(4) and (5)) (see **section 9.2.2**);
- transfers where the consideration is less than £60,000 and a certificate of value is inserted (see **section 2.4.1**);

6.7   INTERNAL REORGANISATIONS

6.7.1   Relief from transfer duty

This relief is available from only transfer duty (but see now FA 1995, s.151 which provides an equivalent relief for leases, see **section 7.17.6**) in respect of purely internal reorganisations. Restrictions arise because the companies concerned must all be in an appropriate 75 per cent beneficial shareholding relationship. This is measured in nominal terms (*Canada Safeway* v. *IRC* [1977] Ch 374).

6.7.2   Body corporate

The relief applies to bodies corporate, this includes:

- unlimited companies;
- foreign companies;

- charter companies;
- guarantee companies;
- certain industrial and provident societies; and
- local authorities.

However, the more unusual entities need to be at the top of the group because they may not have share capital in any relevant sense that is required for subsidiary companies to be members of the group. Certain foreign companies such as Netherlands companies do not have subscriber shares and this can give rise to problems.

6.7.3 Group relationship

The transferor and transferee must be associated. This association must exist prior to the transaction; it is not sufficient that the relationship comes into existence as a consequence of the transaction.

Associated means that either:

- one must be the beneficial owner of not less than 75 per cent of the ordinary share capital of the other; or
- both must have at least 75 per cent of their ordinary share capital owned by a third body corporate.

The *parent company* must have a 75 per cent *economic interest* in the other or both of the other companies, i.e. at least 75 per cent of the profits/dividend rights, and at least 75 per cent of the assets on a winding-up. Also, the parent company must have *control* of the other company or other companies and there must be no arrangements in place whereby some other person could obtain control.

This is a very wide restriction but the Inland Revenue Stamp Taxes Office has stated that the point will not be taken where there is a mortgage over the shares in the relevant companies notwithstanding that the mortgagee or chargee has a power of foreclosure or sale which could alter control.

Other issues possibly affecting the existence of a group which have not been resolved with the Inland Revenue Stamp Taxes Office include convertible preference shares or loan notes, share options and shareholder agreements in relation to joint venture companies. Certain preference shares may have the right to vote if their dividends are in arrears; this may affect control. It is important to note that the arrangements involving a possible change of control do not need to be related to or connected with the transaction for which the relief is being sought.

6.7.4 Beneficial ownership of the shares

The shareholding must be beneficial and this can be lost by:

- contract for sale;
- possibly a contingent contract for sale;
- possibly an option but this may depend upon the interim arrangements relating to dividends (see **section 3.4.3**);
- winding up;
- shareholder arrangements.

It is possible by reason of the amendments contained in the FA 1967 to look through in determining beneficial ownership so that a parent company is the beneficial owner of its sub-subsidiary, etc. However, difficulties frequently arise where shareholdings are less than 100 per cent.

> **Example**
>
> A is the beneficial owner of 80 per cent of which in turn is the beneficial owner of 80 per cent of C, A is deemed to be the beneficial owner of 64 per cent, i.e. 80 × 80, of C. In such a case it is necessary to do a double transfer from A to B and B to C in order to obtain the necessary relief.

The Inland Revenue Stamp Taxes Office has been seeking to establish that where there is some prearranged scheme which requires the extraction of assets prior to the sale to a prospective purchaser, then upon the first step being taken the beneficial ownership is broken for the purpose of s.42 (*Swithland Investments* v. *IRC* [1990] STC 469). It is far from obvious that this was necessarily a correct analysis of the authorities relied upon, but it is clearly prudent to begin the extraction of unwanted assets at as early a stage as possible since even a conditional contract in place at the time of any instrument of transfer may destroy beneficial ownership (*Wood Preservation* v. *Prior* [1969] 1 WLR 1077).

6.7.5 Economic interest test

This is tested in accordance with ICTA 1988, Sched.18. The provisions deem certain loan capital to be *equity* and the rights attaching to them are taken into account in determining the percentage entitlement. The types of security which may cause problems include:

- convertible loan capital;
- convertible preference shares;
- profit sharing loans;
- certain without and limited recourse loans.

It is necessary to include in the letter in support of the application a statement that there are no equity holders within Sched.18 and this is usually accepted as being sufficient.

6.8 ANTI-AVOIDANCE

The FA 1967, s.27(3) (as amended) contains three *arrangements* the existence of which means that the exemption under s.42 will not be available. These are described at **section 6.8.1**.

FA 1967, s.27(3) requires that the instrument is not 'executed in pursuance of or in connection with' one of the proscribed arrangements. There must, therefore, be a causal connection between the document and the arrangement. If the instrument is executed for reasons unconnected with the alleged arrangement it cannot be affected by these anti-avoidance rules. The time for testing whether there is an arrangement must, therefore, be at the time when the decision to execute the instrument or to enter into the transaction which is created or completed by the instrument was taken. The fact that the circumstances change by reason of subsequent events is, in consequence, irrelevant when testing for the availability of the relief.

A crucial question is the meaning of *arrangement*. The Inland Revenue Stamp Taxes Office in SP3/98 sought to equate this with a mere intention or settled expectation. This view is, however, inconsistent with the later *Stamp Taxes Manual* which reverts to the traditional view and importantly requires third party participation in the discussions.

The wider view of SP3/98 has effectively been abandoned in practice and the current legal position is that propounded in the *Times Newspaper* case [1973] Ch 155 which indicates there must be some element of *necessity* in order to constitute an arrangement not a mere *possibility*. The judge said (at p. 109):

> If I may refer again to the wording of the section it speaks of 'an arrangement whereunder . . . the consideration for the transfer of conveyance was to be provided directly or indirectly' by a person other than an associated company. The words quoted must, in my judgement, mean that the arrangement contemplated is one necessarily involving the provision of the consideration or some part of it by the person in question, and it is not enough for the Crown to say that it may or will probably do so.

The key word here is *necessarily*. This, at the very minimum, requires some involvement by specific third parties. It is difficult to see how this can possibly apply where there are no discussions with potential purchasers or there are substantial commercial risks that the transaction may not proceed because the price may not be right or stock market movements may mean that the offer become unattractive and the underwriters or sponsors to the issue are entitled to cancel the arrangements.

6.8.1 The three mischiefs

The type of arrangemens that fall within the anti-avoidance rules are:

- ceasing to be associated;
- previous conveyance;
- provision of the consideration.

6.8.2 Ceasing to be associated

Section 27(3) provides that the relief is not available if the transferee is to cease to be associated with the transferor. The first point to note here of course is that it does not apply if the transferor body corporate is to cease to be a subsidiary. Thus a hiving up of assets prior to a subsidiary leaving the group does not fall within this restriction (but in certain circumstances such as the liquidation of the parent company it may trigger a clawback charge). The issue here is whether the beneficial ownership in the shares of the subsidiary company has been lost at the time of the instrument of transfer. Even though there is a possibility of a subsidiary company leaving the group, this does not mean that assets transferred to it will necessarily not qualify for the exemption pursuant to s.42.

6.8.3 Previous conveyance

Section 27(3)(*b*) is concerned with subsale and similar arrangements which are rarely relevant. This provision is normally concerned more with the acquisition rather than the disposal of assets but may arise in predisposal planning such as where as part of the proposed sale of a joint venture or partnership the outside interests are to be acquired in order to facilitate the sale of the entire business.

Example

Where A PLC is acquiring assets from B PLC it is A PLC's intention, not communicated to the other party to the contract, i.e. B PLC, that all or part of the assets will be transferred from A PLC to relevant subsidiaries as part of a post-acquisition reorganisation. Where the property is transferred directly by B PLC to the relevant subsidiaries the transaction may qualify for treatment as a subsale within SA 1891, s.58(4) or (5) but the relief from s.42 is not available notwithstanding that the only stampable limb of the transaction is the contract between A PLC and its relevant subsidiaries (*Escoigne Properties Ltd* v. *IRC* [1958] 1 All ER 406). B PLC is actively involved by conveying to the relevant subsidiaries at the direction of A PLC and this is regarded as sufficient *arrangement*, i.e. third party involvement to fall within s.27(3)(*b*).

6.8.4   Provision of the consideration

The other major difficulty in relation to s.42 is the question of the provision of consideration. There seems to be no difficulty where an asset is transferred in consideration of inter company indebtedness left outstanding for the mere book entry. The difficulties really arise where actual consideration is involved, particularly the movement of cash. It was the Inland Revenue Stamp Taxes Office view that in certain circumstances loans obtained by the transferee company could amount to the provision of consideration when used to discharge the inter company indebtedness.

This approach has been relaxed and the use of outside money even when charged upon the assets transferred will not, of itself, cause a loss of the relief. SP3/98 indicates that provided that the transfer is not part of some larger scheme for the property to leave the group without payment of full stamp duty the utilisation of money borrowed from outside the group on normal commercial terms should not preclude the availability of the relief.

The provision also extends to the receipt of all or part of the consideration by an outside party. This was intended to reverse the effect of *Shop and Stores* v. *IRC* [1967] 1 All ER 42 where property was transferred to a subsidiary company for an issue of shares. The shares were sold to a third party for cash. The Inland Revenue Stamp Taxes Office argument that the consideration was the cash received from the third party was rejected. The amendment means that the onward sale of the shares would now be caught as the receipt of the consideration. However, this point is virtually unused in practice as the Inland Revenue Stamp Taxes Office does not ask the right questions about the consideration; its main safeguard is that the sale of the shares may break the 75 per cent group in most cases.

The Inland Revenue Stamp Taxes Office expects the letter in support of the application to include a statement to the effect that it is the intention of the transferee company to retain the assets transferred. There is, however, no such requirement in FA 1967, s.42 or s.27. The reason for this Inland Revenue Stamp Taxes Office practice is twofold.

First, s.42 requires that the beneficial ownership of the assets is vested in the transferee at the time of the transfer and the absence of or any qualification of this statement relating to the retention of the transferred asset alerts the Inland Revenue Stamp Taxes Office to the possibility that the beneficial ownership of the assets transferred may not be vested in the transferee company. Where there are arrangements for the onward sale of all or any of the assets involved to an outside purchaser the Inland Revenue Stamp Taxes Office may contend that at the time of the execution of the transfer the transferee had lost the beneficial ownership. This problem can be overcome by ensuring that the internal agreement and transfer are executed at as early a stage as possible during the negotiations and before the exchange of any contract for the onward sale of the property so that there cannot be any serious suggestion of loss of beneficial ownership.

Second, where the statement is omitted or qualified there may be an inquiry by the Inland Revenue Stamp Taxes Office as to whether there is to be an onward sale and the use of the proceeds thereof to pay or discharge the consideration under the internal transfer with the suggestion that the use of such *outside* money involves an arrangement for the possession of the consideration by the non-associated purchaser. This problem can be avoided by ensuring that there is no flow of cash from the transferor that can be regarded as directly or indirectly deriving from outside purchase money. This can be most easily achieved by leaving the internal consideration outstanding as an intercompany balance repayable on demand and not discharging that indebtedness out of the purchase monies, see also **section 6.9.2**. However, Statement of Practice SP3/1998 indicates that the problems in this area have been much relaxed.

6.9   PROBLEMS AND S.42

6.9.1   Liquidations

The liquidation of a company temporarily suspends beneficial ownership of its assets, even where it is solvent (*Ayerst* v. *C and K Construction* [1976] AC 167). This has three consequences for claims for exemption pursuant to FA 1930, s.42 (as amended):

- Where the company is a *parent* of either or both of the transferor or transferee bodies corporate there may not be a stamp duty group.
- Where it is the liquidation of the transferor company it may not be possible to pass the beneficial ownership from the transferor to the transferee body corporate (but see on preliquidation contracts *Escoigne Properties* v. *IRC* [1958] AC 549).
- A liquidation of any company may now de-group the transferee and trigger a clawback charge (but see **section 6.10.1**).

The appointment of a receiver does not affect beneficial ownership.

In some situations where creditors have been satisfied or adequately provided for, the Inland Revenue Stamp Taxes Office may accept that the beneficial ownership has passed into the parent company. This loss of beneficial ownership can be a problem where a liquidator is hiving down assets to a new company with a view to sale. It can also cause problems where assets are being transferred to a subsidiary company as a preliminary step in a reconstruction such as pursuant to the Insolvency Act 1986, s.110 because the transferee will leave the stamp duty group on the winding up of the parent.

These issues do not necessarily apply to receivers and administrative who have an *intention* to sell the subsidiary company but do not have the risk of an *arrangement* under SP3/1998; until they begin to talk to prospective purchasers.

6.9.2 Using borrowed money to pay

It is the arrangement relating to the provision of the consideration that is the most frequent cause of difficulty in relation to obtaining exemption under s.42. The Inland Revenue Stamp Taxes Office now take a more relaxed view where the transferee borrows money from outside the group and this by itself does not involve provision of the consideration by the outside lender (SP3/1998) even when secured by a charge, but the terms of the Statement of Practice need to be carefully considered.

6.9.3 Refinancing issues

These frequently involve properties already mortgaged being transferred into a new subsidiary. The restructuring of the mortgages is no longer by itself an issue (SP3/1998).

6.10 CLAWBACK AND S.42

Where relief has been obtained under any of the relevant provisions, i.e. FA 1930, s.42 (as amended) on or after 24 April 2002 with limited exemptions for transfers and leases pursuant to agreements entered into on or before 17 April 2002, the relief may be cancelled by FA 2002, s.111.

The clawback provisions apply where an instrument transferring UK land from one company to another company has obtained relief pursuant to FA 1930, s.42 and within a period of two years beginning with the date on which the instrument was executed the transferee ceases to be a member of the same group as the transferor whilst continuing to hold any estate or interest in the land including interests in land derived from the property so transferred the stamp duty previously exempted is clawed back.

Transfers of land include the grant or surrender of estates or interest in land so that surrenders of leases within a group will give rise to the charge but not transfers by way of dividend *in specie* or most distributions in a winding up which are not subject to *ad valorem* stamp duty and are exempted from the connected company provisions by FA 2000, s.120. The clawback does not apply to other property in the transfer. There are stringent penalties imposed for failure to report the event and to pay the tax within 30 days and these and the powers of recovery against other companies and directors raise serious compliance and due diligence issues (see **section 11.13**).

The references to the *same group* are to companies which are associated within the relevant provisions, i.e. associated for the purpose. This would seem to have the effect that although when seeking relief the stamp duty group is on a limited basis since it is necessary to establish a minimum group to provide the linkage between the transferor and the transferee the clawback provision looks at the wider group. In consequence, where there is a drop down of an asset from a parent to a subsidiary company this will be the stamp duty group for the purposes of obtaining the exemption.

However, if the parent company transfers the shares in the transferee company to a third wholly-owned subsidiary company, although this was not part of the original stamp duty group, the companies will remain within the group so that the clawback provision will not apply. That is likely to give rise to interesting problems of due diligence where there have been numerous intra-group reorganisations with the relevant two year period.

On the other hand, in such a situation if the shares in the parent company are sold to a third party by the group holding company the transferor and transferee would appear to remain associated so that the clawback would not apply although they have ceased to be part of a larger group.

The interest charge will run only from the clawback event not from the date of the original exemption. However, as the companies would be within the connected company provisions of Finance Act 2000, s.119 and s.121 the stamp duty will be calculated upon the market value of the property concerned plus any rent payable under the lease and not the actual consideration passing.

6.10.1   Sale of transferor

The clawback does not apply where the transferor leaves the group. This exclusion is necessary since there may be a plan to sell a subsidiary company from which assets are being extracted prior to the sale. In this situation the subsequent departure of the transferor will mean that the transferor and the transferee cease to be associated but since the asset remains within the group the clawback does not apply. However, it would appear that if within the remainder of the two year period the transferee subsequently leaves the group, the clawback provision will apply. This raises interesting issues where the transferor body corporate was a subsidiary of the transferee body corporate and passed the land upwards prior to a sale of the shares in the transferee. It seems that a subsequent disposal of the shares in the transferor will not trigger a clawback charge because the relevant group was limited to the two companies.

6.10.2   Liquidations

The clawback provision does not apply if the transferee company ceases to be a member of the same group as the transferor by reason of the winding-up and liquidation of the transferor company or of any parent company direct or indirect of the transferor. This is an important exclusion from the charge and may be available in relation to certain types of company reorganisations as well as commercial liquidations.

6.10.3   Reconstructions

Clawback also does not apply if the parties cease to be members of the same group as a result of a reconstruction that qualifies for exemption pursuant to FA 1986, s.75. This would include certain types of reorganisation pursuant to the Insolvency Act 1986, s.110 and certain types of demergers that do not involve liquidation. The type of transaction envisaged is a transfer of assets by the existing company to a new company which issues share to the members of the existing company.

However, this relief is not total exemption from the clawback since it is provided that if the relevant company ceases to be a member of the group formed by the new company within the balance of the two year period the clawback provision would apply.

For example, where a company is put into liquidation and the shares in the transferee company are transferred to a new company which issues shares to the members of the existing company, the clawback provisions do not arise because the transfer is in connection with a liquidation.

6.11   PARTITIONS AND RECONSTRUCTIONS

6.11.1   The charge

Many reorganisations of companies are carried out under Insolvency Act 1986, s.110 and involve a liquidation with a movement of assets to one or more new companies in consideration of the value of shares by the new companies to the shareholders of the existing company and normally the assumption by the new company of the liabilities of the old company. Substantial transfer duty may be involved calculated not merely by reference to the value of the new company's consideration shares (SA 1891, s.55) but also including the liabilities assumed by reason of SA 1891, s.57. Where shares are issued by the new company Companies Act 1985, s.88 requires a written contract or the particulars thereof to be duly stamped with any duty chargeable under FA 1999, Sched.13 para.7. Formal transfers of land or shares in subsidiary companies will also be dutiable.

6.12   EXEMPTION FROM CONVEYANCE OR TRANSFER ON SALE DUTY

The FA 1986, s.75 provides for exemption from transfer on sale duty in very limited circumstances.

6.12.1   A scheme of reconstruction

The stampable contract or transfer must be executed in pursuance of a scheme of reconstruction. The relief will apply only to a *reconstruction* in a narrow sense and many forms of reorganisation of companies such as amalgamation will not qualify for exemption.

It is necessary to show:

* substantial identity of shareholders; and
* substantial identity of the business involved.

It has been suggested that if the scheme involves the injection of new money by way of share capital this is not a reconstruction (*Crane Freuhauf* v. *IRC* [1975] STC 51). Hitherto this has been tested by reference to the circumstance immediately before and immediately after the transfer in question (*Crane Freuhauf* v. *IRC* [1975] STC 51).

However, two cases move away from that single event to the overall scheme as evidenced in the *Swithland case* [1990] STC 469 by the Taxation of Chargeable Gains Act 1992, s.138 clearance letter. In that case the sale of certain assets to an outside party some time prior to the reorganisation meant that there was not the necessary identity of business involved. In *IRC* v. *Kent Process* [1989] STC 245 a sale of the consideration shares about one year after the reorganisation was part of the same scheme because it was in the contemplation of the parties at the initial stages even though there was no contract to sell them at the time. The cases are inconsistent with principle and cannot fit the 'once for all at the time of execution' nature of stamp duties.

6.12.2   Location of acquiring company

The registered office of the acquiring company is in the UK. There is no restriction as to the place of incorporation or registered office of the company being reconstructed.

6.12.3   Redeemable shares

The consideration for the acquisition must consist only of the issue of shares other than redeemable shares (apart from the assumption of or discharge by the acquiring company of liabilities of the target company). The restriction upon redeemable shares applies even where the target company

137

has pre-existing redeemable shares. These will require special treatment such as redemption prior to sale or reorganisation

6.12.4   Shares issue

The shares must be issued to all of the shareholders in the target company and after the reorganisation none of the shares in the acquiring company may be held by a person who was not a shareholder in the target company. This means that the treatment of the persons who incorporate the acquiring company and their subscribers' shares have to be carefully planned.

6.12.5   Register of members

The *issue* to holders means putting the correct shareholders on the register of members of the acquiring company (*Oswald Tillotson* v. *IRC* [1933] 1 KB 134; *Brotex* v. *IRC* [1933] 1 KB 158; *Murex* v. *IRC* [1933] 1 KB 173). Renounceable letters of allotment are not sufficient. As this means the persons on the target company's register nominees, even if merely bare trustees for the persons on the target company register cannot be registered. The share registration is the crucial factor.

The proportion of shares of the acquiring company held by any shareholder must be the same as the proportion of shares held in the target company and adjustments need to be made to take account of subscriber shares. The consideration shares of the acquiring company need not be issued upon a strict arithmetic pro rata basis amongst the target company shareholders provided that upon initial registration including subscriber or existing shareholdings the correct proportions are maintained. Each such shareholder must be registered for the correct proportion of any combination of preference shares and ordinary shares issued in respect of ordinary shares in the target company. For example, should one shareholder take only preference shares another take only ordinary shares this will mean the exemption is not available.

6.12.6   Discharge of debts

Consideration involving the discharge of the debts of the target company may be ignored.

6.12.7   Avoidance shemes

The reorganisation must be effected for bona fide commercial reasons and not form part of a scheme or arrangement which has as the main purpose or one of the main purposes the avoidance of liability to stamp duty, income tax, corporation tax or capital gains tax. No advance clearance procedure is made available. In practice, clearance pursuant to Taxation of Chargeable Gains Act 1992, s.138 is usually sufficient, but disclosure of the overall scheme may jeopardise the argument that there is a scheme of reconstruction (see *Swithland Investments Ltd* v. *IRC* [1990] STC 469).

6.12.8 Acquisition of an undertaking

There must be the acquisition of the whole or part of an undertaking. Not every asset of a company will be regarded as 'part of an undertaking' (*Baytrust Holdings* v. *IRC* [1971] 3 All ER 76; *Gomme* v. *IRC* [1964] 3 All ER 497). Further, the assets transferred must constitute a *business* and not mere investments not amounting to a business in themselves. The holding of shares can amount to a business, such as shares in subsidiary companies held by a group parent company. Minority shareholding in trading companies can qualify as part of a holding company's business.

The Inland Revenue Stamp Taxes Office claims that the transferred assets must amount to a going concern in their own right which must be taken over and carried on by the acquiring company in essentially the same form. Relief may not be available where the assets transferred do not as such amount to a business. The correctness of this view of the Inland Revenue Stamp Taxes Office is open to question.

6.13 REDUCED TRANSFER DUTY

The FA 1986, s.76 provides that for certain reorganisations involving acquisitions of a company's undertaking or part thereof stamp duty under the head 'Conveyance or transfer on sale' is reduced from 4 per cent to 0.5 per cent. This merely reduces the rate of duty, not the chargeable amount. Where liabilities are taken over, in computing the amount of duty SA 1891, s.57 continues to apply. Duty will be charged by reference to the total notional consideration, i.e. the value of shares issued plus cash paid plus the nominal amount of any liabilities taken over. This must, of course, be apportioned between the various assets on Stamps Form 22 and Companies Form 88.

The reduction in rate applies where the acquiring company acquires the whole or part of the undertaking of the target company. It does not require a scheme of reconstruction or amalgamation. Substantial identity of shareholders and the liquidation of the target company are not required. The reduced rate will apply to partitions between various shareholders, or possibly certain types of demergers, provided that the other conditions of the section are satisfied. It may also be available when establishing joint venture operations carrying out amalgamation of two or more companies or transactions where new outside cash may be involved so that there is no scheme of reconstruction. The conditions to be satisfied are explained under the following headings.

6.13.1 Undertakings

There must be an acquisition of the whole or part of an undertaking (see **section 6.12.8**).

6.13.2 Registered office

The registered office of the acquiring company must be in the UK. There are no restrictions as to the registered office or place of incorporation of the target company.

6.13.3 Consideration in shares

The consideration for the acquisition (except such part as consists of the assumption or discharge of liabilities of the target company) must consist of either solely the issue of shares other than redeemable shares, or non-redeemable shares plus cash not exceeding 10 per cent of the nominal value of the consideration shares. It is important to note that restriction of the alternative consideration to cash (i.e. money actually paid over – not debt or inter-company loan notes) is limited to the nominal (not the market) value of the shares issued. Problems may occur where the consideration shares are issued at a premium. Usually the transaction will qualify as a transfer of a going concern for VAT. However, if a VAT charge arises, payment in cash will exceed the 10 per cent permitted. Careful planning is required to avoid the cost of VAT arising and destroying the claim for the relief.

6.13.4 Target company

The consideration shares must be issued to the target company or to all or any of its shareholders. The reference here to *shareholders* is likely to refer to persons on the register of the target company. This reference to *any* share-holders linked with the absence of any requirement for a scheme of recon-struction shows that the reduced rate may apply to arrangements for the division of a company between various groups of shareholders.

6.13.5 Third party companies

Where the transferee company is associated with another company there must be no arrangement between the transferor company and that other company relating to the consideration shares. This restriction applies only for transfers of land on or after 24 April 2002.

This would apply where, for example, a company owning land transfers the land to a new company, the shares in which are owned by a third party. If there are arrangements pursuant to which the consideration shares issued to the company whose undertaking is being transferred are, for example, to be sold to the third party or to be bought back by the transferee company the relief is not available. The charge applies only to restrict the relief in respect of transfers of land, other assets remain within the reduced rate, but the charge will apply even where the land is only a small part of the transfer of business into a joint venture.

This, and the question of share arrangements, raises serious questions concerning the availability of relief where land is injected into a joint venture. Frequently such formations of joint ventures have either complex share rights or shareholder agreements which contained pre-emptive or similar rights. Such structures may be *arrangements* and since there merely have to be arrangements and such arrangements need not be limited to current disposals and would, prima facie, include *arrangements* affecting how parties will exercise their votes in particular circumstances. This could be a serious obstacle unless some forms of sensible operating concessions are published by the Inland Revenue Stamp Taxes Office.

6.13.6   Issue of shares

The shares must be *issued*. The target company or its registered shareholders must be put on the register of members of the acquiring company. Renounceable letters of allotment, the change to nominees on the register, or from nominees to beneficial owners who were not on the register as members of the target company will not be acceptable to the Inland Revenue Stamp Taxes Office.

6.14   REDUCED TRANSFER DUTY CLAWBACK

Where, within two years beginning on or after the 24 April 2002 or the preceding two years whichever is the shorter, there is a change of *control* of the company at a time when it still owns the land or an interest derived therefrom, the additional 3.5 per cent tax becomes payable (FA 2002, s.113). There are stringent penalties imposed for failure to report the event and to pay the tax within 30 days and these and the powers of recovery against other companies and directors raise serious compliance and due diligence issues (see **section 11.13**).

Control is widely defined in terms of Income and Corporation Taxes Act 1988, s.416 and control changes if the company becomes *controlled* by a different person, by a different number of persons or by two or more persons at least one of whom is not the person or one of the persons by whom the company was previously controlled. This is very wide ranging and it seems that even the movement of a few shares may produce a different number of persons or different grouping of persons who are in control and thereby trigger the clawback. Share options, convertible loan stocks and other matters are relevant in determining who has control for these purposes. Although an amendment to the Act provided that simply because a *loan creditor* temporarily acquires control by reason of changes in the assets of the company or other factors and this does not, of itself, affect the control of the person who immediately prior thereto, controlled the company this is not to trigger the clawback, the exercise of rights in relation to share acquisition clearly are factors that could trigger the charge.

6.14.1   Exempt transfers not on sale

The clawback is not triggered where the change of control arises as a result of any of the transactions within the Stamp Duty (Exempt Instruments) Regulations 1987. This will include factors such as changes of trustees and distributions of shares in the course of administering an estate. Important practical exemptions will be the exemption for gifts which will include distributions and dividends *in specie* and distributions in the course of a winding-up that are not subject to stamp duty by reason of SA 1891, s.57. It would seem, therefore, that although liquidation may affect the beneficial ownership of the shares, it will not of itself trigger the charge as control will remain, and the subsequent disposal of the shares by the liquidator will not trigger a clawback provided that the winding-up process is carefully handled.

6.14.2   Intra-group relief

The clawback is not triggered where the change of control is itself exempt by reason of FA 1930, s.42. However, if within the balance of the two year period the company to which the shares are transferred itself ceases to be a member of the same group as the company whose undertaking was acquired the clawback will operate.

Example

Thus if A transfers its undertaking to B for an issue of shares and subsequently A transfers the shares in B to associated company V this, of itself does not trigger a clawback. However, if within the relevant two year period the shares in B are transferred outside the stamp duty group the clawback is triggered. It is important to note that the references to *group* for these purposes are to a group as defined for the purposes of s.42, i.e.

---

is to the limited group for the stamp duty relief not the group as a whole. This might appear to raise problems if the shares in A are transferred outside the group; however, in such a case it is probable that this control of B will not change within the basic clawback provisions.

6.14.3 Share takeover

There is no clawback where the change of control arises by reason of a takeover that qualifies for the very narrow relief in FA 1986, s.77 which requires the same shareholders to remain interested in the company. However, if within the balance of the two year period a change of control of the new holding company occurs the clawback will operate.

6.14.4 Loan creditors

The interests of certain creditors are relevant upon the issue of control such as where they are entitled to more that 50 per cent of the company's assets. It is, however, provided that there is not a change of control triggering a clawback simply because the entitlement of loan creditors to the assets increases beyond the threshold.

6.15 DUE DILIGENCE AND COMPLIANCE AND CLAWBACK

The clawback event is reportable, under penalty, and details have to be supplied to the Inland Revenue Stamp Taxes Office together with payment of the duty upon the market value within 30 days after the event.

The due diligence process upon share purchases and warranties and indemnities are important problems that have to be addressed. The clawback tax is recoverable not only from the company acquiring the land and the transferor or lessor but also any company that at the time of the execution of the relevant instrument or at any time subsequently was a member of the same group as the company acquiring the land and was its direct or indirect parent company. This means that the tax is technically recoverable from foreign companies.

Example

Where A owns shares in B which owns shares in C which owns shares D and there has been a transfer of property from C to D followed by a transfer of shares in D to A, a purchaser of the shares in company B will be exposed to the possibility of a claim for the tax against company B if the transferor and transferee do not pay. Controlling directors, which would appear to include shadow directors, of any of these companies are personally liable for the tax.

This liability may be a problem if at the time of the clawback the relevant company is outside the jurisdiction or is insolvent or in liquidation. The need to investigate whether companies other than the one being acquired have been involved in any transaction to which s.42, s.151 or s.76 might have applied will need to be carried out with problems of escaping from the restrictions of SA 1891, s.117.

This is a big problem area for solicitors in seeking the protection of clients who are buying companies. This is particularly difficult since at the time of the share purchase the clawback event may not have occurred and it is necessary to seek protection against a future possible transaction. The usual warranties that all documents are duly stamped would not be appropriate since the charge would not necessarily be in respect of documents appropriate to the company being acquired or its subsidiaries.

Moreover, at the time of the transactions the documents may be duly stamped it is only retrospectively that they become dutiable. It is also obviously necessary before embarking upon any reconstruction of a group to investigate whether there may been any exemptions obtained within the preceding period commencing on the 24 April, 2002 or preceding two years whichever is the shorter. It is also necessary to consider whether the reorganisation itself will begin the clock running on possible clawback provisions in relation to land transfer during the reconstructing operations.

However, legal issues arise in relation to protecting purchasers and the impact of SA 1891, s.117 has to be considered. This renders void any indemnity or contract relating to the absence or insufficiency of stamp on documents.

There is no authority on how wide ranging this provision is, but clearly straightforward indemnities are vulnerable and vendors may renege upon the obligation. The statute itself does provide that any person who has paid the tax may recover that amount from the transferee or lessee company, provided that it is solvent.

It is likely that if the tax has not been paid this is because the transferee is unable to pay and in the case of overseas companies there is the question of whether the statutory indemnity would be rejected by a foreign court as enforcing the tax law of another country. Payments made under these provisions are not deductible in computing any income profits or losses for tax purposes so that there may be questions as to whether the amount of any tax so paid and not recovered can form part of the base cost of the shares in any other company acquired.

CHAPTER 7

Leases and agreements for leases of land

7.1 COMPARISONS WITH FREEHOLD

Unlike a freehold, which continues virtually indefinitely, a lease to create an estate in land, must be for a term of years absolute as defined by LPA 1925, s.205(1)(xxvii). The conveyancing problems affecting freeholds, and in their wake the stamp duty considerations, relate primarily to the change of ownership of the same estate. Each lease is a separate entity with its own birth, life, and inevitable death being the creation of a new interest frequently requiring to be registered and therefore duly stamped for an effective legal title to be created (Land Registration Act 1925, s.123 and s.123A).

7.2 COMPLEXITIES OF LEASEHOLD

The greater complexities of leasehold conveyancing are reflected in a greater number of stamp duty aspects needing consideration at each stage in the life of a lease. Thus *ad valorem* duty will normally be payable on the creation of a lease, may well be payable on a subsequent assignment, or a variation of its terms, and may even be payable on its premature death by surrender. (The duties on the assignment or the surrender of a lease are charged under either the head 'Conveyance or Transfer on sale' or the head 'Conveyance or Transfer not on sale' which are considered elsewhere.)

An agreement to sell a leasehold interest attracts stamp duty pursuant to FA 1999, Sched.13 para.7 in respect of severable fixtures (*Lee* v. *Gaskell* (1876) 24 WR 824) and falls into charge pursuant to FA 2002, s.115 where the consideration exceeds £10 million and no stamped transfer is produced within 90 days.

Being governed by a separate head of charge leases have their own exemptions and reliefs, so the grant of leases may complicate subsales and other reliefs from conveyance on sale duty (see **Chapter 6**).

It must not be forgotten that the grant of a sublease for the whole of the term of the lease is not a lease but is an assignment (*Milmo* v. *Carreras* [1946] KB 306) potentially dutiable as a conveyance upon sale with stamp duty upon any premium. Where the *sublease* reserves a *rent* then it will be treated for stamp duty purposes as a premium payable by instalments and the dutiable amount calculated in accordance with SA 1891, s.56 which is likely to produce a substantially higher charge than the stamp duty that would have been payable if it had been a sublease.

A lease, to take effect at law, must be by deed (LPA 1925, s.52; *City and Permanent Building Society* v. *Miller* [1952] Ch 840) unless it is to take effect in possession for a term not exceeding three years at the best rent reasonably obtainable without a fine, in which case it may be granted in writing, or even orally (LPA 1925, s.54). An agreement to grant a lease must also be made in writing – a written memorandum of an oral agreement is no longer effective (LP(MP)A 1989, s.2; *First Post Homes* v. *Johnson* [1995] 4 All ER 355). An option for the grant of or to renew a lease must now be exercised in writing (*Spiro* v. *Glencrown* [1991] 2 WLR 931).

It must also, as mentioned above, be for a term of years absolute: the length of the term must be fixed and certain before it starts, even though it may thereafter be brought to a premature end by, for example, the operation of a break clause in the lease, or by forfeiture or can be renewed or extended by the exercise of an option. A lease at a rent or premium determinable on death or marriage is not a lease for an uncertain term, as the provisions of LPA 1925, s.149(6) turn such a creature into a fixed term of 90 years determinable by notice after the unhappy event (*Skipton Building Society* v. *Clayton* (1993) 66 P&CR 223).

If, however, there is a lease which in other circumstances is to continue until the happening of an uncertain event, it is invalid (*Lace* v. *Chantler* [1944] KB 368 where a tenancy for the duration of the war was held to be invalid). This does not apply where the lease is granted for a maximum term which is expressed to be terminable on the happening of an earlier event such as the giving of a notice to quit (break clauses being unilateral events are not the same as surrenders *Barnett* v. *Morgan* [2000] 1 EGLP 8(HL)) subject to the possible intervention of the Landlord and Tenant Act 1954.

7.3 LEASE OR LICENCE

The head of charge 'Lease or Tack' is limited to leases or agreements for lease of land. It does not apply to licences to occupy land, nor does it apply to leases or hire of goods. In consequence, the distinction between a lease and a licence, so important to the question of security of tenure, has equal significance in the stamp duty context of the transaction. Since the drastic reduction of the scope of 'Bond, Covenant, etc' duty by FA 1971, s.64 there has been no *ad valorem* head of charge which can be considered applicable to licence fees, and the only possible duty payable on a licence used to be the fixed covenant duty of 50p where the licence was by deed. The grant of a licence to occupy land is not the creation of property for the purposes of SA 1891, s.60 and FA 1999, Sched.13 para.1 (*Thames Conservators v. IRC* (1886) 18 QBD 279) and so is not dutiable as a conveyance even where consideration is provided.

However, licences are not entirely free from stamp duty issues. For example, a contract to sell or the assignment of a licence is the disposal of property subject to stamp duty (*Western Abyssinian Mining Syndicate v. IRC* (1935) 14 ATC 286) usually upon the contract to sell pursuant to FA 1999, Sched.13 para.7. It also may mean that the transaction relates to UK land so that any other dutiable property being transferred or leased will be subject to penalties from 30 days after execution even where the documentation is executed offshore (FA 2002, s.114).

Whether or not the parties have created a licence or a lease is a matter of construction in each case, but it should be remembered that the courts look at the substance of the transaction not necessarily at the name the parties have chosen to give it (*Addiscombe Garden Estates v. Crabbe* [1957] 3 All ER 563), and, if the arrangement confers exclusive possession upon the occupier and otherwise contains terms appropriate to a lease, it may be held to have created a tenancy, even though called a licence (*Street v. Mountford* [1985] 2 WLR 877). There may, however, be differences between arrangements relating to business property and those affecting domestic arrangements with the former being easier to create licences (*Dresden Estates v. Collinson* (1987) 281 EG 1321). Difficult issues of classification can arise under building arrangements where developers who are entitled to the benefit of an agreement for lease are allowed into occupation of the premises in order to carry out the building works; in practice they may have the equivalent of exclusive occupation and if they are paying a fee or fees the Inland Revenue Stamp Taxes Office may claim that the licence to enter and to build is in law some form of tenancy. For other stamp problems related to building agreements see **section 7.12.3**.

It is noted elsewhere (**Chapter 4**) that the definition of a *conveyance* is wide and it can, depending upon the context, be wide enough to embrace the grant of a lease (*IRC v. Littlewoods Mail Order Stores Ltd* [1963] AC 135; *Escoigne Properties Ltd v. IRC* [1958] AC 549) but in general references to the stamp duty to *conveyances* do not include the grant of leases, and in the latter case the point was made that a premium payable in respect of a lease should be chargeable under the quite separate head of charge for leases. This head of charge applies to the grant of a lease at full consideration in rent or premium, or a combination of the two, the duty varying with the length of the lease, and the amount of any premiums paid and to any instrument increasing the rent (FA 1999, Sched.13 paras. 10–13 and para.20). All these aspects have to be considered in turn.

7.4   THE ADMINISTRATION OF LEASE DUTY

It should be remembered that legal leases for a term of seven or more years are subjected by FA 1931, s.28 to the requirements of a PD stamp (see **section 11.11**). Agreements for leases for a term of seven or more years may be similarly produced, in which case it is not necessary further to produce the lease granted in pursuance of the agreement.

7.5   BACKGROUND

For the purposes of investigating titles in relation to agreements for lease executed prior to 19 March 1984, these were stampable only if they were for a term not exceeding 35 years, SA 1891, s.75(1). In relation to leases for a term not exceeding 35 years executed prior to that date, these were not subject to stamp duty if the agreement for lease was duly stamped. A legal lease made subsequently to and in conformity with such an agreement, provided that it had been properly stamped, bore a further duty of 5p (SA 1891, s.75(2)), with the duty paid on the agreement being denoted on the legal lease.

Agreements for legal leases for terms in excess of 35 years escaped duty under s.75, and could not be caught under the head of charge 'Lease or Tack' until the agreement was completed by the grant of a legal lease. This gap led to the employment of an agreement for a lease for a term in excess of 35 years as a component in various stamp duty avoidance schemes.

In its simplest form, a freehold or long lease would be denuded of its value by the creation of an agreement for a long lease (or underlease) at a substantial premium. The reversion, now virtually worthless, and the lease agreement, would, by separate but more or less simultaneous transactions, end up together in the hands of the ultimate purchaser.

After grudgingly allowing passage of such schemes, the Inland Revenue, faced with an increasing deluge, finally set its face against them and was upheld in its contention that such schemes were ineffective in accordance with the *Ramsay* principles (*Ingram* v. *IRC* [1985] STC 835 Ch D). It is a matter of speculation whether this decision would stand today in the light of *Craven* v. *White* [1988] STC 476 and would appear to have been effectively overruled by *MacNiven* v. *Westmoreland Investments Ltd* [2001] STC 237.

However, prior to *Ingram,* Parliament had already taken steps (FA 1984, s.111) by extending the provisions of what is now FA 1999, Sched.13 para.14 to all agreements for leases, no matter how long. The 35 years retains practical significance since FA 1984, s.111 provides that where there is a sale of an interest with grant of a lease subject to an agreement for lease for a term exceeding 35 years the transfer or lease must bear a stamp denoting that the agreement for lease has been duly stamped.

7.6 PRESENT POSITION

Where there is an agreement for a legal lease of which equity will give specific performance, equity, looking upon that as done which ought to be done, considers the lease to be as good as granted. This equitable lease, as between the original contracting parties, is virtually as good as a legal lease (*Walsh* v. *Lonsdale* (1882) 21 Ch D 9 but see *Warmington* v. *Miller* [1973] 2 All ER 372; *Cornish* v. *Brook Green Laundry* [1959] 1 QB 394; *Rushton* v. *Smith* [1976] QB 480; *Boorman* v. *Griffiths* [1930] 1 Ch 493). Being a contract for the disposition of an interest in land, it must be in writing and signed by both parties in accordance with LP(MP)A 1989, s.2.

Part performance of a prior oral agreement is no longer possible: the effect of the LP(MP)A 1989 is to make an oral agreement for the sale of an interest in land a nullity. With registration of the interest against the landlord's title and possibly with the protection of an overriding interest within LRA 1925, s.70 equitable tenants are virtually in the same position as if they had taken a formal grant. The main practical problem is whether they require legal title for the purposes of a mortgage. In consequence, many relatively short leases remain uncompleted and unstamped (see **section 11.6.2**), but this may cause difficulties in certain situations such as litigation between landlord and tenant (see **section 7.12.3**).

All written agreements for lease are now dutiable as if they were leases. Duty on the subsequent legal lease, in conformity with the agreement, is then reduced (or as the case may be, extinguished) by the deduction therefrom of the duty paid on the agreement (FA 1999, Sched.13 para.14) and must bear a denoting stamp. If there is no written agreement for lease the lease must bear a certificate to that effect.

This charge to stamp duty upon contracts for lease applies even though the agreement to grant the lease is subject to the satisfaction of a condition, or where the agreement for lease is hidden as part of a larger arrangement such as a building agreement which provides that a lease in the form in a schedule to the agreement will be granted if the building works are completed satisfactorily (although it is a matter of construction of the instrument whether such an arrangement is a conditional agreement or the so-called condition is part of the consideration (*Eastham* v. *Leigh and London* [1971] Ch 871); on whether the building works are part of the stampable consideration see **section 7.12.3**), or there is a written notice exercising an option to call for the grant or renewal of a lease.

Various points concerning the credit mechanism for stamp duty paid upon the agreement for lease require to be noted:

- The credit is available only if the lease is in conformity with the agreement for lease or relates to substantially the same property and is for the same term as the agreement.

- If by reason of the rules relating to contingent payments or the market value rules of FA 1994, s.241 and s.242 (see **sections 2.15** and **4.13**) the stamp duty paid on the agreement for lease exceeds the stamp duty charged on the lease, although no duty is payable upon the lease there is no right to a repayment of the excess duty paid upon the agreement for lease.
- The stamp duty paid upon the agreement for lease is not recoverable if the lease is not granted such as may occur where the agreement for lease is made subject to a condition precedent (e.g. the obtaining of acceptable planning permission) which is not satisfied. The failure of a condition of this nature does not usually fall within the repayment provisions. In this context the line between an escrow and a delivered conditional agreement is not always understood in practice by the Inland Revenue Stamp Taxes Office and the duty is not always claimed.
- There are special rules for late stamping penalties and late payment interest (see **section 11.9**).
- Problems may arise in litigation where the lease has not been granted and the agreement for lease has been left unstamped. It seems that the judiciary is being encouraged to be more zealous in raising stamp duty issues in landlord and tenant matters, including social housing (SA 1891, s.14 (see **section 11.6.2**).

A particular difficulty arises out of this two-stage process for the collection of stamp duty and the new rules contained in FA 1994, s.241 and s.242 and FA 2000, s.121 which respectively impose a charge to stamp duty upon the market value of the relevant property where the consideration consists of shares or other property or is wholly or partially unascertainable (see **section 2.15**) or the lessee is a company connected with the lessor (see **section 7.12.4**). As the market value of the relevant property is to be ascertained immediately before the time of the execution of the relevant instrument (i.e. both the agreement for lease and the lease), it will be necessary to have valuations at both of those times even where the two instruments are presented for stamping together. It may well be that where there is only a brief interval of at most a few months between the two instruments the Inland Revenue Stamp Taxes Office may, in practice, be prepared to accept a single professionally prepared valuation, but this may not necessarily be the case.

There may, for example, be difficulties in this approach where there have been substantial building operations and improvements to the relevant property in the intervening period which can have important stamp duty consequences where there is a variable premium or rent where the stamp duty is calculated by reference to the market value or market rent. The carrying out of the building works or the pre-let or conditional subletting arrangements may enhance the value either of the land being leased or of the passing rent. In such cases there may be stamp duty benefits in granting the lease early before the value of the land has increased or the rent may have become clearer because of pre-sublets or other arrangements.

Moreover, as the Inland Revenue Stamp Taxes Office has indicated that it is prepared to consider only reasonably up to date professional valuations, any greater interval between the execution of the two instruments will almost inevitably require the two valuations to be performed.

7.7   DENOTING STAMPS

The stamp duty regime relating to agreements for lease has given rise to certain requirements as to denoting stamps.

- Where there is the transfer of a freehold or leasehold interest or the grant of a new lease subject to or with the benefit of an agreement for lease or underlease for a term exceeding 35 years, the conveyance or transfer or new lease must bear a stamp denoting that the agreement for lease has been duly stamped (FA 1984, s.111). This can also apply where the lease or underlease has been granted but not registered so that it takes effect as an agreement for lease (LRA 1925, s.123 and s.123A). Purchasers of an interest immediately reversionary on a lease can insist on the lease being duly stamped (*Whiting* v. *Loomes* (1887) 17 Ch 10) and should do so in the case of an agreement for lease since not only may they encounter difficulties in registering their title, but even if this is not the case they may have to stamp the agreement and pay interest and penalties if they wish to sue the tenant for breach. Attempts to deal with this by way of indemnity will be void (SA 1891, s.117).
- A lease granted on or after 20 March 1984 must bear a stamp denoting either that any written agreement for lease to which it gives effect has been duly stamped or that there is no such written agreement.

7.8   LATE STAMPING PENALTIES AND LATE PAYMENT INTEREST

Leases and agreements for lease executed on or after 1 October 1999 are instruments subject to the full range of penalties and interest for stamping outside the 30 day period and for instruments executed on or after 24 July 2002, since they will relate to UK land, the penalty and interest will run from 30 days after execution abroad (FA 2002, s.114). However, if an agreement for lease is presented for stamping together with the lease the penalties for late stamping and the interest charge do not begin to accrue until 30 days after the execution of the lease (FA 1994, s.240). This mitigation presupposes that there is a formal lease and the position is that if the agreement for lease is presented for stamping without the lease, the normal penalty and interest rules apply and these begin to accrue 30 days after execution of the agreement for lease.

In consequence when the parties exchange the agreement for lease they must consider whether to take the risk of deferring the payment of the stamp duty upon the agreement for lease with the related cash flows benefits since this may not qualify for the deferred penalty and interest rules should it be necessary to stamp the agreement before the lease is granted. For example, the tenant decides to defer the stamping of the agreement for lease but subsequently discovers that it is necessary to stamp the agreement in order to bring proceedings against the landlord for specific performance when the lessor refuses to grant the lease; or the agreement lease is conditional and no lease is granted because the conditions are not satisfied but it is necessary to stamp the agreement for lease in order to produce it in evidence in a dispute with the Inland Revenue. In such cases interest and penalties will have accrued (see **section 11.9**).

7.9 FIXED DUTIES ON LEASES AND AGREEMENTS FOR LEASE

There are certain fixed duties charged upon leases although in practice the scope for these has diminished significantly as a result of the changes to the charges to *ad valorem* stamp duty in relation to premiums consisting of other property (FA 1994, s.241) and unascertainable premiums and rents (FA 1994, s.242) and leases deemed to be granted at the market value (FA 2000, s.121).

Where there is a furnished tenancy of a dwelling house or apartment for a fixed term of less than a year and the rent does not exceed £5,000 per annum (FA 1999, Sched.13 para.11) there is no duty payable, otherwise the stamp duty is £5. Furnished lettings for a fixed term of one year are by no means unusual and it would appear desirable to ask for a reduction of one day to save the *ad valorem* charge otherwise payable.

There is a fixed duty of £5. The situations where this is likely to arise are leases without premium or rent such as upon a grant to a nominee (assuming that FA 2000, s.121 does not apply) or as a gift (although as such a lease may be a *conveyance* for these purposes it is arguable that it may be certified as exempt pursuant to the Stamp Duty (Exempt Instrument) Regulations 1987 subject to which adjudication would appear to be necessary).

7.10 *AD VALOREM* STAMP DUTIES ON LEASES AND AGREEMENTS FOR LEASE

7.10.1 Value added tax

When calculating the amount of any premium or rent subject to stamp duty the dutiable amount includes any VAT that is payable or which may become payable as a result of the exercise of the option to tax (see VATA 1994, Sched.10; for a further discussion see **section 2.16**).

The Inland Revenue Stamp Taxes Office do not in practice claim stamp duty upon potential VAT in relation to a lease or agreement for lease where the rent is exempt and there is a covenant by the landlord not to exercise the option to tax; nor where the lease or agreement for lease is entered into between companies in the same VAT group (although since FA 1995, s.151 such a lease may be exempt from stamp duty see **section 7.17.6**). It remains to be seen whether the clawback provisions in FA 2002, s.111 will be applied by the Inland Revenue Stamp Taxes Office to the VAT upon the rent and/or premium. It is assumed that they will be so applied. Where the rent is initially exempt but is expressed to be inclusive of any VAT which may become payable as a result of the exercise of the option to tax, it is considered that the amount of the rent cannot be increased by the exercise of the option to tax so that the claim to stamp duty is related to the rent actually reserved.

A particular issue arises in relation to VAT which is reserved separately from the rent (for example, the formulation of a rent of '£100 plus VAT') or where the rent is expressed to be exempt. In such cases it is arguable that the VAT which will or may become payable if the option to tax is exercised is not a sum reserved as *rent*. In this situation the Inland Revenue Stamp Taxes Office has indicated that it may take the point that the VAT is not rent but other consideration for the grant of the lease falling within SA 1891, s.56. In this case the stamp duty will be charged upon the VAT as a premium by reference to a sum calculated in accordance with s.56, namely, the aggregate VAT which will or may become payable over the term of the lease or 20 years whichever is the shorter. It should be noted that this approach at current rates of stamp duty produces a higher charge to stamp duty than a charge upon a like sum as rent. However, this point rarely arises in practice, since it is normal conveyancing practice to include actual or potential VAT as part of the rent in order to give additional protection to the landlord.

7.11   THE PREMIUM

The most straightforward case to consider is the grant of a lease at a premium with a modest or nominal ground rent reserved. As noted above, to take effect as a legal estate, it must be granted by deed. Full *ad valorem* duty is payable on the premium at 4 per cent (unless a certificate of value for the lower rates of stamp duty is inserted – FA 1999, Sched.13 para.12(2)).

The head of charge imposes 'the same duty as a conveyance on a sale for the same consideration'. This does not have the effect of making the lease or agreement for lease subject to stamp duty as a conveyance; it merely means that the duty is calculated in the same way as conveyance on sale duty. In consequence, where the premium consists of shares or securities the duty is calculated in accordance with SA 1891, s.55; and where the premium consists of or includes sums payable periodically the amount subject to duty is calculated in accordance with SA 1891, s.56 (*Quietlece* v. *IRC* [1984] STC 95 and **Chapter 2** for a detailed consideration of the relevant rules for calculating conveyance on sale duty applicable here).

A lease for less than adequate consideration such as a low premium or a low rent used to be treated by FA 1910, s.74(5) as a voluntary disposition on the grounds that it conferred a substantial benefit on the lessee, and was consequently stamped on its full adjudicated value (*IRC* v. *Littlewoods Mail Order Stores Ltd* [1963] AC 135). Subject to FA 2000, s.121, this is no longer a danger since 19 March 1985 (FA 1985, s.82) but fixed duty may be payable and adjudication may still be required unless the lease is certified as a voluntary disposition pursuant to the Stamp Duty (Exempt Instrument) Regulations 1987 (SI 1987/516).

7.12   ILLUSTRATIONS OF PREMIUMS

7.12.1   Third party payments

It should be noted that the head of charge expressly states that the consideration can move to a person other than the lessor. If payment is made to the lessor's nominee it will not, therefore, escape the charge, as where the lessor of a new building requires the lessee to pay the premium, or part, direct to the builder.

Similarly payments by persons other than the tenant may constitute a premium for these purposes. For example a payment by a settlor who directs that the lease be granted to trustees of a settlement is a stampable premium. These issues must not be overlooked when completing Particulars Delivered and other forms (SA 1891, s.5).

7.12.2   Other property

Prior to FA 1994 the stamp duty charge was limited to premiums consisting of 'any money, stock or security'. However, in order to counteract certain mitigation arrangements FA 1994, s.241 (now FA 1999, Sched.13 para.12(2)) provided that the effect from 1 May 1995 stamp duty under the head 'Lease or Tack' should be chargeable upon 'any property'. This has considerably increased the number of transactions subject to *ad valorem* stamp duty.

For example, transactions now subject to *ad valorem* duty include the grant of a lease of Blackacre in consideration of the surrender or assignment of the lease of Whiteacre; the transfer of the freehold of Greenacre in consideration of the grant of a lease-back of Greenacre (whether or not for a full rent and whether or not for a payment of cash by way of equality).

In these cases the grant of the lease is subject to *ad valorem* stamp duty upon an amount equal to the market value of the other property transferred. The other property transferred is subject to stamp duty on the value, if any, of the new lease. The charge upon the lease or agreement for lease is restricted where the consideration for its grant consists of or includes the surrender of a lease of the same premises, since the value of this is excluded from the stampable premium (SA 1891, s.77(1) and FA 2000, s.128(3)). Multiple charges to stamp duty may arise by reason of these and other provisions in relation to variations of leases that involve a surrender and regrant which is considered as a special topic at **section 7.15**.

The drafting of these arrangements may influence the amount of stamp duty (see **Chapter 3**).

7.12.3   Building works

An element to be ignored is any consideration consisting either of 'a covenant by the lessee to make, or of his having previously made, any substantial improvement of or addition to the property demised to him, or of any covenant relating to the matter of the lease' (SA 1891, s.77), unless the covenant is such that if it were contained in a separate deed it would be chargeable with *ad valorem* stamp duty (Revenue Act 1909, s.8). However, this does not necessarily exclude a charge to stamp duty in relation to arrangements for the construction of a building.

Problems can arise in the case of the construction of a new building both for the grant of leases and in relation to the purchase of freehold building plots. The cost of the building works is likely to form part of the stampable premium where the works are carried out at the expense of the tenant, the builder and the lessor are the same person and the tenant is not entitled to call for the grant of the lease until the building works are completed. The charge does not arise where the tenant employs a builder who is not the landlord. Notwithstanding that there may be a covenant by the tenant to carry out the building works as the payments are not made to the landlord they are not treated as consideration for the granting of the lease.

These also may be an important issue should the Inland Revenue Stamp Taxes Office claim that fitting out costs borne by the tenant are part of the premium. It has been accepted by the Inland Revenue Stamp Taxes Office that a covenant to carry out building works is not *other property* for the purposes of FA 1994, s.241 and so it is not taken into account in calculating the stamp duty. If all of these conditions are not fulfilled so that there is not a single contract for the lease of the completed building, the building costs do not form part of the stampable premium (*Paul* v. *IRC* [1936] SC 443; *Prudential Assurance Co* v. *IRC* [1992] STC 863). It is contended by the

Inland Revenue Stamp Taxes Office that if the lessor and the builder are connected, such as members of the same group of companies, this is sufficient, but this is generally regarded as an incorrect interpretation of the decision in *Mclnnes* v. *IRC* [1934] SC 424 (see *Paul* v. *IRC,* supra).

If the building has been completed by the date of the grant of the lease, all payments to the builder will be dutiable. Duty will not however, be payable if the lease is granted before the building is erected and the building is subsequently put up under a separate agreement (see for example *Kimbers* v. *IRC* [1936] 1 KB 132). Moreover, as with a freehold there will be no duty payable on the value of the building, notwithstanding that the lease is completed after its erection, provided that it is preceded by an agreement for a lease before building commences and the actual construction is carried out under a separate and independent contract.

This view was set out originally in the Board of Inland Revenue Statement of Practice published in [1957] *Gazette* 450, as clarified by the Inland Revenue Statement of Practice SP10/87 dated 22 December 1987; it does not appear in the latest Statement of Practice SP8/93. However, it is considered to be a correct statement of the law (see *Cory Brothers Ltd* v. *IRC* [1965] 1 All ER 917).

In theory, when calculating the premium, any lessor's costs paid by the lessee should be included, but as a matter of practice, the Revenue ignores them [1959] *Gazette* 95.

7.12.4 Deemed premiums

FA 2000, s.121 imposes a charge to stamp duty by reference to a market value premium where the lease is granted to a connected company. Obviously the value of any such premium will depend upon the level of the rent; a lease at a full reviewable rack rent will prima facie have no market value. However, there is a potential problem if the Inland Revenue Stamp Taxes Office should spot the point where the lease is for a ground rent for an undeveloped site; if the lease is granted after the development has been completed the rent will be relatively low and there is a potential market value premium, i.e. what the lease would fetch if sold on the open market. The point is arguable since it is not appropriate that tenants should pay stamp duty upon their own expenditure and it has to be put to the Inland Revenue Stamp Taxes Office that there is some equity or interest in the tenant which depresses the value of the lease granted. The Inland Revenue Stamp Taxes Office, however, is not consistent in its views in this area, and because the existence of the building works is not disclosed by solicitors or the issue investigated by them the point is not frequently raised in practice notwithstanding SA 1891, s.5.

The clawback provisions for relief from lease duty obtained pursuant to FA 1995, s.151 (see **section 7.18.2**) may produce a deemed premium. FA 2002, s.111 provides that if the lessee leaves the stamp duty group within two years after the grant of the lease the stamp duty relief is cancelled and stamp duty is payable as if the lease had been granted at market value. Where the rent for the intra-group lease was below market rent there may be some value in the lease which might emerge as a dutiable premium. It should be noted that the reporting obligations for clawback require the company to give details of market value and the amount of stamp duty payable. In consequence it is necessary to raise this issue with the Inland Revenue Stamp Taxes Office (FA 2002, Sched.34 para.6 with the penalty pursuant to Taxes Management Act 1970, s.98(5) for failure to do so).

7.12.5   Variable premiums

The position is somewhat more complicated where the premium consists of or includes a variable amount, such as where the premium is a multiple of the amount of net lettable area of the building when completed, or is a sum related to the rents derived from the letting of the building when completed. The issue here is whether the Inland Revenue Stamp Taxes Office can find a prima facie sum within the scope of the contingency principle (see **section 2.14**) such as a maximum square footage or a minimum rent for the purposes of calculation of the premium, they will claim stamp duty upon those figures. If not, FA 1994, s.242 provides that where the premium for the grant of a lease is wholly or partially unascertainable the stamp duty is to be calculated by reference to the market value of the lease or agreement for lease – two market valuations will be required (see **section 7.6**). Section 242(3)(*a*) provides that for these purposes the cases where consideration or rent cannot be ascertained at any time do not include cases where the consideration or rent could be ascertained on the assumption that any future event mentioned in the instrument in question were or were not to occur. This means that if the general contingency rules produce a prima facie sum they will claim the stamp duty upon that sum and not the market value (see **section 2.16**). The drafting of such arrangements can have a significant impact upon the stamp duty costs (see **Chapter 3**).

7.12.6   Reverse premiums

There is no stamp duty under this head in respect of a reverse premium, i.e. an inducement paid by the landlord to the tenant to take the lease. The payment is moving with the lease not in the opposite direction to the grant and so is not consideration for the grant. However, there may be indirect stamp duty consequences of such an arrangement. Frequently such arrangements are linked to a higher initial rent than would be payable upon normal market terms. Such higher rent will, of course, affect the amount of stamp duty payable. Such increased cost to the tenant should be taken into account when negotiating the amount of the reverse payment if the tenant is not to be out of pocket.

7.13   CERTIFICATES OF VALUE FOR SMALL PREMIUMS

Having calculated the premium in accordance with the above, the lessee (or assignee of an existing lease) may, as with the purchaser under a conveyance on sale, take advantage of a certificate of value (see **section 2.4**). The premium duty will thus be nil if the lease or assignment is certified at £60,000. The certificate on the grant of a lease is to the effect that the transaction thereby effected does not form part of a larger transaction or of a series of transactions in respect of which the amount or value or the aggregate amount or value of the consideration *other than rent* exceeds the stated amount.

The rental element is thus ignored in calculating the capital sum passing, but is assessed separately for duty in accordance with the provisions appearing below. It must, however, be carefully noted that the associated ground rent must not exceed an average of £600 per annum, this current limit having been set by FA 1982, s.128. If the average rent does exceed this figure, no certificate of value can effectively be given and full *ad valorem* duty will be charged on the whole of the premium, no matter how small.

It should be noted that the restriction on the use of certificates of value applies only where there is a larger transaction between the same parties. In consequence the relief is available where, for example, a developer agrees to acquire a freehold interest upon which he constructs a block of flats and directs the freeholder to grant leases to tenants of the flats. In such a case each lessee would, if the circumstances are appropriate, be entitled to the benefit of a certificate of value. Where the freehold reversion is conveyed to a management company at the direction of the developer for a token sum, subsale relief is available pursuant to SA 1891, s.58(4) and FA 2002, Sched.36 and may be entitled to the benefit of a certificate of value as a conveyance on sale.

7.14   THE RENT

There is no statutory definition of rent for the purposes of stamp duty. The term therefore bears its normal meaning of a payment made by a tenant to a landlord for the exclusive possession of the land (*T & E Homes* v. *Robinson* [1976] STC 462; *Gable Construction Co* v. *IRC* [1968] 1 WLR 1426). If the payment is not reserved out of the land, it is not rent (*Hill* v. *Booth* [1930] 1 KB 381) but this leaves open the question of whether the sums in question are a premium payable periodically dutiable in accordance with the computational provisions in SA 1891, s.56 (see **section 2.11**).

7.14.1 Service and other charges

Leases frequently provide for the lessee to make periodic payments to the lessor of service charges incurred or to be incurred, and for the recovery of insurance premiums paid by the lessor to insure the building demised, or against loss of rent, or both. Such payments are frequently stated to be reserved as additional rents in order to allow the landlord to recover outstanding sums as rent in arrears.

At one time insurance and service charge *rents* were aggregated with the ordinary rent for computing the duty. The Inland Revenue have, however, stated that this practice may have been of dubious legality and they will no longer treat additional rent of this nature as dutiable ([1981] *Gazette* 648) unless a single sum for both rent and services is reserved. Since the abolition of covenant duty by FA 1971, s.64 no duty at all may be payable by the lessee on such additional periodical payments under the lease whether or not reserved as rent.

Following *Quietlece Ltd* v. *IRC* [1984] STC 95 which held that SA 1891, s.56 applies to leases and agreements for lease as well as to conveyances, there is an argument that such periodical sums, if constituting consideration for the grant of the lease (and not consideration for other obligations, benefits or services) could constitute a *periodical premium* with stamp duty of up to 4 per cent becoming payable upon the capital amount calculated in accordance with SA 1891, s.56 (see **section 2.11**). This point is not usually taken in practice by the Inland Revenue Stamp Taxes Office but it has been used by it as a possible means of charging stamp duty upon the actual or potential VAT payable in respect of the basic rent (see **section 2.16**).

7.14.2 Penal rents

Should the lease make provision for a penal rent, or an increased rent in the nature of a penal rent, if, for example, the lessee is in breach of one of his covenants, SA 1891, s.77(1) states categorically that any such increase is to be disregarded in computing the duty.

7.14.3 Average rent

The stamp duty payable upon the rent depends upon a combination of two factors:

1. The length of the lease which determines the rate of stamp duty.
2. The average rent which determines the amount to which the rate is applied. The current scales are imposed by FA 1999, Sched.13 para.12(3).

Term not more than seven years or indefinite:

(a) if the rent is £5,000 or less	Nil
(b) if the rent is more than £5,000	1%

Term more than 7 years but not more than 35 years	2%
Term more than 35 years but not more than 100 years	12%
Term more than 100 years	24%

The above rates are payable in addition to the duty chargeable on any premium. Where there is provision for an escalating rent of a predetermined amount, the duty is assessed on the average rent payable throughout the term.

7.14.4 Calculation of the term

The length of the term is important for two reasons. As the duty is imposed upon the average rent it is necessary to determine the total amount of rent (including actual and potential VAT) that will or may become payable over the term of the lease and then divide this total by the number of years of the term of the lease. The length of the term also fixes the rate. It is important, therefore, to understand the technical stamp duty principles concerning the calculation of the term.

Lace v. *Chantler* [1944] KB 368, referred to at **section 7.2**, shows that an indefinite term cannot exist as a legal entity, and as the arrangement is void no stamp duty would be payable; where stamp duty has been paid it may be possible to recover the duty pursuant to either Stamp Duties Management Act 1891, s.9(7) or s.10 provided that the claim for repayment is made within the prescribed two-year period. In reality, for this purpose the term must be aimed at, and limited to, a periodic tenancy, namely for a certain term not in excess of a year automatically renewable without further ado unless and until either party serves the appropriate notice to quit.

It will be seen from the table given above that an indefinite term is stamped at the rate applicable for a lease not exceeding seven years. Occasionally a fixed term lease contains provision for its automatic extension until either party serves notice bringing it to an end. FA 1999, Sched.13 para.15 provides that the length of the term is to be ascertained by adding to the original fixed term the minimum period which must elapse before the notice can take effect. Again, in similar vein, a fixed term lease may provide for a periodic tenancy to arise on its expiration. In either case, unless the lease specifies the exact date or dates on which the notice may take effect, it should be remembered that the common law rules require a notice to take effect on the expiry of a completed cycle of the period.

It was held in *Cottage Holiday Associates Ltd* v. *Customs and Excise Commissioners* [1983] QB 735 that a time-share lease of 80 years giving the lessee the right to use the accommodation for one week per year was not a single fixed term of 80 years, but a series of 80 separate periods of one week each.

Sometimes the commencement date of the term, as stated in the lease, predates the actual grant. The Inland Revenue's view is that any period prior to the date of the lease is to be ignored in calculating the length of the term, see [1963] *Gazette* 175–6. Thus rent under a lease for, say, 101 years with effect from a commencement date 13 months earlier than the date of the grant will bear a duty at the rate of 12 per cent, not 24 per cent.

The same principle applies to agreements for lease where the term is expressed to commence prior to the exchange of the agreement. However, the situation is likely to cause differences in the amount of stamp duty upon the agreement for lease and the lease, particularly where there is a significant interval between the agreement for lease and the grant of the lease. The former will have a longer term with a possibly higher rate and there may be extra rent (i.e. sums payable in the intervening period) to be included in the averaging process.

The commencement date of the term is often backdated to achieve consistency of end of term dates between similar leases or other units on the same estate or in the same building, as for example where flats in a block are being sold off separately by way of long lease or because of the time which has elapsed between the exchange. In these circumstances there is rarely any question of the liability for rent commencing before the actual date of grant but, even if the rent is also backdated to reflect the taking up occupation by the lessee prior to the grant, the backdated rent is nonetheless disregarded in calculating the length of the term (see also *Alan Estates Ltd* v. *W G Stores* [1981] 3 WLR 892).

7.14.5 Break clauses

Many leases or agreements for lease are expressed to be for a maximum term but contain an option or break clause entitling one or both of the parties to terminate the lease at an earlier date by giving notice to quit. In such cases for stamp duty purposes the lease is treated as being for the maximum term and the break clause is ignored (*Cummins Engine Co Ltd* v. *IRC* [1981] STC 604; *Kushner* v. *Law Society* [1952] 1 All ER 404). A notice to quit or the exercise of a break clause is not a surrender of the lease and so is not dutiable notwithstanding FA 2000, s.128 (*Barnett* v. *Morgan* [2000] 1 EGLP 8(HL)).

7.14.6 Renewals and extensions

If the tenant has a contractual right under the lease by way of option to call for a renewal on the expiry of the present term, the period of any renewed term is ignored in calculating the length of the original term and the stamp duty is chargeable in respect of the length of the lease when granted pursuant to the exercise of the option. Such an option must now be exercised in writing (LP(MP)A 1989, s.2; and see *Spiro* v. *Glencrown* [1991] 2 WLR 931).

As and when the option is exercised the written notice of exercise will be dutiable as an agreement to grant a lease (FA 1999, Sched.13 para.14) and when completed, the renewed lease will bear duty separately in accordance with its length with the appropriate credit against such duty for the stamp duty paid upon the written exercise notice. (There may, however, be a difference between an option to renew and an option to extend; *Baker* v. *Merckel* [1960] 1 QB 657.) It appears, however, that as with an option to renew the Inland Revenue Stamp Taxes Office claims stamp duty only by reference to the original term, notwithstanding the different nature of the option to extend, but the stamp duty issues on other aspects of such options such as their exercise have never been tested in practice.

7.14.7   Mitigation of rent duty

In view of the sharp increases in rates across the bands, particularly from 35 years to more than 35 years, it may be feasible in appropriate circumstances to try to reduce the term so as to take advantage of a lower rate of duty, but still give practical effect to the intentions of the parties with regard to the totality of the length of the term required.

One way is to split up the period for which the parties wish to be bound to each other into two parts, giving the tenant a lease of the first part, being for a term attracting a lower rate of duty, with an option to renew for the balance, which again could be at the lower rate. As this will involve two leases, there will be two separate payments of duty, and although there will be a postponement of one payment there may not necessarily be a net saving in duty.

Reduction, for example, of the duty, by shortening a 14-year term to a seven-year term with an option to renew for a further seven years will be cancelled out by the fresh duty payable on the completed exercise of the option (assuming that there is no change in the rates of duty in the meanwhile). If, however, it is possible to break down a term in excess of 35 years to two terms, neither exceeding 35 years, the effective duty will be reduced from 12 per cent to an aggregate of 4 per cent (2 per cent on each lease). Alternatively, in the case of a lease for 125 years, this can be broken down into two leases for 99 years and 26 years respectively (12 per cent and 2 per cent) or four leases, being three for 35 years and one for 23 years (four leases at 2 per cent).

The drafting of such arrangements will require care. To protect the landlord who is anxious for a tenant to stay for the whole of the period, the tenant's option should be coupled with a put option, i.e. an option in the former's favour. The landlord should remember, however, that, whereas the rule against perpetuities does not apply to an option to renew a lease (*Weg*

Motors Ltd v. *Hales* [1962] Ch 49), the put option will be subject to the rule in Perpetuities and Accumulations Act 1964, s.9(2) that it will be void unless exercised within 21 years.

Another well-tried and tested device is to grant both leases immediately, making the second a reversionary lease to take effect on the expiry of the first. It should be borne in mind that LPA 1925, s.149(3) makes void a term which is to take effect more than 21 years after the date of the grant. The first lease should therefore be for 21 years less two days and the future or reversionary lease should be stated to take effect in possession shortly thereafter such as one day following the termination. Certain commentators suggest that the reversionary lease should take effect in possession immediately after the expiration of the immediate lease. It is considered that such an arrangement could provide the Inland Revenue Stamp Taxes Office with the argument that because the two leases are more or less linked there is a merger of the two leases so that only a single lease is granted, or in reality there is no break so that there is only one lease and not two. Although it may in theory be inconvenient for there to be an interval, albeit very short, between the expiration of the first lease and the reversionary lease taking effect in possession, such an interval of, for example, one day, may be a prudent step in the type of mitigation arrangement.

The rent under the reversionary lease may fall to be ascertained by the market values current at the time when the lease starts, in which case there will be no ascertainable consideration and the duty will be calculated by reference to the market rent of such a lease at the date of grant. In reality, a landlord is unlikely to be willing to accept a reversionary lease which does not provide for payment of a rent at least as high as the highest rent payable under the primary lease. This in turn will doubtless have upwards only rent review clauses, which leads straight back to the rent initially payable under the primary lease as the minimum ascertainable rent payable under the reversionary lease and stampable with exactly the same amount of duty. Even so, as noted above, the aggregate duty will be 4 per cent in lieu of the 12 per cent payable on a term in excess of 35 years.

7.14.8 Calculating the rent

For the *ad valorem* charge to bite, there must be a rent which is ascertainable from the body of the lease at the date of its grant.

7.14.9 Variable rents other than rent reviews

It is unusual in a modern lease for any reasonable term to reserve a fixed rent for the whole term except perhaps in cases where there is a large premium and merely a ground rent but even the ground rent can contain provisions for its increase, and such increasing ground rents can give rise to substantial stamp duty particularly where the lease is for a long term. Solicitors should carry out the arithmetic process and determine the stamp duty charge in advance rather than wait to be shocked when they receive the official calculation.

There are numerous reasons why the parties may require a variable rent, such as where the lessor wishes to guard against inflation and requires rent reviews, or the lease is essentially a fundraising exercise such as a sale and leaseback where the lessor is more concerned with a financial return equivalent to interest rates rather than rental values upon his capital outlay. The lease may be a form of joint venture whereby the landowner and a developer are intending to participate in the profits or income arising from the letting of the completed development; this may be achieved by a rent formula under the head lease whereby the rent reserved to the landlord is a percentage of the rents as profits derived as turnover or an overage arrangement in respect of the underlettings in due course.

There could, for example, be the grant of a reversionary lease at a rent stated to be a percentage of the rents of underleases yet to be created thereout; this is now dutiable upon market rent. The lease could be granted initially at a fixed rent such as a peppercorn rent with a provision for the rent to be reviewed after a specified period of, say, a few months and, thereafter, in accordance with such review, to be the open market rent. In both cases the lease may now attract the duty only on the initial low rent (but see *LM Tenancies plc* v. *IRC* [1998] STC 326 for the suggestion that a reference to the future market rent is to be construed as a reference to the current market rent at the date of the lease). If, however, it is possible to calculate the rent as at the date of the grant, by reference to external criteria or factors, notwithstanding that no fixed sums as such were set forward in the lease, the rent is ascertainable, and therefore dutiable at the normal *ad valorem* rates appropriate to the length of the term of the lease.

The position regarding stamp duty liability and variable rents was changed significantly by FA 1994, s.242 with effect from 7 December 1994 (discussed in more detail at **section 2.15**). Basically the position is governed by the general contingency principle supplemented by the market rent rules of FA 1994, s.242. (The statement on variable rents in [1963] *Gazette* 175–6 has ceased to operate.) The current regime is complicated and it is necessary to understand the general contingency principle as applied in this area not only for the purpose of investigating title but because the statutory regime merely supplements the general principle and does not replace it. The effect of FA 1994, s.242(3)(*a*) is that it is necessary to apply the general principle first in order to determine whether there is a prima facie single rent ascertainable; only if the general principle does not produce an *ascertainable* rent in whole or in part does the statutory market rent scheme apply. Frequently the issue is one of the drafting of the instrument (see **Chapter 3**). Broadly, if the Inland Revenue Stamp Taxes Office can find a maximum sum they will claim stamp duty upon that sum (*Coventry City Council* v. *IRC* [1978] 1 All ER 1107); but where there is either no ascertainable rent or only a minimum or small figure it may seek to apply the market rent provisions.

Unascertainable bears a special meaning of no prima facie sum within the general contingency principle the details of which are considered at **section 2.14**. This means that if there is a single prima facie sum such as a maximum rent or a minimum rent that increases upwards only the stamp duty is charged upon that amount (Inland Revenue *Tax Bulletin,* August 1995) Where this principle does not produce such a sum FA 1994, s.242 provides, among other things, that where the rent reserved by a lease or an agreement for lease is unascertainable, in whole or in part, the stamp duty is to be calculated by reference to the market value of the lease.

The applicability of these provisions is reasonably clear where the rent is totally unascertainable, such as where the lease or agreement for lease is entered into for a rent to be determined solely by reference to a percentage of the rents received from subletting. The effect of the decision in *LM Tenancies* v. *IRC* [1998] STC 326 is that a reference to the future market rent is a reference to the current market rent so that the future rent is *ascertainable* and as a prima facie sum can be found the provisions of FA 1994, s.242 do not apply. Duty is chargeable, in theory, upon the basis of the current rent or current market rent which may be quite low where the lease is granted at an early stage in the building works. This could arise, for example, where the lease is granted to a tenant with the rent to be fixed at the end of the fitting-out period or at the end of a rent holiday. It is in such cases a matter of negotiating the current market rent with the District Valuer.

Ultimately, *unascertainability* of *part of the rent* is a matter of drafting, and where the rent formula includes several components whether it is possible to find a prima facie sum upon general principle for each such component. Where the rent is to be '£x or 10 per cent of the rent received whichever is the larger' or '10 per cent of rent received but to be not less than £x' this is a single minimum rent variable upwards only and it is not *unascertainable*. The stamp duty is charged upon £x (Inland Revenue *Tax Bulletin,* August 1995). However, if the rent formula is '£x plus 10 per cent of the rent received' as no prima facie sum can be found for the 10 per cent component which is an independent element in the rent formula unconnected to the £x basic rent, part of the rent is unascertainable and FA 1994, s.242 applies to charge stamp duty upon the market rent.

7.14.10 Market rent

Apart from stating that the *market rent* is the rent which the lease might reasonably be expected to fetch in the open market, no guidance has been provided as to the principles to be adopted in determining market value, and in consequence there are likely to be some interesting debates on issues of principles of valuation to be adopted with the District Valuer, but it is clear that the lease to be valued is the actual lease granted and not some hypothetical lease. The actual terms, other than the rent, are therefore, important.

7.14.11   Rent reviews

The former practice relating to reviewable rents, set out in [1963] *Gazette* 175–6, treating the transaction as involving two leases has been withdrawn because of the impact of *LM Tenancies* v. *IRC* [1998] STC 326 and FA 1994, s.241.

Although there is a charge upon an instrument increasing the rent (FA 1999, Sched.13 para.20(1)) it is specifically provided that this does not apply to an instrument which merely records the result of the implementation of a rent review provision within the lease (FA 1999, Sched.13 para.20(2)).

The current position depends upon the nature of the review.

7.14.12   Upwards only reviews

The usual provision to the effect that the rent is to be a basic sum but is to be reviewed from time to time and for the period thereafter is to be the higher of the rent previously payable or the then market rent is not within FA 1994, s.242. Landlords, for obvious reasons, would invariably insist on such a one-way ratchet where they can, though the terms of review in a renewal of a lease of business premises imposed by the court under the Landlord and Tenant Act 1954, Part II are at the court's discretion (LPA 1969, s.2). There is a single minimum rent for the whole term and the fact that it may be increased does not mean that the rent is partially unascertainable. Stamp duty is accordingly charged only upon the initial or basic rent pursuant to the general contingency principle.

7.14.13   Floating rents

Where the rent is to vary during the term, and the amounts are ascertainable from the outset, the average rent throughout the term forms the basis of the charge, not just the initial rent. Where, however, the initial rent is ascertainable but, after a pre-agreed period or periods, is to be reviewed in accordance with a stated formula (e.g. open market rent at the date of review whether greater or lower than the initial rent or the rent payable at the time if it may increase or reduce), the future rent is (subject to the effect of *LM Tenancies* v. *IRC* [1998] STC 326) as yet unascertainable. In these circumstances prior to 7 December 1993 only the initial rent attracted the *ad valorem* charge. Such situations, although perhaps less common than previously, are not unusual since the landlord may have agreed that the period to the first review date is a form of rent holiday, or the initial rent may be somewhat higher than the true market rent because the landlord has paid a reverse premium to the tenant as part of an inducement package.

The strict theory of FA 1994, s.242 would suggest that in such cases the stamp duty should be charged upon the market rent, however that is to be ascertained, taking into account the formula for review to market rent. It remains to be discovered how one determines the market rent of a long lease with a variable rental formula. It seems that the Inland Revenue Stamp Taxes Office may be proposing to treat the initial rent as the dutiable figure. This could be based upon one of two approaches. The initial rent could be regarded as the market rent which may well be the case unless either there is a high initial rent because of a reverse premium or there has been a significant delay between the time when the rent was initially agreed and the grant of the lease.

This would seem to be consistent with the decision in *LM Tenancies* v. *IRC* [1998] STC 326 that references to future market rent are to be construed as being references to a sum equal to the current market rent as adjusted in accordance with market changes. This gives a prima facie rent for the whole term. This, of course, indicates that it is frequently in the interests of the parties to take the grant of the lease early before the progress of the planning applications, building works and subletting agreements increase the value of the land and the interests. This basis leaves it open for the parties to dispute the figures with appropriate supporting evidence.

Alternatively, and this is believed to be the basis of the Inland Revenue Stamp Taxes Office view, the initial rent is a prima facie starting figure and falls within the general contingency principle notwithstanding that it may increase or reduce in amount (*Independent Television Authority* v. *IRC* [1960] 2 All ER 487). It is generally considered that this latter view is incorrect, since the general principle requires the same sum to be taken into account on each subsequent occasion when the agreed formula is applied to determine the amount payable; in these cases the initial rent is not usually taken into account in determining the market rent for subsequent periods.

7.14.14 Instrument increasing the rent

It is specifically provided that no stamp duty is payable upon an instrument recording the effect of a rent review (FA 1999, Sched.13 para.20(2)). However there is a special charge (para.20(1)) upon an instrument increasing the rent. If the increase results from a deed of variation rather than pursuant to a predetermined formula in the lease, the deed acts as a genuine subsequent variation of the term of years insofar as the rent is concerned. As will be seen later, sometimes a purported variation of a lease operates as an implied surrender and regrant, but this is not a hazard where merely the rent is concerned; the original lease continues to subsist provided this is the intention of the parties (*Gable Construction* v. *IRC* [1968] 1 WLR 1426). (For deeds varying rent prior to 1 October 1999, SA 1891, s.77(5) and FA 1971, s.64(1)(*a*) imposed stamp duty of the different rates under the head 'Bond Covenant', but which duty was not to exceed the amount which would have been payable under the head 'Lease or Tack'. Currently the charge is purely to lease duty.)

The deed varying the rent is treated as a lease for the amount of the increase for a term equal to the period during which the increase is to operate. It is not always obvious what is the amount of the increase, particularly where there have been rent reviews increasing the initial rent or the rent is a percentage of rents received from underlettings. For example, there may be an initial rent of £100 reviewable upwards only. The latest review was to £5,000 per annum. In such a context the position is that the stamp duty is chargeable only upon the amount by which the increased rent exceeds the actual passing rent at that time. The charge will apply only to the increase over the latest rent review not the increase from the initial rent. In the case of rent sharing arrangements the stamp duty applies only to the amount by which the new rent exceeds the amount of rent currently payable pursuant to the formula as applied to the facts at the time of the deed.

There is no stamp duty payable upon a reduction of rent such as where a tenant pays a lump sum to commute or reduce future rent.

7.14.15 Other variable rents

Reviewable rents are not the only circumstances where a rent may change during the term of a lease; rents may be reserved by reference to movements in interest rates where the market rent rules of s.242 are now likely to apply. Such arrangements are rare in their own right but frequently part of a formula whereby the rent is to be increased to market rent or by a fixed percentage whichever is the greater. In such a case the Inland Revenue Stamp Taxes Office will claim stamp duty by reference to the fixed amount increase as being a prima facie sum within the general contingency principle. In the case of leases for longer terms where the higher rates of 12 per cent or 24 per cent apply to the average rent plus VAT, the amount of stamp duty can be extremely high because of the compounding effect over time. Such arrangements must be approached with great caution on the part of the professional adviser. Fortunately the Inland Revenue Stamp Taxes Office has abandoned the point based upon inflation indexation but other forms of automatic increase of rent will be dutiable on the ascertainable amounts.

7.15 OTHER VARIATIONS OF LEASES – SURRENDER AND REGRANT

Occasionally landlord and tenant agree to what purports to be a variation in the terms of the lease, but which, in the probably unwitting eyes of the parties, has the effect of a surrender of the old lease, followed by a regrant of a new lease. The best example is where the parties agree to a variation in the length of the lease whether extending or reducing the length of the term, or by varying the property demised whether increasing or reducing the subject matter of the lease (*Friends Provident* v. *British Rail Board* [1996] 1 All ER 336) or by granting a new lease of the same premises to the same tenant even where for a different term (*Rhyl UDC* v. *Rhyl Amusements* [1959] 1 WLR 465) and, it seems, inserting an option to extend the term as opposed to an option to review (*Baker* v. *Merckel* [1960] 1 QB 657). As mentioned above, a variation of the rent by deed of variation will only result in an implied surrender and regrant if that is the intention of the parties (*Gable Construction* v. *IRC* [1968] 1 WLR 1426).

As it is frequently possible to achieve the same result by other means that do not involve a surrender and regrant and at considerably lower cost the responsibility of the solicitor is particularly onerous, especially as the position is not helped by inconsistencies in practice by the Inland Revenue Stamp Taxes Office whose approach to the transaction may depend upon how the documentation is drafted and presented to them. However, FA 2000, s.128 dealing with, among other things, closing of leasehold titles at the Land Registry is likely to lead to more charges to *ad valorem* stamp duty, catching those which have hitherto escaped because full particulars were not produced to the Inland Revenue Stamp Taxes Office as required by SA 1891, s.5.

The conveyancing ramifications of an inadvertent surrender and regrant can be serious. If the old lease is registered at HM Land Registry a new registration will be required and a new registration fee will be payable and the application to close or modify the existing title is now dutiable (FA 2000, s.128) and will draw a whole range of issues to the attention of the Inland Revenue Stamp Taxes Office. Attention must also be paid to the rights of third parties such as mortgagees. Although surrender does not prejudice their position, the altered nature of the lease should be properly appreciated and the necessary documentation prepared.

7.15.1 Implied surrenders

Surrender will also arise by implication if the same tenant is given a new lease of the property to commence before the expiry of the existing lease, provided the new lease is itself a valid one. If so, it can be shorter or longer than the one it replaces. The same applies if the landlord grants a new lease to a third party with the consent of the tenant, provided possession also changes. In every case the surrender has the full force of law, even though, by the nature of the surrender, there is no deed or other documentation other than the new lease.

Such arrangements must now be considered in the context of FA 1994, s.243 and FA 2000, s.128. Each case must be carefully investigated to determine whether the new lease is *consideration* of the *surrender* of the existing

169

lease and so there may be issues of surrender on sale and a *hidden premium* as in relation to surrenders and regrants generally (see **section 7.15.3**). Whilst the new lease will not be a stampable instrument in respect of the surrender (FA 2000, s.128(3)) it will bear duty in its own right including rent and any actual or hidden premium including sums paid by the new tenant to the outgoing tenant (*Att.-Gen.* v. *Brown* (1849) 3 Exch 662), but any other documentation such as an application to the Land Registry to close the existing title will be vulnerable to stamp duty in respect of the surrender.

With regard to stamp duty, the effect of FA 1994, s.241 is to raise three potential areas of liability to stamp duty, although the Inland Revenue Stamp Taxes Office is not always consistent in practice in this area but the inclusion of Land Registry documentation in the list of chargeable instruments (FA 2000, s.128) has provided an opportunity for it to see the whole transaction and to take more points. Usually where the leases involved are of a full reviewable rack rent there is no hidden value to give rise to problems of *hidden payments* within s.241 but the points must be investigated to avoid unpleasant surprises later. The issues are considered below.

Two possible areas of charge arise:

1. The existing lease is being surrendered prima facie in consideration of the grant of the new lease.
2. The *regrant* of the existing lease.

7.15.2   Surrender of the existing lease

The existing lease is being surrendered prima facie in consideration of the grant of the new lease. This is deemed to be a *sale* of the existing lease for the market value, if any, of the new lease pursuant to FA 1994, s.241 dutiable upon such value. This may be considerable where the tenant has effected substantial works and improvements on the land under the existing lease

Where the landlord is paying the tenant for the variation that payment will also be dutiable in consideration for the surrender.

The problem may be identifying the stampable document. It must be noted that any dealings with the Land Registry in relation to the title are subject to stamp duty, but there is an exclusion from liability for the deed of variation or the new lease from this particular charge, otherwise the tenant could be paying the landlord's stamp duty on the surrender (FA 2000, s.128).

7.15.3   Regrant

Where there is a *regrant* of the existing lease, there is the question of whether there is a *premium* for the regrant. This can arise in two ways:

- Where the tenant is paying the landlord for the variation, i.e. is paying a lump sum for the variation in the term or as a *premium* for the lease of the additional property this will be regarded by the Inland Revenue Stamp Taxes Office as an actual premium which is dutiable.

• The new lease may be regarded as being granted in consideration of the surrender of the existing lease. If that lease should have value because, for example, it is for a rent lower than market rent or the tenant has carried out substantial improvements and development there is a premium equal to the value (FA 1994, s.241). This can arise where the tenant took the lease for a basic rent and has spent a considerable sum constructing buildings which are subleased for substantial rents. The value of the lease will have increased as a result of the tenant's own work but this fact does not provide any relief from the stamp duty charge. However, SA 1891, s.77(1) and FA 2000, s.128(3) provide that any *hidden premium* represented by the value, if any, of the old lease being surrendered is to be ignored when calculating the stamp duty but only if the old and the new lease both relate to the same premises.

There is also the question of rent duty upon the *regranted* lease. The whole of the rent arising is dutiable and there is no credit or deduction for the stamp duty previously paid in respect of the rent reserved by the existing lease. Unlike the limited charge upon a deed increasing the rent (FA 1999, Sched.13 para.20(1)) the duty is chargeable in full.

This is a wide ranging area and a trap for the unwary. It frequently arises where a tenant, usually of a flat, wishes to extend the term to prevent the unexpired term falling below 60 years which can give rise to several of the above charges where the existing and new leases are at a ground rent which is likely to be the case, and the tenant pays the landlord a lump sum for the extended term.

As the extension of the lease in such a case is done for reasons related to mortgage it may not be possible to escape from these problems by the more efficient routes of either a deed of variation inserting an option to renew the lease in due course which does not attract stamp duty until the option is exercised; or by the grant of a reversionary lease for the extension sought to commence shortly after the existing lease expires by effluxion of time.

It appears that in practice the manner in which the documentation is prepared and presented to the Inland Revenue Stamp Taxes Office may affect the stamp duty position. The *Stamp Taxes Manual* indicates that where there is an express surrender of the existing tenancy and a new lease is granted, the former will be presented by the landlord and the latter by the tenant. In consequence the Inland Revenue Stamp Taxes Office may not see the two documents as being a related transaction, particular if the landlord does not present the deed of surrender. The two sides are not, therefore, seen as involving consideration for each other. It is, however, questionable whether such a course of conduct complies with the disclosure requirements of SA 1891, s.5. Moreover, the need to produce stamped documents to the Land Registry to close and change the title registration may reduce the number of situations where the two sides of the transaction escape the scrutiny of the Inland Revenue Stamp Taxes Office.

The use of a certificate of value in the new lease where the payment made to the landlord for the increase in the term is below £500,000 may be improper in the circumstances. However, where the extension is effected by a deed of variation there is a single instrument setting out the whole transaction and there is a risk that the Inland Revenue Stamp Taxes Office may spot the surrender and re-grant point. However, in such a case FA 2000, s.128(3) provides that the deed of variation as the grant of the new lease is not to be stamped as the instrument of surrender. This privilege is no doubt reserved for the documentation linked to the application to close the title to the existing lease.

7.16 TERMINATION OF LEASES

In general the termination of a lease by lapse of time or by giving notice to quit does not involve a conveyance and the Inland Revenue spare the dying lease on its deathbed from natural causes or where the lease is forfeited for breach of covenant any further exactions.

7.16.1 Surrenders

Not so, however, where there is a surrender to the landlord of a fixed term before its expiry by effluxion of time. FA 1999, Sched.13 para.23 imposes a fixed duty of £5 upon surrenders, which on its own is insignificant provided that the surrender is not *on sale*. If, however, the landlord in effect buys the tenant out or is providing other property within FA 1994, s.241, the surrender will attract *ad valorem* duty as a conveyance on sale. Duty is escaped, apart from the fixed £5, where there is a *reverse premium*: the tenant pays the landlord to relieve the tenant of the lease (*Re Duke of Westminster's Settled Estates (No.2)* [1921] 1 Ch 585).

A surrender of a legal lease, even one for three years or less at the best rent without a fine (which may be granted in writing or orally) must be by deed if it is to take effect at law (LPA 1925, s.52). This is quite distinct from the possibility of surrender by operation of law. Such a surrender is implied where one party, with the consent of the other, does some act inconsistent with the continuation of the lease. Implied surrender may arise where there is delivery up to and acceptance by the landlord of possession of the property. Delivery of the keys with the blessing of the landlord, and with the intention of changing the possession, will suffice.

It is possible to surrender a lease by operation of law without a deed and it was until recently possible to avoid stamp duty even where the landlord provided consideration to the tenant. However, the Inland Revenue Stamp Taxes Office always sought to find a written instrument that could be stamped, such as a memorandum receipt for the premium paid by the landlord.

In order to give the certainty needed in the commercial world, or because there are issues of payments for breaches of covenant or for dilapidations, the parties may believe that it is better to precede the surrender by operation of law with a contract stipulating the terms thereof and the date for completion, and providing for a deed of surrender or surrender by operation of law at the landlord's behest.

Where business premises are involved, such an agreement could fall foul of Landlord and Tenant Act 1954, s.38 which renders void any agreement purporting to exclude the tenant's rights to a new lease (*Joseph v. Joseph* [1967] Ch 78). The agreement should therefore contain a clause binding both parties to seek the leave of the court under LPA 1969, s.5 modifying the Landlord and Tenant Act 1954, s.38, to exclude the tenant's rights. The provision need only be invoked in the event of default. Even when not affected by such provisions since 1989 an agreement to surrender a lease has to be made not merely evidenced in writing signed by both parties (LP(MP)A 1989, s.2).

Unfortunately, in order to counteract the mitigation of stamp duty by surrendering by operation of law FA 1994, s.243 provides that where a lease is surrendered by operation of law any written agreement to surrender is to be stamped as though it were the instrument of surrender, and late stamping penalties and interest will be calculated with effect from 30 days after the date of the actual surrender.

This provision was supplemented by FA 2000, s.128 which provides that any instrument recording the surrender including any statutory declaration or other application to a Land Registry to close the title is dutiable in respect of any consideration provided by the landlord. However, where there is a new lease of the same premises as the lease surrendered the new lease is not dutiable as the instrument of surrender (FA 2000, s.128(3)) since this would have the effect of the tenant paying the stamp duty that would normally be borne in practice by the landlord.

Clearly FA 2000, s.128 is a problem in practice only where the lease in question has been registered. This, for the present, applies only to leases for 21 years or longer. It is, therefore, possible to surrender agreements for lease and leases which have not been registered by operation of law without generating a document liable to stamp duty such as a Land Registry application to close title. Where an unregistered lease has been protected by an entry against the reversionary title it may be that an attempt to remove the restriction would be regarded by the Inland Revenue Stamp Taxes Office as a notification of the surrender within FA 2000, s.128. The parties might, therefore, find it prudent to remove the entry before the surrender. Since this does not convey property it is not within the anti-avoidance provisions of FA 1965, s.90.

7.17 EXEMPTIONS FROM LEASE DUTY

Apart from the small fixed duties upon certain leases considered earlier in this chapter there are certain leases and agreements for lease which are exempt from stamp duty.

7.17.1 Exemption

In any lease of any other property, where there is a fixed term not exceeding seven years or the term is indefinite, i.e. periodic, and the rent does not exceed £5,000 per annum, there is no duty at all (FA 1999, Sched.13 para.12(3)).

7.17.2 Equity sharing schemes

Independently of the enforced sale by local authorities to qualifying sitting tenants under the provisions of the Housing Act 1985, Part V, many local and other statutory housing authorities have developed equity sharing schemes whereby the capital value of a house is transferred to the tenant in stages. Such transactions are structured by the initial creation of a long lease at a premium of (say) half the value of the property on the open market (less discount where appropriate), with the reservation of a rack rent on the other half in value remaining vested in the authority. The tenant then has the right, if able to afford it, to call for a transfer at a later stage of the freehold reversion at whatever value it then has, bearing in mind the premium or premiums already paid by the tenant under his long lease.

This structure could have the adverse stamp duty consequences for the tenant. First, the rack rent reserved on the capital value left with the housing authority could exceed the £600 per annum limit necessary to enable advantage to be taken of a certificate of value on the premium. Secondly, a further tranche of duty could become payable on the ultimate transfer of the reversion at its then market value (possibly less discount).

Bearing in mind that the ultimate purpose is to transfer the freehold in stages, and doubtless also to encourage such transactions, the FA 1980, s.97 as amended by FA 1981, s.108 provides that the initial lease is not to be charged with duty under the heading 'Lease or Tack' but under the heading 'Conveyance or Transfer of Sale'. The lease must contain a statement of the market value of the property of which the premium forms a proportion, and if duty is paid on the full value stated (or, by FA 1981, s.108, the discounted market value) no rent duty is paid, a certificate of value can be used, and there is no further duty payable on the ultimate transfer of the reversion.

Housing associations and housing action trusts establish under the Housing Act 1988, Part III are included in the specified list of housing authorities, leases by which qualify for the above relief. Such leases are not enfranchisable under the Leasehold Reform Act 1967 (Housing Act 1980, s.140, as amended by the Housing (Consequential Provisions) Act 1985, Sched.2 para.44(3)).

7.17.3 Rent to mortgage schemes

Section 202 of the FA 1993 (or s.203 in relation to Scotland) provides that where a person exercises the right to acquire on rent to mortgage terms pursuant to Housing Act 1985, Part V and the freehold is conveyed to him pursuant thereto, for the purposes of conveyance on sale duty the stampable consideration is equal to the price which would be payable pursuant to s.136 thereof. When he acquires a lease under such arrangements the lease is not to be stamped as a lease but as a conveyance on sale.

7.17.4 Certificates of value

For a lease where the premium does not exceed £60,000 and the rent reserved does not exceed £600 per annum, the stamp upon this premium is nil provided that a certificate of value is included.

7.17.5 Charities

No stamp duty is chargeable upon an agreement for lease or lease granted to a charity pursuant to FA 1981, s.129. Adjudication is required.

7.17.6 Associated companies

The FA 1995, s.151 provides an exemption from stamp duty under the head of charge 'Lease' provided that the lessor and the lessee are appropriately associated bodies corporate which includes foreign companies as well as unlimited and guarantee companies, local authorities and certain industrial and provident societies. The position of limited liability partnerships which are bodies corporate has yet to be fought out with the Inland Revenue Stamp Taxes Office which, incorrectly, regards them as transparent, i.e. not corporate entities. The main problem in all of the cases is whether the vehicle has *issued share capital* although this is not a problem when it is the parent company.

7.17.7 Associated

Bodies corporate are associated if one holds beneficially, directly or indirectly, not less than 75 per cent of the issued ordinary share capital of the other or not less than 75 per cent of the issued ordinary share capital of both is held beneficially, directly or indirectly, by a third body corporate. There is no definition of beneficial ownership and the existing cases merely indicate when the beneficial ownership has been lost. These include contracts for sale (*Parway Estates Ltd* v. *IRC* (1958) 37 ATC 164) including conditional contracts and possibly options at least where there is a restriction upon the power of the seller or the granter of the option to take dividends (*Wood Preservation* v. *Prior* [1969] 1 WLR 1077; *J Sainsbury plc* v. *O'Connor* [1991] STC 516). Receivership does not affect beneficial ownership although it is lost on the commencement of a liquidation, even where solvent (*Ayerst* v. *C & K (Construction) Ltd* [1976] AC 167).

The parent company must have at least a 75 per cent economic interest in the lessor and/or lessee companies. This requires that it is entitled to at least 75 per cent of the dividends declared and of the assets available for distribution in a winding up.

This involves consideration of many of the complex provisions in ICTA 1988, Sched.18 which is difficult to apply in the context of stamp duty. These provisions look at the situation over an accounting period and are not appropriate to a single transaction or documentary tax such as stamp duty. In practice the Inland Revenue Stamp Taxes Office does not require the parties to wait until the end of the accounting period. If the situation 'looks right' at the time of the instrument no further investigation or delays will arise.

It is, therefore, important that the letter making the application for exemption states that there are no equity holders within ICTA 1988, Sched.18 in any of the companies involved. The main question is whether there are *non commercial loans* in any subsidiary company at the time, since such loans are, in effect, treated as ordinary share capital and are taken into account to reduce the parent company's shareholding and interest when applying the 75 per cent interest tests. The types of security likely to affect the situation are convertible loan stocks, loans where the interest or principal as related to the value of an asset (although the indebtedness represented by an obligation to make a deferred earnout or overage payment is not thought to be within these provisions), limited recourse finance, excessive interest rates and certain loans arising in connection with the utilisation of capital allowances (ICTA 1988, Sched.18 para.1(5) and (6)). If none of these exist the statement above can be made.

The parent company must control the lessor and/or lessee companies and there must be no arrangement in place whereby some unassociated person could acquire control of the lessee company without acquiring control of the lessor company. The Inland Revenue Stamp Taxes Office has indicated that where there is a mortgage over the shares in any relevant company the mortgagee's powers to foreclose or sell will not be treated in practice as being within this provision, but the fact that it was thought necessary to exclude this situation by concession indicates that the condition is regarded as wide ranging.

Other situations which may give rise to problems include the existence of preference shares which may be entitled to vote if dividends are in arrears, options to subscribe for shares, convertible loan stocks and joint venture or other arrangements whereby other parties have pre-emption or similar rights. Many of these difficulties have yet to be clarified by the Inland Revenue Stamp Taxes Office.

7.17.8 Procedure

The application for the exemption may now be made by letter setting out the relevant facts to satisfy the conditions. No sanctions are imposed if an application is made unsuccessfully because the Inland Revenue Stamp Taxes Office disagrees with the interpretation of the facts such as whether beneficial ownership exists in the shares. In relation to relief for lease duty, in effect, the relief has to be claimed in two stages: initially for the agreement for lease, and subsequently for the lease. For full relief to be obtained the bodies corporate must be associated and all other conditions must be satisfied at both times. If the companies have ceased to be associated at the time of the grant of the lease this will bear full stamp duty notwithstanding that the agreement for lease has been adjudicated as exempt.

7.18   ANTI-AVOIDANCE

The relief is not available where there are certain arrangements in existence. There has been considerable difficulty in determining whether there is an *arrangement* in place at the relevant time. The Inland Revenue Stamp Taxes Office sought to extend its scope by Statement of Practice SP3/98 but this was clearly inconsistent with the existing law and its position was undermined by its own *Manual* which sets out an analysis much closer to the traditional view that an arrangement requires a degree of commercial inevitability and discussion with a third party not a mere intention.

Nevertheless SP3/98 does contain some helpful guidance on certain aspects of the arrangements themselves. The test of whether an arrangement exists is where there is an element of necessity or commercial inevitability that the prescribed circumstances will exist. If the precise outcome has not been agreed or there is a possible risk that the transaction may not be carried through there is no arrangement (*Times Newspapers* v. *IRC* [1971] 3 All ER 98). Importantly third parties must be involved in the planning or discussions for there to be an arrangement. A mere intention to sell or to borrow money is not an arrangement; there must be active discussions with a potential buyer or lender at a reasonably advanced stage before the question of whether an arrangement exists can arise. Forward planning may therefore be beneficial.

7.18.1   The two mischiefs

One of these offending situations arises where there is an arrangement whereby the consideration for the grant of the lease, whether premium or rent, is to be provided, directly or indirectly, or received by some person not appropriately associated as a 75 per cent subsidiary or parent with the lessor and the lessee bodies corporate. This could include situations where the cash for the premium is borrowed from a bank, or where there is to be a sublease granted which will fund the payment of the rent. SP3/98, however, indicates that the former strict line on the use of borrowed money to fund the premium has been relaxed. The use of normal bank borrowing is not regarded as causing a loss of the relief provided that there are no plans for the property to leave the group without the payment of full stamp duty. The full terms of SP3/98 in Appendix A should be studied (see also the drafting principle in **Chapter 3**).

A problem unresolved in practice is the receipt of the consideration. Technically a point may arise where a lease is granted for a rent followed shortly by a sale of the reversion to an unassociated company. This may occur, for example, where they are considering a sale and leaseback financing exercise which can involve disproportionate sums of stamp duty. In order to reduce the stamp duty costs the parties may grant the lease to an associated company seeking to take advantage of the s.151 relief leaving only the sale duty upon the transfer of the reversion to the funder. However, that transfer will entitle the funder as the new landlord to the rent, i.e. a receipt of part of the consideration.

Hitherto the Inland Revenue Stamp Taxes Office has not pursued this point but there are certain cryptic comments in a technically obscure part of SP3/98 (para.14) which hint that it may have the threat in mind for future use. Ideally in such situations the parties should grant the internal lease before opening negotiations with the potential funder so that there are no *arrangements* in place at the time. A subsequent variation of the lease to meet the requirements of the third party may attract stamp duty upon any increase in the rent (FA 1999, Sched.13 para.20) but is not usually otherwise dutiable since a surrender and regrant should not arise (see **section 7.15**).

The other offending arrangement is where the plan is that the lessee is to cease to be a 75 per cent subsidiary of the lessor or the third body corporate. The departure of the lessor from the stamp duty group does not lead to a loss of the relief. Ceasing to be a 75 per cent subsidiary will apply to a sale of the shares or a variation of the rights of shares so that the 75 per cent economic interest is affected and there is to be a change of control. The fact that the lease may be transferred outside the group does not bring the provisions into operation, but it may have implications for the question of whether consideration is coming from outside the group (see above).

7.18.2 Clawback

As FA 1995, s.151(3) as interpreted by SP3/98 failed to prevent people from transferring or leasing assets into companies and selling the shares at a much lower stamp duty cost than an asset sale such as by granting the lease before discussion relating to the sale of the shares opened so that no arrangement existed. FA 2002, s.111 provides that for documents executed on or after 24 April 2002 if the lessee ceases to be within the same stamp duty group as the lessor within two years after the execution of the relevant instrument, which means that the two years will normally commence with the execution of the lease rather than the agreement for lease which, as indicated above, is a necessary consequence of the two stage process of stamping under the lease head of charge, the stamp duty relief is cancelled and the duty is payable upon the market value of the land together with late payment interest from 30 days after the happening of the clawback event. Delay in executing the lease is perilous since it effectively extends the two year period. Waiting until the lessee is about to leave the group can be a false economy.

The lessor and the lessee cease to be associated if either:

- the lessor ceases to be the parent of the lessee; or
- the lessee ceases to be the parent of the lessor; or
- either ceases to be the subsidiary company within the s.151 definition of a third body corporate.

This can arise if:

- the shareholding falls below the 75 per cent level;
- the economic interest falls below the 75 per cent level.

This can happen not only where there is a sale of shares, but also the issue of new shares in any relevant company. Liquidation but not receivership causes a loss of beneficial ownership and can cause a break in the stamp duty group.

The clawback charge does not apply in the following cases:

- *Lessor leaving the group*: the clawback does not apply where the lessor ceases to be associated with the lessee by reason of matters affecting its shares. However, it would seem likely that the Inland Revenue Stamp Taxes Office will not accept that the departure of the lessor from the group terminates the clawback provision totally. No doubt the departure does not of itself trigger the clawback, but if subsequently within the two-year period the lessee leaves the remainder of the original stamp duty group the clawback will operate. For example, if the share capitals of the lessor and lessee are held by a third company, a sale of the shares in the lessor will not operate the clawback, but a subsequent sale of the shares of the lessee is likely to be regarded as being liable to the clawback provisions.

- *Liquidations*: the clawback does not arise simply by reason of the liquidation of the lessor or of any other company above the lessor in the stamp duty group.
- *Reconstructions*: the clawback provisions do not operate where the lessor and the lessee cease to be associated by reason of a reconstruction qualifying for relief pursuant to FA 1986, s.75. However, the two year period continues to run and if the lessee leaves the new group within the balance of the two year period the clawback will apply.

7.18.3   Compliance

The company is required under penalty to notify the Inland Revenue Stamp Taxes Office of the clawback, and to pay the tax within 30 days of the relevant event. If not paid by the lessee company the tax and interest can be recovered from the lessor or any company which was at the time of the instrument or subsequently was a stamp duty parent above the lessee company. Controlling directors are also liable for the unpaid duty and interest (FA 2002, Sched.34 para.8). This liability applies notwithstanding that the lessee company has been liquidated or is insolvent, and the company need not be associated with the lessee at the time.

7.18.4   Share sales and purchases

This clawback of the relief represents a significant due diligence obligation for solicitors involved in negotiations for the purchase of shares in or reorganisations of companies given the range of companies potentially liable to pay the tax. They are required to discover whether the proposed transaction will trigger a clawback or is part of a larger transaction where the clawback is merely deferred. The transaction may itself start a new clawback period running if the relief pursuant to FA 1995, s.151 or FA 1930, s.42 or FA 1986, s.76 is involved. It is, therefore, essential to discover whether any members of the group other than the company being acquired have been parties to an application for s.151 exemption; not merely the company being acquired.

7.19   SALES OF THE LANDLORD'S INTEREST

Where land is sold subject to an agreement for lease for a term exceeding 35 years, the conveyance, transfer or lease shall not be taken to be duly stamped unless there is denoted thereupon the duty paid on the agreement. In the light of the above changes, in particular FA 1984, s.111, the scope for use of equitable leases in an attempt to avoid or minimise duty has disappeared completely and no purpose will be served in rehearsing the devices formally employed, even those considered sufficiently uncomplicated to fall outside the scope of *Ramsay*.

Indeed, the pendulum may have swung further against the taxpayer than the Revenue actually intended: a contract by, e.g. a flat purchaser to take a new lease for a standard 99-year term technically ought to be stamped no later than 30 days after exchange. If not, and there is a delay in completing the matter, the contract will be unusable in any subsequent court proceedings until all duty (and any penalty) has been paid in accordance with the provisions discussed later at **section 11.6.2**.

However, the new provisions contained in FA 1994, s.240 deferring the commencement of late stamping penalties and late payment interest for agreements for leases until 30 days after the execution of the lease provided that both of the instruments are presented for stamping at the same time should alleviate the inconvenience in most cases. The normal rules for late stamping penalties will apply where the agreement for lease is presented for stamping without the lease, such as where the tenant is suing for specific performance of the agreement, or where the tenant has gone into occupation without taking a formal grant and the landlord wishes to sue for breach of covenant for failure to pay the rent and requires the agreement for lease to be put in evidence. Landlords may, therefore, find it prudent to arrange for there to be a counterpart agreement for lease suitably executed so as to qualify as a deemed counterpart lease dutiable only with the fixed duty of £5 (FA 1999, Sched.13 para.19(2)).

7.20 ASSIGNMENTS OF LEASE

Once the lease has been granted, the head of charge 'Lease or Tack' ceases to apply and a subsequent sale or assignment will be treated as a conveyance on sale (with a certificate of value if appropriate) or as a voluntary conveyance (no longer chargeable) if there is an element of gift. No regard is had to the rent payable, only to the capital value of the lease (*Swayne* v. *IRC* [1899] 1 QB 335). In this situation the stampable consideration will not include any sums paid by the outgoing tenant to the incoming tenant to cover dilapidations, or as a reverse premium to take the lease because the rent reserved exceeds the current market rent for the premises.

FA 1999, Sched.13 para.7 should not be overlooked since it will operate to charge stamp duty upon its contract to sell in respect of those fixtures and fittings passing on the sale which are of a purely ornamental or domestic nature and can be removed by the tenant at the end of the lease. In such cases the outgoing tenant is selling the right as against the landlord to sever the fixtures (*Lee* v. *Gaskell* (1876) 24 WR 824). Later sublettings are, of course, a different matter: the head of charge 'Lease or Tack' bites afresh. It should, however, be noted that a sublease for the whole of the remainder of the term of the lease is an assignment not a lease (*Milmo* v. *Carreras* [1946] KB 306) and will bear the appropriate conveyance stamp duty.

Where the consideration for the contract to assign the lease exceeds £10 million the new charge upon contracts for sale of land pursuant to FA 2002, s.115 is prima facie applicable. However, the £10 million threshold is arrived at only in respect of the land so that the consideration attributable to fixtures that have retained their character as chattels is ignored.

CHAPTER 8

Gifts and undervalue transactions past and present

8.1 PRESENT REGIME

Stamp duty is upon basic principles charged upon the amount or value of the actual consideration, including a lease premium or the average rent (see **Chapter 2**). However, this basic principle is becoming increasingly subject to modification especially where land is involved, and, in particular, the duty is being charged upon the value or market value of assets involved in the transaction (see **section 2.9**). Certificates of value can be inserted by reference to the actual consideration and are not in general restricted by the market value being in excess of the relevant threshold. This means that although gifts and sales or leases at above or below market value or market rent will normally attract only the fixed stamp duty of £5 if there is no consideration or *ad valorem* stamp duty only upon the actual consideration or rent, if any, this is not an invariable rule and the exception provides a trap for the unwary conveyancer.

Even where *ad valorem* stamp duty does not arise, such undervalue transfers or leases may require to be adjudicated in order to be properly stamped. In the new compliance regime it is necessary to understand not only the current treatment of *gifts* and undervalue transactions, it is also necessary to understand the previous law on the subject (see **sections 8.6.1** and **8.12**).

8.2 EXEMPTION

In general terms gifts are not subject to *ad valorem* stamp duty (FA 1985, s.82(1)). They attract the fixed duty of £5 as a conveyance or transfer not on sale and require adjudication in many cases (FA 1985, s.82(5)).

A gift can as a matter of statutory interpretation include a transaction at an undervalue or overvalue (*Re Baroness Bateman* [1925] 2 KB 429; *Plaut* v. *Steiner* (1989) 5 BCC 352). Such transactions may give rise to legal issues in other areas such as company law where they may involve unlawful dividends or returns of capital (*Aveling Barford* v. *Perion* [1989] BCLC 626) as well as possibilities of challenge pursuant to the insolvency legislation. General tax law also has many provisions dealing with transactions at other than the proper price. Solicitors embark in this area at their peril, since the tax advice of accountants having been given is not necessarily a total protection for the lawyer if things go wrong. This is particularly so in the area of stamp duty which has judicially traditionally be regarded as the responsibility of solicitors and this responsibility is likely to increase if, as seems probable, the modernised land stamp duty is administered through solicitors.

The writer would advise that, given the responsibility for the tax efficient implementation of the transaction even where not advising upon tax, the prudent solicitor should enquire of the tax advisers upon precisely what taxes they are advising. In order to avoid the risk of not achieving the intended tax result or producing a higher than anticipated stamp duty charge the arrangements including the drafting should be put before the accountants or tax advisers for review even if only as a matter of self defence. For convenience in the remainder of this chapter the word *gift* will include any transaction at other than the market value or market rent.

The provisions require an understanding of how voluntary disposition duty operated by FA 1985. This is considered below in this chapter in relation to investigations of title, but fortunately, in many cases, the charge and the need to adjudicate (SI 1987/516, reg.5) can be avoided by certificates pursuant to the Schedule to the Stamp Duty (Exempt Instruments) Regulations 1987, SI 1987/516 (see **Chapter 10** for a description of the categories and the form of the certificate).

8.3   CHARGEABLE GIFTS – MARKET VALUE RULES

However, not all *gifts* are exempt from stamp duty, and in relation to undervalue transactions this may be charged upon some figure other than the actual consideration passing and the Stamp Duty (Exempt Instruments) Regulations 1987 (SI 1987/516) apply only to instruments falling into charge as a conveyance or transfer not on sale. There are, in consequence, many cases where *gifts* are dutiable and/or require adjudication.

These categories need to be understood since it is proposed that under the revised land stamp duty regime starting in early 2004 such transactions will not be dutiable but will have to be reported by taxpayers under penalty.

Moreover, there is an increasing number of anti-avoidance provisions charge stamp duty upon market value and these apply to gifts. (see **section 4.14**). The most frequently encountered areas for the property lawyer include:

- transfers of property subject to a mortgage including a contingent mortgage given by way of guarantee (SA 1891, s.57; see **section 2.10.3**);
- transfers in consideration of the assumption of liabilities or in satisfaction of a debt (SA 1891, s.57);
- transfers and leases for an unascertainable consideration or rent (FA 1994, s.242); and
- transfers and leases to connected companies (FA 2000, s.119 and s.121).

It is, of course, necessary to understand what constitutes a *gift* for stamp duty purposes where the special rules raise problems as to what is within the exemption and transactions for no consideration fall into two categories:

- transfers where there is a change of beneficial ownership; and
- transfers of bare title where the beneficial ownership remains unchanged such as a change of nominee or trustee.

There are many transactions where there are transfers for no consideration but there is not a change in the beneficial ownership of the property so that there is not a gift. Such transfers may be governed by the same head of charge in FA 1999, Sched.13 namely 'Conveyance or Transfer not on sale', but the principles relating to gifts and those other transfers are fundamentally different. For example, changes of trustees or transfers to nominees are dutiable as conveyances not on sale, but they are not gifts and the rules relating to the need for adjudication and the exemptions and in particular the appropriate categories for certification pursuant to the Stamp Duty (Exempt Instruments) Regulations 1987, SI 1987/516 are different.

The stamp duty position of transfers where beneficial ownership does not change is included in the relevant parts of Chapter 10 dealing with the fixed duties. This chapter is concerned with the former category.

Gifts in the strict sense apply to transfers for no consideration which operate to pass the beneficial interest. This can include dividends *in specie* (*Wigan Coal and Iron* v. *IRC* [1945] 1 All ER 392). Other situations can include variations of or releases of interests in trusts. These are prima facie exempt from all stamp duty and the need to adjudicate if certified pursuant to the Stamp Duty (Exempt Instruments) Regulations 1987 (SI 1987/516).

8.3.1 Undervalue transactions

Subject to the special rules set out below, such transactions will attract stamp duty upon the actual price or rent payable (FA 1985, s.82 repealing FA 1910, s.74(5)). However, because of the machinery of repeal certain instruments require adjudication although this has been modified and the fixed £5 stamp duty is not payable and adjudication is not require for instruments falling within the Schedule to the Stamp Duty (Exempt Instruments) Regulations 1987, SI 1987/516.

Where these are dutiable as sales, adjudication is not required, but leases at an undervalue do require adjudication where the lease vests beneficially in the lessee; where the lease is granted by the lessee as a nominee the duty is prima facie £5 subject to FA 2000, s.121; as there is no change in beneficial ownership there is no voluntary disposition within FA 1985, s.82. However, where beneficial ownership in the lease vests in the tenant because it is at an undervalue it would have been a voluntary disposition under the old law (FA 1910, s.74(5)) and in consequence requires adjudication to be duly stamped.

The relief from adjudication for undervalue transactions in FA 1985, s.82 applies only to conveyances on sale and it seems clear that this exclusion does not apply to instruments dutiable as leases. It seems that an agreement for lease at an undervalue is not a *conveyance* for the purposes of voluntary disposition duty and does not require adjudication although any lease granted pursuant thereto does need to be adjudicated (FA 1985, s.82).

8.3.2 Transfers for no consideration

A gift can be made only by deed or by delivery of the asset which can include taking all steps necessary to vest title to the asset in the intended donee (*Re Rose* [1949] Ch 78; *Re Rose* [1952] Ch 499; *Milroy* v. *Lord* (1862) 4 De F and J 264), although in certain cases imperfect gifts may be perfected by the subsequent vesting of title in the intended donee (*Strong* v. *Bird* (1874) Land Registry 18 Eq 315). In certain cases oral declarations of trust may be valid but as *Cohen & Moore* v. *IRC* [1933] 2 KB 126 indicates the subsequent appointment of the trustees vesting the property is a conveyance and subject to whatever stamp duty is appropriate (although there are extensive exemptions from the £5 fixed duty – see **Chapter 10**) including *ad valorem* duty where a sale is involved. Oral declarations of trust relating to land are void (LP(MP)A 1989, s.2) but they may form the basis of a constructive trust when suitably acted upon (*Yaxley* v. *Gotts* [1999] 2 WLR 1217). The broad effect is that where land is involved a written instrument will usually be required.

However, a transaction for what appears to be no consideration is not necessarily a gift within the Stamp Duty (Exempt Instruments) Regulations 1987, SI 1987/516 and exempt from stamp duty. Nor is it a gift simply because there is no consideration or payment moving either from the transferee or to the transferor since a third party may be paying or receiving the price (see for example lease premiums at **section 7.11**). It may fall into charge depending upon the facts.

For example a transfer by a liquidator to the members in the winding up of the company or by a trustee to a beneficiary is not a gift but a transfer in satisfaction of the rights of the transferee and dutiable £5 on a transfer not on sale but exempted by different categories in the Stamp Duty (Exempt Instruments) Regulations 1987, SI 1987/516. Where land is involved the connected company provisions of FA 2000, s.119 apply to such transfers but there are limited exemptions in s.120 thereof.

The rules as to what constitutes a *gift* for stamp duty purposes requires investigation because it may:

- affect the validity of titles prior to April 1985;
- mean that an *ad valorem* charge arises; and/or
- mean that a need for adjudication may still arise on what might be thought to be an instrument free from stamp duty or subject only to fixed stamp duty of £5.

However, there are two main areas where notwithstanding the absence or inadequacy of the consideration *ad valorem* stamp duty is charged.

8.4   THE STAMP ACT 1891

Subject to FA 2000, s.119 described below, the SA 1891, s.57 provides that a transfer of property that is, among other things, subject to a mortgage or charge is to be stamped as a sale for a consideration equal to or increased by the amount of the mortgage and outstanding unpaid interest. This can operate to convert a gift into a sale dutiable accordingly. However, this is an area where knowledge of the official practice is important and detailed study of the *Stamp Taxes Manual* and Statement of Practice SP6/90 (see **Appendix A**) is beneficial.

Problems can be encountered or avoided at basic levels such as putting the matrimonial home into joint names or into trust. Where there is a cash consideration there is a basic sale and the duty is calculated upon the actual consideration plus the amount of the mortgage unless, it seems, the seller indemnifies the purchaser against liability upon the mortgage although this latter point is not clear in practice. Where there is a gift of property subject to a mortgage this is subject to stamp duty upon the amount of the mortgage unless the donor indemnifies the donee against liability upon the mortgage (Statement of Practice SP6/90 para.8).

Where there is a gift of a part interest in the property then by concession only part of the mortgage is brought into charge. This is the part equivalent to the proportion of the property passing. For example, where there is a gift of a half share in a house with a mortgage of £100,000 only £50,000 is brought into charge and a certificate of value for nil stamp duty can be included.

Where the mortgage exceeds £120,000 (or the proportionate share exceeds £60,000) two courses are open to the donor; namely:

- the transferor may agree to indemnify the transferee within Statement of Practice SP6/90 para.8; or

- the transferor may make a number of small gifts falling below £60,000 utilising certificates of value because it has long been accepted that gifts being legally independent cannot form a larger transaction or a series of transactions.

8.5 FINANCE ACT 2000

It is important to note that transfers and leases to connected companies are dutiable upon the market value of the property and not the actual consideration. This includes, among other things, gifts, sales and leases at an under-value and transfers in consideration of the issue of shares. The provisions can have important adverse consequences where parties are seeking capital gains tax relief upon the incorporation of a business. While the advice is to rely upon Taxation of Chargeable Gains Act 1992, s.162 the stamp duty will be linked to the gross market value of the assets (SA 1891, s.6, s.55 and s.57) subject to relief for exempt assets such as goodwill, intellectual property and goods. Attempts to escape from these consequences by means of gifts or transfers within Taxation of Chargeable Gains Act 1992, s.165 will not succeed where land is involved since this will be stamped upon market value.

It is important to note that connected companies include corporate trustees since trustees are connected with the settlor. For conveyances there are exclusions from the charge where the corporate trustee is a commercial professional trust such as a bank trustee company or the company is not otherwise connected with the trustees, i.e. its shares are owned by persons unconnected with the settlor.

Groups and associated companies are connected but there are limited exemptions for dividends *in specie* and distributions in a winding up (FA 2000, s.120). In other cases it will be necessary to seek to utilise the relief for intra-group transactions or reconstructions (see **section 6.7**).

8.6 COMPLIANCE

The problems arise in practice because FA 1985, s.82(5) provides that an instrument:

(a) in respect of which stamp duty would have been chargeable by virtue of FA 1910, s.74 apart from this section, and

(b) on which stamp duty is not chargeable under FA 1999, Sched.13 Part I (conveyance or transfer on sale)

shall not be deemed to be duly stamped unless it has, in accordance with SA 1891, s.12, been stamped with a particular stamp denoting that it is duly stamped or that it is not chargeable with any duty.

This issue has been substantially modified in practice by the Stamp Duty (Exempt Instruments) Regulations 1987, SI 1987/516 which provide that an instrument certified as a gift within category L in the Schedule to the regulations is both exempt from the fixed duty of £5 (reg. 2(2)) and from the need to be adjudicated (reg. 5).

However, FA 1985, s.82(9) provides that the requirement for adjudication was not applicable in the case of an instrument which is certified in accordance with regulations to be issued under FA 1985, s.87(1) and (2).

These regulations were issued with effect from 30 April 1987 and apply to any instrument bearing a certificate in accordance with the provisions of the Schedule to the Stamp Duty (Exempt Instruments) Regulations 1987, SI 1987/516 in which case it now avoids both the requirement for adjudication and the fixed stamp of £5 (regs. 2(2) and 5; see further **Chapter 10**).

However, the relevant certificate contained in category L, applies only to a conveyance for no consideration in money or money's worth nor for any consideration falling within SA 1891, s.57. This means that there were and remain certain instruments still technically requiring adjudication pursuant to FA 1985, s.82(5) as set out above.

For example a lease of the family farm granted to trustees at a low rent if not dutiable upon market value pursuant to FA 2000, s.121 technically requires to be adjudicated in order to be *duly stamped*. The need to adjudicate where the certificate is not included remains.

8.6.1 Previous position

The present position does, however, require a working knowledge of the previous law in order to understand when an instrument is subject to the fixed duty and is exempt or may require adjudication as well as for investigating old titles.

The SA 1891 omitted any provision for imposing stamp duty on *inter vivos* voluntary dispositions, apart from the fixed charge payable on what was then a conveyance of any other kind, i.e. not on sale. Sales at an undervalue paid duty upon the price, not the value of the purchased property. This happy state of affairs lasted until 1910 when by FA 1910, s.74(1) a voluntary disposition became subject to a full *ad valorem* duty on the value of the property transferred by requiring it:

> to be chargeable with the like stamp duty as if it were a conveyance or transfer on sale with the substitution in each case of the value of the property conveyed or transferred for the amount or value of the consideration for the sale.

The charging provisions were, however, not limited solely to transactions by way of gift or for no consideration; s.74(5) brought into charge transactions where the consideration was less than the value of the property so that the conveyance conferred a *substantial benefit* on the transferee. The effect of this was that conveyance on sale duty was payable upon the greater of the purchase consideration or the market value of the property. Since the view of the Inland Revenue Stamp Taxes Office, which was affirmed by the Privy Council in *Lap Shun Textiles Industrial Co* v. *Collector of Stamp Revenue* [1976] AC 530, was (and remains) that arm's length negotiation was only good evidence and not conclusive proof that the transaction had been carried out at market value, the head of charge was of considerable extent and caused significant practical inconvenience, including the costs of valuation in disputes with the Inland Revenue Stamp Taxes Office.

In 1983 the Inland Revenue published a consultative document on the scope for reforming stamp duty and of the resultant changes introduced by FA 1985. The most radical was undoubtedly the abolition of *ad valorem* duty on gifts by s.82(1) with the simple words, 'the stamp duty chargeable by virtue of s.74 of the FA 1910 (gifts *inter vivos*) is abolished'.

The reform affects all instruments executed on or after 26 March 1985, or executed on or after 19 March 1985 and stamped on or after 26 March 1985. Instruments executed before this remain fully stampable, and although with the passage of time the relevance of FA 1910 will fade, for the time being at least, voluntary transactions may well be found on investigation of title to unregistered land and on first registration of title when it will be important to see that the proper stamp duty was then paid (but see *Re Weir and Pitts' Contract* (1911) 55 Sol J 536).

Moreover, given the full extent of the head of charge it may be difficult to discover whether older instruments are properly stamped, but this problem will disappear once title has been registered since it is now clear that the registration of an unstamped or insufficiently stamped instrument is effective to pass full title (*Re Nisbet* v. *Shepherd* [1994] 1 BCLC 300; *International Commercial* v. *Adham* [1994] 1 BCLC 66).

8.7   PRESENT-DAY ISSUES – ILLUSTRATIVE PROBLEMS

8.7.1   Exchanges on favourable terms

Since 7 December 1993, FA 1994, s.241 has treated such instruments as being subject to *ad valorem* stamp duty under the head 'Conveyance as Transfer or Sale' and so henceforth excused from the requirement for adjudication by FA 1985, s.82(5)(*b*). Other instruments, however, may still technically require adjudication where the mutual values are not equal. A lease at an undervalue may have previously been within the charge to voluntary disposition duty and not being within Category L of the Stamp Duty (Exempt Instrument) Regulations 1987, SI 1987/516 would seem to require adjudication. Partitions of land falling within FA 1999, Sched.13 para.21 for unequal consideration would also seem to fall within the requirement for adjudication.

A certain doubt remains in relation to instruments where a certificate of value is used but the price is less than the value of the property and so within the former FA 1910, s.75(5). Such an instrument does not bear a stamp and so may not be *chargeable* under the 'Conveyance on Sale' head. However, this point does not seem to be correct since the instrument is chargeable but then exempted, and the Inland Revenue Stamp Taxes Office does not appear to take any such point in practice (see also Stamp Duty (Exempt Instruments) Regulations 1985, SI 1985/1688).

8.7.2   Deeds of gift of land

A gift may take the form of a direction by a contracting purchaser to the vendor to convey the property directly to the donee such as trustees of a settlement if the donor/purchaser joins in the conveyance, that document enshrined two transactions, the purchase and the gift (see FA 1981, s.4(*a*)) and there would formerly have been the risk of a double payment of duty (*IRC* v. *Baddeley* [1955] AC 572) but now the gift element is exempt, if certified, and only sale duty in respect of the first leg is payable.

Subsale treatment is not available since the second leg is prima facie not a sale unless it falls into statutory provisions deeming it to be a sale, such as FA 2000, s.119. If, however, the conveyance was direct from the vendor to the donee, without the donor being a party, duty was attracted either on the transaction as conveyance on sale, or as a voluntary conveyance, whichever yielded the higher revenue.

However, care is needed since if the transferee/donee is a corporate trustee the market value charge upon transfers to connected companies may apply pursuant to FA 2000, s.119 unless the trustee falls within the limited exemptions for corporate trustees in s.120. Cumulative duty is not likely to arise since the gift being deemed to be a sale at market value, subsale treatment pursuant to SA 1891, s.58(4) is likely to apply.

This practice was, of course, consistent with the unpublished practice of the Inland Revenue Stamp Taxes Office adopted hitherto in relation to subsales which did not comply with the technical requirements of SA 1891, s.58(4) and (5) when the only single highest duty is claimed, but the *Stamp Taxes Manual* hints that this long standing practice may have been changed without public notice so that the aggregate stamp duty will be claimed but the Inland Revenue Stamp Taxes Office rarely sees the whole documentation in order make the claim for all duties. In consequence, pending clarification of the position, solicitors acting for subpurchasers and similar parties should seek some form of undertaking from their immediate seller to bear any additional stamp duty over that which their client would normally expect to pay; such agreements do not fall within SA 1891, s.117 (see **section 11.6.4**).

A gift in consideration of marriage is not a conveyance on sale, but the existence of the marriage consideration prevented such a gift from being treated as a voluntary disposition (s.74(5)). No *ad valorem* duty was therefore payable. For exemption from the fixed stamp duty of £5 and the need to adjudicate the regulations require that the transfer is either to a party to the marriage or his or her nominee or to the trustees of a settlement made in consideration only of the marriage.

8.7.3 Voluntary declarations of trust

Declarations of trust are subject to the fixed duty of £5 unless operating as conveyances on sale (*Chesterfield Brewery* v. *IRC* [1899] 2 QB 7) or deemed conveyances on sale pursuant to the connected company rules (FA 2000, s.119 and s.120).

8.7.4 Powers of appointment

The definition of a conveyance (FA 1999, Sched.13 para.16(2)) includes:

> every instrument whereby any property, or any estate or interest in any property, is transferred to or vested in any person.

These words were held in *Stanyforth* v. *IRC* [1930] AC 339 and *Fuller & Shrimpton* v. *IRC* [1950] 2 All ER 976 to be wide enough to cover the exercise of a general power of appointment. Powers of appointment are not only now free from *ad valorem* duty but also from the former fixed head of charge applicable when no beneficial interest passed. Sight, however, should not be lost of the possibility of an appointment as a new trustee doubling up as a conveyance to the new trustee of the trust property.

Similarly an appointment to a beneficiary may operate as a voluntary conveyance. In either case the appointment prima facie remains liable to a fixed duty of £5 and the latter to adjudication, unless, being executed on or after 1 May 1987, it is certified in accordance with Category A or F in the Schedule to the Stamp Duty (Exempt Instruments) Regulations 1987, SI 1987/516.

8.7.5 Releases and disclaimers

A distinction must be drawn between a release of property and a disclaimer. A disclaimer is no more than the rejection of a proffered gift, and unless made specifically in favour of another, no property passes as a result of the rejection. As no property passes, there is no *conveyance* and no *ad valorem* duty was ever payable as a gift, nor even the fixed duty as a conveyance or transfer not on sale (*Re Paradise Motors Ltd* [1968] 1 WLR 1125; *Re Stratton's Disclaimer* [1958] Ch 42 at p. 49). If however by deed, a disclaimer, before 26 March 1985, would have attracted a fixed duty of 50p under the separate head of 'Deed of any kind whatsoever not described in this Schedule' but is no longer dutiable.

192

A release or renunciation of property otherwise than on sale attracts the fixed duty of £5 (FA 1999, Sched.13 para.22, see **section 10.13**). In consequence a deed of release for no consideration attracts the fixed duty.

A release previously attracted *ad valorem* duty as a gift (and still will if for consideration) if the result was or is to effect a transfer of property to someone else, even though the property passing may not be identical (*IRC* v. *Buchanan* [1958] Ch 289). A unilateral release without any consideration passing would now fall within the general exemption given by s.82(1), but a mutual release, with property changing hands either way, as where for example the end result would be a mutual exchange of securities, would still attract *ad valorem* duty as a conveyance on sale (*Oughtred* v. *IRC* [1960] AC 206; *Lloyds Bank plc* v. *Duker* [1987] 1 WLR 1324). To cope with this residual possibility, where the variations are made within two years after death, FA 1985, s 84 gives further exemption from *ad valorem* duty. There must not, however, be consideration:

> in money or money's worth other than consideration consisting of the making of a variation in respect of another of the dispositions (s.84(2)).

Even when *ad valorem* duty was payable, it had to be shown that the release had the effect of allowing an interest in land or other property to fall into possession, giving a hitherto unenjoyed right to the property, or enlarging an existing right. If the interest, the subject of the release, was not a property right as such it would not have been dutiable.

A release does not always operate as a conveyance (*Cormack's Trustee* v. *IRC* [1924] SC 819 which is still relevant where the release is for a consideration). Where such a voluntary release is executed it is not exempted from the fixed duty of £5 and being formerly dutiable as a voluntary disposition it requires adjudication since it is not within the Stamp Duty (Exempt Instruments) Regulations 1987, SI 1987/516 (reg.2(2)) notwithstanding that it is a voluntary disposition.

The definition of conveyance requires either property to be transferred or to be vested in some person. In consequence the *disappearance* of property does not involve a conveyance. Thus the release of a debt or of a restrictive covenant or an option does not pass property, and there is no conveyance on the redemption of preference shares (but note the charge upon the purchase of own shares pursuant to FA 1986, s.66).

Thus, for example, it has been held by the Court of Appeal (*Pritchard* v. *Briggs* [1980] Ch 338) that a right of pre-emption over land, being no more than a right of first refusal, confers only a personal contractual right, and is not an interest in land. It would follow that the release of such a right, even if made for consideration before or after FA 1985, was not, and is not dutiable *ad valorem.*

Again, where existing and potentially competing rights are rearranged so as to change the right to priority, as for example by a deed of postponement or *pari passu* between different mortgagees of the same property, no new property rights are being created. They have therefore never been dutiable either as voluntary transactions or as conveyances on sale. Following the decision of the House of Lords in *Williams & Glyn's Bank Ltd* v. *Boland* [1981] AC 487, recognising the priority under a resulting trust of a beneficiary in occupation over a later legal mortgagee, the practice has arisen of requiring an existing or potential occupier not appearing on the legal title to agree in writing to postpone whatever beneficial interest he or she may have in the property to the building society or other lender. No question has ever arisen of the occupier's rights to the land being transferred to anyone else and, at the worst, the consent to postponement attracted a fixed duty of 50 pence if by deed until the abolition of the fixed duty payable on deeds.

8.7.6 Charities

An *inter vivos* gift to a charity, like any other gift, must be the subject of adjudication. It should be remembered however that charities were exempted from the increases in *ad valorem* duty imposed by FA 1974, s.49 and totally exempted from *ad valorem* duty and fixed conveyance and lease duty on conveyances or transfers executed on or after 22 March 1982 but adjudication is required (FA 1982, s.129). The Stamp Duty (Exempt Instruments) Regulations 1987, SI 1987/516 do not apply.

8.7.7 Surrenders

A voluntary surrender of a lease was formerly chargeable with *ad valorem* duty under the same principles if the lease had a capital value. Otherwise it bore a 50p stamp if by deed. Surrenders of leases are now surrounded by a wide area of anti-avoidance legislation which requires careful investigation in those areas where the landlord is or is deemed to be providing consideration (see **section 7.15**). Surrenders of leases even on a voluntary basis are subject to stamp duty upon the market value of the lease when made to a connected company (FA 2000, s.119 unless relief pursuant to FA 1930, s.42 is available – see **section 6.7**). Written agreements to surrender leases upon sale, if valid, are dutiable (FA 1994, s.243) as are instruments evidencing the surrender or the purposes of the Land Registry (FA 2000, s.128). Moreover, where the surrender of the lease is made or consideration of other property such as the grant of a new lease or a surrender and regrant arises by operation of law pursuant to a deed of variation (*Gable Construction* v. *IRC* [1968] 1 WLR 1426; *Friends Provident* v. *British Rail* [1996] 1 All ER 336) the transaction may be subject to multiple charges to stamp duty pursuant to the land exchange provisions in FA 1994, s.241. Surrenders are discussed in greater detail in **section 7.16.1**.

8.8 VOLUNTARY LEASES

There was never any express charge on voluntary leases as such, but this has been changed by FA 2000, s.121 which imposes a charge upon the market value of a lease granted to a connected company (unless exempt pursuant to FA 1995, s.151 – see **section 7.17.6**).

However, even where this charge does not apply the fixed duty of £5 may apply (FA 1999, Sched.13 para.13) and it may be necessary to adjudicate (FA 1985, s.82(5)) since leases are not within the Stamp Duty (Exempt Instruments) Regulations 1987, SI 1987/516 in certain contexts a lease may be a conveyance (*Att.-Gen.* v. *Brown* (1849) 3 Exch: 662; *Escoigne Properties Ltd* v. *IRC* [1958] AC 549) although as a matter of general stamp duty terminology conveyances and leases are separate categories and the reference to a *conveyance* does not include *lease*.

If property was demised without a premium, or at no rent, or if whatever was paid under either or both was inadequate, the lease would have been treated as attracting *ad valorem* duty as a voluntary disposition (*IRC* v. *Littlewoods Mail Order Stores Ltd* [1963] AC 135); however, the correctness of these comments was never challenged because they offered the opportunity of mitigating stamp duty in many situations and rarely produced an actual charge in practice so that it was in the interests of lessees to adopt them. These benefits are now irrelevant and it may be worthwhile questioning the decisions should the point ever be raised by the Inland Revenue Stamp Taxes Office). Although now not subject to such duty it should be adjudicated.

An agreement for lease is dutiable as a lease, regardless of the length of the term (FA 1999, Sched.13 para.14) but as a voluntary agreement is a contradiction in terms, it is difficult to see how duty could be levelled on a document whereby a party agrees to give a lease to a donee at a later stage. If under hand such a document would fail as an imperfect gift, though it has been suggested *obiter* that a document executed as a deed with no payment would perhaps be enforceable by specific performance (*Mountford* v. *Scott* [1975] Ch 258 per Russell LJ, at p. 265).

8.9 MORTGAGES

Until 1971 the creation and transfer for value of a mortgage was chargeable, not as a conveyance on sale but under the head of 'Mortgage, Bond, Debenture, Covenant' (except where these are *marketable securities* within SA 1891, s.122 which remain potentially dutiable upon transfer unless exempt as loan capital of a company within FA 1986, s.79). Various rules applied, depending on whether the mortgage was a primary security, a collateral security or an equitable mortgage. The discharge of a mortgage was also chargeable. The various rates all had one feature in common: they were substantially less than the full *ad valorem* charge on a conveyance on sale.

All the above duties were abolished by FA 1971, s.64 but it had previously been held in *Anderson* v. *IRC* [1939] 1 KB 341 that a voluntary transfer of mortgage was dutiable as a conveyance on sale under FA 1910, s.74 attracting a higher rate of duty. This left the paradoxical situation whereby, after 1971, sales of mortgages were completely exempt but gifts of mortgages, until 1985, attracted full duty.

8.9.1   Present-day problems with mortgaged property

As with other gifts, a voluntary disposition of property subject to an existing mortgage is no longer dutiable *per se*, but if the donee assumes any responsibility for the repayment of the mortgage, even contingently, the Inland Revenue can charge duty on the amount secured thereby as a conveyance on sale of the property in consideration of taking over the mortgage debt, i.e. there is a partial sale (SA 1891, s.57).

Where there is a gift of part of the property subject to the mortgage, such as a transfer of a half share in the matrimonial home by one spouse to the other, in practice the Inland Revenue Stamp Taxes Office claims stamp duty only upon that proportion of the mortgage which the gifted interest bears to the whole property and permits the inclusion of a certificate of value for that amount. In consequence where there is a gift of a one-quarter share in property subject to a charge by a parent to a child a certificate of value for the nil rate can be included provided that the amount currently secured by the mortgage does not exceed £240,000.

The difficulty lies in determining when the donee assumes the liability in whole or in part for the mortgage. Where an express indemnity is given the position is clear. However, the Inland Revenue Stamp Taxes Office takes the view that there can be an implied indemnity (see Statement of Practice SP 6/90). Parties should note the benefits to be derived by making the appropriate entries upon the Land Register pursuant to Land Registration Act 1925, s.28.

If however there is a *sale* of the equity of redemption, duty will be paid on the aggregate of the price paid to the vendor and the amount outstanding on the mortgage debt, SA 1891, s.57 stating that the debt charged on the property is to be deemed 'the whole or part . . . of the consideration'.

Since it came into force, no duty has been payable on a release or discharge of a mortgage, even if voluntary under the FA 1971, s.64(1)(*c*).

8.10   DIVIDENDS *IN SPECIE*

It has been held that a dividend *in specie* by a company was a voluntary disposition (*Wigan Coal and Iron Co Ltd* v. *IRC* [1945] 1 All ER 392; *Associated British Engineering Ltd* v. *IRC* [1940] 4 All ER 278) and so would have been subject to *ad valorem* stamp duty accordingly. Such transfers are now exempt if certified pursuant to category L of the Stamp Duty (Exempt Instrument) Regulations 1987, SI 1987/516; otherwise they are dutiable £5 and require to be adjudicated.

Occasionally the Inland Revenue Stamp Taxes Office contends that a company cannot make a gift *inter vivos* for these purposes. The point is considered to be wrong and is, of course, totally inconsistent with their practice between 1910 and 1985 and the argument which they succeeded with in the two cases above.

On occasion the company's articles of association may require the declaration of a cash dividend to be satisfied by the distribution of specified property (see, e.g. reg. 105 of Table A, Companies (Tables A to F) Regulations 1985, SI 1985/805) and the views of the Inland Revenue in relation to the difference between dividends and distributions may require a similar type of resolution. It is considered that this does not create a sale giving rise to an *ad valorem* charge pursuant to SA 1891, s.57 since there is no pre-existing debt to be discharged by the transfer of the property (*Re Bradford Investments* No 2 [1991] BCLC 688). However, the declaration of a cash dividend without any reference to the transfer of the property will involve two stages: the creation of a debt and its subsequent discharge, which falls within SA 1891, s.57.

It is considered, however, that a declaration of an interim dividend which does not create a debt, since it is not effective until paid, does not fall within s.57. From time to time the Inland Revenue Stamp Taxes Office has taken the nonsensical point that where the dividend *in specie* is made to another company which includes a carrying cost for the asset in its accounts as a sale because the accounts prove that there had to be a debt or cost. However, this as a proposition has no justification whatsoever.

More important are the principles imposing *ad valorem* stamp duty upon transfers of land to connected companies (FA 2000, s.119). These prima facie apply to dividends of land *in specie* within a group but there is a specific exemption for dividends in Case 7 in FA 2000, s.120(8) provided that the property was acquired by the distributing company by means of a duly stamped transfer. In other case relief the intra-group transfers pursuant to FA 1930, s.42 may be available since that provision overrides the charge pursuant to FA 2000, s.119 (see **section 4.14**). Moreover, the Inland Revenue Stamp Taxes Office has accepted that where there is a dividend *in specie* of land subject to a mortgage SA, 1891, s.57 does not convert this into a *sale* for the amount of the mortgage, provided that the transferees do not agree expressly or impliedly agree to indemnify the transferor company and the terms of Statement of Practice SP6/90 are observed (see **Appendix A**).

8.11 DISTRIBUTIONS IN A WINDING-UP

Distributions in a winding-up are not gifts or voluntary dispositions since they are in satisfaction of the rights of the members in the winding up. In consequence they are dutiable £5 as a conveyance not on sale unless certified pursuant to Category I in the Schedule to the Stamp Duty (Exempt Instruments) Regulations 1987, SI 1987/516. However, this category draws attention to the fact that the distributions may be dutiable as a sale. This can arise where the property is subject to a charge or the shareholders agree to indemnify the liquidator against outstanding liabilities of the company (SA 1891, s.57; **section 2.10.3**).

8.12 OLD TITLES

Sometimes it may not be apparent on the face of it that an earlier transfer or conveyance should have been stampable as a voluntary disposition: it may appear to have been a conveyance or transfer for consideration but in reality conferred a substantial benefit upon the transferee, thus rendering the whole value of the property liable to *ad valorem* duty, not just the stated consideration (FA 1910, s.74(5)). Whether or not there has been a substantial benefit is a question for the Commissioners to decide, and they are entitled to ignore any apparent good faith between the parties.

In *Lap Shun Textiles Industrial Co* v. *Collector of Stamp Revenue* [1976] AC 530, a Privy Council decision on very similar Hong Kong legislation, an arm's length commercial transaction in good faith but at only one-third of the property's true value, was held dutiable on the full value.

Bearing in mind, as mentioned above, that the only stamp which is conclusive is an adjudicated stamp, the implications of the *Lap Shun* decision could pose serious problems for later purchasers whose title depends on the adequacy of the stamp duty recorded as paid on documents of title which have not been adjudicated. How are they to know that there was no similar element of benefit rendering the recorded stamp useless? This is perhaps one of those areas where, as happens occasionally in conveyancing, ignorance is bliss (see further *Re Weir and Pitts Contract* (1911) 55 Sol J 536).

8.13 OLD EXEMPTIONS

Certain documents were specifically exempted from the *ad valorem* charge on voluntary dispositions (FA 1910, s.74(6)) for the reason that no beneficial interest was transferred. Transactions so exempted were as follows:

(a) A transfer for a nominal consideration and to secure the repayment of a loan
In essence, such an arrangement has always been regarded by equity as a mortgage and, in a different context, it has been noted that mortgages *per se* are no longer dutiable (FA 1971, s.64).

(b) An appointment of a new trustee
[This is dealt with more specifically in **Chapter 7** on the fixed heads of duty.]
An appointment, however, of an original trustee seemed to fall outside the scope of this particular exemption and carried full *ad valorem* duty if at the same time it had the effect of declaring or perfecting the trusts.

(c) The retirement of a trustee
By the Trustee Act 1925, s.39 this must be by deed (and with the consent of the other trustees, of whom, if individuals, there must be at least two left). The deed stamp has now been abolished, but if reliance is placed on the implied vesting declaration in the Trustee Act, s.40 in favour of the continuing trustees, the instrument must contain a certificate under the Stamp Duty (Exempt Instruments) Regulations 1987, SI 1987/516 or be stamped 50p as a conveyance or transfer not on sale.

(d) Where no beneficial interest passed
This is no more than a statement of general principle more specifically illustrated by the other examples listed.

(e) A transfer made to a beneficiary by a trustee or other person in a fiduciary capacity under any trust, whether expressed or implied
Such a transfer attracted a 50p fixed duty stamp as a conveyance of any other kind until 1 May 1987. Thereafter the fixed duty stamp is only payable if it is not certified under the Stamp Duty (Exempt Instruments) Regulations 1987, SI 1987/516.

(f) A disentailing assurance by a tenant in tail converting his fee tail to a fee simple

(g) Divorce
It was unclear whether conveyances on a divorce were *voluntary*, i.e. without consideration (*Re Abbott* [1983] Ch 45) and so outside the 'Voluntary Disposition Duty' head of charge. No point appears to have been taken by the Inland Revenue Stamp Taxes Office in this area. See now FA 1985, s.83.

CHAPTER 9

Trusts and wills

9.1 *TRUSTEE*

There is an important distinction, at least in stamp duty, between a nominee or bare trustee and a trustee in the strict sense. The point underlies many stamp duty issues such as:

- whether there is an exempt appointment of a trustee (Stamp Duty (Exempt Instruments) Regulations 1987, SI 1987/516 Category A) or merely a change of nominee dutiable £5 as a conveyance or transfer not on sale; or
- whether there is a transfer of land to a nominee connected company which is exempt from stamp duty or a transfer of land to a corporate trustee which is dutiable *ad valorem* upon market value unless the conditions for exemption are strictly observed (FA 2000, s.119 and s.120).

> Distinctions such as these must be noted and will continue into the revised land stamp duty regime commencing in early 2004.

Stamp duty legislation provides no guidance upon the point, but general law would indicate that a nominee is a person who merely holds the legal title for some person absolutely and has no power or discretion but must act under the direction of the absolute beneficial owner (*Cowan de Groot* v. *Eagle Trust* [1991] BCLC 1045). Successive, as opposed to joint, interests and ability to take decisions on his own initiative would point towards a *trust*, see also Trusts of Land and Appointment of Trustees Act 1996.

Stamp duties are not charged upon trusts declared by wills (see FA 1999, Sched.13 para.17(2)) and the vast majority of trusts and settlements are created voluntarily, i.e. without consideration), so that on the basis that *ad valorem* stamp duty on voluntary dispositions has been abolished (FA 1985, s.82; see **Chapter 8** for certain problem areas) it might be thought that there were no significant stamp duty issues in respect of trusts and wills after 18 March 1985. However, this is not an entirely accurate appraisal of the situation; there are both historical issues and current problems in relation to stamp duty.

Not all dealings in trust assets or interests are voluntary in the sense that there is no consideration. Where there is a consideration, such as upon the variation of a trust and an estate such deeds of family arrangement are not in general sales (*Henniker* v. *Henniker* (1852) 1 E & B 54), but this is not an invariable rule and where the necessary conditions for a sale exist the relevant instrument whether a contract for the sale of an equitable interest (FA 1999, Sched.13 para.7 – including foreign equitable interests as in *Farmer* v. *IRC* [1898] 2 QB 141) or a conveyance completing the transaction (*Oughtred* v. *IRC* [1960] AC 206) is dutiable.

After FA 1994, s.241 which enlarged the definition of *sale* for land transactions there is an increased risk that the variation or partition of a trust or an estate may be a sale possibly attracting two charges to *ad valorem* duty where land is involved on both sides of the transaction (see **section 4.13**). It is, however, an open question whether an equitable interest in a trust which holds is itself *land* for the purposes of stamp duty whatever may be the position for other areas of law.

It is thought that an equitable interest is, like a share in a partnership, a separate asset from the interests in the trust assets and so is not land, particularly where the trust investments are a mixture of land and other assets. However, the terms of any transaction need to be considered in order to determine whether in the particular circumstances it does involve land.

There are also anti-avoidance provisions such as FA 1965, s.90 and, in particular, the connected company charge pursuant to FA 2000, s.119 and s.121 which include transfers of land into and out of the settlement, and which, with very limited exemptions, apply to dealings with or by trustees. These charges may apply upon the transfer or leasing of property into a trust, dealings in equitable interest and transfers of property out of the settlement or testamentary trust.

Moreover where, as is probable, the estate of the deceased or the trust fund includes or may receive interests in shares and loan stock of companies, questions of the much wider liability to the directly enforceable stamp duty reserve tax can arise (see FA 1986, s.87 and following). It has been from time to time the view of the Inland Revenue Stamp Taxes Office that the definition of *chargeable securities* contained in FA 1986, s.99 (as amended) is probably sufficiently wide to encompass interests in shares and other securities held as part of a trust fund; however it appears that at present this view, which would in many cases be incorrect, is not taken.

9.2 WILLS AND INTESTACIES

The areas relating to wills where stamp duty may arise are:

- variations of the estate of the deceased;
- transfers of assets to specific legatees and devisees;

- appropriation of assets in satisfaction of legacies;
- dealings in interest in the estate after the variation.

9.2.1 Variation of estates of deceased persons

It has long been possible for beneficiaries under a will or on intestacy to rearrange by agreement between themselves their respective testamentary or statutory entitlements. Provided the rearrangement takes place within two years after the death, no further capital taxation is levied (IHTA 1984, s.142 and TCGA 1992, s.62). However, stamp duty at the full *ad valorem* rate was payable either on any element of gift or on consideration in kind deemed to be dutiable, as, for example, a mutual transfer of shares.

The liability to *ad valorem* stamp duty on such rearrangements was eliminated by FA 1985, s.84 which provides that an instrument of variation executed by the beneficiaries within two years after a person's death relating to any of the dispositions under the will or under the law relating to the intestacy, shall not be chargeable to stamp duty as a 'conveyance or transfer on sale'. Liability on any voluntary element is disposed of by s.82.

There is however a proviso in s.84(2): if the variation is made for any consideration in money or money's worth other than consideration in money's worth consisting of the variation in respect of another of the dispositions, *ad valorem* duty is still payable, although it should be noted that many forms of consideration in money's worth involved in the variation of estates will not give rise to a *sale* for the purposes of stamp duty notwithstanding the enlarged meaning of this term particularly where land is involved.

In consequence the reference to consideration in the form of other interests in the estate does not enlarge the *ad valorem* stamp duty charge.

The instrument of variation must have been executed on or after 26 March 1985 and was liable both to a fixed duty of 50p and adjudication until 1 May 1987. Instruments executed thereafter should take advantage of the Stamp Duty (Exempt Instruments) Regulations 1987 and, by containing the appropriate declaration, avoid both.

9.2.2 Transfers and appropriations

Less substantial variations can take the form of appropriations of property in or towards the satisfaction of a legacy. *Jopling* v. *IRC* [1940] 2 KB 282 held that such an arrangement was potentially liable to *ad valorem* stamp duty where it required the consent of the legatee (Administration of Estates Act 1925, s.41) but not it seems where there was an express power of appropriation in the will dispensing with the need for such consent. The FA 1895, s.84(4) provides that where there is an appropriation in or towards the satisfaction of a general legacy the money is not liable to duty under the head 'Conveyance and Transfer on sale', and s.84(5) provides for a similar exemption where on an intestacy property is appropriated by a personal representative in or towards the satisfaction of the interest of the surviving spouse in the estate, including certain matters within the Intestates' Estates Act 1952.

9.2.3 Subsequent dealings

Once the asset has left the estate, or the dealing with the interest is after the variation or appropriation, the documentation will be subject to stamp duty on normal principles. These dealings are in equitable interests and dispositions have to made in writing (LPA 1925, s.53(1)(c)) and any written contract for sale is prime facie dutiable pursuant to FA 1999, Sched.13 para.7. In addition the connected company rules in FA 2000, s.119 can apply to transfers out of estates and trusts subject to limited exclusions in s.120 (see **section 4.14**).

Moreover, any transfers of the legal title by the executors may operate as a conveyance completing an earlier transaction and be subject to *ad valorem* stamp duty where the earlier arrangement was a sale (*Oughtred* v. *IRC* [1960] AC 206).

9.3   TRUSTS

Stamp duty (and, where shares and other securities are involved, stamp duty reserve tax) arises in relation to trusts:

- upon the establishment of the trust and the vesting of property;
- the appointment and retirement of trustees;
- vesting assets in the trustees;
- changes of investments by trustees;
- dealings in equitable interests in the trust; and
- distribution by trustees to beneficiaries including exercises of powers of appointment and revocation.

Some of these may still involve *ad valorem* charges to stamp duty. For example, in some situations a variation of trust may produce a conveyance on sale dutiable as such (*Oughtred* v. *IRC* [1960] AC 206; *Henniker* v. *Henniker* (1852) 1 E&B 54).

In relation to current transactions, there are occasions when trusts arise pursuant to a commercial bargain where the presence of consideration leads to an imposition of *ad valorem* duty.

Examples may arise from pension arrangements, co-ownership where not all the beneficiaries wish to or are capable of holding the legal estate, or partnerships where some only of the partners hold the partnership property for the benefit of the others.

The recent extension of the head of charge 'Conveyance or Transfer on sale' to include exchanges of land for both land and any other property may mean that inappropriately worded instruments which are appropriating trust property on a division of the fund and so falling outside the revised partition rules in FA 1999, Sched.13 para.21 may now attract *ad valorem* stamp duty, or fall within the connected company charge pursuant to FA 2000, s.119 unless exempted by s.120 thereof.

9.3.1 Creation of trusts

The whole concept of a trust is based on equity's insistence that one follows the dictates of one's conscience (as interpreted by equity). Looking at the substance of the transaction rather than the form, equity (as opposed to statute) does not require any formalities to be observed on the creation of a trust. All that is necessary for a trust to arise is the presence of the three certainties of:

* intention;
* subject matter; and
* objects.

If the property and interest therein to be the subject matter of the trust are ascertainable, the beneficiaries identified or identifiable by reference to a sufficiently certain formula, and above all, it is clear from the words or deeds of the person making the disposition that a trust is intended, a trust will come into being.

Thus an oral declaration by the settlor of an intention thenceforth to hold stated property upon trust for stated beneficiaries will create an immediate and valid trust, as in *Paul* v. *Constance* [1977] 1 WLR 527 where there was an oral declaration of trust concerning money in a bank account by the use of the words, uttered by the settlor to the beneficiary, 'The money is as much yours as mine'. It will immediately be appreciated that, in the above situation, although there is undoubtedly the creation or passing of a beneficial interest, there is no document to bear stamp duty (*Chartham (T) International* v. *Pagarani* [2001] 2 All ER 492.)

Equity's permissive view has long been modified by statutory provisions requiring the observance of written formalities in many cases, and in practice an oral declaration of trust is only unaffected by statute when limited to personalty. The LPA 1925, s.53(1)(*b*) states:

> . . . a declaration of trust respecting any land or any interest therein must be manifested and proved by some writing signed by some person who is able to declare such trust or by his will.

Like s.40 of the same Act, before its repeal by LP(MP)A 1989, s.2(8), the above provision is evidential only and does not require that the trust should necessarily be declared by writing. There must be written evidence of the declaration signed by the competent party at some stage, or probably some act of reliance upon the oral arrangement which can be utilised to establish a constructive or similar trust which does not require writing (LPA 1925, s.53(2); LP(MP)A 1989, s.2(6); *Yaxley* v. *Gotts* [1999] 2 WLR 1217; *Binions* v. *Evans* [1972] 2 All ER 70).

The LPA 1925, s.136 requires transfers of legal title to *choses in action* to be in writing. If the settlor does not do everything possible, according to the nature of the property given, to vest the property in the trustees (as in *Re Rose* [1949] Ch 78), equity will not interfere to perfect the trust. This is because, in the absence of consideration given by a beneficiary, there is an imperfect gift and (in the absence of an estoppel or the creation of a constructive trust which does not require writing), as was said in *Milroy* v. *Lord* (1862) 4 De GF & J 264, 'there is no equity in this Court to perfect an imperfect gift'.

In certain situations trustees may be ordered by the court not to enforce a deed of covenant unless there is separate consideration as partner within the marriage consideration (*Re Kay's Settlement* [1939] Ch 329; *Re Cooks Settlement Trusts* [1965] Ch 902).

The position may differ where the proposed trustees are the personal representatives of the deceased settlor who thereby become vested with the legal estate (*Strong* v. *Bird* (1874) LR Eq 315) or the legal title otherwise *accidentally* vests in them (*Re Ralli* [1964] Ch 288).

It remains to be seen how far the judges who were trained upon the now repealed doctrine of part performance bring back a similar set of principles relabelled *constructive trust*. It is immaterial when the written memorandum is produced, and even pleadings in litigation have been accepted as sufficient.

It may be thought that duty can be avoided, even on a declaration of trusts of land, by first making an oral declaration, which cannot be stampable, and then following it with written confirmation at a later stage. The difficulty with this course of action is that until there is a written declaration, the trust remains unenforceable by court action, and the Inland Revenue Stamp Taxes Office may seek to contend that the written memorandum is dutiable as *the conveyance* itself, on the grounds that the oral declaration concerning land, being unenforceable by court action, cannot effectively create an enforceable trust so that the written record is the first written instrument which affects the title (*Oughtred* v. *IRC* [1960] AC 206).

It is, however, considered that this view if put forward by the Inland Revenue Stamp Taxes Office is untenable because such arrangements are valid, albeit unenforceable by the court (*Forster* v. *Hale* (1798) 3 Ves 696; *Rochefoucauld* v. *Boustead* [1897] 1 Ch 196) and the position differs from that of a transaction which is void unless effected in writing.

This also means that the legislative requirement may be invalid pursuant to the human rights legislation as an obstacle to the protection of validly created property rights. This is a fundamental issue as to how far the rules of evidence and procedure can continue to regulate property ownership and its protection. The transfer may, therefore, be dutiable as the completion of a prior transaction such as where the settlor has agreed to purchase the property and directs a transfer to the trustees to be held as part of the trust fund. This could also apply where the settlor has orally declared himself a trustee of the benefit of the contract.

Alternatively, the Inland Revenue Stamp Taxes Office may consider both oral declaration and subsequent memorandum or formal appointment of the trustee and vesting to be 'all one transaction' as in *Cohen and Moore* v. *IRC* [1933] 2 KB 126 where an oral declaration of trust (made when voluntary transactions were still dutiable) was followed by a deed of appointment of new trustees which also recited the oral trusts. It was held that the deed of appointment was dutiable as a written, as opposed to an oral, settlement. It was observed, however, in that case that the deed of appointment was already in draft at the time of the oral declaration, and it is a requirement of the rules relating to memoranda recording earlier oral and valid transactions that these documents attract *ad valorem* duty only if it was always the intention of the parties that there should be a written record of the transaction.

In consequence, if there is no such intention which may be evidenced by there being a reasonable interval between the declaration and the memorandum, coupled perhaps with the settlor in the meantime behaving in a manner consistent with trusteeship, there may well be a good chance that the memorandum will not be dutiable. This may be important in practice where parties are seeking to avoid the *ad valorem* charges upon transferring or leasing land to corporate trustees within FA 2000 s.119 to s.121, but this may be difficult given the general requirement for writing for land transactions.

In the meantime, the beneficiaries will not, in the case of land, be able to enforce the trust by court action. Beneficiaries under personalty trusts face merely the evidential handicap of proving the fact of the oral declaration. Such declaration made in the presence of a respectable witness coupled with a statutory declaration by him should suffice, although such a declaration particularly if acknowledged by the signatures of the parties, may become a stampable record.

Different considerations arise where it is intended that the nominated trustees shall take over the control and management of the property to give effect to the trust. In these circumstances, notwithstanding the presence of the three certainties, the trust will be imperfectly constituted until such time as the property is properly vested in the trustees by the manner appropriate to the nature of the property. Until this happens and the property is in their hands, the trustees are trustees of nothing (*Richards* v. *Delbridge* (1874) LR 18 Eq 11).

Cash and goods can be transferred by delivery, but land must be conveyed or assigned by deed, shares by a stock transfer form or directives through CREST where the default liability to the principal charge to stamp duty reserve tax will apply (FA 1986, s.87) unless appropriate steps are taken to enable the utilisation of those transaction indicators or *flags* which indicate that the transaction is for one of the relevant reasons not liable to stamp duty reserve tax.

Solicitors should note that stamp duty reserve tax is directly enforceable and it is required under penalty that appropriate records are maintained so that upon audit by the Inland Revenue the parties can substantiate their utilisation of the particular flag.

Where the trust is to be managed by a fresh set of trustees appointed specifically for that purpose it was usual to effect the settlement by two documents, and where there was a strict settlement governed by the Settled Land Act 1925 two deeds were essential (Settled Land Act 1925, s.4).

Writing is also required in relation to will trusts even, it seems, where the personal representatives are the same as the trustees. A written assent in favour of themselves is required in order to prove that they have ceased to act as personal representatives and are acting as trustees for sale (Administration of Estates Act 1925, s.36(4) and (7); *Re King's Will Trusts* [1964] Ch 542; *Re Hodge* [1940] Ch 260); but not it seems if they purport to sell as personal representatives (Re *Pander* [1921] 2 Ch 59). One document constitutes the trust instrument appointing the trustees and declaring the trusts of the settlement, and the other, or others, the document or documents whereby the property is effectively transferred to the trustees.

The question then arises as to which of the documents should bear *ad valorem* stamp duty, the trust instrument or the conveyance(s) or transfer(s). The short answer is that, apart from a strict settlement governed by the Settled Land Act which stipulates that the trust instrument shall bear any *ad valorem* stamp duty which may be payable (Settled Land Act 1925, s.4(3)(e)), it does not matter (*Re Robb's Contract* [1941] Ch 463); and in such a situation SA 1891, s.58(3) provides that where there are several instruments of conveyance for completing the purchasing trustees' title to the property sold only the principal instrument of conveyance is to bear the *ad valorem* stamp duty.

In support of this SA 1891, s.61(2) permits the parties to select the principal instrument of conveyance but this power to choose has been severely limited by *Parinv Investments* v. *IRC* [1998] STC 306. Most settlements are, of course, voluntary and therefore, in general, no longer dutiable *ad valorem*. Consideration, however, is not unknown in the shape of a financial inducement to persuade the tenant in tail in remainder to bar the entail, and resettle on further trusts.

Nevertheless, in practice, the instrument to be stamped should be that which actually gives effect to the passing of the beneficial interest, and this view was supported by FA 1910, s.74(6) when in force, which stated that *ad valorem* duty was not payable on a conveyance or transfer made for effectuating the appointment of a new trustee or under which no beneficial interest passed in the property conveyed.

Where the settlor first executes a trust deed, showing a clear intention that nominated trustees are to be given the task of managing the property, then, as mentioned above, the trust cannot become operative for so long as it remains incompletely constituted. Where, therefore, the trust deed is followed by a conveyance or transfer vesting the property in the trustees, it is the conveyance or transfer which completes and gives effect to the trust, and thus bears any *ad valorem* duty.

If, on the other hand, the settlor first conveys the property to trustees on trusts yet to be declared, no beneficial interest passes as there is an immediate resulting trust back to the settlor (*Vandervell* v. *IRC* [1967] 1 All ER 1). The conveyance or transfer will thus bear a fixed duty of £5 only as a 'Conveyance or transfer not on sale' (unless it falls either within FA 1965, s.90 as a conveyance in contemplation of a sale when it is dutiable as a sale for market value or with in FA 2000, s.119 and s.120).

The Stamp Duty (Exempt Instruments) Regulations 1987, SI 1987/516 do not apply to a conveyance to trustees on the creation or in anticipation of a trust, but only to the appointment of a new or the retirement of an existing trustee. In such a situation subsequent attempts to create an effective trust are likely to require to be carried out in writing in order to comply with LPA 1925, s.53(1)(*c*). The trust instrument, when executed, will have the effect of shifting the beneficial interest away from the settlor and into the hands of the beneficiaries, and thus bear the full *ad valorem* charge, but after 19 March 1985 only if for a stampable consideration.

FA 1999, Sched.13 para.17 contains the following head of charge:

Declaration of use or trust

(1) Stamp duty of £5 is chargeable on a declaration of any use or trust of or concerning property unless the instrument constitutes a conveyance or transfer on sale.

(2) This does not apply to a will.

The duty is £5 provided it is not a declaration of trust on sale (but see *Chesterfield Brewery Co* v. *IRC* [1899] 2 QB 7 for an illustration of a declaration of trust dutiable *ad valorem* as a sale).

9.3.2 Appointment and retirement of trustees

The SA 1891 also imposed a fixed duty of £5 on the appointment of a trustee, or on the appointment or execution of power of attorney, other than by will. This head has been abolished by FA 1985, s.85 but, as noted in Chapter 10, on fixed duties, the deed of appointment may well double as a conveyance or transfer not on sale in which case a certificate under the Stamp Duty (Exempt Instruments) Regulations 1987, SI 1987/516 will be needed to avoid the fixed duty of £5 otherwise payable.

Prima facie the above heads of charge give rise to a nugatory burden of duty. In reality, if for consideration or if voluntary before 19 March 1985, either the declaration of trust or the transfer or conveyance to the trustees could result in the imposition of full *ad valorem* duty on the value of the property forming the subject of the trust.

It follows from the above that any written instrument which creates the trust (or which is treated as creating it) will be treated as a conveyance (though, since 19 March 1985, only if for stampable consideration as enlarged by the provisions for land transactions by FA 1994, s.241 and FA 2000, s.119 and s.121) chargeable as a conveyance on sale such as where the trust property is subject to a mortgage (SA 1891, s.57; SP6/90).

It will also be recalled that an express declaration of that which would otherwise be implied in a contract for sale receives the same treatment as a conveyance on sale, or possibly as an agreement for the sale of an equitable interest in property chargeable as a conveyance on sale under FA 1999, Sched.19 para.7 (*Chesterfield Brewery Co* v. *IRC* [1899] 2 QB 7; *Peter Bone Ltd* v. *IRC* [1995] STC 921).

9.3.3 Vesting the trust property

The vesting of the property whether on the initial appointment or subsequent appointment is a conveyance and is subject to stamp duty depending upon whether it is *on sale* or not. Obviously, insofar as the trustees purchase or change investments they will pay stamp duty in the same way as any other purchasers. The question is the vesting of property by a settlor or testator.

As indicated above the *gift* which can include a lease to the trustees may be dutiable *ad valorem* or it may complete one or more transactions which is liable to *ad valorem* stamp duty (*Oughtred* v. *IRC* [1960] AC 206) or be dutiable *ad valorem* pursuant to the connected company provisions in FA 2000, s.119 and s.121 (see **sections 4.14** and **7.12.4**). A classic illustration would be where the settlor has agreed to purchase the property and directs the seller to transfer the property directly to the trustees. Such a purchase and sub gift does not escape stamp duty as a subsale since the second limb, i.e. the gift to the trustees, is not a sale for the market value of the property, SA 1891, s.58(4) (as amended). It is, therefore, dutiable as a conveyance pursuant to the initial sale.

If not perfecting an actual or deemed sale, the instrument is prima facie subject to the fixed stamp duty of £5 within FA 1999, Sched.13 as a 'conveyance or transfer not on sale' but there is an exemption where the instrument contains the appropriate certificate pursuant to Stamp Duty (Exempt Instruments) Regulations 1987, SI 1987/516 Category A which applies to a conveyance not on sale vesting of property (there are possibilities for the automatic vesting of property pursuant to Trustee Act 1925, s.40) subject to a trust in the trustees of the trust on the appointment of a new trustee, or in the continuing trustees on the retirement of a trustee.

9.4   VESTING PROPERTY ON SALE OR LEASE

The difficult issues arise around when the vesting of assets is *on sale* or deemed sale (as in FA 2000, s.119 and s.120) or a lease including leases to connected companies for which there are no exclusions for corporate trustees particularly in the case of land. In general the property moving into the trust will be by way of gift with no obvious consideration and the vesting in new or continuing trustees will usually not be for a relevant consideration.

However stamp duty pursuant to the head of charge 'conveyance or transfer on sale' is extremely wide and includes the following normally regarded as *gifts*.

9.5   GIFTS

General gifts, i.e. transfers for no consideration, are subject to the fixed stamp duty of £5 as a conveyance not on sale (FA 1985, s.82) unless certified pursuant to the Stamp Duty (Exempt Instruments) Regulations 1987, SI 1987/516. This will, prima facie, include the vesting of property by the settlor in the trustees, which falls within category A.

However, as described in Chapter 8 certain *gifts* remain dutiable *ad valorem* even where the transferees are trustees. These include:

- Transfer of property subject to a mortgage or charge within SA 1891, s.57 unless the donor or settlor indemnifies the trustees as set out in Statement of Practice SP6/90 (especially para.8) (see **Appendix A**).
- Transfers of land to corporate trustees (FA 2000, s.119) unless within the limited exemptions in s.120 thereof (see **section 4.14**);
- Leases to corporate trustees for which there are no exemptions (FA 2000, s.121). The procedure should be for the lease to be granted to individual trustees when s.121 does not apply and the individuals retire in favour of the corporate trustees within the exemption in s.120.
- The transfer of the property to the trustee may come from another trust. Although in general transfers out of trusts or from one trust to another are not dutiable because they are not sales (see also Stamp Duty (Exempt Instruments) Regulations 1987, SI 1987/516, Category A) this not invariably the case and certain transfers and leases by trustees out of settled property are dutiable upon market value pursuant FA 2000, s.119 and s.121 with a limited exemption for transfers to beneficiaries pursuant to the terms of the trust provided that the transferee did not acquire his or her interest in the trust for value (FA 2000, s.120, Case 5). Alternatively, the instrument may perfect an earlier transaction that is a sale (*Oughtred* v. *IRC* [1960] AC 206). The background to the instrument cannot be ignored since the duty may be chargeable even though the

property transferred does not correspond precisely with the interest in the property involved in the previous uncompleted transaction so that a sale of a limited equitable interest may be completed by a transfer of the legal title (*Oughtred* v. *IRC* [1960] AC 206). (See also *Parinv Investments Ltd* v. *IRC* [1998] STC 305 for the suggestion that the instrument may be dutiable notwithstanding that there is some earlier writing completing the transaction).

Certain of these provisions require careful planning in order to avoid unnecessary charges even where there are individual trustees. For example, they may wish to hold the land in a nominee company or where it is part of a business to be beneficially owned in a company wholly owned by them. In these cases the exemptions in FA 2000, s.120 will not apply, because, for example, in the former case the nominee company will be holding for the benefit of the trustees and not, as s.120 requires, for the transferor.

9.6 RESERVING A BENEFIT OR INTEREST

A difficult area arises where the settlor wishes to vest the property in the trustees whilst reserving some benefit for themselves whether by way of contract or otherwise or wishes to dispose of only a partial interest in the property. Here the conveyancing mechanics imposed by the general law or the machinery adopted by the parties can affect the stamp duty costs significantly.

This is particularly so following FA 1994, s.241 treating *land exchanges* as potentially dutiable sales or chargeable leases (see **section 7.12.2**) especially as the Inland Revenue Stamp Taxes Office relies strictly upon the conveyancing principles in order to maximise the stamp duty.

It is not always possible to transfer land reserving an interest or simply gifting a partial interest. This type of problem will frequently arise where the settlor wishes to transfer the freehold of their home to the trustees but retaining a leasehold interest or the right to continue to reside there. Such arrangements are likely to create leases for life rather than licences (*Skipton Building Society* v. *Clayton* (1993) 66 P&CR 223) and there may be an intention to grant or reserve a lease for a fixed term for the settlor.

The Inland Revenue Stamp Taxes Office takes an aggressive position on this area and has contended that where there is a transfer of the title to trustees who agree to delay delivery of vacant possession indefinitely this is a lease for life (i.e. for a term of 90 years) and is not a licence to occupy, since it confers exclusive possession upon the transferor/donor.

It is currently possible in England to create valid leases in this situation (see on dealings between nominees and beneficial owners, *Lady Ingram* v. *IRC* [1999] STC 37; and *Rye* v. *Rye* [1961] 2 All ER 146 but there may be difficulties in Scotland *Kildrummy* v. *IRC* [1990] STC 657).

There are, therefore, issues as to whether there is a contractual relationship between the settlor and the trustees (*Nichols* v. *IRC* [1973] STC 497; [1975] STC 278; *Park* v. *IRC* [1970] 1 WLR 686; (*No.2*) [1972] Ch 3. Such arrangements may now involve sales and leases for dutiable consideration (see FA 1994, s.241).

The Inland Revenue Stamp Taxes Office may take the view that there is a sale and leaseback rather than just the gift of a reversionary interest. Pursuant to FA 1994, s.241 the stamp duty upon the transfer will be charged upon the market value of the lease which may be substantial if little or no rent is reserved and upon the lease for a premium equal to the value of the land transferred (less any actual consideration provided) plus upon any rent reserved. The Inland Revenue Stamp Taxes Office does not accept the argument that the land transferred is to be valued subject to the obligation to grant the leaseback.

The above is relatively straightforward where settlors intend merely to divest themselves of their beneficial interest and remain nominal owner of the property now subject to the trust, as where they remain the legal estate owners of land, or the registered proprietor of stocks and shares.

9.7   TRANSFERS SUBJECT TO DEBTS, MORTGAGES AND LIABILITIES

The SA 1891, s.57 enlarges the area of stampable consideration in two ways. It provides that where any property is conveyed (the same rules apply to the charges under the lease head of charge; see *Gingell* v. *Perkins* (1850) 4 Exch 720; *Quietlece* v. *IRC* [1984] STC 95) to any person in consideration, wholly or in part:

- in satisfaction of any debt due to the transferee; or
- subject either certainly or contingently to the payment or transfer of any money or stock, whether a charge on the property or not the debt money or stock is to be treated as the whole or part of the consideration chargeable with *ad valorem* duty.

It is, however, the second limb of SA 1891, s.57 concerned with the assumption of liabilities that causes the greatest hardship in relation to the computation of stamp duties. It should also be noted that there are only limited restrictions on the scope of the charge to the value of the property concerned. The duty is generally calculated by reference to the face value of the liabilities taken over. Where the transfer relates to property subject to a mortgage then the face value of the mortgage is added to the consideration paid to the equity of redemption (see **section 2.10.3**).

9.8   RESTRICTIONS ON CHARGEABLE AMOUNT

The charge under SA 1891, s.57 does not extend to liabilities that are inherent in the property transferred (*Swayne* v. *IRC* [1899] 1 QB 335; [1900] 1 QB 172), so that no liability arises on the assignment of a lease in respect of future rents, nor in the case of partly paid shares in respect of the uncalled liability, nor upon the assignment of a contract to purshase land where all or part of the consideration remains outstanding.

The amount of the stamp duty is restricted to the market value of the property transferred in two cases, namely:

- where the property is conveyed to a creditor and the value of the property is less than the amount discharged (FA 1980, s.102); and
- in the case of a foreclosure order the duty is not to exceed the value of the property (FA 1898, s.6).

Importantly for trustees paragraph 8 of Statement of Practice 6/90 provides (see **Appendix A**):

> Such an implied covenant may be negated if there is evidence that it was the intention of the parties at the time of the transfer that the transferor should continue to be liable for the whole of the mortgage debt. Where evidence of such a contrary intention exists, the transfer would again be treated for stamp duty purposes as a voluntary disposition. (Note the importance of LRA 1925, s.28 in relation to implied indemnities and the need for appropriate entries upon the land register.)

Basically if the settlor agrees to indemnify the trustees against liability in respect of the mortgage the instrument can be certified as exempt from stamp duty as a gift.

9.9   LAND TRANSACTIONS

The FA 2000, s.118 and s.119 to s.121 make certain land transfers into sales or transactions subject to *ad valorem* stamp duty by reference to market value. These are:

- land transferred as consideration in a land exchange but with a credit in certain cases (see **section 4.13**);
- transfers of land to a *connected body corporate* whether or not for a consideration with certain exemptions for transfers to nominees, certain corporate trustees and dispositions out of settlements (see **section 4.14**);
- leases of land to a *connected body corporate* whether or not for a consideration but without the benefit of the exemptions for nominee trustees and settlements (see **section 7.12.4**).

9.10   STAMP DUTY RESERVE TAX – AVOIDING UNNECESSARY CHARGES

A key issue in tax efficiency in establishing or vesting property in a trust is the avoidance of unnecessary stamp duty reserve tax. This tax is generally neglected by solicitors upon the relatively justifiable basis that it is predominantly a Stock Exchange tax collected through CREST. Unfortunately it also applies to off-market transactions and to shares in private companies.

Hitherto omissions to comply with the requirements of the tax have generally escaped the sanctions because of the inadequacy of the Inland Revenue Stamp Taxes Office's audit resources; but with the delegation of the audit of the proposed extended land stamp duty regimes to the Inland Revenue generally, errors in stamp duty reserve tax will be more frequently detected.

Familiarity with its provisions will, therefore, become a prerequisite for solicitors dealing with trusts and estates, but detailed analysis of the tax is outside the terms of this book.

It sometimes happens that a settlor agrees to purchase property and directs the vendor to transfer the property directly to the trustees of a settlement. This instrument completes two transactions and as, except in relation to land transfers it does not meet the conditions for subsale relief pursuant to SA 1891, s.58 it attracts:

- *ad valorem* stamp duty for the sale; and
- the fixed stamp duty of £5 as a gift unless certified pursuant to the Stamp Duty (Exempt Instruments) Regulations 1987, SI 1987/516.

However, where the conditions of FA 2000, s.119 apply the subsale relief may be available because there is a deemed sale at full market value.

Where the property is shares if the original purchaser directs a stock transfer form to the trustees then technically:

- the stock transfer form attracts ad valorem stamp duty in relation to the initial sale although exempt pursuant to the Stamp Duty (Exempt Instruments) Regulations 1987, SI 1987/516 in respect of the second limb;
- the stock transfer form completes two transactions and is dutiable in respect of both unless the conditions for subsale relief pursuant to SA 1891, s.58(4) are strictly observed (*Fitch Lovell Ltd* v. *IRC* [1962] 1 WLR 1325). It will be dutiable in respect of the sale but as the second leg is not a sale for full value the relief is not available. By entering into the purchase contract the settlors incur a liability to the principle charge to stamp duty reserve tax which is cancelled only by a duly stamped transfer to the settlor or a bare trustee for the settlor or the mortgagee in certain limited circumstances (FA 1986, s.87). The transfer is to the trustees. Technically as the transfer is not to the settlor although stamped in full the conditions for the cancellation of the charge are not satisfied. The Inland

214

Revenue Stamp Taxes Office tends to take this type of point in similar circumstances when it becomes aware of the facts.

In general there are few direct exemptions from the principal charge to stamp duty reserve tax; such exemptions as are available are totally dependent upon proper organisation of the stamp duty documentation. It is provided that the liability to the principal charge to the tax is retrospectively cancelled if within six years there is a duly stamped transfer to the relevant and correct party.

Failure to transfer to the correct party or to produce the correct documentation leaves the charge in place together with the penalties and interest for non-declaration and late payment. *Duly stamped* includes not only instruments subject to *ad valorem* stamp duty but also instruments subject to only the fixed duty or exempt altogether from duty; but the instrument has to be produced. It is no defence to a claim for stamp duty reserve tax that the stamp duty would have been nominal or nil. The stamp duty position must be properly dealt with including where necessary formal adjudication. In consequence where there is a transfer of shares to trustees it is necessary to investigate whether more than one transaction will be completed by the stock transfer form and whether one or two or more transfers in appropriate to minimise the stamp duty reserve tax charge.

9.11 AVOIDING UNNECESSARY DOCUMENTATION

It should be apparent that stamp duty can be saved in those cases where there is a sale in stamp duty terms where the transfer of ownership to the trustees can be carried out without documentation, provided the trust deed is executed first, as until the transfer takes place the trust is incompletely constituted. Cash, paintings, gold, jewellery and all manner of other chattels fall within the category of property transferable by physical delivery.

An acknowledgment of receipt by the trustees may be pounced upon by the Revenue as an instrument of transfer if it is able to say that it is *all one transaction* with the original trust declaration (such as where it was possibly in draft at the time of the oral declaration of trust (*Cohen and Moore* v. *IRC* [1933] 2 KB 126; or it was always intended to have a written memorandum). The Inland Revenue Stamp Taxes Office may seek to argue that the writing contained in the receipt is intended to prove the trustees' title to such property since a receipt may operate as a stampable memorandum (on receipts see, *Garnett* v. *IRC* (1899) 81 LT 633).

Unfortunately, it is difficult to envisage any potential saving where the order of the transactions is the other way round and the conveyance to the trustees precedes the declaration of the trusts. Once the legal and beneficial ownerships have become separated, albeit by resulting rather than express trust, a subsequent disposition of the beneficial interest cannot be made orally for reasons shortly to be discussed.

9.12 CONSTRUCTIVE AND RESULTING TRUSTS AND DRAFTING

The formalities for the creation of a trust of land do not affect the creation or operation of resulting, implied or constructive trusts (LPA 1925, s.53(2)). By their very nature such trusts arise without the formality of documentation recording their existence, but as they invariably attach themselves silently to a conveyance of the affected property, the conveyance itself will bear any duty payable, as in the case of a conveyance to co-owners who are also to take beneficially, whether or not the trusts for themselves are expressly declared.

However, as the decision in *Peter Bone Ltd* v. *IRC* [1995] STC 921 clearly shows, expressly recognising the implied, constructive and resulting trust by stating the trust relationship in the instrument is likely to convert a non-dutiable document into a stampable instrument. Relying upon the implied trust is not dutiable (*Angus* v. *IRC* (1889) 23 QBD 579; *West London Syndicate Ltd* v. *IRC* [1898] 2 QB 507) but making it an express trust is stampable (*Peter Bone Ltd* v. *IRC* [1995] STC 921).

9.13 DISPOSITIONS OF TRUST PROPERTY – DEALINGS IN EQUITABLE INTERESTS

A trust arises, however, whenever one person holds property subject to an obligation, enforceable by equity, to use the property in whole or in part for another. The classic example is where the legal estate or interest in, say, land or shares is vested in the trustee or trustees with a direction to hold upon stated trusts for the beneficiaries.

It has long since been recognised that the rights of the beneficiaries, though originally *in personam* only against the trustees, have acquired the status of interests in property enforceable historically against the whole world, save for the time honoured bona fide purchaser for value of the legal estate without notice, actual or constructive, of a prior equitable interest in the property, or those deriving title through such a person.

This rule has been substantially displaced by the doctrine of overreaching as enshrined in LPA 1925, s.2 whereby purchasers of a legal estate in land can ignore equitable interests regardless of notice provided they take the appropriate safeguards, e.g. by paying their money to the appropriate number of trustees in the case of a trust for sale or strict settlement.

Nevertheless, pending overreaching, the equitable rights arising out of the trust remain firmly interests in property, as illustrated with a vengeance by the House of Lords in its decision in *Williams & Glyn's Bank Ltd* v. *Boland*

[1981] AC 487. This aspect of the decision is reinforced by LP(MP)A 1989, s.1(6) and s.2(6) both of which define an interest in land for the purposes of the sections as: 'any . . . interests . . . in or over land or in or over the proceeds of sale of land'.

As property rights these equitable interests can in turn be held on a sub or derivative trust for further beneficiaries. On the creation of a trust, and the subsequent disposition thereof, beneficial interests in property are created or are disposed of, and, if the dealing is *inter vivos,* they are or were potentially subject to *ad valorem* duty, either as conveyances on sale if dutiable consideration if given, or deemed to be given by the legislation such as the connected company charges pursuant to FA 2000, s.119 and s.121.

Once a trust has been properly created, a separate problem arises on a subsequent disposition of the property. For so long as the trust exists, the legal or other interests held by the trustees can in general be freely transferred to other trustees without *ad valorem* duty, as no beneficial interest will pass and may be exempt from the fixed duty (Stamp Duty (Exempt Instruments) Regulations 1987, SI 1987/516, Category A.)

However, this is not an invariable rule. For example, although variations of trusts do not normally involve sales (*Henniker* v. *Henniker* (1852) 1 E & B 54) this depends upon the facts of the case, and in such situations a transfer between trustees may complete an earlier transaction and be dutiable accordingly (*Oughtred* v. *IRC* [1960] AC 206; *Parinv Investments* v. *IRC* [1998] STC 305). It is a moot point as to whether a fraudulent conveyance of trust property to a purchaser in bad faith with the intention (unfulfilled) of depriving the beneficiaries should bear an *ad valorem* stamp!

However, in relation to dealing, a beneficial interest upon sale *ad valorem* stamp duty can arise in two ways. The FA 1999, Sched.13 para.7 charges *ad valorem* stamp duty upon a written agreement for the sale of an equitable interest, and para.1 thereof charges duty upon a formal written assignment of the beneficial interest for consideration or any other instrument giving effect or recording such a transaction (*Oughtred* v. *IRC* [1960] AC 206). The question is how far such arrangements are legally effective if carried out orally. Unfortunately for the taxpayer LPA 1925, s.53(1)(*c*) states:

> . . . a disposition of an equitable interest or trust subsisting at the time of the disposition, must be in writing signed by the person disposing of the same, or by his agent thereunto lawfully authorised in writing or by will.

Unlike s.53(1)(*b*) of the same Act, the requirement of writing is not merely evidential, it is a matter of substance, and an oral disposition if voluntary will have no legal effect whatsoever. If consideration is given, however, an oral disposition may be treated by equity as a contract to transfer the beneficial interest at a later stage, at least in those cases where a written contract is not required (LP(MP)A 1989, s.2).

Being an oral contract it cannot bear duty under FA 1999, Sched.13 para.7 as a contract chargeable as a conveyance on sale, but the problem still remains as there can be no completion of the contract in the form of the effective passing of the full equitable title without writing.

The LPA 1925, s.53(2) and LP(MP)A 1989, s.2(6) provides that writing is not required for the effective creation of implied, resulting or constructive trusts (see on the current law *Yaxley* v. *Gotts* [1999] 2 WLR 1217). It is well established that where equity would order specific performance of the contract once payment in full is made (*Michaels* v. *Harley House (Marylebone) Ltd* [1999] 3 WLR 244 for part payment and vendor's liens) the equitable and beneficial interests pass to the purchaser, i.e. a constructive or implied trust arises in his or her favour (*Walsh* v. *Lonsdale* (1882) 21 Ch D 9).

This raises the question of the interaction of the charging provisions and LPA 1925, s.53(1)(c) which requires writing for the effective disposition of the equitable interest. *Oughtred* v. *IRC* [1960] AC 206 has been regarded as authority for the proposition that s.53(1)(c) prevails over s.53(2) and notwithstanding the constructive trust the equitable interest does not pass until the first written instrument dealing with the property.

However, this analysis must now be regarded as incorrect. The case was concerned with the situation where the vendor had only an equitable interest and could not control the legal title being a life tenant. The case does not deal with issues where the vendor has access to the legal title, such as the purchaser of land in a subsale situation or where the title is held upon trust for the vendor absolutely, at least if the owner of the legal title is bound to transfer the title at their direction or joins the contract agreeing to transfer the legal title.

In *Neville* v. *Wilson* [1997] Ch 144 the Court of Appeal held that the constructive trust operated to pass the equitable interest notwithstanding the absence of writing. This means that the decision in *Oughtred* v. *IRC* [1960] AC 206 is no more than a doubtfully valid application of the Memorandum Rules (see **section 1.12**).

Moreoverer, if instead of transferring the beneficial interest direct to the intended donee, donors instruct their trustees to hold the donors' beneficial interest for the donee in lieu of the donor, this is in substance also a disposition of the equitable interest, since it is an effective equitable assignment (*Re Tyler* [1967] 3 All ER 367; *Letts* v. *IRC* [1957] 1 WLR 201) and the direction to the trustees must be in writing if it is to be effective *Grey* v. *IRC* [1960] AC 1. If written, the direction will of course bear *ad valorem* duty on any consideration paid.

Trustees are, of course, entitled and possibly should be advised to refuse to act upon the basis of such written directions or other assignments unless they are duly stamped (see **Chapter 11**). A purchaser may, therefore, find it necessary to pay the stamp duty in order to obtain effective control of the property as against the vendor.

Instead of directing the trustees to hold for another, the beneficiary may, if the sole beneficiary, instruct the trustees to convey the property direct to an intended purchaser. It does not matter whether this instruction is in writing or given orally, as it is not the type of direction which passes the beneficial interest being merely a mandate to the trustees to transfer, the title passes by the conveyance by the trustees to the donee, conferring upon the donee the legal title for the donee's own use. The transfer of the legal title takes with it the equitable interest without the need for a separate written instrument. As such the conveyance, rather than the direction, will be stampable (*Vandervell v. IRC* [1967] 2 AC 291).

An interest in a trust fund is a *chose in action,* enforceable only by court action against the trustees at the instance of a beneficiary. Purchasers or assignees of a *chose in action* must remember to protect their interest by giving notice to the person obliged to distribute the property. There may, of course, be questions whether such notices are in substance equitable assignments (*Brandt's (Wm)* v. *Dunlop Rubber Co* [1905] AC 454).

It is thought that in order to be an equitable assignment the notice would require to be signed by at least the transferor or seller. In the case of a legal *chose in action* express written notice must be given to the debtor, trustee or other person from whom the assignor would have been entitled to claim the debt or *chose in action* (LPA 1925, s.126). An equitable interest in a trust fund should be protected in exactly the same way under the rule in *Dearle* v. *Hall* (1828) 3 Russ 1. Since 1925 the notice to the trustees must be in writing (LPA 1925, s.137) and to give maximum protection should be served on all the trustees (*Re Wasdale* [1899] 1 Ch 163).

Failure to serve notice may cause the donee to lose priority in the event of a subsequent dealing with the same interest. The same principles apply in registered land where the interests rank as minor interests. Any question of priority is governed by the rule in *Dearle* v. *Hall* in the same way as unregistered land.

9.14 CREATION OF DERIVATIVE TRUSTS

As an alternative to disposing of their equitable interest outright, the assignors may care to create a derivative or subtrust, leaving themselves as a buffer between the head trustees and the ultimate beneficiary. Thus if beneficiaries have, say, a life interest in property which they wish to sell to another, instead of assigning the interest outright they can convey it to a new set of trustees to hold on the stated trusts, or continue to hold it themselves as trustee, having moved the beneficial interest down one step by a declaration of trust. In either case the original trustees will remain owners of the legal estate and interest, and liable to account for the income to the new trustees of the life interest or the original life tenant, as the case may be. Original or new trustees in turn must pass the income down the line to the beneficiary.

If trustees of the life interest are to be appointed, exactly the same principles as above apply in properly constituting the trust, but as the subject matter of the conveyance to the trustees is a subsisting equitable interest, the conveyance must be in writing to satisfy LPA 1925, s.53(1)(c) or pass the equitable interest by constructive trust where this is permitted without writing (*Neville* v. *Wilson* [1997] Ch 144). This applies even though the property in the hands of the head trustees consists of property capable of transfer by delivery. Similar principles to those discussed above also apply in determining whether the contract, if any and if in writing, to dispose of the equitable interest is within FA 1999, Sched.13 para.7 or the assignment to the trustees or the declaration of trust bears the *ad valorem* stamp.

Where, however, the former beneficial life tenant chooses to remain trustee, he can make the declaration of trust orally, at least if the property out of which the trust has been created is personalty. If the trust is of land, unless a bare trust or a strict settlement governed by the Settled Land Act 1925 is involved, the legal estate will be held on trust for sale by the original trustees. As such, the property is treated by equity as personalty by the application of the doctrine of conversion. Nevertheless, the safer view appears to be that the beneficial interests are still in land until sale actually takes place. Certainly the interest of a tenant in common in equity under a trust for sale was held in *Cooper* v. *Critchley* [1955] Ch 431 to be an interest in land for the purpose of LPA 1925, s.40(1) before its repeal by LP(MP)A 1989, s.2. The LPA 1925, s.53(1)(b) governing the formation of trusts in land (which has not been repealed) is very similar in wording and purpose to the old s.40.

9.15 THE INTERNAL REARRANGEMENT OF BENEFICIAL INTERESTS

In the compliance regime applicable on and after 1 October 1999 trustees and executors dealing with beneficiaries who are not the original beneficiaries but are, for example, assignees of the original beneficiary should ensure that any documentation dealing with the change of the equitable interest is duly stamped. Under the present regime if trustees need to rely upon documentation to justify their conduct they may find themselves having to pay the stamp duty, penalties and interest upon such documents notwithstanding that they are not parties to the instruments in question (see **section 11.11**).

It should be remembered that a release of a beneficial interest under a trust will amount to a disposition if in writing and its effect is to move or create a beneficial interest in favour of another. Thus if instead of a life tenant selling his or her interest to the remainderman, he or she purports for consideration to surrender or release it, the effect is the same: the reversion is accelerated and falls into possession immediately (*Platts Trustees* v. *IRC* (1953) 34 ATC 292).

Before 19 March 1985 an *ad valorem* charge was payable on both gifts and sales but, in the case of a gift, the desired result could have been achieved by the trustees exercising their powers of advancement under the Trustee Act 1925, s.25 with the requisite consent of the life tenant. The consent of the life tenant to the arrangement is not a release of an interest (*Re Pauling's Settlement* [1962] 1 WLR 56). The powers are limited by the statute to the advancement of one half only of the actual or presumptive entitlement of the reversioner, but in a properly drawn trust deed these powers can and should be enlarged. The exercise of a power of advancement has never been a dutiable transaction.

Where the alteration of the equitable interest is effected with the assistance of the court pursuant to the Variation of Trusts Act 1958 the court order is a conveyance subject to stamp duty, possibly *ad valorem* and requires to be adjudicated (*Thorn* v. *IRC* [1976] 1 WLR 915; see also Practice Note [1966] 1 WLR 1455). Consequent upon the abolition of voluntary disposition duty by FA 1985, s.82 such arrangements not normally being *sales* (*Henniker* v. *Henniker* (1852) 1 E & B 54) will not normally attract *ad valorem* stamp duty but this is not a universal principle and sale duty may arise in the particular circumstances (*Oughtred* v. *IRC* [1960] AC 206).

Issues may arise where the trust asset concerned is land since trustees, settlors and beneficiaries are *connected persons* and the transfer of land to a company is potentially subject to *ad valorem* stamp duty pursuant to the connected company provisions in FA 2000, s.119 with only the limited exemption in s.120, Case 4 which applies where, among other things, the beneficiaries did not acquire the interest for money or money's worth.

It may be difficult to satisfy this requirement where the exchange or release of interest may represent money's worth, there being no exclusion for the making of the variation such as appears in FA 1985, s.84(2) for variations on death. The grant of a lease by trustees to a company may be dutiable upon market value pursuant to s.121 thereof and it is vital to note that there are no exemptions from this charge which applies even where the company is simply a nominee for the trustees or the beneficiary.

Instead of one party wishing to rearrange the beneficial interests so that an advantage is conferred on another, there may be a rearrangement of the interests under which neither party gains. It no longer matters that a voluntary substantial benefit may be conferred on one party (FA 1985, s.82) but if the consideration moving between the parties consists of shares or cash the transaction may be caught as a conveyance on sale (*Oughtred* v. *IRC* [1960] AC 206) and the same problems arise where interests in land are involved in the exchange or variation after 7 December 1993 (FA 1994, s.241).

The exchange of purely equitable interests in other property, however, does not constitute a sale as there is no chargeable consideration. Should any equality money be payable, a certificate of value can be given limited to the amount paid if within the appropriate limits.

9.16 INVESTIGATIONS OF TITLE

The historical issues are the usual problems of investigations into past titles or transactions. For example, where the enforceability or the vesting of property in the trustees or the construction of a trust created prior to 19 March 1985 may be called into question or examined, or where on a transfer or on a sale of the beneficial interest thereunder the issue may arise of whether the relevant documents required in evidence have been correctly stamped so as to be admissible (SA 1891, s.14(4)), so that a working knowledge of the old law will still be necessary to check the adequacy (or lack thereof) of the duty which should have been paid at the relevant time.

Similarly, where there are issues of whether trustees have acted properly in giving effect to a transaction which was carried out or is evidenced by unstamped or even stamped paper, the adequacy of that stamp may be an issue.

Notwithstanding the comments made in *Marx* v. *Estates and General Investments Ltd* [1976] 1 WLR 380 that the parties may act on the basis of an unstamped instrument, it was also pointed out that they thereby incur the risk that they may have to stamp the document if they need at any time to justify their conduct in court, and questions of penalties upon the relevant parties may arise (SA 1891, s.15(3)).

CHAPTER 10

The fixed duties

10.1 INTRODUCTION

Fixed duties are those imposed upon an instrument of a specified or limited amount regardless of the size or value of the transaction carried out by means of or the value of the property transferred or vested by that instrument. Thus a transfer of stock into the name of a nominee where this is dutiable as a 'conveyance or transfer not on sale' attracts only the fixed duty of £5 regardless of the value of the stock transferred. These were increased to £5 in all cases, including those leases formerly subject to the fixed stamp duty of £2, for instruments executed on or after 1 October 1999.

Example

It appears from current proposals for modernising land stamp duties that fixed duties are to be abolished as from early 2004 but it will be necessary to report all transactions which currently attract a fixed duty and are not taxable.

The report will act as a check for the Inland Revenue Stamp Taxes Office that *ad valorem* stamp duty is being properly paid – failure to report will no doubt attract some form of directly enforceable penalty upon audit.

A working knowledge of these principles is and will remain essential in order to make accurate returns.

It is vital to note that a knowledge of the principles relating to the fixed duties and the exemption is also currently important where shares are involved. The principal charge to stamp duty reserve tax (FA 1986, s.87) is wider than the stamp duty upon sales. It contains few exemptions and such reliefs as are available are obtained indirectly by producing a duly stamped stock transfer form within the prescribed time limits. Payment of £5 stamp duty or obtaining an exemption can cancel a much larger charge to stamp duty reserve tax.

In addition a knowledge of the Stamp Duty (Exempt Instruments) Regulations 1987, SI 1987/516 is helpful to the efficient operation of certain non-Stock Exchange transactions in listed securities through CREST. This tax is reportable and directly enforceable under penalties and interest. Currently few transactions are reported and these failures in tax compliance usually escape the attention of the Inland Revenue Stamp Taxes Office. It would, however, seem to be imprudent to assume that this happy state of errors escaping unnoticed will continued into the new regimes.

10.2 THE SCOPE OF FIXED DUTIES

The scope of the fixed duties is explained under the following headings.

10.2.1 Exemption

The FA 1985, s.85 and Sched.24 reduced the number of fixed duties. Doubtless the object of the exercise was to jettison as many nominal imposts as possible, the yield being out-weighed by the cost of collection. The main purpose of the retention of certain fixed duties of £5 is to enable the Inland Revenue Stamp Taxes Office to investigate whether *ad valorem* stamp duty is chargeable.

The Stamp Duty (Exempt Instruments) Regulations 1987, SI 1987/516 removed a wide range of instruments from the charge to the fixed duty as a 'conveyance or transfer not on sale' and, in certain cases, from the need to have the instrument adjudicated, provided that it is appropriately certified.

10.2.2 Conversion to *ad valorem* stamp duty

Numerous provisions have replaced the fixed duty of £5 with an ad valorem charge. In particular the fixed duties have been replaced by *ad valorem* charges in relation to the following situations:

- FA 1965, s.90 imposes a charge to *ad valorem* stamp duty upon transfers in contemplation of a sale whether this is to a potential purchaser or a third party such as a nominee (see **Appendix B**);
- FA 1994, s.241 has abolished the old fixed duty and special treatment for instruments formerly falling within the 'Exchange and excambion' head of charge; these are now dutiable as sales (see **section 4.13**);
- FA 1994, s.241 also enlarges the charge to lease premium duty to include premiums consisting of 'other property' which would formerly have attracted only the fixed duty (see **section 7.12.2**);
- FA 2000, s.118 has changed the position of land transferred as the consideration land in a land exchange, Since this subjects the transfer of the

consideration to stamp duty as a conveyance on sale the fixed stamp duty of £5 is not payable even where the reduction in the stamp duty payable operates to reduce the stamp duty back to nil which will usually be the case in land exchanges (see **section 4.13.3**);

- FA 1994, s.242 has imposed a charge to *ad valorem* stamp duty upon conveyance on sale and leases where all or part of the consideration is 'unascertainable' (see **section 2.15**);
- FA 2000, s.119 has imposed a charge to *ad valorem* stamp duty upon certain transfers to 'connected companies' which formerly might have attracted the fixed duty of £5 although there are certain limited exemptions for transfers to nominees in FA 2000, s.120 (see **section 4.14**);
- FA 2000, s.121 imposes a charge to *ad valorem* stamp duty to leases to 'connected companies' even where there is no consideration or the company is merely a nominee (see **section 7.12.4**).

There is a certain amount of pressure to present instruments subject only to the fixed duty of £5 to the Inland Revenue Stamp Taxes Office if only to enable it to investigate whether the instrument is liable to *ad valorem* stamp duty. Obviously such an instrument is unstamped and therefore inadmissible in evidence and subject to the other difficulties of such instruments.

In particular an instrument liable to the fixed duty of £5 is not subject to the late payment interest charge regime, but is subject to late stamping penalties regime in full in accordance with the normal principles of SA 1891, s.15B, namely:

- A maximum penalty of the amount of the stamp duty, i.e. £5 if presented within the first 12 months; and
- A penalty of £300 if presented after the 12 month period.

This arises because the penalty for the first period is restricted to the amount of the stamp duty so that the ceiling of £300 is irrelevant. However, after the expiration of the 12 month period the minimum penalty of £300 becomes potentially applicable. The Inland Revenue Stamp Taxes *Office Manual* indicates that no late stamping penalty will be levied if the documentation is presented within the 12 month period. Thereafter the level of late stamping penalty is a matter of individual review, but the £300 minimum penalty may be claimed.

10.2.3 Dating documents

Solicitors will also welcome the relief given from the small chore involved in presenting such documents for stamp duty. In the shadows, however, of this particular reform lurks a slight risk: the possibility of fraud arising out of the loss of the valuable notarial function of the stamp. Hitherto, the necessity to present for stamping every conceivable deed within 30 days of its execution gave a guarantee at least as to the document's minimum age. Now, in the case of a document completely released from any head of charge, as for a example a deed of covenant or most powers of attorney, it can be spirited by the unscrupulous out of thin air and, by being backdated, lay apparent claim to a bogus antiquity. Such activities are, however, manifestly criminal offences and even assisting in them could have serious consequences for the parties' professional advisers (*Saunders* v. *Edwards* [1987] 2 All ER 657).

Parties may, however, backdate the execution of an instrument or state that the instrument is to take effect from a prior date without such obviously fraudulent intention. Such an arrangement is, of course, legally ineffective, the instrument cannot take effect prior to its execution and cannot be expected to rewrite history (*Saywell* v. *Pope* [1979] STC 824).

Where the parties state that the transaction is to take effect from an earlier date, possibly with the seller being deemed to have acted as the purchaser's agent in the intervening period, this does not mean that the transaction took place earlier and in strict law is merely an accounting arrangement between the parties requiring an adjustment to the price (*Metal Box Plastic Films* v. *IRC* [1969] 3 All ER 1001).

10.2.4 Not on sale

It should nevertheless be borne in mind that many of the transactions enshrined in documents apparently subject to (or formerly subject to) a fixed duty may quite independently attract *ad valorem* duty as a conveyance on sale, a deemed conveyance on sale, or a contract chargeable as a conveyance on sale or as a lease premium pursuant to FA 1994, s.241.

The question of what is a '*sale*' or chargeable premium for these purposes particularly in relation to land transactions has been considered earlier (**sections 4.13** and **7.12.2**) and the following paragraphs must be read with that concept in mind.

It follows that fixed duties only come into play when there is no *ad valorem* duty payable, as, for example, when there is no passing or transfer of a beneficial interest, or no ascertainable or chargeable consideration.

Into this category of non-sales also fall conveyances for a consideration other than cash or those items treated as *cash* for the purpose of the charge to stamp duty, e.g. marriage or services (such as the grant of an option to acquire shares to an employee where no cash is paid for the option), agreements to carry out building works, conveyances where no beneficial interest passes, and conveyances or transfers of property (particularly of registered stock or securities) by way of security where the transfer on the face of it is absolute, whether or not accompanied by a memorandum of deposit. Subject to the necessity for a constant reminder of the above, the following documents are those which a conveyancing lawyer may meet and which still bear a nominal fixed duty.

10.3 CONVEYANCES

10.3.1 Conveyance or transfer otherwise than on sale

FA 1999, Sched.13 para.16 imposes stamp duty of £5 on a conveyance or transfer of property otherwise than on sale. For these purposes 'conveyance or transfer' includes every instrument, and every decree or order of a court or commissioners, by which any property is transferred to or vested in any person (see further **Chapter 4** on the meaning of *conveyance*).

It has been said that this definition should be construed *reddendo singula singulis*, the words *transferred to* being read with the word '*instrument*' and the words '*vested in*' being read with the words *decree or order*, but this has since been questioned, and it appears that an instrument creating property *de novo* such as an instrument granting put and call options may fall within this head of charge when not dutiable as a conveyance on sale pursuant to FA 1999, Sched.13 para.1 and SA 1891, s.60.

Transfers not on sale within the £5 charge include transactions such as:

- a transfer to a residuary legatee in satisfaction or part satisfaction of his share of residue;
- a transfer to a specific legatee;
- a transfer to a person entitled on intestacy (not being in satisfaction or part satisfaction of the spouse's fixed net sum);
- a transfer to a beneficiary under a settlement on distribution of the trust funds or by way of exercise of a power of advancement;
- a transfer by the liquidator of a company to shareholders in satisfaction of their rights in winding up;
- a conveyance or transfer to a pecuniary legatee or in satisfaction of a statutory legacy of the fixed net sum to the spouse of an intestate made under the statutory power of appropriation with the consent of the legatee is no longer dutiable as a conveyance on sale, (FA 1985, s.84) and is now dutiable under this head, where the personal representatives appropriate property to pecuniary legacies without the consent of the legatee under a clause in the will or otherwise, the contractual element then being missing;
- gifts, including dividends in specie (see **Chapter 8**);
- change of trustee;
- a transfer to or by or upon a change of nominee. A transfer not on sale, and where no beneficial interest passes, to a mere nominee of the transferor, or from one nominee to another nominee of the same beneficial owner;
- not all transfers to nominees will attract the fixed duty of £5; for example, a lease to a nominee which is a connected company dutiable *ad valorem* pursuant to FA 2000, s.121; or where executed in connection with depositary or clearance schemes may attract stamp duty or stamp duty reserve tax of 1.5 per cent;

- mortgages. Transfers of property by way of security where on the face of it the transfer is to be absolute, including retransfer on repayment of the loan. It is not possible since 1925 to mortgage a freehold or a leasehold by way of absolute transfer (LPA 1925, s.85 and s.86) but this method remains suitable for registered securities and *choses in action*. The Revenue is apparently not impressed with the argument that if the transaction is in reality a mortgage, it ought to be totally exempt under FA 1971, s.64;
- certain transfers exempted from conveyance on sale duty such as divorce arrangements and variation of wills and trusts;
- an exchange of property other than involving exchange of land or shares, both of which are dealt with under the separate head of charge 'Conveyance or Transfer on Sale' (FA 1994, s.241 – see **section 4.13**; and *J&P Coates Ltd* v. *IRC* [1897] 2 QBD 423 respectively).

10.4   EXEMPTIONS FROM THE FIXED DUTY FOR CONVEYANCES

Certain instruments are exempt from the fixed duty of £5 under this head of charge.

10.4.1   Certification

The FA 1985, s.87 provided machinery whereby regulations may be issued by the Commissioners of Inland Revenue and/or the Treasury under which upon insertion of an appropriate certificate an instrument ceases to be liable to a fixed duty. This power has been exercised in the Stamp Duty (Exempt Instruments) Regulations 1987 SI 1987/516 relieving many instruments executed on or after 1 May 1987 otherwise subject to the fixed conveyance duty of £5 pursuant to the following heads of charge:

- conveyance or transfer not on sale;
- declarations of trust;
- dispositions in Scotland;
- transfers in connection with matrimonial breakdown (FA 1985 s.83); and
- transfers in connection with variations of estates on death (FA 1985, s.84).

It is provided that the exemption is dependent upon the required certificate being included in the instrument which:

- shall be certified to be an instrument of the relevant kind; and
- shall not be treated as duly stamped if it is not so certified.

An instrument which is certified in accordance with these regulations shall not be required under FA 1985, s.82(5) or s.84(9) to be stamped in accordance with SA 1891, s.12 with a particular stamp denoting that it is duly stamped or that it is not chargeable with any duty.

10.5   EXEMPT CATEGORIES (A–N)

A.   The vesting of property subject to a trust in the trustees of the trust on the appointment of a new trustee, or in the continuing trustees on the retirement of a trustee.

The fixed duty on appointments was abolished by FA 1985, s.85. A deed of appointment or retirement however will impliedly (if not expressly) vest the trust property in the new or continuing trustees (see also Trustee Act 1925, s.40). This applies only in relation to trustees in the strict sense – transfers to nominees and bare trustees, changes of nominee and transfers by nominees to beneficial owners are not within this exemption and remain subject to the fixed duty of £5 as a 'conveyance or transfer not on sale'. The distinction is related to the question of whether the fiduciary has any powers or discretions which he may exercise (a trustee) or is totally under the control of the bene-ficial owner and has no power to act upon his own initiative (*Cowan de Groot Properties Ltd* v. *Eagle Trust* [1991] BCLC 1045). The point is important upon this issue and whether the transfer is dutiable as a transfer to a con-nected company pursuant to FA 2000, s.119 since the exemptions for trustees and nominees in s.120 thereof are different.

In some cases the vesting of property in a trustee may be dutiable as a sale and so outside the scope of this exemption. The main areas are:

- Where the trustees have agreed to purchase the asset from the transferor.
- Where the property is acquired by the trustees subject to a mortgage where SA 1891, s.57 may apply to convert this transfer into a sale. However, SP6/90 provides guidance as to when a transfer subject to a mortgage escapes this charge (see **Appendix A**).
- Where the conveyance or lease is to a corporate trustee which is a con-nected company (FA 2000, ss.119–21, see **sections 4.14** and **7.12.4**). An exemption certificate would not be appropriate in such a case unless the corporate trustees fall within the exemptions from the charge pursuant to FA 2000, s.120 which apply to a corporate trustee which is either:

  (a)   a person carrying on a business which consists of or includes the management of trusts; and is to hold the estate or interest as trustee acting in the course of that business; or

  (b)   as to hold the estate or interest as trustee and, apart from the Taxes Act 1988, s.839 (trustees as connected persons), would not be connected with B.

B.   The conveyance or transfer of property the subject of a specific devise or legacy to the beneficiary named in the will (or his nominee)

This does not apply to a transfer in satisfaction of a legacy which is within category D.

C. The conveyance or transfer of property which forms part of an intestate's estate to the person entitled on intestacy (or his nominee)

D. The appropriation of property within FA 1985, s.84(4) or s.84(5)

Formerly an appropriation for which the consent of the beneficiary is needed was treated as a conveyance on sale until the FA 1985, when duty was limited to a fixed 50p. The current position is:

- Where property is appropriated by a personal representative in or towards satisfaction of a general legacy of money, stamp duty under the heading conveyance or transfer on sale not be chargeable on an instrument giving effect to the appropriation (FA 1985, s.84(4));
- Where on an intestacy property is appropriated by a personal representative in or towards satisfaction of any interest of a surviving husband or wife in the intestate's estate, stamp duty under the heading mentioned in subsection (1) above is not chargeable on an instrument giving effect to the appropriation.

An interest in the intestate's estate:

  (a) includes a reference to the capital value of a life interest which the surviving husband or wife has under the Intestates' Estates Act 1952 elected to have redeemed, and
  (b) in Scotland, includes a reference to prior rights (within the meaning of the Succession (Scotland) Act 1964) but not to such rights as are mentioned in subsection (7).

- Where in Scotland, on an intestacy or otherwise, property is appropriated by a personal representative in or towards satisfaction of the right of a husband to *jus relicti*, of a wife to *jus relictae* or of issue to *legitim*, stamp duty under the heading conveyance on sale is not be chargeable on an instrument giving effect to the appropriation (FA 1985, s.64(5)–(7)).

An appropriation in satisfaction of a pecuniary legacy used to be regarded as a sale until FA 1985, s.84 on the grounds that if made under the statutory powers conferred by the Administration of Estates Act 1925, s.41 the consent of the beneficiary was required. Where, however, the executors are entitled to appropriate property, for example, under a power in the will, no consent is needed; so there was no *sale*. It is noteworthy that the element of consent in the context of a compulsory purchase order is somewhat fictitious, particularly where the Lands Tribunal determines the compensation. A compulsory purchase is nevertheless a sale for stamp duty purposes at such consideration as may have been agreed or ascertained at the date of the sale, or upon the market value pursuant to FA 1994, s.242.

Another appropriation arose where a surviving spouse on an intestacy took the family home in satisfaction of the statutory legacy. Where, however, the property appropriated was worth less than the statutory legacy, and was vested in her in satisfaction of her statutory entitlement, the Inland Revenue took the view that the surviving spouse, like a residuary legatee, was absolutely entitled to the property and the personal representatives had therefore to do as requested: there was no element of consensual bargain and thus no stamp duty on the assent as a conveyance on sale. Exemption to both kinds of appropriation is now given respectively by FA 1985, s.84(4) and (5).

Again, a deed of family arrangement may attract duty as a sale, as in *Oughtred* v. *IRC* [1960] AC 206, where a son orally agreed to surrender a reversionary interest to his mother, who was life tenant of the property, in return for other shares owned by the mother. The deed of transfer affecting the property, the subject of the reversion, was held to be a conveyance on sale in return for the mother's shares. It should be remembered that shares constitute consideration for the purposes of whether there is a *sale*. If, however, the mutual exchange is of equitable interests, there is no 'consideration' and therefore no sale, but if before 19 March 1985, one party received a 'substantial benefit', the transaction would have been dutiable *ad valorem* under FA 1910, s.74 as a gift.

Post-death variations, provided they are made within two years after the death and there is no consideration in money or money's worth other than the actual variation of the dispositions, are now expressly exempted from ad valorem duty (FA 1985, s.84). *Inter vivos* deeds of variation are not affected by this reform.

E. The conveyance or transfer of property which forms part of the residuary estate of a testator to a beneficiary (or his nominee) entitled solely by virtue of his entitlement under the will

Assents of land, if under hand, have long since been exempt from all duty if to a person to whom the property was devised. Other instruments of transfer now join them.

F. The conveyance or transfer of property out of a settlement in or towards satisfaction of a beneficiary's interest, not being an interest acquired for money or money's worth, being conveyance or transfer constituting a distribution of property in accordance with provisions of the settlement.

Vesting property in beneficiaries absolutely entitled or trustee pursuant ot the exercise of a power of appointment or advancement does not usually involve a *sale* and would attract the fixed £5 if not certified under this category. Variations of trusts are not usually *sales* (*Henniker* v. *Henniker* (1852) 1 E & B 54) but a transfer by trustees to a beneficiary on a variation may be dutiable as a conveyance or transfer on sale where the transferee acquired his interest by way of purchase (*Oughtred* v. *IRC* [1960] AC 260). It must also be noted that a transfer of land out of a trust falls within the charging provisions in FA 2000, s.119 where connected companies are involved subject to an exemption where there is a transfer by trustees who are not nominees or bare trustees. The charge does not apply where:

- The transfer or vesting is a conveyance or transfer out of a settlement in or towards satisfaction of a beneficiary's interest.
- The beneficiary's interest is not an interest acquired for money or money's worth. Where there was such a previous sale the transfer may also complete that previous sale of the interest (*Oughtred* v. *IRC* [1960] AC 206); there is, therefore, a potential double charge to stamp duty upon the agreement to sell the equitable interest (FA 1999, Sched.13 para.7 – see **section 5.3**) or any assignment of the interest and upon the extraction of the land from the settlement. This may apply even where the interest is in an overseas trust (*Farmer* v. *IRC* [1898] 2 QB 141) and depending upon the circumstances as the instrument may relate to land in the UK the late stamping penalty may run from 30 days after execution (FA 2002, s.114) as well as the late payment interest charge (SA 1891, s.15A).
- The conveyance or transfer is a distribution of property in accordance with the provisions of the settlement (FA 2000, s.120, Case 4).

G. **The conveyance or transfer of property on and in consideration only of marriage to a party to the marriage (or his nominee) or to trustees to be held on the terms of a settlement made in consideration only of the marriage**

Since marriage is not '*other property*' the provisions of FA 1994, s.241 do not apply to treat such transfers as sales. It should, however, be noted that the charge to *ad valorem* stamp duty upon the market value of land pursuant to FA 2000, s.119 can apply to transfers to corporate trustees since a trustee is connected with the settlor. That charge overrides the exemption for gifts in the case of land.

H. **The conveyance or transfer of property with in FA 1985, s.83(1) (i.e. divorce and separation arrangements)**

A court order transferring property is included in the definition of a 'conveyance on sale', and a transfer by one spouse to another following an order will be stamp able *ad valorem* (subject to a certificate of value) if made for financial consideration and where shares are involved may attract the principal charge to stamp duty reserve tax (FA 1986, s.87). If, however, no consideration was given, it was the practice of the Inland Revenue to treat the conveyance as liable to a fixed duty as a conveyance not on sale. The same applied to transfers independently of a court order where made in settlement of the recipient spouse's claim to capital or maintenance, as the abandonment of and forbearance to pursue a claim, though consideration for contract purposes, does not rank as dutiable consideration (*Re Abbott* [1982] 3 All ER 181).

The position of separated or divorcing parties was regularised and clarified by FA 1985, s.83 which provides that (conveyance or transfer on sale) duty shall not be chargeable on an instrument by which property is conveyed or transferred from one party to a marriage to the other if the instrument:

- is executed in pursuance of an order of a court made on granting in respect of the parties a decree of divorce, nullity of marriage or judicial separation; or
- is executed in pursuance of an order of a court which is made in connection with the dissolution or annulment of the marriage or the parties' judicial separation and which is made at any time after the granting of such a decree; or
- is executed in pursuance of an order of a court which is made at any time under the Matrimonial Causes Act 1973, s.22A, s.23A or 24A; or
- is executed at any time in pursuance of an agreement of the parties made in contemplation of or otherwise in connection with the dissolution or annulment of the marriage, their judicial separation or the making of a separation order in respect of them.

The transfer may also be made by agreement between the parties at any time, either before or after dissolution, annulment or judicial separation, and before those proceedings are commenced.

I. The conveyance or transfer by the liquidator of property which formed part of the assets of the company in liquidation to a shareholder of that company (or his nominee) in or towards satisfaction of the shareholder's rights on a winding-up

This exemption is not available where the shareholders accept the assets in satisfaction of a debt owed to them by the company in liquidation, or where the shareholders assume outstanding liabilities of the company as consideration for the transfer (*Henty & Constable Brewers Ltd* v. *IRC* [1961] 3 All ER 1146). Such an arrangement is treated by SA 1891, s.57 as a conveyance on sale. For example, a transfer by the liquidator to the members of freehold property which is subject to a mortgage (even it seems a charge to secure a guarantee of another company's indebtedness) and the shareholders assume liability for a mortgage, or a transfer of property where the members agree to discharge outstanding trade liabilities of the company would be stampable as sales. This applies even where the mortgage or charge was given by way of security for a guarantee and remains a contingent or prospective liability of the time of the transfer.

However, the general indemnity against unknown liabilities which is usually given to liquidators at the end of the winding-up as part of their discharge order does not result in the loss of their exemption. On going into liquidation the company ceases to be the beneficial owner of its assets and in consequence the transfer does not pass beneficial ownership from the company in liquidation (*Ayerst* v. *C&K (Construction) Ltd* [1976] AC 167).

Hitherto there has been no indication in practice that the Inland Revenue Stamp Taxes Office considers taking the point that being a transfer of land for an unascertainable consideration it is subject to ad valorem stamp duty upon the market value pursuant to FA 1994, s.242 (see **section 2.15**).

The liquidation may not trigger the clawback of any previous exemptions obtained pursuant to FA 1930, s.42; FA 1995, s.151 or FA 1986, s.76 but the position should be investigated since there is an obligation under penalty to report the occurrence of a clawback event (FA 2002, ss.111 and 113). A distribution of land by a liquidator may fall within the *ad valorem* stamp duty charge pursuant to FA 2000, s.119 but s.120(8) thereof provides for an exemption in Case 7 where:

- B is a company;
- the transfer or vesting is, or is part of, a distribution of assets (whether or not in connection with the winding up of the company); and
- the estate or interest was acquired by B by virtue of an instrument which is duly stamped.

The transfer will be not eligible for relief pursuant to FA 1930, s.42 (as amended) unless executed pursuant to a preliquidation agreement (*Escoigne Properties* v. *IRC* [1958] 1 All ER 406) even though the company in liquidation is a wholly owned subsidiary of its shareholder. It seems that in practice the Inland Revenue Stamp Taxes Office permits the use of this category to exempt transfers on the winding up of a unit trust scheme provided that a liquidator has been formally appointed.

J. **The grant in fee simple of an easement in or over land for no consideration in money or money's worth**

K. **The grant of a servitude for no consideration in money or money's worth**

L. **The conveyance or transfer of property operating as a voluntary dispositions *inter vivos* for no consideration in money or money's worth nor any consideration referred to in SA 1891, s.57**

The first points to note are the limitations to the concept of '*gift*' for these purposes (see also **Chapter 8**). It does not apply here the transaction is otherwise dutiable such as a sale at an undervalue which is stampable on the price. It applies to dividends *in specie* by companies (*Wigan Coal and Iron Co* [1945] 1 All ER 392), but it does not apply to transfers of property subject to a mortgage where SA 1891, s.57 applies. This charge does not apply where the transferor agrees to indemnify the donee or transferee against liability in respect of the mortgage in accordance with the provisions set out in Statement of Practice SP6/90 (see **Appendix A**).

The rules relating to gifts have been substantially modified where land is involved. The FA 2000, ss.119 and 121 provided that, among other things, gifts of land including gifts by way of lease to a connected company is stampable *ad valorem* upon the market value (see **sections 4.14** and **7.12.4**). This also applies leases and certain transfers to corporate trustees. The charge also applies to gifts of land to companies where the parties are seeking to take advantage of the capital gains relief pursuant to the Taxation of Chargeable Gains Act 1992, s.165. There are, however, exemptions for gifts to corporate trustee by way of conveyances, but not for leases, pursuant to FA 2000, s.120. In situations within the exemptions in s.120 the certificate procedure can be adopted.

M. The conveyance or transfer of property by an instrument within section 84(1) of the Finance 1985. This applies to instruments varying dispositions on death such as deeds of family arrangement)

This deals with instruments of post-death variation. Before the repeal of duty on voluntary dispositions a document varying the disposition of property under a will or intestacy was normally liable to *ad valorem* duty as a voluntary disposition, or occasionally as a conveyance on sale where, e.g. a transfer of shares was involved (*Oughtred* v. *IRC* [1960] AC 206).

Variations of estates on death are not normally sales (*Henniker* v. *Henniker* (1852) 1 E & B 54) but this depends upon the precise circumstances (*Oughtred* v. *IRC* [1960] AC 206) and the extension of the definition of '*sale*' in relation to land transactions by the FA 1994, s.241 has increased the scope of the *ad valorem* charge.

Moreover, it must be noted that the principal charge to stamp duty reserve tax applies to transfers for value which is wider than sales (FA 1986, s.87). This principal charge can, therefore, apply to variations of estates where shares and loan stocks are involved; but it is cancelled where a duly stamped transfer is produced which includes an instrument that is certified as exempt pursuant to this category. The instrument must, however, be produced. It is not sufficient to claim that no duty would have been payable had it been executed.

Where, within the period of two years after a person's death, any of the dispositions (whether effected by will, under the law relating to intestacy or otherwise) of the property of which he or she was competent to dispose are varied by an instrument executed by the persons or any of the persons who benefit or would benefit under the dispositions, conveyance or transfer on sale duty is not chargeable on the instrument, provided that the variation is not made for any consideration in money or money's worth other than consideration consisting of the making of a variation in respect of another of the dispositions.

The relief applies whether or not the administration of the estate is complete or the property has been distributed in accordance with the original dispositions. FA 1985, s.4 makes such instrument dutiable with the fixed duty of £5 but requires that it be adjudicated. This category exempts from that the fixed duty and the adjudication requirement.

N.   A declaration of use or trust of or concerning a life policy or property representing benefits, or benefits arising under, a life policy

10.6   FORM OF CERTIFICATE

If a document falls within one of the above categories the appropriate certificate should be completed and signed, and the document then sent direct to the Registrar or other person who needs to act upon it. Some of the categories (D, L and M) formerly required adjudication but this requirement has now been abolished: none of the documents is to be sent to the Inland Revenue Stamp Taxes Office or to be sent for adjudication.

A conveyance on which *ad valorem* duty is avoided solely by virtue of the inclusion of a certificate of value does not fall within this category; it falls under the head of charge 'Conveyance or Transfer on sale' and the certificate gives a total exemption insofar as the document deals with the transfer of ownership.

The form of the certificate which must be signed by the transferors or grantors or by their solicitor or duly authorised agent (but note not the transferee or grantee or his representative or agents) should be in the form:

> I/We hereby certify that this instrument falls within category . . . in the Schedule to the Stamp Duty (Exempt Instrument) Regulations 1987.

Where the certificate is not inserted into the instrument or endorsed thereon it should carry sufficient information to identify the instrument to which it refers and may be itself executed or endorsed on the instrument after the execution of that instrument. The named must insert a statement of the capacity in which he or she signs; that he or she is authorised to sign and that he or she gives the certificate from their own knowledge of the facts stated in it.

Three points require notice:

- In the absence of the certificate, the fixed duty remains payable.
- In the absence of the certificate adjudication may be necessary in order to be *duly stamped* for stamp duty purposes.
- In the absence of the certificate the instrument even though not liable to any stamp duty will not be *duly stamped* and this may mean that the

liability to the principal charge to stamp duty reserve tax which arises where the instrument involves chargeable securities will not be cancelled.

10.7 DISPOSITIONS IN SCOTLAND

FA 1999, Sched.13 para.18 provides that the following are chargeable with duty as a conveyance on sale:

- a disposition of heritable property in Scotland to singular successors or purchasers;
- a disposition of heritable property in Scotland to a purchaser containing a clause declaring all or any part of the purchase money a real burden upon, or affecting, the heritable property thereby disponed, or any part of it;
- a disposition in Scotland containing constitution of feu or ground annual right.

A disposition in Scotland of any property, or any right or interest in property, that is not so chargeable is chargeable with stamp duty of £5.

10.8 DECLARATION OF USE OR TRUST NOT ON SALE

Stamp duty of £5 is chargeable on a declaration of any use or trust of or concerning property unless the instrument constitutes a conveyance or transfer on sale. This does not apply to a trust declared by a will (FA 1999, Sched.13 para.17). It makes no difference whether or not the declaration is by deed.

It has, however, been noted in Chapter 9 on trusts that, as a declaration of trust by its nature is intended to pass or create a beneficial interest, it will be chargeable to full *ad valorem* duty as a conveyance on sale if for an appropriate consideration, but no longer if made voluntarily; this can be a problem where the property is charged (SA 1891, s.57 but see Statement of Practice SP6/90).

This *ad valorem* charge extends to an express declaration of that which is in any event implied in a contract for sale, namely the creation of beneficial interests in favour of the purchaser (*Chesterfield Brewery Co* v. *IRC* [1899] 2 QB 7). A declaration of trust by a vendor in favour of the purchaser for a cash consideration is a conveyance on sale (*Peter Bone Ltd* v. *IRC* [1995] STC 921). In such cases it may be necessary to produce the declaration of trust for stamping in order to prove that any later transfer to the beneficial owner is not a conveyance on sale but is merely a transfer under which no beneficial interest passes (*Parinv* v. *IRC* [1998] STC 305). It may, however, destroy the benefit of subsale relief and expose the parties to penalties if not disclosed in such a case (see **section 11.3.1**).

10.9 DUPLICATE OR COUNTERPART

FA 1999, Sched.13 para.19 provides that a duplicate or counterpart of an instrument chargeable with duty is chargeable with duty of £5. Apart from the case of a counterpart lease and it would seem a counterpart agreement for lease the duplicate or counterpart of an instrument chargeable with duty is not duly stamped unless:

- it is stamped as an original instrument; or
- it appears by some stamp impressed on it that the full and proper duty has been paid on the original instrument of which it is the duplicate or counterpart.

There are no provisions identifying what is the counterpart or duplicate but since in general there has to be an instrument bearing the *ad valorem* stamp duty in existence when the instrument is presented it would seem that the original is the one which is first produced to the Inland Revenue Stamp Taxes Office.

This is not to be confused with the former deed stamp, as a duplicate or counterpart whether under hand only or of an instrument taking effect as a deed is chargeable under this head.

10.9.1 Counterpart Leases

The need for a duly stamped original does not apply to the counterpart of an instrument chargeable as a lease, if that counterpart is not executed by or on behalf of any lessor or grantor. The requirement that the original lease should be stamped before the counterpart can be stamped only with the fixed duty of £5 does not apply to the counterpart of an instrument chargeable as a lease, if that counterpart is not executed by or on behalf of any lessor or grantor.

This special treatment would appear to extend to a counterpart agreement for lease since this is an instrument stampable as a lease. This would appear to be a useful protection for landlords who may need to rely upon an unstamped agreement for lease prior to the grant of the lease such as when suing the tenant for specific performance of the agreement for lease or breach of the building agreement particularly since the lease will not be available to defer the commencement of the late stamping penalty and the late payment interest charge.

It remains to be seen whether the Inland Revenue Stamp Taxes Office will accept this argument in relation to a 'counterpart building agreement' with a draft lease scheduled thereto when there are two documents and only the tenant has signed the landlord's documentation.

10.10   EXCHANGES AND PARTITIONS

The position regarding exchanges of land and transfers on leases of land in consideration of any other property, whether land or not, was fundamentally changed by FA 1994, s.241. Such transfers are now dutiable *ad valorem* under the head of charge 'Conveyance or Transfer on sale' and are discussed at **section 4.12.2**). If a contract for sale is completed, not by payment of money or chargeable consideration but by an exchange of land, and this was not expressly contemplated in the original contract, the deed of exchange will be viewed by the Inland Revenue Stamp Taxes Office, and with the court's blessing, as a conveyance on sale completing the original contract (*Portman* v. *IRC* (1956) 35 ATC 349 but see Sargent J. in *Re Duke of Westminster's Settled Estates* [1921] 1 Ch. 585 at p. 591 to the contrary – this decision was not cited in the *Portman* case.)

It should, however, be possible to escape this consequence if the original two contracts of sale are rescinded and replaced by an agreement to exchange the properties (*Cottingham* v. *Central Land Board* [1957] 8 P&CR 339). The moral is therefore repeated: having entered into a contract to buy, if the parties wish to give effect to their agreement by exchanging land instead of handing over cash, the original agreement must be amended or supplanted by an agreement to exchange. It is, however, necessary to be aware of the former rules for the purposes of investigating titles.

10.10.1   Exchanges pre Finance Act 1994 changes

In the case specified in SA 1891, s.73 the duty was payable in accordance with that section, and in any other case was 50p. This provided that, upon the exchange of real or heritable property for other real or heritable property, or upon the partition or division thereof, where any equality money in excess of £100 was paid or agreed to be paid, the conveyance or deed of exchange was to be charged with the same *ad valorem* duty as a conveyance on sale for the consideration paid as equality money. The effect was to exempt from *ad valorem* stamp duty a document or deed of exchange where the equality money or consideration paid does not exceed £100.

The scope of SA 1891, s.73 in any other case was strictly limited to the exchange of realty for realty and in the case of *IRC* v. *Littlewoods Mail Order Stores Ltd* [1963] AC 135 it was held that an exchange of a freehold for a leasehold did not fall within this head of charge but was chargeable as a conveyance of any other kind and was subject to the fixed 50p duty payable under that head. It has already been observed in the discussion on dutiable consideration in Chapter 4 on the conveyance on sale (**section 4.12.2**) that shares rank as chargeable consideration and, if the exchange is of one lot of shares for another, so far from being exempt under SA 1891, s.73 there is, on the contrary, a double charge for stamp duty, the exchange being considered to be a sale of one lot for another and vice versa (*J & P Coats Ltd* v. *IRC* [1897] 1 QB 778).

If the exchange was of property other than freehold land, there are three points to note. The first was that only the fixed duty was payable regardless of the size of the equality payments.

The second was that, as in *J & P Coats Ltd* v. *IRC* [1897] 1 QB 778 (exchange per shares) the property, the subject of the exchange, may be classified as dutiable consideration, i.e. be treated the same as cash. There is, however, a longstanding but unpublished practice of the Inland Revenue Stamp Taxes Office that in certain cases such mutual transfers of shares may be treated as a single sale with one stock transfer form attracting the *ad valorem* duty and the other bearing the fixed conveyance duty of £5. This may, it now seems, be in the view of the Inland Revenue Stamp Taxes Office, a matter of drafting (*Connell* v. *Begej* (1993) 39 EG 125).

The third point was that should the trap just mentioned be avoided because the property exchanged was not treated as consideration there was not the charge within s.73. This third point, however, was of little significance since where there was an exchange or partitions of freehold land within the charge of s.73 a certificate of value could be given for equality money up to £60,000, quite regardless of the worth of the property exchanged which, by its nature, did not rank as part of the consideration.

10.10.2   Post Finance Act 1994 changes

The effect of the land exchanges and the *single sale* issue provisions is that, prima facie, an exchange of freehold land for freehold land or for any other property is no longer an exchange subject to the fixed duty of £5 as a 'conveyance or transfer not on sale' but is now potentially a double sale, each of which is subject to *ad valorem* stamp duty. However, it seems that notwithstanding their initial stance in the Notes to the FA 1994 the Inland Revenue Stamp Taxes Office is prepared to accept that it may be possible to arrange matters in such a way that what is in substance a mutual transfer of real properties is, subject to the implications of and the relief provided for by FA 2000, s.118 in fact dutiable as a *single sale* (see **section 4.13.3**).

In fact given the drafting of FA 2000, s.118 it may be necessary to prepare the documentation as a *single sale* in order to obtain the benefit of the reduction provided for the consideration land in s.118. It seems that in order to obtain the benefit of this *single sale* approach it is necessary to draft the contract and conveyance as a transfer of the property in consideration of a cash sum to be satisfied by the transfer of the other property or properties and a payment of a cash balance.

There may be difficulties in drafting the formal Land Registry transfer or conveyance of the other property forming the consideration. It seems that the

Inland Revenue Stamp Taxes Office is not prepared to accept a transfer made *as consideration for* or *in consideration of* the transfer of the first property as qualifying as a single sale. However, by subjecting the transfer of the consideration land to *ad valorem* stamp duty with a credit FA 2000, s.118 has removed this type of transfer from liability to the fixed duty of £5 since it is deemed to be a conveyance on sale.

In relation to those cases where FA 1994, s.241 does not apply and the instrument is not obviously a sale but where there is equality money (i.e. where it is a case of part exchange) the legislation would seem to raise some doubt as to whether this type of transaction constitutes a *sale* either in whole or in part. This is significant since if the transaction is not a sale because the whole of the consideration for the transfer does not fall within that which qualifies a transaction as a sale the purposes of stamp duty then the instrument is subject only to the fixed stamp duty of £5 under this head and there is no *ad valorem* stamp duty upon the cash or other component in the consideration whereas such consideration would attract *ad valorem* stamp duty if there is such a concept as a *part sale* for the purposes of stamp duty.

Certain cases suggest that such a transaction is in part a sale and is probably under SA 1891, s.4(*b*) to the extent that the consideration is cash, dutiable as such, but such cases may be capable of being explained as the parties agreeing a price in cash part of which is to be satisfied by the transfer of property. Where there is no pre-agreed cash sum but the agreement is for part exchange or barter with cash equality the transaction would appear not to be a sale in any respect.

It appears that this was formerly not the view of the Inland Revenue Stamp Taxes Office which, whilst regarding the position as *anomalous*, did not treat such exchanges of property other than interests in land with cash equality as *part-sales* and claim only £5 duty under the previous head as a 'conveyance or transfer not on sale'. This view seems difficult to justify on the cases but it has considerable technical merit to support it and these technical arguments do not appear to have been put forward in the cases so that their authority may be somewhat limited on this point.

In relation to the former head of charge 'Exchange or excambion' considered above, no *ad valorem* duty would seem to be payable apart from the specific provisions of now repealed provisions in SA 1891, s.73 (as unamended) which charges duty upon any equality payment as a conveyance on sale. In other words, SA 1891, s.73 can be regarded as a particular charging provision indicating that a consideration consisting only partially of cash does not involve a part sale and a sale is limited to situations where the consideration consists solely of cash or its equivalent for stamp duty purposes.

However, it seems from the Inland Revenue *Tax Bulletin* for August 1995 that this view may have been changed. The wording in the *Tax Bulletin* is slightly ambiguous but it does contain a suggestion that the Inland Revenue

Stamp Taxes Office may now be looking to put forward the *part sale* argument notwithstanding the previous technical analysis in this paragraph.

In most situations this narrow interpretation of part-exchanges not being sales seems to be favourable to the taxpayer. In particular, it means that should any value added tax arise on the transaction, it will not be subject to stamp duty. The position may, however, be disadvantageous in certain *subsale* situations when one stage of the transaction is a part exchange since not all stages will be sales. However, the continued extension of the definition of *sale* in relation to land transactions such as FA 1994, s.241 and FA 2000, s.118 has eased these problems significantly.

The former difficulties which arose when a developer agreed to purchase land and having carried out the development entered into a part exchange with the sub-purchaser have been overcome and the conditions for subsale relief which require the payment by the subpurchaser of a full *cash* consideration will now have been satisfied, provided that the relevant contracts and transfer are so drafted that the transfer in question is stampable as a sale pursuant to FA 1994, s.241.

Subject to the view set out above being correct, a conveyance of land in consideration of cash payment plus the grant of a leaseback of all or part of the same land would seem to be dutiable as a sale in respect of the cash payment, no duty arising in respect of the leaseback by reason of FA 1900, s.10. This provision surprisingly appears to have been left unchanged by the FA 1994, s.241. The leaseback could now attract duty in respect of the land being transferred as consideration for the grant since this is now a dutiable premium. However, in cases where the lease is granted in respect of land other than that conveyed with a cash equality sum being paid by the lessee to the grantor such cash attracts lease premium duty.

If a mutual transfer of property of this type is very beneficial to one party the Revenue could formerly claim duty on the conveyance to that party as a voluntary disposition *inter vivos* and, notwithstanding the abolition of that duty by the FA 1985, such an instrument would now require to bear a denoting stamp and £5 duty under this head. The Stamp Duty (Exempt Instruments) Regulations 1987, SI 1987/516 would seem to be inapplicable as the transfer was made for valuable consideration.

10.10.3 Partitions or divisions post Finance Act 1994

A partition of property is essentially an arrangement whereby there are mutual exchanges of equitable or beneficial interests in jointly owned property with the result that any instrument transferring part of the property to its new individual as opposed to former joint owners is a transfer for consideration. There is no statutory definition for the purposes of the head of charge but the Inland Revenue Stamp Taxes *Office Manual* states:

4.458. Partition or Division

A partition or division of any estate or interest in land may take place when there are mutual exchanges of part of formerly jointly-owned property; and as a result there is a transfer for consideration of that property.

This raises two issues, namely:

- the exchange of equitable interests in a single jointly owned parcel of land; and
- the division of numerous jointly owned assets amongst co-owners such as on the dissolution of a partnership.

A partition is not a sale (*Henniker* v. *Henniker* (1852) 1 E & B 54; as to partitions and dissolutions of partnership see *Macleod* v. *IRC* (1885) 12 R (Ct of Session)) but FA 1999, Sched.13 para.21 provides that stamp duty of £5 is chargeable upon an instrument effecting a partition or division except where on the partition or division of an estate or interest in land consideration exceeding £100 in amount or value is paid or given, or agreed to be paid or given, for equality, the principal or only instrument by which the partition or division is effected is chargeable with the same ad valorem duty as a conveyance on sale for the consideration, and with that duty only. As the duty is under the sale head the lower rates of stamp duty are available where the equality payment does not exceed the £500,000 threshold.

Where there are several instruments for completing the title of either party, the principal instrument is to be ascertained, and the other instruments shall be charged with duty, as provided by SA 1891, s.58(3) and s.61 (but see *Parinv* v. *IRC* [1998] STC 305).

It should be noted that the former charge pursuant to the repealed SA 1891 s.73 has been enlarged. Formerly limited to partitions of freehold land, it now applies to the partition of any interest in land including a partition of a leasehold interest. The effect of the enlargement of is that equality payments on partitions of leases are now dutiable *ad valorem*.

On recent Inland Revenue Stamp Taxes Office practice it is important to ensure that any partition of land is not expressed as being in consideration of the mutual transfer of the parties' undivided interests in the estate or land, since following FA 1994, s.241 this may be regarded by the Inland Revenue Stamp Taxes Office as a series of mutual *sales*, dutiable accordingly. By reason of the *Portman* case (1956) ATC 349 it will be necessary to ensure that any preliminary contracts to divide the land or assets are suitably drafted and do not refer to one of the parties transferring his undivided interest in part of the relevant asset to the other party who thereby becomes solely entitled to that part, in consideration of the latter transferring his part interest in the single or another asset with like consequences.

Such drafting may now attract *ad valorem* conveyance on sale duty at up to the 4 per cent rate probably upon both sides of the transaction. A contract in this form is likely to give rise to a claim by the Inland Revenue Stamp Taxes Office that the formal deed of partition bears *ad valorem* stamp duty as implementing one or more exchanges of interests in land and any written contract may be dutiable pursuant to FA 1999, Sched.13 para.7.

Where such a partition gives rise to charges to value added tax it is thought that any cash paid is a payment by way of tax and not by way of equality and so is not subject to stamp duty, although it seems that the Inland Revenue Stamp Taxes Office may take the opposite view.

It would appear from the terms of the partition head of charge that upon the partition of any property other than any estate or interest in land no charge to *ad valorem* duty can arise even though there may be an equality payment. It must, however, be noted that what is expressed to be a partition of assets including property other than land may not be a partition within this head of charge but an exchange or transfer of an interest in land in consideration of other property which constitutes a *sale* pursuant to FA 1994, s.241.

This does, however, depend upon the circumstances of the particular case and the structuring and drafting of the documentation. However, the mere existence of a consideration consisting of or including cash or shares does not automatically take the instrument out of the relevant fixed duty head and into the head 'Conveyance or Transfer on Sale.' Thus a partition of property not involving a partition of any estate or interest in land within FA 1999, Sched.13 para.21 is not necessarily dutiable *ad valorem* even though there may be a cash payment to produce a correct pro rata partition.

10.11 PARTNERSHIP ISSUES

In *MacLeod* v. *IRC* (1885) 12 R (Ct of Sess) 1045 which concerned property upon the winding up of a partnership, under which one of the partners received cash, it was held that the instrument was not dutiable as a sale and was properly chargeable with the fixed duty of only £5 as a conveyance or transfer not on sale. (See also *Henniker* v. *Henniker* (1852) 1 E&B 54; *Christie* v. *IRC* (1866) LR 2 Ex 46.)

The Inland Revenue Stamp Taxes *Office Manual* states:

4.463. Partition on the Dissolution of a Partnership

A dissolution of a partnership is the most common transaction which falls within the Partition or Division provisions. The most straightforward partnership dissolution is the final winding up when the partnership ceases to trade and its assets are sold. The partnership liabilities are satisfied out of the sale proceeds and the balance is divided among the partners in accordance with the Articles of the partnership. A document under which property is partitioned on the winding up of a partnership is not dutiable as a sale, but is chargeable under the provisions of Partition or Division (*Macleod* v. *IRC* [1885] 12 R 1045, 22 SLR 674).

4.464.   Distribution of Partnership Assets *In Specie*

The winding up of a partnership may be arranged by distributing part or all of the partnership properties among the partners instead of selling all the partnership assets and then distributing the net proceeds. Such a distribution may fall within FA 1999, Sched.13 para.21. If it is done precisely in accordance with the Articles of the partnership the division may attract no more than £5 fixed duty. These cases need careful examination to ascertain the precise position before assessment of the stamp duty due. Any deviation from the previously agreed method of winding up the partnership may give rise to a liability to *ad valorem* duty.

The comments do not apply in relation to a limited liability partnership which pursuant to the Limited Liability Partnership Act 2000 is a body corporate although incorrectly the Inland Revenue Stamp Taxes Office regards such vehicles as *transparent*.

10.12   LEASES

This head of charge has merited its own chapter. It will be remembered that after FA 1994, s.241 and s.242 it is rare indeed for a legal lease to avoid *ad valorem* duty, but that in certain limited circumstances, where the lease is not subject to *ad valorem* duty, a nominal fixed duty only may be payable (see **Chapter 7**).

Substantial changes in the charging of stamp duty have been made by FA 1994, s.242 where the premium or rent is in whole or in part unascertainable; such lease or agreements for lease now attract *ad valorem* stamp duty charged upon the market value (see **section 2.15**). However, prior to 7 December 1994 (for the question of investigations of title to leases granted prior to that date), *ad valorem* duty was escaped if it was impossible at the date of the lease to calculate with arithmetical precision the consideration which would, or at some stage in the future might become, payable, the fixed lease duty was £2.

In appropriate circumstances this fixed duty might be charged in addition to *ad valorem* duty, for example, where there was a lease with a fixed rent for a stated number of years (which will bear *ad valorem* duty) to be followed by a rent ascertainable only on review at the end of the stated period, and the review could be either upwards or downwards. For the second period there would be the former additional fixed lease duty of £2. If rent, both initially and on review, was unascertainable, there will be two fixed lease duties, making a total payable of £4. Unascertained service charge rent also attracts the fixed duty of £5 (Inland Revenue Press Release dated 12 November 1985).

10.13   RELEASE OR RENUNCIATION NOT ON SALE

FA 1999, Sched.13 para.22 charges stamp duty of £5 on a release or renunciation of property unless the instrument constitutes a conveyance or transfer on sale. However, many cases of releases or renunciation not on sale may be exempt as conveyances within the Stamp Duty (Exempt Instrument) Regulations 1987 SI, 1987/516.

This includes releases of life interests which result in the vesting of the interest in remainder not sale (*Platt's Trustees* v. *IRC* [1953] ATC 292). This charge to fixed duty of £5 and *ad valorem* stamp duty does not apply to releases of personal obligations even where there is consideration, such as release of a debt or restrictive covenant (*Cormack's Trustees* v. *IRC* [1924] SC 819). The charge requires an interest in property. A disclaimer is not a release and is no longer dutiable even if effect by deed.

It is not every release which is to be treated as a release on sale simply because consideration is given. There must be a release in the nature of an assignment, e.g. of an interest in property (*Scottish Equitable Life* v. *IRC* (1894) 22 R (Ct of Session) 85) probably such an interest as would, if the property were land, constitute an estate in the land. An undertaking not to work coal in a particular area, has been held not to be such a release (*Great Northern Railway* v. *IRC* [1899] 2 KB 416). A release from liability for breach of trust in the appointment of a new trustee would fall under the head but only in respect of the fixed duty of £5. The release of interests upon retirement from or dissolution of a partnership may fall into this head of charge (*Garnett* v. *IRC* (1899) 8 LT 633).

10.14   RENUNCIATION

Renunciation, which in Scotland appears to be the equivalent of a surrender (FA 2000, s.128(1)) is in England an expression commonly used in connection with legacies as synonymous with disclaimer. But they differ fundamentally. Disclaimer is simply the rejection of a proffered gift and operates by way of avoidance (*Re Stratton's Disclaimer* [1958] Ch 42; *Re Paradise Motors Ltd* [1968] 1 WLR 1125). The person disclaiming has no say in what happens to the gift. It is not a transfer of property at all and attracts *ad valorem* duty.

Renunciation by contrast normally involves the acceptance of the thing renounced, and the nomination of some other person to take. It should, however, be noted that where a person has a right to be allotted shares in a company such as a person who has exercised an option to subscribe or who has sold assets to a company whether upon a new incorporation or otherwise, in consideration of the undertaking to issue shares a written direction to the company to issue the shares to another person is not a renunciation but is an assignment of his contractual right to be allotted the shares (*Letts* v. *IRC*

[1957] 1 WLR 201) and if undertaken for a relevant consideration the letter or other written directions concerning the allotment or issue will be dutiable as a conveyance or transfer on sale. Moreover, it is the view of the Inland Revenue Stamp Taxes Office that the right to be allotted shares is not 'stock or marketable securities' within the 0.5 per cent rate of stamp duty so that the transfer will be subject to *ad valorem* stamp duty at up to the 4 per cent rate but will be eligible for the inclusion of a certificate of value if the consideration is below a relevant threshold. The problem does not arise if pursuant to the terms of the original subscription arrangements the shares are to be allotted and issued

In this last sense the word is now very commonly used in connection with the allotment of shares and debentures although following the introduction of CREST and the principal charge to stamp duty reserve tax such letters of allotment have fallen out of use. It may be effected either by letter of allotment exempt from duty as an agreement under hand or as a deed, and where the rights are renounceable not later than six months after issue they are exempt from duty otherwise payable under the head 'Bearer Instruments' (FA 1999, Sched.15 para.15) and in most cases are exempt from stamp duty under the head 'Conveyance or Transfer on sale' (FA 1963, s.65 but see FA 1985, s.81). It should be noted that many dealings in such renounceable letters of allotment or similar instruments which are not subject to bearer instrument duty will be subject to stamp duty reserve tax (FA 1986, s.89).

10.15   SURRENDERS NOT ON SALE

FA 1999, Sched.13 para.23 provides that stamp duty of £5 is chargeable on a surrender of property unless the instrument constitutes a conveyance or transfer on sale.

A surrender involves the giving up on termination of an estate or interest, and is most frequently encountered in connection with the termination of leases, and the termination of life or similar interest in a settlement. The fixed duty is £5, but it will be remembered that a surrender of an interest may operate as a conveyance on sale in exactly the same way as a release, if the effect is to cause a beneficial interest to become accelerated in the hands of another, as where a remainder or gift over falls into possession as a result.

It has been held under former legislation that a surrender for no consideration was a conveyance operating as a voluntary disposition not dutiable under this head but chargeable as a conveyance on sale. It now appears to be the view of the Inland Revenue Stamp Taxes Office that such a surrender can qualify for exemption from both stamp duty and the need for adjudication if certified as being within category L of the Stamp Duty (Exempt Instruments) Regulations 1987, SI 1987/516.

Where the surrender is made in consideration of a cash or similar consideration paid or including other interests in land to the person effecting the surrender such as by a landlord to a tenant the instrument of surrender will be dutiable *ad valorem* as a conveyance on sale; but where the payment is made by the person effecting the surrender as an inducement to the other party to agree to the termination, such as by a tenant to the landlord in order to escape from an onerous lease, this is not a sale.

10.16   SURRENDER OF LEASE

A surrender of a lease whereby the landlord pays chargeable consideration to the tenant is in effect a sale by the tenant of his lease to the landlord and is chargeable as such *Phillips* v. *Phillips* (1840) 11 A & E 796, but not where the tenant pays to the landlord compensation to take the lease off the tenant's hands (*Re Duke of Westminster's Settled Estates (No 2)* [1921] 1 Ch 585). A surrender of a lease, to take effect at law, must be by deed unless the surrender arises by operation of law, as where the tenant hands back the lease and keys to the landlord, with the landlord's full consent, and vacates the premises.

Where there is a surrender of a lease by operation of law any written agreement to surrender may now fall within this head of charge pursuant to FA 1994, s.243. Although an agreement to surrender a lease is not a surrender (*Weddell* v. *Capes* 150 ER 341), s.243 now provides that where there is a surrender by operation of law of a lease any written agreement for surrender will become retrospectively stampable. As all agreements to surrender must be in writing (LP(MP)A 1989, s.2) this is clearly a major cost on surrenders of leases.

However, the charge to stamp duty applies only for written contracts and the Inland Revenue Stamp Taxes Office no longer claims stamp duty upon written proposals for a surrender by operation of law. However, the anti-avoidance legislation has been extended to the Land Registry documentation lodged after a surrender by operation of law. FA 2000, s.128(1) treats any instrument evidencing a surrender as a conveyance and this applies to Land Registry documentation. It would seem that strictly any documentation supporting an application to close the title to the surrendered lease will be liable to the fixed stamp duty of £5 pursuant to this head unless the surrender is to a connected company when it is dutiable as a sale for market value pursuant to FA 2000, s.119 subject to any relief that may be available pursuant to FA 1930, s.42 (see **section 6.7**).

It must, however, be noted that by reason of FA 1994, s.241 which imposes an *ad valorem* stamp duty charge where land is transferred or deemed to be transferred in consideration of other property where the surrender involves a surrender of a lease or other interest in land, if part of a larger land transaction such as a surrender of an existing lease being a conveyance in consideration of the grant of a new lease of other premises, the surrendered lease may itself represent stampable consideration for other land transfers and grants of interest in land. The surrender which may include a surrender and regrant arising by operation of law pursuant to a deed varying the lease (see **section 7.15**) may also by reason of the transfer of other interests in land become a surrender on sale dutiable accordingly (see **section 7.15.2**).

10.17 GENERAL EXEMPTIONS FROM FIXED DUTIES

10.17.1 Section 64 of FA 1971 (as amended)

This as *preserved* by FA 1999, Sched.13 para.25 exempts from all stamp duties, including the fixed conveyance duty, all instruments of transfer by way of security and their reconveyance and the transfer of such instruments. No stamp duty is payable upon the transfer of any mortgage, or the money secured thereby, provided that it is not a marketable security within SA 1891, s.122.

This is a wide ranging exemption since debentures can be issued by entities other than bodies corporate such as individuals, partnerships and clubs. Moreover, since such entities and private companies cannot obtain a listing for their securities these cannot be *marketable* for these purposes. Many debt instruments issued by plc's are not suitable for listing on the Stock Exchange and so are within this exemption even when not exempt pursuant to FA 1986, s.79.

These provisions do not apply to the transfer of property which is subject to a mortgage or charge which is, prima facie, dutiable as a sale pursuant to SA 1891, s.57.

10.17.2 Registered social landlords

No stamp duty is chargeable under this on a conveyance or transfer of an estate or interest in land, or on a lease of land, to registered social landlords, etc. (FA 2000, s.130(1)).

10.17.3 Disadvantaged land

No stamp duty will be chargeable on a conveyance of land or transfer of an estate or interest in land, or a lease of land, if the land is situated in a disadvantaged area and the relief is ever implemented (FA 2001, s.92(1) and Sched.30), expected to be March or April 2003.

10.18   CHARITIES

Conveyances and leases to charities are exempted from fixed duty under the head 'conveyance or transfer not on sale', but adjudication is required (FA 1982, s.129).

10.19   HISTORIC BUILDINGS

No stamp duties are chargeable on any instrument whereby property is moved between funds for the maintenance of historic buildings, but adjudication is necessary (FA 1980, s.98; FA 1982, s.129; FA 1983, s.46).

10.20   LETTER OR POWER OF ATTORNEY

The former multiplicity of fixed duties on various powers or letters of attorney was finally abolished by the FA 1985. However, it must be borne in mind that what is in form a mandate by a creditor to a debtor to pay a third party may operate as an equitable assignment upon the sale of the debt (*Diplock* v. *Hammond* (1854) 5 De G M and G 141).

Upon this basis a power of attorney given by a vendor to a purchaser pursuant to an uncompleted sale contract is a conveyance on sale unless in the form of a *default* arrangement to the effect that the purchaser is empowered to execute the conveyance only if the vendor fails to do so when requested in accordance with the terms of the contract. It is irrevocable as an authority to protect the interest of the purchaser pursuant to both the Powers of Attorney Act 1971 and at common law and has been regarded as an equitable assignment since it confers effective control over title to the property to the purchaser.

Third parties taking transfers executed pursuant to such a power of attorney should ensure that it has been duly stamped since they may be exposed to the stamp duty, late stamping penalty and late payment interest charge should they need to rely upon the power of attorney such as when seeking to register the transfer at the Land Registry, and any indemnity given by the other party will be void (SA 1891, s.117).

A power of attorney or power of sale in a mortgage may be similarly irrevocable but is not an equitable assignment or conveyance since there is not uncompleted sale at the time of the execution of the mortgage documentation and there is no sale in contemplation for the purposes of FA 1965, s.90.

CHAPTER 11

Payment of the duty, administration, compliance and due diligence and title investigation

11.1 VOLUNTARY TAX AND INCENTIVES TO STAMP

Stamp duty has been described as a voluntary tax since:

- there is no obligation in stamp duty legislation requiring the use of written instruments; this is a matter of the general law and the wishes of the parties;
- there is no enforceable obligation to present documentation for stamping; there are merely certain *incentives* or indirect pressures;
- apart from bearer instrument duty and stamp duty reserve tax, stamp duty is not directly enforceable.

However, there are problems in leaving a document unstamped:

- registration of title to certain property such as land and shares requires properly stamped documents and penalties are imposed upon persons registering unstamped or insufficiently stamped instruments (SA 1891, s.17; LRA 1925, s.14);
- insufficiently stamped instruments are strictly inadmissible in evidence (SA 1891 s.14(4); *Bar News,* August 2001). This applies to the new charge upon contracts for the sale of land for a consideration in excess of £10 million which although initially admissible in evidence cease to be so admissible once the 90 day period or any extension thereof has expired (FA 2002, s.115);
- purchasers may query title and there are prohibitions upon attempts to prevent requisitions on stamping of documents of title and the giving of stamp duty indemnities (SA 1891, s.117);
- penalties for late presentation (SA 1891, s.15B);
- interest for late payment (SA 1891 s.15A);
- the need for an adjudicated instrument;
- the need for denoting stamps;
- the particular issues of duplicates and counterparts other than leases;
- the obligation to deliver a *PD* form;

- stamp duty reserve tax penalties and interest where this tax is not paid and a duly stamped transfer of the shares is not produced within the prescribed time limits (FA 1986, s.87).

The voluntary nature of the tax means that many errors in stamp duty are not made known to or discovered by the Inland Revenue Stamp Taxes Office, which lacks the resources at present to investigate in depth the documents and forms presented to it. This is, however, gradually changing. Increasing pressure is being exerted upon other Government departments, including the Inland Revenue, to be more zealous in their attitude towards stamp duty by requiring documents to be presented for stamping.

The provisions relating to the subsale repayment of stamp duty in FA 2002, Sched.36 require the production of all documents in the chain of transaction in support of the application. The clawback of stamp duty reliefs, provided for in FA 2002, ss.111 and 113, imposes a positive obligation under penalty to report the transaction and to pay the stamp duty.

The proposed reforms for early 2004 will make the tax reportable and directly enforceable supported by formal audits possibly extending to solicitors' files.

11.2 TIME FOR PAYMENT

11.2.1 Instruments executed on or after 1 October 1999

Theoretically stamp duty should be paid on chargeable instruments before execution. However, SA 1891, s.15 (as amended) provides that an unstamped or insufficiently stamped instrument may be stamped after being executed on payment of the unpaid duty and any interest or penalty payable (see **section 11.7**).

11.2.2 Execution

This 30 day period of grace for the late payment interest charge and late stamping penalties starts from the date of execution of the document, which may sometimes be other than the apparent date. However, it must not be overlooked that an unexecuted or unsigned instrument can be a *conveyance* for the purposes of stamp duty such as the blank stock transfer form in *Fitch Lovell* v. *IRC* [1962] 3 All ER 685 (note the penalties for dealing in such forms in FA 1963, s.67).

The date of execution is taken to mean not the date when the document is first signed by one or other of the parties, but the date upon which it first becomes an effective instrument. The SA 1891, s.122(1) provides that in relation to instruments not under seal *executed* means signed, and s.122(1A) (inserted by FA 1994, s.239) provides that a deed shall be treated as executed when it is delivered or if it is delivered subject to conditions, when the conditions are fulfilled.

Thus in the case of a conveyance or any other deed, the document does not become effective until fully delivered. Delivery at law, however, is not mere physical delivery of the document on completion to the purchaser/donee/lessee, but consists of the sealing of the document with an intention to be bound thereby.

For some guidance on the Inland Revenue Stamp Taxes Office view of *execution* see the Press Release dated 10 July 1992, which states:

> Execution is a process involving signature and unconditional delivery of the instrument. Delivery requires the use of acts or words sufficient to show that the person executing the instrument intends it to bind him or her as a deed. It need not necessarily require the instrument to be physically handed over at that point, though physical delivery may be a condition for delivery in some cases.

In this context it is clear that:

- the position in a particular case will depend on the precise circumstances;
- instruments will not be executed . . . if they are delivered in escrow (i.e. the instrument is not to become binding until certain conditions have been fulfilled) . . .

As the law stands at present most deeds are executed in escrow: the document is delivered at the time of sealing, but only upon condition that it is not to be operative until some condition is performed (*Alan Estates* v. *WG Stores Ltd* [1981] 3 All ER 487).

In the meantime, pending fulfilment of that condition, the party which has sealed the document cannot withdraw and remains bound by the seal. The most common escrow is the execution by a vendor of the conveyance prior to completion but subject to the payment of the outstanding balance of the purchase price. The condition must be satisfied within a reasonable time (for example no later than the service of a completion notice as in *Glessing* v. *Green* [1975] 1 WLR 863), but as soon as this happens the deed becomes fully delivered. Delivery then relates back to the date of the initial sealing, making that the real date of the conveyance rather than the date of actual completion.

This state of affairs has been considerably modified by LP(MP)A 1989, s.1. A party to the deed is able to authorise another to deliver it on his or her behalf without the current requirement of doing so only by deed and, in connection with a transaction involving the disposal or creation of an interest in land, it is conclusively presumed in favour of a purchaser that the party's solicitor or licensed conveyancer is authorised to deliver the instrument on his behalf. The document will then be correctly dated as at completion. In the meantime the client will be able to withdraw it, even though this may put him in breach of contract. Escrows will only arise as the result of a deliberate decision.

The relevance of the true date of a deed lies in the 30 day time limit for presentation of the document for payment of stamp duty. When faced with the problem caused by this principle the court has held that, for stamp duty purposes at least, the date of the escrow can be ignored: the 30-day time limit runs from the date of actual completion (*Terrapin International* v. *IRC* [1976] 1 WLR 665 see also *Crane Fruehauf* v. *IRC* [1975] 1 All ER 429 at p. 434; *BTR* v. *IRC* [1986] STC 437).

Unfortunately for certainty this decision was not followed for other purposes by the Court of Appeal in *Alan Estates Ltd* v. *WG Stores Ltd* [1981] 3 W LR 892, which applied the older principle of retroactive delivery and dating (*Re Devonshire* (1952) 31 ATC 399; *Byrne* v. *IRC* [1935] IR 664). The advantage therefore of LP(MP)A 1989, s.1 will be to settle the argument once and for all.

An escrow must not be confused with a conditional agreement such as an agreement for lease which is dependent upon obtaining planning consent. Such an instrument is dutiable at once not when the condition is satisfied and a conveyance delivered pursuant to a conditional agreement to sell is stampable forthwith (*Ridge Nominees* v. *IRC* [1961] 3 All ER 1108). In the case of conditional sales including the new charge upon land sales for more than £10 million, but not conditional agreements for lease, the stamp is refundable if the contract is subsequently annulled, rescinded or otherwise not substantially carried into effect.

11.3 DUE STAMPING AND DISCLOSURE

11.3.1 Routine stamping *over the counter*

The standard method of payment is to present or send the document to the local Inland Revenue Stamp Taxes Office. At the counter the document is rapidly appraised by a member of the Revenue's staff and *marked* with the amount of duty. The duty is then paid and the document is impressed with a stamp showing the amount and the date of payment together with any interest or penalty. The vast majority of instruments are stamped in this way. The process is relatively informal and does not involve an investigation of the facts and circumstances surrounding the instrument.

In consequence a heavy compliance obligation is imposed upon not merely the parties to an instrument but also their professional advisers and other parties involved in the preparation of the document. The SA 1891, s.5 (as amended) requires that, under penalty, a document must set out all facts relevant to the liability to and calculation of the amount of stamp duty. Penalties of up to £3,000 are imposed upon the parties and the persons involved in the preparation of the instrument, including the professional advisers, if this requirement is not observed; particularly if the inaccurate information is fraudulent.

Where it is inappropriate to set out all of the facts in the instrument itself the parties may submit the instrument with covering letter setting out all of the relevant facts.

The sanction for issues of certificates of value is also provided for by s.5. This disclosure requirement also applies to forms delivered to the Inland Revenue Stamp Taxes Office such as the Particulars Delivered Form as well as the documents themselves such as a Land Registry Transfer or stock transfer form. This means that the parties' advisers are under a duty to know the law and the Inland Revenue Stamp Taxes Office's views and practices.

This is particularly important in the area of what is the stampable consideration which is not always the same as the consideration in the normal sense, for example:

- Premiums for leases which includes not only payments for the lease but also certain payments to third parties (*Att.-Gen.* v. *Brown* (1849) 3 Exch 662).
- VAT and Transfer of a Going Concern where the agreement contains provisions for the payment of VAT if the transaction is for some reason not a transfer of a going concern (see [1999] *Gazette* 15 January 1999).
- Contingent payments such as earnouts and overage arrangement (see **Chapter 2**). In this and the preceding case the parties should include a statement that the consideration includes an undertaking to pay the VAT, if due, or the overage payment when determined.
- Agreements to procure the repayment of the debts of the company whose shares are being sold owed to the vendors and others.

However, other areas of stamp duty fall within s.5. For example, when sub-purchasers present a Land Registry Transfer for stamping as eligible for subsale relief pursuant to SA 1891, s.58(4) or (5) they are representing that there are no circumstances or facts inconsistent with that claim such as there are no powers of attorney or other instruments which are dutiable but unstamped (see **section 6.1**). Failure to refer to these ancillary documents would appear to breach SA 1891, s.5. As the documents are likely to be scrutinised by the Inland Revenue Stamp Taxes Office where there is a claim for repayment of stamp duty paid pursuant to FA 2002, s.115 the failure to reveal these documents may be discovered and their discovery is likely to mean that both the subsale relief and the repayment claim will fail.

In contrast to the process of adjudication mentioned below, there is no conclusive presumption that the amount of stamp duty paid in pursuance of the marking is correct, and in theory it is up to anyone who may later on have to depend upon the validity of the stamp to satisfy himself that the amount paid was in fact correct. A subsequent purchaser of property must of course be satisfied that all prior instruments have been duly stamped otherwise he may experience difficulty in registering or proving title.

11.3.2 Adjudication

The formal process for obtaining a definitive stamping of a document is known as *adjudication* (SA 1891, s.12 (as amended)). The process is also available where the parties believe and wish to establish beyond argument that the documentation is not dutiable. The document is submitted for more detailed consideration. However, the process takes place entirely by correspondence. There is no provision for a formal hearing before an independent tribunal. Having appraised the documentation the Inland Revenue Stamp Taxes Office will indicate its view on whether the instrument is dutiable and, if so how much.

The taxpayer is entitled to dispute this view or the amount in correspondence. Telephone discussions or requests for meetings are rarely productive since the Inland Revenue Stamp Taxes Office will normally terminate the discussion with the comment that it wishes to consider the position and will get back to the taxpayer. Eventually a final position will be taken and the only recourse for the taxpayer is an appeal to the High Court (see **section 11.5**).

Notwithstanding that the Inland Revenue Stamp Taxes Office has taken its decision in an adjudication, the stamp duty is still not enforceable and the taxpayer can withdraw the documentation from the Inland Revenue Stamp Taxes Office.

However, such a course of conduct has to be carefully considered:

- In certain circumstances such a withdrawal attracts a penalty of £300 (Stamp Act 1891, s.12).
- Should it prove necessary to re-present the instrument for stamping the Inland Revenue Stamp Taxes Office is unlikely to take a sympathetic approach to late stamping penalty.
- The taxpayer may lose the right to appeal since an appeal must be launched within 30 days after the end of the adjudication process and there is apparently no power for this period to be extended (SA 1891, s.13).

11.3.3 *Compulsory adjudication*

As a matter of law certain instruments must be adjudicated, i.e. they are expressed to be duly stamped only if adjudicated. Such instruments are not duly stamped even though they bear the correct amount of stamp duty unless the adjudication stamp has also been impressed. Those affecting the conveyancer are:

- Conveyances between associated companies where relief is claimed under FA 1930, s.42 (as amended).

- Agreements for lease and leases granted between associated companies where relief is claimed under FA 1995, s.151(as amended).
- Conveyances and leases to charities which, since 22 March 1982, are now totally exempt from duty (FA 1982, s.129).
- Conveyances in consideration of a debt. Until 1980 if a creditor (such as a mortgagee) accepted a transfer of property in discharge of the debt, duty was payable under SA 1891, s.57 on the whole amount of the debt released, notwithstanding that the debt may well have been at a face value for an amount greater than the value of the property, but in reality a bad or dubious debt. Now, by virtue of FA 1980, s.102 where the debt would exceed the value of the property conveyed, the consideration shall be treated as being limited to the value of the property.
- Certain instruments subject to the fixed duty of £5 unless certified under the Stamp Duty (Exempt Instruments) Regulations 1987, SI 1987/516 (FA 1985, s.82 and s.87) (see **Chapter 10**).
- Company takeovers and reconstructions within FA 1986, s.75 to s.77.
- Transfers and leases to registered social landlords (FA 2000, s.130).
- Transfers and leases of disadvantaged land should the relief ever be fully implemented (FA 2001, s.92 (as amended)).
- Voluntary dispositions: The requirement for adjudication was maintained by FA 1985, s.82 included, endorsed, or physically attached to the instrument concerned. The regulations do not apply however to a gift subject to a mortgage and the donee takes over a certain or contingent liability for repayment: adjudication remains necessary, together with the risk of an *ad valorem* charge.
- Deeds of family arrangement and similar instruments varying the beneficial entitlements under a will or intestacy are treated the same way as voluntary dispositions: they remain subject to adjudication and a £5 stamp as a conveyance of any other kind if not certified under the regulations (FA 1985, s.84).
- An appropriation by a personal representative in or towards satisfaction of a general legacy of money or, on intestacy, in or towards satisfaction of any interest of a surviving spouse in the intestate's estate (FA 1985, s.84). These are treated in exactly the same way as deeds of family arrangement.

Adjudication may be a lengthy process, and if there is a transfer of registered land to be adjudicated, or a conveyance or lease taken within an area of compulsory registration, there is a real risk that the Revenue will not have dealt with the matter within the priority period given by the transferee's search, or the two month time limit for compulsory registration.

On the other hand the Registrar, like any other person who gives effect to an unstamped instrument, incurs the risk of a fine of £300 under SA 1891, s.17 if he proceeds with registration prior to the payment of the duty. In addition Land Registration Act 1925, s.14(3) expressly imposes a duty on the Registrar to satisfy himself that all *ad valorem* duty has been paid.

To meet the problem, Land Registration Rules 1925, r.94 and r.95, as applied in practice, provide that priority will be preserved if the original document and a certified copy are lodged with the Registry within the priority period, with a request for the return of the original for adjudication. An undertaking must also be given to relodge the document when adjudication has been effected.

This practice has been modified. With effect from 5 April 1994 the Land Registry has stated that it will no longer be a requirement that an applicant seeking priority must lodge the original instrument. Henceforth a certified copy of the instrument may be lodged with the application together with a covering letter explaining the situation and confirming that the original instrument will be sent to the Land Registry promptly on its return from the Inland Revenue Stamp Taxes Office.

There appears to be an informal, unpublished practice that upon provisional stamping of the instrument upon the basis that any excess duty will be refunded the Land Registry will register the transfer or lease. On occasion where an instrument is being adjudicated for an exemption registration has been offered upon the basis of solicitors' undertakings to pay any duty assessed.

However, this does not appear to be offered generally and where parties anticipate that there may be delays in the stamping process it is usually convenient to complete by means of a declaration of trust which is nominated as the principal instrument for the purposes of stamping and to transfer the legal title from nominee as bare trustee to beneficial subject to the fixed duty of £5. Registration can then proceed notwithstanding problems in the stamping of the declaration of trust.

11.4 PAYMENT OF THE STAMP DUTY

Upon payment of the duty in accordance with the making or the adjudication the document will be *stamped*.

On conveyancing and associated documents all paid stamp duties are recorded by the affixation by the Inland Revenue on the document concerned of an impressed stamp indicating the amount of duty paid and the date of payment. Prior to FA 1971 certain stamp duties were dealt with by way of adhesive stamp; none of these are currently in force. Power has been taken to introduce other methods of *stamping*, but this power has not been and is unlikely to be exercised.

General supervision of the administration of stamp duties is under the auspices of the Commissioners of Inland Revenue. Documents must be either personally delivered or posted for stamping (with the appropriate remittance) to any one of the various offices maintained for that purpose in England and Wales.

The mechanics for the payment of stamp duty in relation to land transactions is to be significantly changed in early 2004.

In addition to stamps relating to the duty there are other types of stamp frequently encountered upon conveyancing documents. These include adjudication stamps which indicate that the document has been through the formal stamping process and is either not subject to stamp duty or bears the correct account of stamp duty. Such stamps mean that in the absence of fraud the amount of duty paid cannot be challenged.

Denoting stamps indicate that although the instrument upon which it is impressed would normally be expected to bear stamp duty that duty has been borne by some other instrument or a related document has been duly stamped. The existence and need for such stamps is an important practical issue since notwithstanding that the document bears an impressed stamp of the correct amount the absence of such other stamps may mean that it is not *duly stamped* and is strictly subject to the same restrictions upon use as a totally unstamped instrument. Investigations of title and due diligence require, therefore, the search for such stamps.

11.5 APPEALS

It is possible to appeal against the decision of the Inland Revenue Stamp Taxes Office (SA 1891, s.13). Appeals against stamp duty are by way of case stated to the High Court. It is possible to produce further evidence before the High Court although such appeals are usually concerned with points of law or the construction of the documentation.

The request for a case stated must be made within 30 days after the issue of the assessment in the adjudication. Appealing merely as a delaying tactic to put off the day of reckoning is potentially pointless as the appeal can only be made on payment of the assessed duty and any interest and penalty (SA 1891, s.13(1)) although it is probable that this requirement is no longer valid because it is a denial of access to the courts contrary to the Human Rights legislation. If the appeal is successful the stamp duty is repayable together with interest.

Appeals are possible against late stamping penalties because there is a reasonable excuse for the delay in presenting the instrument and against the amount of the penalty. Basically such appeals are made to the Special Commissioners although where there is also an appeal against liability of the amount of the stamp duty the penalty appeal may be taken together with this directly to the High Court.

11.6 INCENTIVES TO STAMP

11.6.1 Registration of title

In certain cases registration is necessary to pass legal (but not necessarily equitable) title (*Brown & Root Technology Ltd* v. *Sun Alliance and London Assurance Ltd* [2000] 2 WLR 566) and the title to property such as land or shares cannot be registered until a duly stamped transfer is presented. Duties are imposed upon registrars to ensure that the documents presented are properly stamped with penalties for failure (SA 1891, s.17; LRA 1925, s.14). However, title passes upon registration of insufficiently or unstamped documentation (*Nisbet* v. *Shepherd* [1994] 1 BCLC 300). There is increasing evidence that in practice the official bodies such as the Land Registry and Companies House are being more rigorous in their stamp duty enquiries. The registrar can insist that the instrument be presented to the Inland Revenue Stamp Taxes Office for adjudication and formal assessment of the stamp duty (*Maynard Consolidated Kent Collieries* [1903] 2 KB 121; *Conybear* v. *British Briquette* [1937] 4 All ER 191).

This person seeking registration will normally be the purchaser or tenant who wishes naturally to obtain fully protected title to the asset being purchased or the land being leased. It will in practice, therefore, normally be the person seeking to register transfers of land or transfers of shares or the tenant who will be required to pay the stamp duty in order to obtain registration thereby receiving the full legal title to the property.

The pressure to pay the stamp duty is indirect since it is the registrar who is liable to penalty if an insufficiently stamped instrument is recorded and the penalties and interest are imposed upon the person presenting the instrument for stamping outside the 30 day period.

A purchaser is entitled to call for a properly stamped chain of title documents and the absence or insufficiency of stamping may entitle him to repudiate the transaction. The position cannot be prevented by seeking to preclude requisitions as to stamping or dealing with it by indemnities (SA 1891, s.117). This can give rise to considerable difficulties for solicitors acting for third parties such as mortgagees or subpurchasers (particularly where powers of attorney to execute documents are involved) since any inadequacy of the stamping of documents in the chain of title may affect their title and security should they seek to enforce (see **section 11.6.2**).

Example

Non-registration can have stamp duty side effects.

Non-registration of a new lease for a term of 21 years or longer within 60 days after the grant of the lease means that the legal title reverts to the

---

landlord and the lease takes effect as an agreement for lease (LRA 1925, s.123A).

This links into FA 1984, s.111 which provides that where there is a transfer of the reversionary interest to an agreement for lease for a term exceeding 35 years or the grant of a lease subject to an agreement for lease for a term exceeding 35 years the transfer or lease must bear a special stamp denoting that the agreement for lease has been duly stamped.

This gives rise to problems such as:

- Purchasers of the reversion or overriding interest may have problems in obtaining stamping and registration of their titles unless they pay the *ad valorem* stamp duty upon the agreement for lease.
- Tenants may be forced to stamp the agreement for lease before the lease is granted and this means that the rules for the postponement of late stamping penalty and late payment interest upon agreements for lease do not apply and these charges relate back to the exchange of the agreement for lease.
- In order to obtain late registration of the lease the tenant may have to pay substantial penalties and interest.

11.6.2 Evidence

One of the most effective encouragements to pay duty is that the unstamped document cannot be used in evidence in any proceedings (except criminal) or be available for any purpose whatever (SA 1891, s.14(4)).

The Bar Council has now effectively made it the duty of the advocate to draw the attention of the court to the absence of stamp upon the other side's documents so that professional advisers who fail to warn their clients that the documentation is on risk of challenge or who fail to spot the absence of stamp upon the other side's evidence is failing in their duty to the client who may lose the case or the opportunity of obtaining or making a favourable settlement if the point is not spotted.

This means that solicitors, advocates and barristers need to appreciate the subtleties of stamp duty and be able to identify a document that may be liable to stamp duty and to understand the impact that the drafting and structuring of a particular document may have affected the stamp duty (*Peter Bone* v. *IRC* [1995] STC 921). Unless, therefore, the parties to an unstamped but stampable document choose voluntarily to abide by it, failure to stamp makes the document ineffective until such time as the outstanding duty is paid, together with any penalty and interest.

An example is a building agreement may frequently include an agreement for lease and is accordingly stampable but with the benefit of deferral of stamping, interest and penalties (FA 1999, Sched.13 para.14; FA 1994, s.240 (as amended)). Should there be a dispute relating to the building works before the lease is executed the party relying on the document will be required to stamp it and pay interest and penalties from 30 days after the execution of the agreement and this may include the landlord who would normally expect to pay only the fixed stamp duty of £5 upon the counterpart lease.

In the case of agreements for the sale of land for more than £10 million dutiable pursuant to FA 2002, s.115 after 90 days are admissible in evidence unstamped until the expiration of that period or any extension thereof granted by the Inland Revenue Stamp Taxes Office. After that date they cease to be admissible if unstamped.

This may be a cause of anxiety for persons such a mortgagees and sub-purchasers or lessees whose security is 'retrospectively under threat' and their solicitors should take steps to avoid this situation arising.

It may well be, however, that the taxpayer may choose to take a calculated risk that the document is unlikely ever to be needed in evidence, and deliberately not pay the duty.

In the context of conveyancing a good example would be a short-term lease which the lessee is forbidden, or does not intend, to assign, and where he has no reason to suspect that the landlord will attempt to derogate from his grant or breach his covenant for quiet enjoyment. It is submitted that there is nothing improper or unprofessional in solicitors advising their clients of the advantages and disadvantages of paying duty in such circumstances, and leaving the decision to the client (*Marx* v. *Estates and General Investments Ltd* [1976] 1 WLR 380). If, of course, the lease is to be the subject of a later assignment, the assignee will be entitled to insist upon the outstanding duty penalties and interest being paid before completion.

Such inadmissibility affects conveyancers since ultimately title depends upon being able to produce admissible evidence to any court. This is important in all litigation not merely title issues. Obviously schemes designed to mitigate tax may involve the creation of stampable documentation and the Inland Revenue is beginning to take a more aggressive approach to the stamping of documentation put before it or the Special Commissioners (*John Lewis plc* v. *IRC* [2000] STC (SCD) 494; *BMBF* v. *IRC* [2002] STC (SCD) 1450).

These issues are of considerable practical importance since persons who are not parties to the instrument such as mortgagees may need to stamp it in order to protect their rights.

For example, mortgagees may find it difficult to enforce their security if the mortgagor has not stamped the documentation in the root of title. Similarly trustees or debtors or insurance companies who have paid out money to third parties on the basis of unstamped assignments may have difficulties in producing evidence to justify the payment if the evidence point pursuant to SA 1891, s.14(4) is raised. However, there may be human rights issues of the right to a fair trial and the protection of property in relation to a regime that prevents persons from producing evidence of their title to the property because they or someone else have failed to stamp the document.

Such persons and receivers and liquidators, are entitled to act upon unstamped documents such as assignments but they do so at their peril since if they need to rely upon the document to justify their conduct in paying money or transferring property to the assignee they may be required to stamp up the documentation and pay any the late payment interest charge and late stamping penalties as the price of so doing (*Marx* v. *Estates and General Investments Ltd* [1976] 1 WLR 380).

This provision is related to the best evidence rule which requires that where the parties rely upon a written instruments or where their rights are based upon a written document they must produce that document duly stamped and cannot rely upon copies or secondary evidence or seek to prove their rights by other means not relying upon the instrument. There may also be difficulties for parties who having received an unstamped assignment seek to establish their title by relying upon any prior contract. Such a course of conduct may be in breach of the best evidence rule which would appear to require evidence of the best, i.e. legal title (but see *BMBF* v. *IRC* [2002] STC 1450 where the Inland Revenue did not raise this point although taking the stamp duty objection).

Difficulties can arise where the original has been lost but if any link in the chain of title rests upon secondary evidence such as a certified copy (there being satisfactory evidence that the original has been lost), there is a rebuttable presumption; that the original was duly stamped (*Marine Investments* v. *Haviside* (1872) LRR 5 HL 624). If there is evidence or the circumstances surrounding the instrument suggest that it was still unstamped at the time it was lost such as because it was executed and retained offshore, secondary evidence of its contents is not admissible. Secondary evidence of an unstamped original can be produced where the document is in the possession or under the control of a person who cannot be served with a witness summons to produce the document such as parties outside the UK.

By virtue of the adversarial system of our courts, the parties in a civil action can to a very large extent themselves agree to waive the formal requirements of the strict rules of evidence, and invite the court to accept something which may otherwise be potentially inadmissible or agree as a fact that a particular situation is the correct position. However, in relation to an unstamped or an insufficiently stamped document, it is the positive duty of the judge to refuse its admission (SA 1891, s.14(1); for cases where this has happened see *Routedge* v. *McKay* [1954] 1 WLR 615; *Stokes* v. *Costain Property Investments* [1983] 2 All ER 681). The objection may be cured on payment even at this late stage of the unpaid duty, the interest and penalty payable and 'the further sum of £1 (SA 1891, s.14(1)).

In practice the court would accept the personal undertaking of the solicitor for the party concerned to present the document for stamping and to pay all duties and penalties attracted (*Re Coolgardie Goldfields Ltd* [1900] 1 Ch 475; but see *Lloyds and Scottish* v. *Prentice* (1977) 121 SJ 847 for a suggested restriction upon this where there is a suspicion of tax evasion; see also *Saunders* v. *Edwards* [1987] 2 All ER 651). It is quite a different matter to expect a subsequent purchaser of the property to acquiesce in accepting such a document.

There may also be problems where the client is exposed to difficulties because it may be necessary to register or rely upon the document after the trial and pay the stamp duty which has been missed during the hearing and which could have fallen upon some other party.

As this is merely a rule of evidence and does not affect the substantive issue the absence or insufficiency of stamp does not affect its admissibility in trials and arbitrations outside the UK; but it applies to foreign instruments which fall into the stamp duty charges pursuant to SA 1891, s.14(4) (see **section 1.19**).

11.7 PENALTIES FOR LATE PRESENTATION FOR STAMPING

Penalties are imposed upon persons who produce an instrument to the Inland Revenue Stamp Taxes Office more than 30 days after its execution (SA 1891, s.15B).

Penalties are revised as from 1 October 1999. Subject to the special cases mentioned below:

- Where the instrument is presented for stamping more than 30 days after execution but within 12 months after the 30 days there is a penalty of the lower of £300 or a sum equal to the stamp duty. Where the instrument is subject only to fixed duty of £5 in practice no penalty is claimed in this period.
- Where the instrument is presented more than 12 months after the expiration of the thirty days, i.e. 13 months after execution the penalty is the higher of £300 or the amount of the stamp duty. It seems that if the instrument is presented more than two years after execution the full penalty will be claimed subject to any appeal. This minimum penalty also applies to instruments attracting fixed duty of £5 and the Inland Revenue Stamp Taxes Office requires the parties to justify any claim for a reduction from £300 on an individual basis.

No penalties are chargeable if there is a reasonable excuse for the delay. The Inland Revenue Stamp Taxes Office has power to mitigate the late stamping penalty. Regulations have been issued for the assessment, enforcement and appeals against penalties. The Inland Revenue Stamp Taxes Office has issued the Compliance Chapter in their *Manual* setting out their views and various press releases and leaflets contain further details of their approach where the stamp duty is small.

11.7.1 Clawback and penalties

No penalties should arise where relief from stamp duty for land transfers and leases has been obtained pursuant to FA 1930, s.42, FA 1995, s.151 or FA 1986, s.76 is clawed back pursuant to FA 2002, s.111 or s.113.

Appeals are now permitted against both the imposition of penalties (because there is a reasonable excuse for the delay) and the amount thereof (FA 1999, s.13).

11.8 SPECIAL CASES ON LATE PENALTIES

11.8.1 Business sale agreements

These are now subject to the regime in full. There is a risk that when a transfer of land is presented for stamping the Inland Revenue Stamp Taxes Office may call for the agreement in order to:

- impose late stamping penalties and the late payment interest charge; and
- collect stamp duty upon property within the agreement not included in any documents presented.

11.8.2 Lease assignment trap

The presentation of the assignment of leases for stamping is providing an unpleasant surprise for the unwary. Such an assignment, although frequently subject only to the fixed stamp duty of £5 or nil because being at a fully reviewable rack rent it will have no value, it is often only one of the assets involved in the sale of a business. There is increasing evidence in practice that the Inland Revenue is seeking production of any related business sale agreement which may attract substantial stamp duty upon other assets, including, in particular, tenant's fixtures pursuant to FA 1999, Sched.13 para.7, together with related interest and penalties.

11.8.3 Large land sale contracts

The FA 2002, s.115 imposes a charge to *ad valorem* stamp duty upon contracts for the sale of land for a consideration in excess of £10 million (or £8,500,000 plus VAT) where a duly stamped transfer is not produced within 90 days after the contract or such longer period as the Inland Revenue Stamp Taxes Office may allow. The 30 days for late stamping penalties and the late payment interest charge run only from the expiry of the 90 days or such longer period as is granted by the Inland Revenue Stamp Taxes Office. It is currently assumed that the late payment interest charge and late stamping penalties which will have started to accrue will be cancelled where the 90 day period is retrospectively extended (if this is permitted) by the Inland Revenue Stamp Taxes Office, but the position is not clear.

11.8.4 Execution offshore

In general the late stamping penalties do not arise until 30 days after the document comes into the UK (SA 1891, s.15B). However, in relation to instruments executed on or after 24 July 2002 which *relate to* land situate in the UK the penalties begin to run from 30 days after execution. The words *relate to* have been said to be of the widest application (*Maples (Paris) Ltd v. IRC* [1908] AC 22) and this has been extended by s.116 so that the penalty will apply to the entire stamp duty upon the instrument not merely that part of the stamp duty which arises in connection with the consideration or value apportioned to the UK land.

It appears that the Inland Revenue Stamp Taxes Office has modified its initial view that even commercially related contracts are within the new penalty regime although these are technically in law separate transactions. A transaction involving a sale of UK and a separate contract for the sale of the business carried out on that land will not, it seems, attract the new penalty regime upon the business sale contract even if it can established that one would not have been signed unless the other were signed at the same time provided, however, that the contracts are legally independent. It remains to be seen whether the Inland Revenue Stamp Taxes Office will take a reasonable approach to the mitigation of the stamp duty upon foreign property involved in the transaction.

Late payment interest runs from 30 days after execution even though the document remains offshore, and this is not limited to transactions relating to land in the UK.

The effect of the changes in the FA 1999 and FA 2002 is that there will rarely, if ever, be any advantages in executing documentation relating to UK land offshore, especially where registration is compulsory or essential to the obtaining of full title.

11.9 AGREEMENTS FOR LEASE

11.9.1 The relief

Where an agreement for lease is presented for stamping at the same time as the lease granted pursuant to and in conformity with it and the appropriate duty is paid on the agreement of the lease then for the purposes of calculating penalties the agreement for lease is treated as having been executed at the time when the lease was executed. In other words, in general, the agreement for lease will not attract penalties and interest provided that:

- it is presented for stamping together with the lease; and
- both are presented within 30 days after the execution of the lease.

The conditions are cumulative.

11.9.2 The problems

There are various points to watch in this apparently simple act of generosity. In particular delay in granting the lease will effectively prolong the two year period for clawback of any relief pursuant to FA 1995, s.151 for intra-group leases.

The normal penalty rules apply where the documents are presented more than 30 days after the date of the execution of the lease. In such a case it seems that the penalties and interest on the agreement for lease will be calculated by reference to the date when the lease was executed, provided that the two instruments are presented together.

The agreement for lease remains dutiable in full so that, for example, if it attracts a higher rate of duty than the lease as in the illustration above there is still no credit or refund in respect of the higher level of duty. The fact that the actual lease has been granted and the precise rent may be known is not taken into account in computing the stamp duty payable upon the agreement for lease or in determining the market value and market rent of the premises which remains to be determined as at the date when the agreement for lease came into existence.

The mitigation of penalties only applies where the lease is actually granted. If for any reason the parties execute the agreement for lease and do not grant the lease but at some time it becomes necessary to stamp the agreement for lease this relief will not apply since there cannot be a simultaneously presentation of the agreement for lease and the lease itself. There is, therefore, an incentive to execute the formal lease at a time when the agreement may need stamping because that by itself will avoid the penalties and interest on the agreement for lease.

However, this is not always possible particularly where the parties to the agreement for lease are in dispute or the parties are in dispute with the Inland Revenue concerning the deduction of expenses upon the abortive lease. This may arise, for example, where the parties rely upon the agreement for lease and the landlord wishes to sue for arrears of rent or breach of covenant or one of the parties is suing for specific performance of the agreement to grant the lease.

Particular problems arise where the lease cannot be granted, such as where there is a conditional agreement for lease which does not become effective because conditions are not satisfied. This will remain subject to penalties as from 30 days after its execution.

Solicitors who have failed to discuss these risks with clients in relation to the agreement for lease may, justifiably, find themselves in difficulties in relation to the additional costs incurred by reason not only of the interest and penalties but also because their client, such as the landlord or the purchaser of shares in one of the companies involved, has to pay the stamp duty which would normally fall upon the tenant when registering the lease.

11.9.3   Interest for late payment of stamp duty

As from 1 October 1999 a new interest charge applies in relation to *ad valorem* stamp duty where the stamp duty is not paid within 30 days after the execution of the document. The late payment interest charge does not apply to instruments subject only to the fixed duty of £5. This applies even where the instrument is presented within the 30 days and no late presentation penalty is incurred. It applies notwithstanding that the delay is because there is an adjudication or valuation involved and the delay is down to the Inland Revenue Stamp Taxes Office in failing to respond promptly during the negotiations. It also applies where the instrument is executed offshore and runs whilst the documentation is held offshore.

The interest can be avoided or reduced by depositing a sum with the Inland Revenue Stamp Taxes Office within the 30 days. However, the interest like the penalty is payable only if the document is actually stamped. For example, if the instrument is executed and retained offshore and remains unstamped neither interest nor penalty is payable.

Unlike penalties the late payment interest charge cannot be mitigated so that, for example, where additional stamp duty becomes payable under the new practice in relation to Transfer of a Going Concern for VAT the late payment interest charge applies to the additional amount of stamp duty as from 30 days after the documentation not 30 days after the VAT becomes payable pursuant to the delivery of the tax invoice.

11.9.4   Clawback and interest

FA 2002 s.111 and s.113 provide for the clawback of exemptions from stamp duty for sales and leases of land pursuant to FA 1930, s.42; FA 1995, s.151; or FA 1986, s.76. The interest upon such tax runs from 30 days after the occurrence of the clawback event.

11.10   DENOTING STAMPS

An indirect pressure to have documents stamped are the statutory requirements that documents are only duly stamped if they bear a stamp indicating
that the correct stamp duty has been paid upon some other instrument. These
include:

- counterparts and duplicates indicating that the original is stamped;
- conveyances where the contract pursuant to which they are executed is
  dutiable under FA 1999, Sched.13 para.7 indicating that the written
  agreement has been stamped; and
- transfer or leases of interests subject to an agreement for lease for a term
  exceeding 35 year indicating that the agreement for lease has been
  stamped.

11.11   *PARTICULARS DELIVERED* STAMPS

Regardless of the question of stamp duty, there is a separate provision, under
FA 1931, s.28 that particulars of every conveyance on sale or grant of any
lease of land or agreement to lease for a term of seven years or more, or the
transfer on sale of any such lease, shall be produced by the purchaser or
lessee to the Commissioners within a period of 30 days after its execution.

If the conveyance, lease, or transfer has been executed abroad, particulars
must be produced within 30 days after the instrument is first received in Great
Britain.

Practitioners will be only too well aware of the need to show on Form
Stamps L(A) 451 details of the parties, the property and the consideration.
The form is presented with the instrument upon which the *Particulars delivered*
(PD) stamp is affixed. As with failure to pay stamp duty, failure to produce
particulars renders the document inadmissible in evidence (apart from criminal proceedings), this being the effect of FA 1931, s.28 which declares that
an instrument not produced as required by the section is not to be deemed
duly stamped. In this context the entitlement under a certificate of value to
take advantage of a nil rate of duty is irrelevant.

To speed up the conveyancing process a modified procedure was introduced
with effect from 1 January 1986, by the Stamp Duty (Exempt Instruments)
Regulations 1985, SI 1985/1688, introduced under FA 1985, s.89. These cut
out the need to send certain transfers of registered land, or conveyances or
assignments which are the subject of compulsory first registration, first to the
Stamp Duty Office for the PD stamp to be affixed, If the transfer bears no
stamp duty at all as it is certified at £60,000, the usual form L(A) 451 is completed as hitherto, but sent direct to the District Land Registry, which will
then check that no stamp duty is payable and that the PD form has been

properly completed. The same time limit of 30 days applies, but the object of the exercise is clearly to allow solicitors to accompany the application for the affixation of a PD stamp with the application for registration of the transfer.

Any transfer which needs adjudication or which does not contain a certificate of value must be sent to the Inland Revenue Stamp Taxes Office as hitherto, as must a new lease reserving a rent, even though an allowable certificate of value is given for the premium.

The object of the PD form seems to be not merely to enable district and other valuers to be apprised of current property prices in assessing claims for compensation and calculating values for the purposes of capital taxation upon death or voluntary disposition but also draw the attention of the Inland Revenue Stamp Taxes Office to the consideration for stamp duty purposes which may not always be apparent upon the face of the transfer or lease. Failure to include the correct stamp duty details in the form will incur penalties (see **section 11.3**).

11.12   TITLE INVESTIGATION

The new compliance regime introduced for instruments executed on or after 1 October 1999 has significantly increased the risks attaching to less than comprehensive investigation of title. There is a tendency to take the view that once a title to land has been registered the issues of stamp duty upon the transfer itself and any antecedent documents in the direct or indirect chain of title are irrelevant.

Whilst it is well established that legal title only passes upon registration (*Brown and Root* v. *Sun Alliance* [2000] 2 WLR 566), it is also well established that legal title passes upon registration even where the instrument is unstamped or insufficiently stamped (*Lap Shun Textiles Industrial Co* v. *Collector of Stamp Revenue* [1976] AC 530; *Nisbett* v. *Shepherd* [1994] 1 BCLC 300).

However, it is not every document which requires to be registered, and on occasion parties may find that inadequately stamped documents may prevent them from obtaining registration of title. Moreover, even the curtain of registered title may have to be lifted on occasion.

Solicitors who do not appreciate the technical conditions of stamp duty may not raise the correct requisitions upon stamp duty may jeopardise their client's interests or, more interestingly, expose themselves to penalties for failing to set out all relevant information in the documentation or forms such as PD forms or Land Registry TR1 as required by SA 1891, s.5. Basic investigations of stamp duty issues can save the client considerable stamp duty, for example whether any equipment attached to the land has retained its character as chattels and so is exempt from stamp duty if not included in the conveyance (which in turn may make the instrument either eligible for a certificate of value and the lower rates of stamp duty or below the £10 million threshold for the new regime for stampable contracts for the sale of land pursuant to FA 2002, s.115) (see **section 5.8**).

A basic illustration of the types of problem which can arise in relation to subsales which affect quite fundamentally the stamp duty upon house purchases whether of newly constructed houses or part exchange and similar schemes. The problems of subsale relief for land transactions have been increased by FA 2002, Sched.36. The detailed conditions for subsale relief are considered at **section 6.1** but for present purposes it is noted that the relief is not available to parties where the first or any intermediate purchaser has obtained an instrument which constitutes a *conveyance* for stamp duty purposes.

The width of the definition of a stamp duty *conveyance* is considered at **section 4.3**, and it is clear that in their anxiety to protect their clients solicitors may destroy the relief for their clients or other parties in the chain or make the title strictly unsaleable except under payment of substantial stamp duty, interest and penalties.

Example

A contracts to sell land to B who after constructing several houses sub-sells these houses separately to C, D and E. A has granted a power of attorney to B to execute transfers and B has utilised this power of attorney to produce the transfers to C, D and E. C's transfer is challenged by the Land Registry or his mortgagee and it is presented to the Inland Revenue Stamp Taxes Office for adjudication who take the points that:

- The power of attorney is a conveyance liable to *ad valorem* stamp duty as completing the sale between A and B. In consequence C cannot prove that his Land Registry Transfer is properly executed without needing to rely upon a *conveyance*.
- The Land Registry Transfer is not properly stamped. Technically where the conditions for subsale relief are not strictly satisfied the conveyance to the subpurchaser is liable to the aggregate of stamp duty for all transactions completed by the instrument (*Fitch Lovell Ltd* v. *IRC* [1962] 1 WLR 1325) and there are certain comments in the *Stamp Office Manual* which indicate the Inland Revenue Stamp Taxes Office may take the point. C is, therefore, potentially liable not only to his own stamp duty, but also that payable in respect of the sale from A to B.
- The solicitors for C in presenting the transfer without drawing the attention of the Inland Revenue Stamp Taxes Office to these issues and, in particular, the absence of stamp upon the power of attorney, have failed to disclose all relevant information as required by SA 1891, s.5.

C's mortgagee may feel reluctant in taking the title as security because of these stamp duty risks.

The author is frequently approached by solicitors who believe that where there is a contract of sale the execution of a declaration of trust does not attract stamp duty. Unfortunately for them it is a conveyance on sale dutiable accordingly (*Chesterfield Brewery Co* v. *IRC* [1899] 2 QB 7). Subsale relief has, therefore, been prejudiced and the subpurchaser is upon risk unless his or her solicitor asks the right questions and takes appropriate steps by insisting that the doubtful documents are adjudicated. Attempts to protect the client by indemnities or undertakings to pay the stamp duty will be void within SA 1891, s.117.

11.12.1   Land sales and the £10 million threshold

In the new regime for contracts for the sale of land for a consideration in excess of £10 million (see **section 5.8**), apart from the questions of whether the conditions for the subsale relief have been strictly complied with, the amount of stamp duty may depend upon the correct questions being asked and the documents organised accordingly.

11.12.2   Backward, sideways and forward obligations for solicitors

Where subsales are involved, the amount of stamp duty which a purchaser or subpurchaser may have to pay depends upon the amount of the consideration and duty paid upon the earlier contract. Where there are subsales of part there will need to be discussions with the related subsale purchasers as to the allocation of the credit upon the part of the land.

The stamp duty repayment to purchasers and subpurchasers depends upon both the stamp duty paid and the numerous conditions being satisfied including subsequent contracts and transfers which may be below the £10 million threshold. Sellers who may be seeking the benefit of the credit or repayment mechanism in FA 2002, Sched.36 will find it necessary to monitor subsequent transactions in order to ensure that they are not prejudiced.

Solicitors must, therefore, investigate prior transactions closely and monitor subsequent transactions in order to protect their client's position. This may require a warranty that the purchaser will not do anything to prejudice the seller's stamp duty position.

Investigations of title in subsale of part of the land even where these are below the £10 million threshold will involve discovering whether any prior contracts have born or are liable to stamp, the amount of the original consideration allocated to the part of the land which they are acquiring since this may affect the amount of stamp duty upon the contract and/or the transfer, whether that stamp duty has been paid and, in particular, whether there are any circumstances or documents which might prejudice the stamp duty position of the client purchaser.

Solicitors acting for mortgagee will need to know what will happen if the contract becomes stampable and potentially inadmissible in evidence if unstamped after the 90 day period expires.

All of these issues have to be considered in the context of the restrictions imposed upon obtaining protection from the absence of stamp by SA 1891, s.117. For example, it would appear clear that a simple attempt by a mortgagee to pay the stamp duty and provide that it is to be added to the principal sum secured will be vulnerable to striking down pursuant to SA 1891, s.117.

11.13   SHARE TRANSACTIONS

Solicitors dealing with purchases of shares cannot overlook land stamp duties. Usually this position is covered by some provision in the share sale arrangements that the target company's documents of title are duly stamped. In some situations there may be an indemnity from the vendor to the target company regarding the stamp duty but this may be vulnerable to the provisions of SA 1891, s.117 rendering indemnities void. It is an open question whether s.117 applies to strike down warranties relating to stamp duty in the share sale contract between the vendor and purchaser.

These duties to the client to investigate the stamp duty position of companies to be purchased have been enlarged by FA 2002, s.111 and s.113 which clawback the stamp duty reliefs for land transactions obtained pursuant to either FA 1930, s.42 (intra-group sales); FA 1995 s.151 (intra-group leases) or FA 1986, s.76 (certain reorganisations), where the companies cease to be relevantly associated at a time the transferee/lessee company still has an interest in the land within a two year period after the execution of the instrument for instruments executed on or after 24 April, 2002.

This liability for the stamp duty which becomes payable is imposed upon not only upon the transferor/lessor and the transferee/lessee companies but also upon other companies (*third company*) who were at the time of the instrument or have in the intervening period subsequently been above the transferee/lessee in the stamp duty group. In addition the liability continues to run notwithstanding subsequent changes of ownership or control of the third company and certain reconstructions.

Appropriate questions need to be raised concerning intra-group land transactions and care is needed in seeking to protect purchasers of shares because of the restriction upon stamp duty protections represented by SA 1891, s.117.

Where as part of tidying up title either presale or as a consequence of enquiries made by a prospective purchaser, such as where previous transactions have remained uncompleted or dealt with *informally*, and the legal title is in the wrong name such tidying process may have stamp duty consequences. For example, although the transfer or lease may qualify for exemption purchase to FA 1930, s.42 or FA 1995, s.151 as it is *unconnected* with the sale it may start a two-year period for the purposes of clawback of the relief pursuant to FA 2002, s.111.

Alternatively the transfer may fall foul of FA 1965, s.90 as a transfer in contemplation of a sale. There is an obvious problem of the duality of purpose behind the transfer, i.e. completing the old transaction and preparing for the new transaction. It is unclear whether such duality of purpose is sufficient to exclude the application of s.90. It is considered that the actual sale excludes s.90, but if the point is pressed, on balance, the current judiciary is likely to be willing to find in favour of the Inland Revenue Stamp Taxes Office.

11.14 WASTED STAMPS

Occasionally a stamped instrument may turn out to be a useless document: it may have been absolutely void from the beginning; it may be found to be unfit for the purpose originally intended as the result of an error or mistake in the document; it may remain incomplete and inadequate for its purpose because it was stamped before it was executed by all necessary parties, and one or other necessary party subsequently can or will not complete the transaction; it may be accidentally spoiled; or it may subsequently become void, e.g. for want of enrolment or registration within the time required by law (Stamp Duties Management Act 1891, s.9(7)).

The relief is not available in cases apart from those listed, so that where an instrument which is subsequently rescinded for misrepresentation, for example, has been stamped the duty cannot be recovered. There are several other situations listed in Stamp Duties Management Act 1891, s.9 but with the exception of s.9(1), relating to spoiled prestamped instruments, the bulk of these reliefs are largely redundant in practice.

In these circumstances application can be made to the Inland Revenue for an allowance in respect of the wasted duty. There are, however, limitations upon the making of a refund:

- the application must be made within two years after the stamp has been spoiled or become useless; and
- in the case of an executed instrument no legal proceeding has been commenced in which the instrument could or would have been given or offered in evidence (proviso to Stamp Duties Management Act 1891, s.9(7)).

The above two limitations do not apply to a claim for reimbursement of duty paid on a contract treated as a conveyance on sale by FA 1999, Sched.13 para.7 or FA 2002, s.115, when the transaction is never completed.

11.15   MISTAKEN PAYMENT

Occasionally parties may pay *ad valorem* stamp duty incorrectly. They may overlook the fact that there is an exemption for conveyances or lease to charities or be unaware of the exemption for lease between associated companies. In such cases it may be possible to reclaim the stamp duty paid. Stamp Duties Management Act 1891, s.10 provides that where a party has inadvertently used a stamp of greater value than was necessary or has inadvertently used a stamp where none was necessary may apply to the Commissioners within two years after the first execution of the instrument and the duty may be cancelled upon payment of the proper stamp duty. This is, of course, drafted in relation to prestamped instruments, but it seems that in practice duty has been recovered notwithstanding that the instrument was stamped after execution.

11.16   INCIDENCE AND INDEMNITIES – INSTRUMENTS EXECUTED ON OR AFTER 1 OCTOBER 1999

11.16.1   Liability for the stamp duty

There is no provision as to who is liable to pay the stamp duty apart from:

- FA 1999, Sched.13 para.7 which imposes the charge to stamp duty upon certain contracts for sale states that the purchaser is liable for the stamp duty, but there is no provision dealing with the stamp duty upon any transfer or assignment executed pursuant to a contract whether dutiable pursuant to FA 1999, Sched.13 para.7 or not.
- FA 2002, s.115 which imposes stamp duty upon agreements for the sale of UK land for a consideration in excess of £10 million where there is not a stamped conveyance after 90 days states that the stamp duty is payable by the purchaser.
- Bearer instruments which have their own special compliance package in FA 1999, Sched.15.

The position, therefore, appears to remain the same as previously; namely, the person who seeks to rely upon the instrument and so is the person actually presenting the instrument to the Inland Revenue Stamp Taxes Office even though they are not a party to the instrument is a person who should pay the duty. This will usually be the purchaser or tenant.

However, this is not the universal situation and in certain cases no party may be particularly anxious to present the instrument for stamping unless and until there is some dispute either with a party to the instrument or with the Inland Revenue or some official body which takes a stamp objection to the instrument being produced, or as a consequence third parties may find themselves and the obligation of paying stamp duty in respect of documents to which they are not party is one respect of transactions in which they have no real interest.

Trustees in dispute with the Inland Revenue may have to pay stamp duty in respect of the assignment of equitable interests behind the trust made between beneficiaries.

Trustees and personal representatives who have paid out upon the basis of unstamped assignments or deeds varying beneficial interests and legacies may have to pay the stamp duty interest and penalties if sued for breach of trust by other beneficiaries or legatees.

A debtor who pays out upon the unstamped assignment of a debt could be in difficulties if later sued and wishes to put forward the assignment of the debt as part of a defence.

Probably those most likely to be affected are mortgagees who may find that in order to enforce their security against the particular asset they will have to stamp an assignment from a third party to the mortgagor. This would arise where an asset was purchased but the documentation was unstamped at the time that the purchaser sought to utilise the asset as security for the loan of the purchase price.

Unless the mortgagee takes the point that it is not prepared to advance money unless and until the underlying documentation is duly stamped the mortgagee may be the position that when enforcing security it is necessary for it to pay someone else's stamp duty. This is a particular problem where pursuant to FA 2002, s.115 a contract for the sale of UK land for more that £10 million becomes retrospectively stampable after 90 days and consequently inadmissible in evidence until stamped.

A landlord suing a tenant pursuant to a building agreement which is dutiable as an agreement for lease may find that he has to pay *ad valorem* stamp duty on the agreement for lease together with full late stamping penalty and late payment interest since it is not presented together with the lease which has not been granted although he would normally expect to pay only £5 stamp duty upon his counterpart lease. A landlord should either:

- insert a term into the building agreement or agreement for lease that the tenant will pay all stamp duty so that he will be liable in damages for breach of contract; or
- execute the agreement with a counterpart which is dutiable as a counterpart lease bearing only the fixed stamp duty of £5.

Persons receiving title in a subsale context where the first purchaser is proposing to use a power of attorney granted to him/her by the original vendor. Such a power of attorney is dutiable and so a conveyance on sale. Where, in a subsale situation, the first purchaser has obtained a power of attorney which operates as a conveyance on sale for the purposes of stamp duty the subpurchaser should require the power of attorney to be stamped since should any later party question the execution of the Land Registry Transfer pursuant to the power of attorney any indemnity to stamp up the power of attorney by the first purchaser would be void. Also failure to disclose its existence may be a breach of the disclosure requirements of SA 1891, s.5 (see **section 11.3**). Prudent purchasers should be asking whether the vendor intends to complete using a power of attorney and ask for it to be adjudicated.

11.16.2 Liability for late stamping penalties

This becomes an even more acute problem when dealing with the question of late stamping penalties. The position here has been made even more obscure then under the previous regime. The original SA 1891, s.15 contained a table of persons who are liable to the penalty. That table has disappeared from the new legislation and there is no longer any specific person named as a person liable for the penalty (apart from bearer instruments).

In relation to the late stamping penalty regime there is the question whether the fact that the person presenting the document is not party to it but is a person such as a mortgagee has, simply because he is not a party to the documentation, a reasonable excuse for not presenting the document within the 30 days and so should be excused the penalty or is a justification for mitigating the amount thereof. In a sense, as the mortgagee might not have the power over or custody of the document, there might be in excuse for not having stamped at the proper time.

However, it is likely that the court would be more sympathetic to the possible argument that the Inland Revenue Stamp Taxes Office is likely put forward; namely, the mortgagee or, indeed, any third parties, should avoid such problems concerning the proffered security and insist upon the document being stamped before advancing the money and taking the charge over the relevant asset or otherwise acting on the basis of the document. It is, therefore, most unlikely that the fact that person presenting the document is not party to the instrument will necessarily qualify as a reasonable excuse from liability to be the penalty.

The position remains open and there is no definitive guidance in the Inland Revenue Stamp Taxes *Office Manual* as to how this situation is viewed officially. It seems that the Inland Revenue Stamp Taxes Office takes the view that the penalty is simply the price that has to be paid for stamping a document out of time and that it does not matter who presents the document.

11.16.3 Liability for the late payment interest charge

The late payment interest charge is similarly without any statutory guidance as to who is liable for the interest charge. Presumably, this liability falls upon whichever person is required to present the document.

Therefore, as in the above illustration, if a mortgagee is presenting the document late for stamping he will be the person who has to pay the interest charge.

There is no power to mitigate the interest charge or to excuse from liability.

11.16.4 Indemnities

The question then arises whether a person who is not party to the instrument is entitled to some form of indemnity in respect of the payment of interest and penalty upon the document. To this possible claim for an indemnity there are two objections:

- SA 1891, s.117 contains a prohibition in relation to an indemnity on account of the absence or insufficiency of stamping of any instrument. This section renders indemnities in respect of improperly stamped documentation in a chain of title void.
- Although there is, broadly, an equitable right to an indemnity to a person who has discharged the indebtedness of another, it is difficult to imply a right of indemnity upon the basis that the person has satisfied the liability of another party when apart from the case of a purchaser pursuant to a stampable contract within FA 1999, Sched.13, para.7 or FA 2002, s.115 there is no person who is primarily or solely responsible for payment of the stamp duty which is unenforceable, i.e. there is no indebtedness to be discharged.

This would mean, for example, that if a prospective mortgagee raised objection to the proposed security because there was unstamped document such as a power of attorney or agreement for lease or option pursuant to which the property was purchased in relation to the mortgaged property any indemnity by the mortgagor to indemnify the mortgagee should it prove to be necessary to stamp a document in the enforcement process would find that than indemnity was void, even assuming that the mortgagor was not insolvent at the time and could afford to pay the stamp duty. Similarly a provision that the mortgagee could add any stamp duty to the principal debt would be struck down by this section.

It seems, however, that an agreement between the parties to share or deal with stamp duty upon their own instrument is not affected by SA 1891, s.117 which appears to be aimed at the situation of documentation involving third parties.

It would seem that the new regime has rendered the penalty and interest compliance sanctions even more severe than previously. The obvious point is that potentially affected persons should ensure that all relevant documentation has been properly stamped.

CHAPTER 12

The future

12.1 INTRODUCTION

Significant changes are expected over the next decade in relation to electronic conveyancing moving away from paper transfers of title much as has happened in relation to trading in securities on the Stock Exchange.

Obviously, a move away from a paper or document based transfer structure to transactions effected by electronic means will have fundamental implications for the future of stamp duty which is a documentary tax.

As part of this process, a substantial *modernisation* of stamp duties for land transactions has been proposed. This was initiated by a Consultation Document in the spring of 2002. Limited draft clauses began to be published in the autumn of 2002, with details to be in the Finance Bill 2003 and publication of the consequent regulations and return forms in the late summer of 2003. The draft clauses indicate that much of the existing stamp duty regime will be continued in the new legislation.

This would lead to a commencement date, currently not expected to be before early 2004. The effect is that there will be three areas of stamp duty, which will apply to shares as part of the land-rich company regime. These are:

- stamp duty reserve tax for shares primarily, but not solely, when traded on the stock exchange;
- stamp duty upon shares primarily, but not solely, when dealt in off-exchange; and
- modernised stamp duty for land and property deriving its value from land.

For solicitors there are, in effect, two areas of change that have to be noted:

- the scope of the tax; and
- the compliance and due diligence implications for particular transactions.

There is also an ancillary area that will represent a very tight deadline for solicitors, namely the transition from the present to the modernised system. This will require a thorough knowledge of both the existing and the proposed changes in order to advise clients whether to accelerate transactions and bring them into effect under the present regime or to defer them into the new regime depending upon which produces the more favourable outcome.

12.2 THE SCOPE OF THE TAX

It was originally suggested that there would be two regimes applicable to land: one regime for residential conveyancing and another for commercial properties. However, there will be considerable overlap at certain levels between the two regimes. An example might be the purchase of a site for development, which may fall into the large transaction or commercial property regime, even though ultimately it will emerge as many individual properties within the other regime. At present there is no suggestion for such a split system; residential and commercial land operate within a single regime. Should there be two systems it may be that the compliance requirements and any subsale relief that will be factored into the new system will require solicitors within the residential system to investigate back in order to see whether the transaction started in the commercial regime and how any subsale relief would operate as a result of such a transition. Separate return forms and separate events operating as a tax trigger will be involved.

It seems that the tax will be based upon the transfer of land, including the grant of leases and any transfer of value into or out of land. This is considerably wider than the present regime of conveyances and options and leases and include, pre-emption rights, easements and profit. It would seem that the granting, variation and cancellation of restrictive covenants, the release of options over land and variation are to be taxed. It was originally proposed that the grant and surrender of licences would also be within the charge but this is under review.

12.2.1 Tax trigger

The draft clause defines the transaction by reference to *conveyance*, *grant* and similar terminology i.e. the execution of the instrument transferring legal title, as at present. However, to discourage persons from resting on contract and subselling it is provided that where short of *completion* the contract to sell, lease, vary the restrictive covenant, etc. is substantially performed the charge will arise. This is when the person obtains the economic benefit of the land the kind such as where the constructive trust arises upon payment, and presumably the purchaser and lessee goes into occupation.

It would appear that this uncertain terminology means that the tax is likely to be triggered by payment rather than transfer of title within the paper or computer system. This will give rise to difficult questions of what amounts to *payment* or the satisfaction of the consideration particularly where significant deposits are involved, i.e. when the constructive trust arises. There will be

280

significant problems where the consideration consists of or includes the issue of shares which satisfy the consideration and therefore trigger the tax much earlier than at present. It would seem that the contract as the tax point has been rejected since this would accelerate the payment of the tax to a commercially and politically unacceptable early date.

12.2.2 Property deriving value from land

The charge is not limited to land in the UK as such. It is contemplated that there will be a charge in relation to property deriving its value from land such as shares in land owning companies whether incorporated in the UK or abroad.

Share transfers in these cases may well attract stamp duty appropriate to land rather than to share transactions or lose the benefit of the exemption for transfers of shares in foreign companies executed abroad. It is, of course, going to be an extremely difficult problem for solicitors to be aware of whether there are any changes in the ultimate ownership of interests in companies.

The proposal is also to extend the tax to dealings in trusts including foreign trusts which hold land in the UK as well as partnerships owning land. There will be many fine issues of definition that will need to be borne in mind and problems of valuation in order to determine whether the vehicle or the interest in question derives from a *land rich entity*.

It is proposed to bring back the double charge on exchanges of land. It will no longer be possible to obtain the benefit of the single sale treatment by suitable drafting. This will extend to land exchanges in the widest sense such as variation of leases that amount to surrender and re-grant. There will be stamp duty upon the surrender and upon the regrant. Other variations of leases including termination by notice to quit may also operate to transfer value such as increases of rent and rent reviews or commutation of rent by payments of lump sums to the landlord and these may well give rise to a charge because of the movement of value involved.

12.3   CALCULATING THE TAX

The charge is by reference to the considerations so the gift may be free of stamp but no doubt the current anti-avoidance rule for transactions with connected companies and other arrangements will be continued into the new regime. The charge is upon 'money as money's worth' and is to include a charge upon services, including certain building works, with special provisions for employees. As SA 1891, s.57 is brought forward it remains to be seen how far the other computational provisions are carried with the new regime. A copious amount of stamp duty baggage is expected.

The lower rates of stamp duty may remain but a new concept of *linked transactions* and payment of tax by instalments will significantly restrict the opportunities of making use of these reliefs.

Since the tax is so much wider than a straightforward cash consideration there will be considerable areas of valuation. Given that it is proposed the tax will be payable, as at present, within 30 days of the tax event, parties will need to be very quick in preparing their best estimate of the valuation calculating the tax and making a deposit in order to minimise interest and penalties if the tax bill should prove higher than their original estimate. It seems likely that any such valuations will need to be prepared on a reasonable basis. There will no doubt be penalties for wilful default and neglect in preparing the tax return and a pure guestimate of the tax unsupported by a reasonable valuation is likely to give rise automatically to interest and penalty charges.

One area of difficulty concerns periodical payments and contingent arrangement such as rents, instalments and overage and earnout payments. Here the consideration is not known or will be payable over a period of time. It seems that the current favoured proposal is to move to a payment of the tax upon an estimated basis with subsequent adjustment. The return form will presumably contain a requirement that the solicitor completing it gives an indication of when each instalment is to be made and the estimated amount thereof. This will enable the Inland Revenue Stamp Taxes Office to monitor the transaction and pursue taxes, presumably via solicitors who will need to maintain contact with their clients in order to ensure that the tax is paid on time.

One particular problem concerns rent under leases. The current proposal is that the amount of rent payable under the lease will be aggregated as a lump sum and taxed as a premium. This will give rise to a significant increase in the amount of stamp duty. It is unclear at present whether there will be any form of discounting for rent under long leases. The idea appears to be that the rent is really a premium payable by instalments and should be taxes accordingly. Thus there will be a significant change from a 20 year lease with a rent of £100,000 a year currently dutiable £2,000 (ignoring value added tax) to a premium of £2 million (i.e. 20 × £100,000) which will be dutiable at 4 per cent, i.e. £80,000. The draft clauses are silent upon these topics.

12.3.1   Exemptions and relief

Small transactions will be outside the scope of the tax unless they relate to a major interest in land, i.e. freeholds and leases largely as an administrative exercise. Currently it seems that disadvantaged land, mortgages, wills and variation of estates and transactions connected with matrimonial breakdown currently exempt will continue to be exempt. Charities are not mentioned, nor are company reorganisations.

No mention is made of any form of subsidy relief, even though the charge upon substantial performances of uncompleted contracts will lead to a cascade tax effect like unrecovered VAT.

12.4 COMPLIANCE

The tax will be directly enforceable and there will be an obligation, under penalty, to report the transaction within 30 days of the trigger event. The tax will also have to be paid within that same 30-day time limit.

Where there are uncertainties such as valuations or contingencies a solicitor will be required to make a best estimate on reasonable justifiable grounds of the amounts involved, make a best estimate of the tax and arrange for it to be paid. The administration will be through completion of a form. Unlike the present forms such as the PD 01 Companies Form 88 or Land Registry TR1 which have stamp duty implications the new forms will be audited from time to time by the Inland Revenue.

At present many errors escape because the forms are completed incorrectly. However, the sort of errors that now creep into the forms will be discovered with the consequent sanctions being applied. The relaxed approach to conveyancing will no longer be a viable option and incorrect advice on completing the return given to a client will attract retribution even if the solicitor is not accountable for the tax. Detailed investigations, due diligence valuations and other matters will be required and a comprehensive understanding of how the consideration or chargeable amount is determined will be fundamental. The sanctions could be quite severe since it has been suggested and not denied by the Inland Revenue Stamp Taxes Office that one possible sanction for errors discovered on audit will be a removal of the right of access to the Land Registry computer thereby preventing the carrying out of conveyancing activities in the future.

The purchaser or lessee or other person making the payment or providing the services will be liable for the tax but it seems likely that it will be collected through solicitors, as 'accountable persons' who will be responsible under penalty for ensuring that the form is returned on time and will be accountable for the tax if the stamp duty reserve tax model is followed. That is to say they will be required to pay the tax personally unless they can show that they have taken reasonable steps to collect the money from the client but have been unable to do so. The draft clauses so far published do not include the provision, but it should be noted the accountable persons for stamp duty reserve tax did not emerge until the detailed regulations were published after the Finance Act 1986.

12.5 TITLE ISSUES

At present title cannot be registered until stamp duty has been paid and denoted upon the document. This will continue, title will not be accepted by the Land Registry unless a receipt from the Inland Revenue Stamp Taxes Office can be produced. Documents where the tax has not been paid in respect of any relevant transaction or stage in the transaction may not be admissible in evidence, although this may become quite an acute issue of human rights in terms of improper demands of access to the Court and impeding a right to a fair and proper trial of private property issues; but this is not clear at present.

The reform will, depending upon the compliance regime and whether solicitors are to become accountable, represent a fundamental change to the approach required from solicitors and other conveyancers in relation to land transactions. There are important potential implications for client relationships, record keeping and ensuring that the tax is paid on time, particularly where instalments or variable contingent consideration is involved.

Although much of the matters may be delegated to other parties such as valuers and accountants for the planning and mitigation arrangements, it would seem that the frontline responsibility could easily rest with solicitors as the persons to be regarded as responsible for completing the form as well as investigating that the stamp duty position of prior title and prior stages in the transaction have been properly dealt with. The direct enforcement of the tax means that errors, whether omission or commission, will be fully open to the Revenue whereas at present they are not investigated.

Inland Revenue Stamp Taxes Office Statements of Practice

- **SP 5/78** Conveyance in consideration of a debt
- **SP 6/90** Conveyances and transfers of property subject to a debt: SA 1891 s 57
- **SP 11/91** Stamp duty and value added tax (VAT) – interaction
- **SP 8/93** Stamp duty: new buildings
- **SP 3/98** Stamp duty: group relief

SP 5/78 CONVEYANCE IN CONSIDERATION OF A DEBT (8 NOVEMBER 1978)

Stamp duty on an instrument transferring property in consideration of the discharge of a debt owing to the transferee is governed by the provisions of SA 1891 s 57. The Board of Inland Revenue are advised that where the value of the property transferred is less than the amount of the indebtedness agreed to be discharged, the latter is the proper measure of the consideration for stamp duty purposes. The practice of the Office of the Controller of Stamps will be regulated accordingly and the value of the property transferred will not be treated as limiting the consideration in respect of which stamp duty is charged.

SP 6/90 CONVEYANCES AND TRANSFERS OF PROPERTY SUBJECT TO A DEBT: SA 1891 S 57 (27 APRIL 1990)

Introduction

1. Since the abolition of the duty on voluntary dispositions in 1985, many enquiries have been received about the stamp duty chargeable on conveyances etc subject to a debt where *no* chargeable consideration (*eg* money or stock) unrelated to the debt is given by the transferee. This Statement of Practice sets out the Board's view of the correct stamp duty treatment of such conveyances.

2. For the sake of completeness it should be noted that where chargeable consideration unrelated to debt *is* given by the transferee, s 57 renders the conveyance liable to *ad valorem* duty on the aggregate of that consideration and the debt whether the transferee assumes liability for the debt or not (*IRC v City of Glasgow Bank* (1881) 8 R (Ct of Sess) 389, 18 SLR 242).

SA 1891 s 57

3. The most commonly misunderstood applications of s 57 arise where:

    (*a*) a mortgaged property held in the name of one spouse is transferred into the joint names of both spouses;

    (*b*)   a mortgaged property held in the name of one spouse or in their joint names is transferred into the sole name of the other;

    (*c*)   a mortgaged business property, frequently farmland, is conveyed from a sole proprietor to a family partnership or from a family partnership to a fresh partnership bringing in other members of the family.

4.   The critical question is whether the transaction to which the conveyance gives effect is or is not a sale. If it is, s 57 will apply and the conveyance will be chargeable to *ad valorem* duty on the amount of the debt assumed. If it is not, then s 57 will not apply and *ad valorem* duty will not be payable.

Express covenants

5.   Where property is transferred subject to a debt, the transferee may covenant, either in the instrument or by means of a separate written undertaking, to pay the debt or indemnify the transferor against his personal liability to the lender. Such a covenant or undertaking constitutes valuable consideration and, in view of s 57, establishes the transaction as a sale for stamp duty purposes.

6.   Where the transferor covenants to pay the debt and the transferee does not assume any liability for it, no chargeable consideration has been given and there is no sale. The transfer would then be a voluntary disposition – *ie* an unencumbered gift capable of being certified as Category L under the Stamp Duty (Exempt Instruments) Regulations 1987 (SI 1987/516) – and so exempt from the 50p charge that would otherwise arise.

Implied covenants

7.   Where no express covenant or undertaking is given by the transferee, the Board are advised that, except in Scotland, a covenant by the transferee may be implied. That makes the transaction a sale, as in para 4.

8.   Such an implied covenant may be negated if there is evidence that it was the intention of the parties at the time of the transfer that the transferor should continue to be liable for the whole of the mortgage debt. Where evidence of such a contrary intention exists, the transfer would again be treated for stamp duty purposes as a voluntary disposition.

9.   Where property in joint names subject to a debt is transferred to one of the joint holders (though with no cash passing), a covenant by the transferee to indemnify the transferor may be implied even where both parties were jointly liable on the mortgage.

Amount chargeable

10.   Where a conveyance of property subject to a debt is chargeable to *ad valorem* duty and the express or implied covenant by the transferee relates only to part of the debt, only the amount of that part is treated as chargeable consideration within s 57. A certificate of value under FA 1958 s 34 (4) may, where appropriate, be included in the conveyance where the relevant amount of the debt does not exceed the amount certified.

Other provisions

11. The foregoing does not affect any statutory exemption from duty that may apply, *eg* that for transfers to a charity (FA 1982 s 129) and that available for certain transfers of property from one party to a marriage to the other in connection with their divorce or separation (FA 1985 s 83(1) and Stamp Duty (Exempt Instruments) Regulations 1987, Category H).

Procedure

12. Where the applicant is satisfied that the conveyance or transfer is made on sale, it may be sent or taken for stamping with a remittance for the duty payable. If the transfer contains an appropriate certificate of value – see para 10 – it may be sent direct to the Land Registry in the usual way if appropriate. In either case, if the amount of the debt outstanding is not given in the conveyance or transfer the amount should be stated in a covering letter.

13. Where the conveyance or transfer contains a covenant by the transferor to pay the debt (see para 6) and is certified as within the Stamp Duty (Exempt Instruments) Regulations 1987, Category L it should also be sent direct to the Land Registry if appropriate.

14. In any other case where the applicant believes that the conveyance or transfer effects a voluntary disposition – see para 8 – it should be presented for adjudication accompanied by a statement of the facts and any supporting evidence.

SP 11/91 STAMP DUTY AND VALUE ADDED TAX (VAT) – INTERACTION
(12 SEPTEMBER 1991)

1. This statement is a revised version of the statement about stamp duty and VAT issued on 22 July 1991, and replaces it.

Introduction

2. To comply with a judgment of the European Court of Justice in June 1988, standard rate UK VAT has been applied to non-residential construction with effect from 1 April 1989 (FA 1989, s.18). VAT is compulsory on sales of buildings treated as new for this purpose, which are mainly buildings under three years old that have been completed after March 1989. And owners of non-residential property were given the option from 1 August 1989 of charging VAT on sales of old buildings and on leases.

3. These new charges have prompted a number of enquiries about the relationship between stamp duty and VAT where both taxes arise on a sale or lease of commercial property or, occasionally, other assets.

Sales of new non-domestic buildings

4. The Board are advised that for stamp duty purposes the amount or value of the consideration for a sale is the gross amount inclusive of VAT. Therefore where VAT is payable on the sale of new non-residential property, stamp duty is calculated on the VAT-inclusive consideration.

Other non-domestic transactions

5. Transactions in non-residential property other than sales of new buildings are exempt from VAT. These include:

    - sales of old buildings
    - the assignment of existing leases, or the creation of new leases, in old or new property.

However, the vendor or lessor can elect to waive the exemption.

6. The Board have received legal advice that:

    - where the election has already been exercised at the time of the transaction, stamp duty is chargeable on the purchase price, premium or rent including VAT;
    - where the election has not been exercised at that time, VAT should similarly be included in any payments to which an election could still apply (which will depend on the facts of each case).

7. The Board propose to follow this advice, which will result in a change of practice: in the past, the Inland Revenue Stamp Taxes Office did not seek to include the VAT element in the stamp duty charge in cases where an election to waive the exemption from VAT had not yet been exercised. The new practice applies to documents executed on or after 1 August 1991.

8. Neither a formal notice of election made to HM Customs & Excise, nor any notification to the purchaser or lessee that such an election has been made, will attract stamp duty.

Rent

9. Where VAT is charged on the rent under a lease, and is itself treated as rent under the lease, stamp duty at the appropriate rate according to the length of the term will be charged on the VAT-inclusive figure. If the lease provides for payment of VAT on the rent otherwise than as rent, duty will be charged on the VAT element as consideration payable periodically (Stamp Act 1891 s 56). In either case the rate of VAT in force at the date of execution of the lease will be used in the calculation.

10. In the case of a formal Deed of Variation or similar document varying the terms of the original lease so as to provide for payment of VAT by way of additional rent, further stamp duty may be payable (Stamp Act 1891 s 77(5)).

Agreements for leases

11. Paragraphs 5 to 10 above also apply to an agreement for lease if that is the instrument to be stamped (Stamp Act 1891 s 75).

Procedure

12. Applicants for stamping are requested to make clear, either in the conveyance or lease document itself, or in a covering letter to the Inland Revenue Stamp Taxes Office, whether the property is commercial or residential.

13. Deeds of Variation etc (para.10 above) should be presented for adjudication together with a copy of the original lease.

No VAT on stamp duty

14. It is sometimes suggested that stamp duty might itself attract a charge to VAT. This is not the case. The value for VAT depends on the amount (consideration) obtained by the supplier from the purchaser, less the included VAT itself. Stamp duty is paid by the purchaser/lessee of property direct to the Inland Revenue and not to the supplier; it does not therefore form part of the consideration for VAT purposes.

SP 8/93 STAMP DUTY: NEW BUILDINGS (12 JULY 1993)

This statement sets out the practice the Board of Inland Revenue will apply in relation to the stamp duty chargeable in certain circumstances on the conveyance or lease of a new or partly constructed building. It affects transactions where, at the date of the contract for sale or lease of a building plot, building work has not commenced or has been only partially completed on that site but where that work has started or has been completed at the time the conveyance or lease is executed.

This statement reflects the advice the Board have received on this subject in the light of the decision in the case of *Prudential Assurance Company Ltd v IRC* ([1992] STC 863; [1993] 1 WLR 211). The statement does not apply to the common situation where the parties have entered into a contract for the sale of a new house and that contract is implemented by a conveyance of the whole property. This statement replaces the statements of practice issued in 1957 and 1987 (SP 10/87) on this subject which are now withdrawn.

The Board are advised that, whilst each case will clearly depend on its own facts, the law is as follows:

1 Two transactions/two contracts

Where the purchaser or lessee is entitled under the terms of a contract to a conveyance or lease of land alone in consideration of the purchase price or rent of the site and a second genuine contract for building works is entered into as a separate transaction, the ad valorem duty on the conveyance or lease will be determined by the amount of the purchase price or rent which the purchaser or lessee is obliged to pay under the terms of the first contract. In these circumstances it does not matter whether any building work has commenced at the date of the conveyance or lease. The consideration chargeable to ad valorem duty will still be only that passing for the land.

2 One transaction/two contracts

Where there is one transaction between the parties but this is implemented by two contracts, one for the sale or lease of the building plot and one for the building works themselves, the amount of ad valorem duty charged on the instrument will depend on the amount of the consideration, which in turn will depend on whether those contracts can be shown to be genuinely independent of each other.

(i) if the two contracts are so interlocked that they cannot be said to be genuinely capable of independent completion (and in particular where if default occurs on either contract, the other is then not enforceable) ad valorem duty will be charged on the total consideration for the land and buildings, whether completed or not, as if the parties had entered into only one contract.

(ii) if the two contracts are shown to be genuinely independent of each other, ad valorem duty will be charged by reference to the consideration paid or payable for the land and any building works on that land at the date of execution of the instrument. It follows that, where the instrument is executed after the building works are completed, ad valorem duty will be charged on the consideration for the land and the completed building(s).

3 Sham or artificial transactions

This statement does not apply to cases where the transaction concerned, or any part of it, involves a sham or artificial transaction.

Contracts already entered into

Where unconditional contracts have been entered into before or within 28 days of the date of this statement and the duty payable on the resulting conveyance or lease would have been less under the earlier statements of practice, the Inland Revenue Stamp Taxes Office will accept duty in the lesser amount. In such cases the instrument should be submitted together with all the evidence to support the claim that unconditional contracts were entered into within this transitional period.

Procedure for submitting documents

Where a person accepts that a conveyance or lease of a building plot is chargeable on the total price paid or payable for the land and the completed building, it should be submitted for stamping in the usual way together with a covering letter giving the aggregate price and a payment for the duty appropriate to that price.

Where the total price does not exceed the amount up to which the instrument is liable to nil duty (currently £60,000) and a certificate of value is included in the instrument, a conveyance may be sent direct to the Land Registry in England and Wales or, in Scotland, to the Keeper of the Registers of Scotland. A lease will need to be stamped in respect of the rent.

Where the total price exceeds the threshold at which duty becomes payable but the taxpayer takes the view that duty is payable on some smaller sum, the instrument should be submitted to the Inland Revenue Stamp Taxes Office. This applies even where the taxpayer believes that the amount potentially chargeable to ad valorem duty is below the threshold and a certificate of value is included in the instrument. The instrument should be accompanied by a copy of the agreement(s) for sale etc and a letter stating the amount which the taxpayer regards as chargeable consideration, identifying separately any amount attributable to building work. Details of any contractual arrangements not covered by the agreement(s) should also be given in the covering letter.

This statement does not affect in any way a taxpayer's rights of appeal.

SP3/98 STAMP DUTY: GROUP RELIEF

1. Section 42 Finance Act 1930 gives relief from stamp duty for transfers of property between members of the same group of companies. Section 151 Finance Act 1995 similarly gives relief from duty on the grant of a lease between members of the same group.

2. Section 27(3) Finance Act 1967 and Section 151(3) Finance Act 1995 are designed to prevent the use of group relief to avoid stamp duty when property, or an economic interest in it, passes out of the group.
3. This statement sets out the Inland Revenue Stamp Taxes Office's current general practice in order to assist practitioners in determining whether claims to relief might qualify. The treatment of a particular case will of course depend on the precise facts. This statement is for general guidance only; and the facts of a particular transaction may, exceptionally, place it outside the guidelines. It applies also to the equivalent Northern Ireland Legislation.

General

4. Broadly, Section 27(3) and the corresponding provisions in section 151, provide that relief is not to be given if the transfer was made in pursuance of, or in connection with, an arrangement under which:

    (a) all or part of the consideration for the transfer was to be provided or received, directly or indirectly, by a person outside the group; or
    (b) the interest being transferred was previously transferred by a person outside the group; or
    (c) the transferor and transferee were no longer to be part of the same group.

5. The person claiming the relief when the relevant instrument is adjudicated has the onus of satisfying the Inland Revenue Stamp Taxes Office that the intra-group transaction is not carried out in pursuance of, or in connection with, an arrangement of a kind which disqualifies the transaction from relief; Escoigne Properties Ltd v. IRC [1958] AC 549, 564.

'Arrangement'

6. In this context, arrangement means the plan or scheme in pursuance of which the things identified in the subparagraphs of ss27(3) and 151(3) have been or are to be done: Shop and Store Developments Ltd v. IRC [1967] 1 AC 472, 493–494. The arrangement need not be based in contract. It is sufficient if the intra-group transaction is made in connection with the plan or scheme. The intra-group transaction may be the first bi-lateral step by which legal rights and obligations are created in pursuance of the arrangement. If there is an expectation that a disqualifying event will happen in accordance with the arrangement and no likelihood in practice that it will not, relief will be refused.
7. The words in connection with are very broad. In Escoigne, there was a gap of four years between the two steps in issue.

Provision or receipt of consideration by a person outside the group: section 27(3) (a); section 151(3)(a) and (4)

8. Section 27(3)(a) denies relief where the instrument was executed in pursuance of or in connection with an arrangement under which any of the consideration is to be provided or received, directly or indirectly, by a person outside the group. It also denies relief if the arrangement is one under which the transferor or transferee (or a member of the same group as either of them) is to be enabled to provide any of the consideration, or is to part with it, in consequence of a transaction involving a payment or other disposition by a person outside the group. Section 151 lays down similar rules for leases.

9. In some cases, the question arises whether loan finance for the purchase or lease will disqualify an intra-group transaction from relief. It is necessary to look at all the facts of the individual case, but the Inland Revenue Stamp Taxes Office will interpret the provisions in the light of their general purpose of denying relief where the intra-group transaction is a means of saving stamp duty when the property, or an interest in it, moves out of the group. Accordingly, the Inland Revenue Stamp Taxes Office are likely to be satisfied that relief is due if the intra-group transaction is not to be followed by a sale of the property transferred, or an underlease, to a person outside the group. If the intra-group transaction is to be followed by a sale or underlease to a person outside the group, but the claimant can demonstrate the stamp duty will be paid in respect of that transaction in approximately the same amounts as would have been payable if the intra-group transferor or lessor had itself sold the property or granted the underlease, the Inland Revenue Stamp Taxes Office are likely to be satisfied that the intra-group transaction and the transfer or lease out are independent for stamp duty purposes and grant the relief sought.

10. A transaction is not disqualified merely because the transferee within the group obtains a specific loan for the purchase of the asset; or the loan is secured on the asset; or arrangements are made to replace or novate an existing charge on the property transferred. It will be necessary to consider the facts as a whole, especially if the loan finance is not straightforward finance on ordinary commercial terms.

11. Intra-group transactions will be very carefully scrutinised, and relief may be refused, where, for example, the intra-group transaction involves or is to be followed by:

    - the creation of transfer of loan stock or equity capital;
    - a capital reorganisation of the transferee;
    - a guarantee by a third party not associated with the group;
    - the creation of a new charge or financial arrangement whereby title to the property is, or may be, vested in the lender otherwise than in satisfaction of all or part of the debt; or
    - the assignment of the freehold reversion or the intra-group lease to a person outside the group.

12. Similarly transactions will be very carefully scrutinised where:

    - all or part of the consideration for the transaction is to remain outstanding or is represented by intra-group debt, (as the aim and effect may be to reduce the value of the transferee company on a possible future sale outside the group); or
    - the existing shareholders of the transferee include shareholders outside the group and the transaction is to be followed by the declaration of a dividend in specie, or by the liquidation of the transferee.

13. Further assurances by way of statutory declaration – the document in which the claim is made to the Inland Revenue Stamp Taxes Office – will be required in any case in which the property transferred or vested intra-group is the only, or only substantial, asset of the transferee. Information to that effect should be provided in the statutory declaration submitted with the documents.

14. Where group member A has granted a lease to a person outside the group, and subsequently grants an underlease to its fellow group member B, so that the rent already payable by the lessee becomes payable to B rather than A, relief is likely to be given for the intra-group underlease, provided there are no other factors which suggest that relief should be denied.

Property previously conveyed by a person outside the group; section 27(3)(b)

15. Section 27(3)(b) was intended to prevent the avoidance of duty on the transfer of property into a group by means of a sub-sale, so as to take advantage of section 58(4) of the Stamp Act 1891. For example, suppose the property is sold to a group member by a vendor outside the group, but the sale rests in contract without a transfer of the legal title. The group member then sells the property to another member of its own group, and directs the vendor to transfer the legal title to that other member. In accordance with section 58(4) the transfer completing the sale and the sub-sale is chargeable to duty only in relation to the sub-sale (thus relieving the effect of section 4 of the Stamp Act). However, section 27(3)(b) would deny group relief for the transfer.

16. The Inland Revenue Stamp Taxes Office will continue to apply section 27(3)(b) to schemes of this type and to any other scheme where an attempt has been made to avoid the duty payable on the acquisition by the group. However, where an outside vendor sells a property to a member of the group, the sale is completed by a transfer and stamp duty is paid on that transfer, the Inland Revenue Stamp Taxes Office will normally regard any subsequent intra-group transfer as independent, and grant relief for the transfer within the purchaser's group.

Dissociation or demerger of transferee: section 27(3)(c): section 151(3)(b)

17. Before the introduction of section 27(3), almost all the avoidance devices encountered in this area involved the transfer of property to a subsidiary, often created solely as a vehicle for that property, followed by the transfer of the shares in the subsidiary out of the group. Compared with a transfer of the property out of the group, a substantial amount of duty could be avoided even where the subsidiary paid for the property from its own resources. If the consideration for the intra-group transaction remained outstanding or was represented by debt, duty could be reduced further by reducing the value of the shares – hence section 27(3)(a).

18. Section 27(3)(c) was introduced to counter this avoidance in relation to conveyances and transfers on sale. Section 151(3)(b) deals with leases on similar lines.

19. In cases of this kind, the Inland Revenue Stamp Taxes Office will need to be satisfied that the intra-group transfer or lease is not a step in pursuance of an arrangement to demerge the transferee. The existence of such an arrangement may be apparent from company documents, correspondence and other dealings between members of the group and professional advisers, or from discussions or negotiations with the potential purchasers, underwriters or minority shareholders.

20. In practice, the Inland Revenue Stamp Taxes Office will apply these provisions so as to preclude group relief if there is evidence of a plan or scheme to dispose of the subsidiary and there is no practical likelihood that the scheme will not be carried through. It will not be regarded as sufficient for the claimant to contend that such an arrangement which is less than contractual may possibly be frustrated by unforeseen events or unlikely occurrences. Even a contract may be frustrated.

21. As the liability of the relevant instrument must, as a matter of general principle, be determined as at the date of the instrument, the question whether an arrangement of the relevant kind exists must also be determined at that time, although the Inland Revenue Stamp Taxes Office may have regard to what is said and done thereafter to establish the true purposes of stamp duty, it is therefore the existence of the scheme or plan to which these provisions direct attention, not the ultimate outcome of steps which may be taken to implement that scheme.

Inland Revenue Stamp Taxes Office Bulletins

STAMP TAXES BULLETIN ISSUE 1, AUGUST 2001 (EXTRACTS)

When is a Fixture Not a Fixture?

Deductions for Chattels (or Moveables in Scotland)

Where the consideration for the conveyance or transfer on sale of a property includes an amount attributed by the parties to chattels (or moveables in Scotland), that amount will not normally be charged to stamp duty provided the chattels pass by delivery and are not conveyed in the document.

Case law provides that where assets of different character are agreed to be sold for one consideration for the whole, an apportionment between the chargeable and non-chargeable property must be a bona fide one. This is taken to mean that it must be based on the commercial value of the property concerned. A contract for sale based on a false apportionment may be unenforceable because of its improper intent and can therefore have more far-reaching consequences.

Over the last year or so, Stamp Taxes has seen a steady increase in the number of cases where the amount of consideration attributed to items claimed to be chattels is more than a small percentage of the total consideration. This is especially the case where this brings the chargeable amount just below the £250,000 or £500,000 thresholds.

Customers should note that in cases where it appears that an excessive amount of the consideration has been artificially attributed to non-chargeable items a full inventory and breakdown of the consideration will be requested by Stamp Taxes. This is to ensure that all the items claimed as chattels are properly within that description and that the allocation of the consideration is bona fide and not in breach of Section 5 of the Stamp Act 1891.

Stamp Taxes does not provide a comprehensive list of items which are accepted as chattels or moveables since many cases need to be considered on their own merits and case law is evolving in this area all the time. However items which will generally be accepted as chattels or moveables include – carpets, curtains, light shades, pot plants, free-standing kitchen white goods and portable electric or gas fires.

Items which are generally unacceptable as chattels are – Fitted kitchen cabinets and cupboards, fitted kitchen white goods, fitted bathroom sanitary ware, central heating systems, plants growing in the soil, central heating systems and gas fires connected to a piped gas supply.

Loose Plant and Machinery

Plant and machinery may in certain circumstances be treated as 'goods, wares and merchandise' and will then fall within the exception to the charge to stamp duty under Paragraph 7, Sch 13, Finance Act 1999.

The requirement for plant and machinery to be in an actual state of severance at the date of the agreement for sale for it to fall within the 'goods, wares and merchandise' description is an historical one. It stems from case law based on circumstances involving mortgagees in possession. The two main tests as to whether plant and machinery constitutes goods, wares and merchandise are essentially the same as for chattels, namely (1) the degree of annexation to the building or land and (2) the purpose or object of annexation. Stamp Taxes has for many years required customers to certify that plant and machinery claimed as loose plant must be in an actual state of severance if it is to be considered as goods and therefore outside the charge to duty on an agreement for sale. We will no longer insist upon this certification being given.

Where it would be possible for plant and machinery to be relatively easily severed from the property to which it is fixed, say for example by the simple expedient of removing some bolts securing it to the floor or walls, we will no longer insist that this is actually done before it will be considered to be 'loose plant and machinery'.

The position in law has not changed nor does this mean that all plant and machinery suddenly falls within the exception. As in the past, the consideration attributed to fixed plant will be chargeable to stamp duty on the agreement for sale document. Heavy plant and machinery which is integral to a building and plant where its removal would damage the building or land will still be considered fixed plant. This will be particularly relevant in respect of plant such as, for example, escalators and elevators, boilers, furnaces, walk-in refrigerators and restaurant cooking stations, none of which would be likely to be classed as loose plant for stamp duty purposes. Each case will be considered on its own merits. The Stamp Taxes form Stamps 22 will be amended to reflect this new treatment. The equivalent forms used in Scotland and Northern Ireland do not require amendment since they did not previously include the certification requirement.

Stamp Duty on Goodwill and Intellectual Property

With the rapidly changing face of today's business world and the growth of new technology, there are now many different types of assets relating to the trade of a company.

We are receiving an increasing number of enquiries about certain types of 'intellectual property' relating to computer applications.

This is a brief outline of what is and isn't chargeable.

Intellectual property including:

- Domain names
- Databases
- Software applications

All these are not chargeable.

- Goodwill – Traditionally this refers to the rights associated with carrying on the business, the 'good name' and established reputation which brings with it the promise of trade.

Business goodwill is chargeable with stamp duty.

However, if the goodwill is derived from intellectual property, for instance, it is associated with a trademark, then it is exempt from duty under s.129 (2) Finance Act 2000.

- 'Know-how' is not chargeable with stamp duty.

Inland Revenue Stamp Taxes Office Customer Newsletters

CUSTOMER NEWSLETTER, ISSUE 3. JULY, 2002

1. General

1.1 This Newsletter provides guidance on the general application of the legislation at section 115 and Schedule 36 FA 2002. That legislation brings within the charge to stamp duty contracts for the sale of interests in UK land where the purchase consideration in respect of that land exceeds £10 million. Duty is chargeable on such contracts as though they were conveyances.

1.2 The Newsletter also outlines

- the procedures for making applications to extend the 90-day time limit under section 115 (2) FA 2002 to the newly-established Stamp Taxes Contracts Unit located in Manchester, and
- the Inland Revenue's view of the application of the new legislation in a number of specific circumstances.

1.3 The administration of the legislation, including stamping of contracts within the scope of section 115, the processing of applications to extend the 90-day time limit, and the granting of the benefit of sub-sale relief are all matters that will be exclusively dealt with by the Stamp Taxes Contracts Unit in Manchester (see Appendix B). It follows that such matters should not be referred to other Stamp Offices.

2. Background

2.1 In his Budget on 17 April 2002, the Chancellor announced a package of measures intended to counter avoidance of stamp duty on property transactions. These measures are intended to discourage a range of techniques currently used to avoid stamp duty on high-value property deals.

2.2 Under section 115 Finance Act 2002, certain contracts or agreements for the sale of land situated in the UK are brought within the charge to ad valorem stamp duty. This addresses the avoidance of stamp duty on large deals where the parties stop short of executing a formal conveyance of the land, which is the instrument that normally attracts the stamp duty charge, and 'rest' on the contract instead.

2.3 The contracts within the scope of section 115 are those where the amount or value of the consideration given for an estate or interest in land in the UK exceeds £10 million, or where the instrument forms part of a larger transaction or series of transactions relating to UK land in respect of which the amount or value, or aggregate amount or value, of the consideration exceeds £10 million.

2.4 Such contracts will be stampable with ad valorem duty as if they were conveyances on sale, if, upon the expiry of a 90-day period from the date that the contract, including one that is conditional, is entered into, a conveyance or transfer has not been presented for stamping.

2.5 The legislation has effect in respect of contracts or agreements executed after 24 July 2002.

2.6 Where it is envisaged that completion of a transaction by the execution of a formal conveyance of the land will not happen within the 90 day period, the legislation provides for an application to be made to the Commissioners of Inland Revenue to extend this period. The procedure and conditions for such applications are set out at 4. below.

2.7 References in this Newsletter to contracts and conveyances include, for transactions in Scotland, the conclusion of missives and dispositions respectively.

3. The Stamp Taxes Contracts Unit

3.1 A specially dedicated unit has been established in Manchester to deal with all aspects of the operation of the new legislation, including formal applications for extending the 90 day period. Communications should be addressed to:

Stamp Taxes Contracts Unit,
Manchester Stamp Office,
Upper Fifth Floor
Royal Exchange
Exchange Street
Manchester
M2 7EB
DX 719821 Manchester 2
Telephone: 0161 839 6260
Fax: 0161 834 3350

3.2 **A contract that is chargeable under section 115 must be presented for stamping to the Contracts Unit in Manchester only**. The Unit will also be solely responsible for processing applications for extending the 90-day time limit. It follows that the benefit of relief in respect of sub-sales, including, where appropriate, any repayment of duty paid on the original sale or an earlier sub-sale,(see Appendix A of this Newsletter) will also be dealt with by the Unit in Manchester and not by any other Stamp Office.

3.3 The Contracts Unit will be happy to deal with enquiries as to whether a particular contract is, or will be, within the scope of the section 115 charge.

4. Applications to extend the 90 day period

4.1 Section 115 (2)(b) FA 2002 provides that the Commissioners of Inland Revenue may grant an extension to the 90 day period allowed for presentation of a conveyance for stamping where completion of a transaction is not anticipated within that period.

4.2 Applications for an extension should be made in writing, to the Stamp Taxes Contracts Unit, by a responsible officer of the transferee company, which may include a solicitor or accountant acting on behalf of the company and who is aware of the full circumstances of the application, or, where the transferee is not a company, an authorised representative of the transferee, and must contain all of the following:

(a)   the full postal address of the land contracted to be sold;

(b)   the date of the contract;

(c)   the full names and addresses of the vendor and purchaser (if a company, the registered office address and the name of the ultimate parent company are also required);

(d)   the amount of the purchase consideration, specifying amounts already paid and any further amounts that will or may become payable by the purchaser;

(e)   any apportionment of value between land and buildings, on the one hand, and other assets;

(f)   a description of the nature of the transaction, including details of any sub-sales or part sub-sales already in contemplation;

(g)   the anticipated completion date and a full explanation of the reason for requesting an extension;

(h)   where the contract or agreement forms part of a larger transaction or series of transactions in respect of which the amount or value, or aggregate amount or value, of the consideration attributable to land in the UK exceeds £10 million, details of all relevant transactions;

(i)   details of any stamp duty reliefs (e.g. group relief) to be claimed in respect of the transaction.

Note that it is not necessary to provide a copy of the contract with the application, although this may be requested later.

5.   Treatment of applications to extend the 90 day period.

5.1   The Stamp Taxes Contracts Unit will consider all applications to extend the 90-day period, and may seek additional information and documentation before granting an extension.

5.2   The length of the extension granted is a matter for the Unit's discretion having regard to all the facts and circumstances of the case under consideration, and compliance with any conditions that it sees fit to impose (section 115(3)(b)).

5.3   The Unit may, on behalf of the Commissioners of Inland Revenue, refuse to extend the period in any case unless full documentation, including, where requested, a copy of the contract, is provided (section 115(3)(a)). An extension will also be denied if 'the whole, or substantially the whole, of the intended consideration' has changed hands (section 115(3)(c)). 90% or more of the consideration will usually be regarded as 'substantially the whole' for this purpose.

5.4   Applications for an extension should be submitted to the Stamp Taxes Contracts Unit as soon as it is appears likely that a conveyance will not be produced within the 90 day time limit. The Unit will endeavour to process applications within thirty days of receipt. To be certain of knowing the outcome of an application by the 90 day point, an application for extension should be lodged with the Contracts Unit no later than 60 days after the contract is entered into. Where applications are made later than that, if an extension is not agreed by the 90 day point, there may be a short period where the contract is technically in charge because an extension has still to be approved. If, however, an extension is subsequently approved, the contract will again be protected from coming into charge until the extension expires (see section 115(2)(b)).

5.5 Where an extension has been granted, the Contracts Unit will be prepared to consider one or more further applications for extension of the period allowed under section 115(2)(b). When considering such applications, the Unit may request further information and documentation. If a further extension is not granted, the contract will become chargeable to ad valorem duty on the date upon which the existing extension expires.

5.6 When, in due course, legislation is introduced to modernise the Stamp Duty regime, further guidance will be provided as necessary concerning the transitional treatment of extensions granted under section 115(2)(b) that remain outstanding at the date of implementation of the new legislation.

6. Consideration issues

6.1 The figure of £10 million that appears in section 115(1) relates to the amount or value of the consideration given for the sale of an estate or interest in UK land. So a contract for the sale of UK land and other assets for £12 million, only £8 million of which is attributable to the UK land will be outside the scope of section 115.

6.2 The apportionment between UK land and other assets must be made on a just and reasonable basis.

6.3 Where the contract forms part of a larger transaction or series of transactions the aggregate value of which exceeds £10 million attributable to UK land, section 115 will apply. For example, four connected and inter-linked contracts for £3 million each will be within the scope of the provision.

6.4 The £10 million is a VAT inclusive figure. So where the consideration is £9 million plus VAT of £1.575 million, the contract is within section 115.

6.5 Where, when the contract is made, all or part of the consideration is unascertainable, but a maximum, minimum or basic amount can be ascertained, construction of the new legislation as one with the Stamp Act 1891 (para.10, Sch.36) means that the contingency principle applies. So a contract showing consideration of £8 million with a further £4 million contingent upon the happening of some event, will be treated as a contract for £12 million and within the scope of the provision. Where the consideration cannot be ascertained under the contingency principle, section 242 FA 1994 applies (see paragraphs 18–22 of the August 1995 Tax Bulletin article).

7. Subsequent conveyance

7.1 Where stamp duty is paid upon a contract under the provisions of section 115 and subsequently a conveyance is presented for stamping, the conveyance is only chargeable with duty if the duty chargeable on it exceeds the duty paid on the contract (para 5(1)(a), Schedule 36). In this circumstance only the excess duty is payable on the conveyance. The duty paid on the contract will be either denoted on, or transferred to, the conveyance (para. 5(4), Schedule 36).

8. Use of contract in Court proceedings

8.1 Where a contract within section 115 remains unstamped, it will nevertheless be admissible as evidence in Court proceedings until the expiry of the 90 day or extended period granted by the Contracts Unit (section 115(5)(a)).

9. Interest & Penalties

9.1 A contract that is chargeable with duty under section 115 is treated, for the purposes of the late stamping interest and penalty provisions (sections 15A and 15B Stamp Act 1891) as if it had been executed at the end of the 90 day or extended period allowed by the Inland Revenue. Thereafter the normal 30 day limit for presenting a document which has been executed applies before interest and penalties become exigible.

10. Sub-sales

10.1 Section 115 and Schedule 36 FA 2002 introduce a new form of sub-sale relief for contracts that are chargeable under section 115. The relief is similar to the existing relief in paragraph 7(2), Schedule 13 FA 1999 for property sold under an agreement which is sold on before the original purchaser takes a conveyance. The existing scheme of sub-sale relief under section 58(4) and (5) Stamp Act 1891 is preserved unaltered for contracts that are not chargeable under section 115 FA 2002.

10.2 The broad scheme of the new relief is that any duty paid on the original sale contract and any intervening sub-sale contracts is credited against duty payable upon the conveyance. Where the duty paid on the contract(s) exceeds that due in respect of the conveyance(s), repayment of the excess will be made.

10.3 Full details of how the relief operates in conjunction with section 115, together with a series of examples, is set out in Appendix A. The examples do not cover every possible situation that might arise in practice, but the Contracts Unit will be pleased to advise on the application of the law to particular circumstances that are not specifically covered in the Appendix.

Appendix A

Sub-sale relief

Section 115(2) provides for sub-sale relief where duty has not been paid on contracts under section 115. Schedule 36 deals with sub-sale relief where duty has been paid on contracts within section 115. 'Sub-sale' is defined as the situation where a purchaser, or sub-purchaser, under a contract, without having obtained a conveyance of the property contracted to be sold, contracts to sell the whole or part of the property to another person, putting that person in the position to call for a conveyance from the original seller (para. 2, Schedule 36). In these circumstances there will be more than one contract potentially chargeable under section 115. For example, suppose A contracts to sell UK land to B for £11 million, and, before completing the transaction, B contracts to sell the land to C for £12 million, with the land being conveyed by A directly to C. Both the A-B and B-C contracts are within the scope of section 115 (although duty would not, of course, be payable on the B-C contract if completion took place within 90 days). The examples below illustrate how Section 115(2) and Schedule 36 deal with this situation.

Sub-sale relief will be administered only by the Stamp Taxes Contract Unit in Manchester, to which all sub-sale contracts and final conveyances should therefore be sent

1. Sub-sale where no duty paid on the contracts followed by a subsequent conveyance.

In the above example the conveyance from A to C is regarded as made in conformity with both the A–B and the B–C contracts and duty will be payable upon the conveyance for £12 million (section 115 (2))

2. Sub-sale where duty paid on the contract followed by a subsequent conveyance.

A contracts to sell UK land to B for £11 million, and B pays stamp duty on the contract of £440,000 (£11m 3 4%). B then contracts to sell the land to C for £12 million and A conveys the land directly to C.

The conveyance to C for £12 million is only chargeable with duty if the duty chargeable on it (£480,000) exceeds the duty paid on the contract (£440,000) – para 5(1)(a) of Schedule 36. As £480,000 exceeds £440,000, duty of £40,000 must be paid on the A–C conveyance.

In the event that the consideration for the conveyance from A–C is less than the consideration on which B paid stamp duty on the A–B contract, para 6 of Schedule 36 provides for repayment. So if B paid duty on £11 million (£440,000) and the conveyance from A–C was for £9 million (£360,000), para 6(1) applies and B, as the person who paid the duty on the original sale, will be entitled to a repayment of £440,000 − £360,000 = £80,000. This assumes that the £9 million is not less than the value of the property immediately prior to the sub-sale (see s.112 FA 1984).

3. Sub-sale contract for part followed by conveyance where additional duty payable

A contracts to sell UK land to B for £30 million and B pays stamp duty on the contract. Before taking a conveyance however, B contracts to sell one-third of the land to C for £12 million and A conveys one-third of the land directly to C.

The sub-sale to C is in respect of part only of the property that was the subject of the original sale. Duty on the A–C conveyance is chargeable in respect of the amount by which the ad valorem duty chargeable on it exceeds an 'appropriate proportion' of the ad valorem duty paid on the original sale (para 5(2) of Schedule 36)

The appropriate proportion is determined on a just and reasonable basis having regard to the ad valorem duty paid on the original sale together with any intervening subsale. In this example, B paid duty on the original sale of £1.2 million. B has sold ⅓ of the land to C. So the appropriate proportion of duty to be credited on the A–C conveyance might, depending upon the circumstances, be £1.2 million × ⅓ 5 £400,000. Duty on the A–C conveyance is therefore £12 million × 4% = £480,000 – £400,000 = £80,000.

4. Sub-sale contract for part followed by conveyance where duty repayable

Once the whole of a property contracted to be sold in parts has been conveyed, and the aggregate duty chargeable on the conveyances is less than the duty paid on the original sale and the intervening sub-sales, then a repayment is due under para 6 Schedule 36.

For example – A contracts to sell UK land to B for £11 million. B pays duty of £440,000 on the contract. B then parcels the land into 60 parts and contracts to sell them for £200,000 each. Once the final part has been conveyed from A to the 60th purchaser, if the duty chargeable on the conveyances is less than £440,000, a repayment will be due.

The duty on each conveyance is £200,000 × 1% = £2,000. £2,000 × 60 conveyances = £120,000. Therefore a repayment of duty is due to B in the sum of £440,000 − £120,000 = £320,000.

5. Where whole property sold and duty previously paid on original sale (or an earlier sub-sale)

Suppose that A contracts to sell land to B for £11 million but, before taking a conveyance, B contracts to sell the land on to C for £12 million. B pays duty on £11 million, but the conveyance from A to C does not take place. Duty on the B–C contract is chargeable only in respect of the excess of the chargeable consideration on that contract over the chargeable consideration on the A–B contract. So C would pay duty on £1m (£12m − £11m.) @ 4% = £40,000 (paragraph 3(1), Sch. 36)

If, in turn, C, having paid duty on the B–C contract, contracts to sell the whole property on to D for £15million, D will be liable for duty calculated by reference to the excess of £15 million over the higher amount of chargeable consideration on which duty has been paid on an earlier transaction. The higher amount of chargeable consideration in this case is the £12 million on the B–C contract, and so D will pay duty on £3m (£15m. − £12m.) @ 4% = £120,000 (para. 3(2), Sch 36).

6. Where part only of property sold and duty previously paid on original sale or earlier sub-sale

Suppose A contracts to sell UK land to B for £30 million. Before taking a conveyance B contracts to sell one-third of the land to C for £12 million, and subsequently contracts with D to sell the remaining two-thirds of the land for £25 million. B pays duty on the £30 million consideration for the A–B contract.

The sub-sale to C is in respect of part only of the property that was the subject of the original sale. Duty on the B–C contract is chargeable in respect of the amount by which the consideration of £12 million exceeds an 'appropriate proportion' of the consideration on the earlier transaction (paragraph 3(3) Sch. 36). The appropriate proportion is determined on a just and reasonable basis having regard to the subject matter of the sub-sale and the earlier transaction (paragraph 3(4)). In this case C would pay duty on £12m. less £10m. (£30m. × ⅓) = £2m. @ 4% = £80,000.

Similarly, D would pay duty on £25m. less £20m (£30m. × ⅔) = £5m. @ 4% = £200,000.

If D paid the duty but did not take a conveyance from A, but instead sold the whole of his two-thirds of the original property on to E for £27m million, E would be required to pay duty on the amount by which the chargeable consideration on the D–E contract exceeds the higher amount of chargeable consideration on an earlier sale or sub-sale of that property. In this example, the chargeable consideration on which duty was paid by D was £25 million, so E pays duty on £2m (£27 m. − £25m.) = £2m. @ 4% = £80,000.

If D only sold on to E half of the property he bought from B, for £15m million, then the calculation of duty payable by E would need to take into account the higher of the 'appropriate proportion' of the chargeable consideration on the original sale (A–B) and the 'appropriate proportion' of the chargeable consideration on the intervening sub-sale (B–D), as follows:-

B's chargeable consideration £30m.
Appropriate proportion thereof (30m × ⅔ × ½) £10m. (X)
D's chargeable consideration £25m.
Appropriate proportion thereof (25m × ½) £12.5m. (Y)

(Y) is greater than (X), so E pays duty on
£15m − £12.5m. = £2.5m. @ 4% = £100,000
(paragraph 3(1)–(5), Sch, 36)

7. Where part sub-sold and part retained by original purchaser, and duty paid on original contract

Suppose A contracts to sell UK land to B for £15 million. Before taking a conveyance, B agrees to sell one third of the land to C for £7 million and a further third of the land to D, also for £7 million. B pays duty on the £15 million consideration for the A–B contract. Following the principle in 5. above, both C and D would pay duty on £7m less £5m (£15m × ⅓) = £2m @ 4% = £80,000. The conveyance from A to B of the land not agreed to be sub-sold is liable to duty, not on a consideration of £1m, but following the decision in *Maples* v *IRC* [1914] 3KB 303, on £5m, which represents the proportionate value of the land in relation to the original contract price. The conveyance is therefore liable to duty of £200,000 (£5m @ 4%). As the original contract was stamped with £600,000 duty, and £400,000 has been credited against the stamping of the conveyances to C and D, the balance is available to satisfy the liability on the conveyance from A–B.

8. Rate of duty

Where duty is chargeable on a contract within section 115 and, under paragraph 3 of Schedule 36, duty on a sub-sale is chargeable in respect of part only of the consideration for the sub-sale, the rate of duty chargeable on the sub-sale is the rate that would be applicable if the whole of the chargeable consideration on the sub-sale were taken into account.

A contracts to sell UK land to B for £30 million. B pays stamp duty at 4% on the contract. B then contracts to sell the land to C for £30.1 million. Duty is payable by C on the additional £100,000 consideration at 4% under paragraph 3(6) of Schedule 36.

APPENDIX B

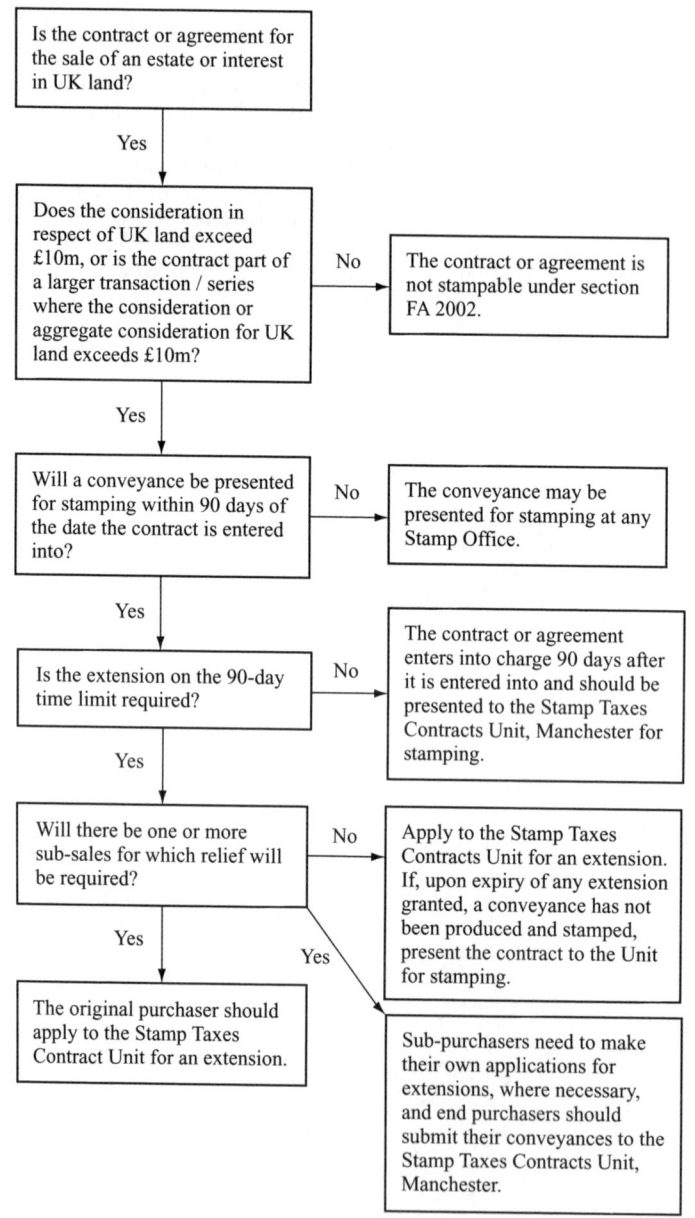

Index